THE SEX CODE

THE SEX CODE
Morals for Moderns

FRANCIS BENNION

WEIDENFELD AND NICOLSON · LONDON

George Weidenfeld and Nicolson Ltd
91 Clapham High Street, London SW4 7TA

ISBN 0 297 82125 3 (paperback)

Typeset by Deltatype Ltd, Ellesmere Port
Printed in Great Britain by Butler & Tanner Ltd, Frome and London

To those not entirely happy in their sexuality.

How much greater would human happiness have been if the gratification of the sexual instinct had never been looked upon as wicked.

*   *   *

The office of morality is to persuade the individual that what is of benefit to society is of benefit to him.

*   *   *

One can only rule men by dogmatic affirmations.

*   *   *

One of the commonest errors of the human intelligence is to insist that a rule should be universally applicable.

*   *   *

A moral code is only accepted by the weak minded; the strong form their own.

From W. Somerset Maugham, *A Writer's Notebook*

Contents

Preface

Grounded in a lifetime of sexual questioning, this book has taken fifteen years to write. The experience of a hundred times that span might have done the subject justice, though I doubt it.

The book's object is to point to a society where morals do not depend on religion, sex is not cheapened, fidelity is upheld, comfort is given where it can be, infants are not punished for curiosity, children can rejoice in being sexual creatures, puberty is an open rite, wimpish youths are not called 'wankers', all adolescents are expected to celebrate their peak of potency, human beauty is fully adored, a stupid man is not termed a 'cunt', the term 'fucking' is revered rather than hijacked as a pejorative adjective, women are allowed sovereignty over their own bodies, nudists are not sneered at (because everybody is one), lesbians and gays are accepted as decent human beings, page three girls (like page seven 'fellas') have become redundant, sex is seen as a human right and glory, and everyone thrives in the Garden of Happy Emotions.

In aid of that outcome, the book offers those who are dissatisfied with religious teaching on sex a suggested code of secular ethics. The accompanying explanations tend to deal at length with debatable areas of morality, such as pornography, prostitution and adolescent sexuality, and to spend little time on topics where opinion is agreed, such as the immorality of rape or bestiality.

I have eschewed footnotes because unlike most of my other published books this is essentially a personal statement or (anagrammatically) testament, rather than an academic production. Although the thoughts of many other writers are gratefully called in aid, this is very much my own account of the secular morality of sex. A list of sources used is given at the end of the book, as is my own very full and perhaps unusually informative index.

In addition to those who unknowingly formed my thought merely by acting as key characters in my life, many people have knowingly helped write this book. The former it would be kind not to specify. With apologies to those of the latter I do not mention, I would single out for special thanks, without holding them in the slightest degree responsible for any statement which is contained, or not contained, in the book: James R. Adams, Dr Martin Bax, Mrs A. Burrows, Dr Martin Cole, Sam Eadie, John Fader, Mrs Vivien Gibson, Keith Gimson, Antony Grey, Dr

xi

John Hart, Mrs J. Herget, Alexander Hill, Professor Edwin Le Fèvre, Jonathan Ledger, Nurse K. S. Manning, Pat Mathewson, Sam Pattenden, Margaret Rogers, George Ross, Donald Smith, Eric Stockton, Dr Harry Stopes-Roe, Jack Sully, Frank Torey, Jane Wendt Whitehead, Edward Wild and Derek Wilkes.

Thanks are due to John Murray (Publishers) Ltd for permission to quote part of the poem 'Senex' from John Betjeman's *Collected Poems*.

Finally I give warm thanks to the Publishers and their staff for friendly and efficient support throughout, to the copyeditor who with high professionalism restrained her own religious convictions in the cause of effective transmission of this secular message, and to the proofreader who displayed standards of erudition in his art that I have not encountered for many years and had thought lost.

Left Bank of the Isis   F. B.
Oxford
Michaelmas Term 1990

I
Ethics and Sex

Preliminary

Most people in the west now find it difficult to accept religious teachings about sex. Yet they reject the idea that 'anything goes'. They dislike promiscuity, for it indicates lack of discrimination and the rejection of quality. They are uneasy about 'permissiveness', for it suggests an absence of standards. This shows that moral principles do exist, though they derive from reason and conscience rather than religion. It is important to work out what they are, since otherwise we do not know how to guide our children or justify to them the standards we follow ourselves. Even adults may feel the need of help on particular ethical issues. Also we must be sure that our legal rules truly correspond to what morality requires. If they do not, we will wish to alter them.

This book aims to supply the need for a guide to secular sexual ethics. It contains a suggested code of sixty principles, which are explained one by one in the chapters that form the body of the book and are then set out together at the end. The author does not expect every reader to agree with all these principles. His object is not to offer moral certainty, or secure universal agreement. It is rather to provide a formulation against which the reader can compare his or her own moral beliefs. If the book assists readers to decide what these are, its purpose will be achieved. The book is limited to western culture because, although believing the sexual nature of humans to be a constant, the author does not consider himself equipped to investigate the ethics of cultures other than his own. If there is anything here of value for other cultures it can be applied by those concerned.

The opening chapter analyses the concept of secular ethics as developed in our western culture. The following seven chapters are the core of the book, because they deal in turn with three central principles of positive sexuality. The first of these suggested principles says we should *accept* our sexual nature, and corrects the sex-negativism instilled by centuries of Judaeo-Christian teaching that sex is sinful. The second says we should *respect* our sexual nature, and not degrade or trivialise it in the way pornography, promiscuity and other features induced by sex-negativism so often do. The third says that all through life we should *fulfil* our sexual nature (though in an ethical manner) and assist others to do the same, because only in that way can the unhappiness arising from repression and frustration be avoided, and the potential for sexual joy realised. Because these three principles are basic to the philosophy set out in this book the chapters that describe them are neccessarily long and detailed. After the eight opening chapters the book goes on to deal in turn with specific aspects of human sexuality.

The Basis of Secular Morality

Secular morality is of universal validity, but in practical terms we may call it the non-believer's guide to conduct. Though its content is uncertain, we know it has a wide application. Most of us nowadays are non-believers. If not devotees of atheism (which itself is a form of belief) we find ourselves, often reluctantly, compelled by our intelligence to an agnostic stance. When it comes to understanding the universe, we admit to being mentally under-equipped.

What then is the basis of secular morality? In his *Encyclopaedia of Religion and Ethics* James Hastings said that ethics is not only of universal application, but refers to constant elements in human nature. Many will accept this as an adequate foundation, but we would do well to add an express reference to conscience. While a particular individual conscience may be an unreliable guide, we are impressed when a thing is treated as a matter of conscience by people in general. The generalised conscience, abstracted from individual human consciences, is of the essence of secular morality. In practical affairs, the morality is mediated by the individual conscience. This process is effective because the latter recognises and is inspired by the intimations of the former.

J. A. Smith, editor of Aristotle's *Ethics*, summed up secular moral philosophy from Plato to John Stuart Mill by saying that good character is the indispensable condition and chief determinant of happiness, the goal of human doing. The end of all action, individual or collective, is the greatest happiness of the greatest number. This utilitarian ethic is the best that sceptics have been able to manage. Since it depends on reason, rationalists will not despise it.

Aristotle said that character is formed by 'habituation', or the repeated doing of acts that have a common or similar quality. Such repetition, acting upon natural propensities or aptitudes, gradually fixes them. If they are to be fixed in a good, rather than a bad, mould this must be done in a certain way. The process is one of assimilation, largely by imitation and under direction and control in youth by the older and wiser. As this goes on there is a growing understanding of what one does, a choice of it for its own sake, a fixity and steadiness of purpose. Right acts and feelings become, through habit, easier and more pleasant. Eventually the doing of them becomes *second nature*. The virtuous character has been formed, which does not mean it will never thereafter be subject to temptation.

2

What then are 'right' acts? Aristotle considered them in two stages. First, they are acts that conform to a rule. This is the right rule, ultimately referable to reason. For the Greeks, moral conduct is in the end reasonable conduct. Second, their 'rightness' is judged by the doctrine of the mean. To do or feel what is right in a given situation is to do or feel just the amount reason requires, neither more nor less. Sometimes, as with sexual joy, reason may countenance an explosion of feeling. To do wrong is therefore to fall short of, or overshoot, a mean determined by the logic of the situation. The repetition of acts which lie in the mean is the cause of goodness of character, and for this rules can be given. J. A. Smith sums up Aristotle's teaching in these words:

The subject-matter of Human Conduct is not governed by necessary and uniform laws. But this does not mean it is subject to no laws. There are general principles at work in it, and these can be formulated in 'rules', which rules can be systematised or unified. It is all-important to remember that practical or moral rules are only general and always admit of exceptions, and that they arise not from the mere complexity of the facts, but from the liability of the facts to a certain unpredictable variation. At their very best, practical rules state probabilities, not certainties; a relative constancy of connection is all that exists, but it is enough to serve as a guide in life.

Undeterred by the saying that there are two species of the unwise, those who give advice and those who do not take it, this book aims to offer such a life guide, limited to the field of human sexuality. As the psychologist Margaret Knight remarked in her 1955 book *Morals Without Religion*, moral teaching cannot be coldly rational: there must be colour and warmth and interest. So the precepts are presented here within a commentary using stories taken from life and practical illustrations.

The eighteenth-century secular philosopher Rousseau believed that people are naturally unselfish and co-operative. If they behave otherwise, he thought, it is because their natural development has been interfered with. 'Man', said Rousseau, 'is naturally good. Only by institutions is he made bad.' This sunny doctrine contrasts with the earlier view of Hobbes that people are essentially selfish. He thought all our behaviour self-interested. If we help our neighbour, it is only because we think our neighbour may thereby be induced to help us when the time comes. The two views are opposite extremes, and no doubt the truth is somewhere in the middle. At whatever point it lies, it postulates the existence of a moral code.

What is behind such a code? What sanction can it have? Here we may find help from the answer given by Margaret Knight to the question 'Why should I consider others?'

because we are naturally social beings; we live in communities; and life in any community, from the family outwards, is much happier, and fuller, and richer if the members are friendly and co-operative than if they are hostile and resentful.

3

To the believer's retort that this omits anything equivalent to the religious reason for doing good, that it is God's will, Margaret Knight gives the sceptic's answer. Why should I do God's will? Why shouldn't I simply please myself? That, she argues, is just as much of a poser as 'Why should I consider others?'

Perhaps a more substantial sanction is that by committing immoral acts we damage the building up and securing of that good character so prized by Aristotle. A system of secular ethics does not pretend, like the Church, that any one of a number of sins is equally 'mortal' whatever the degree of obloquy involved. Common sense insists that some immoral acts are more evil than others. But it does not forbid us to accept that immorality in any degree, quite apart from its adverse effect on other people, is likely to damage the doer also.

This opening discussion on secular morality generally can be summarised in the first precept of our suggested code, as follows.

Though non-believers cannot accept religion, they acknowledge right and wrong. They wish to make the best of themselves, and out of common sympathy also wish the best for their fellow humans. Without any supposed divine command or revelation, they accept that human acts are moral, immoral or morally neutral. They perceive that this indicates the existence, in some sense that is real, of an objective standard of ethics (referred to in this book as 'the ethical code') whose sole base is in human reason and the human conscience.

Secular Sexual Morality

Passing to the area of secular morality dealing with sex, we may begin with a brief look at the current state of sexual ethics in the west. This is usually characterised as a conflict between the virtues of religious moralism and the evils of godless permissiveness. The dichotomy is false, however. Religious moralism is not always, or even usually, truly virtuous. On the other hand the majority of non-believers hold to an ethical standard which is high, though largely unargued and unformulated.

What you and I secretly wish for is the ability to act out our sexual fantasies wherever and whenever they present themselves. They are fascinating and beguiling. We suspect that at the end of life they will be the source of our most heartfelt regrets. Yet though our bodies are constructed for endless physical love-making, our souls require it to be conducted within a moral framework. Ethics, the science of living together on a correct moral basis, is a normative system. Setting forth *oughts*, it is concerned with right and wrong – unfashionable concepts in many quarters today. Yet we had better not forget that some actions are right and others wrong.

Sexual ethics is the set of oughts (or norms) that guides human sexual behaviour. Since right is an absolute, there can be only one true system. The problem we face is to discover it. In any society, norms may be agreed or disputed. If they are agreed, the society will be quiet and settled (though possibly misguided). If they are disputed, the society lacks an ethical system. Since possessing this is the necessary requisite of any successful human community, its plight is then pitiable.

Preparing uneasily to enter the twenty-first century, we citizens of today's western society find ourselves flung into this pitiable plight. We do not possess an agreed system of sexual ethics. So this book describes what does not exist? Precisely. It sets out our system of sexual ethics as many wish it to be, and believe it should be: the norms we need but have not got. What is the point of describing what does not exist as if it did exist? Why, so that it may exist.

In recent years the pendulum of western culture has swung back from the moral permissiveness of the 1960s towards greater strictness, though at bottom sex-negativism has ruled throughout the period as before. It derives from the fact that our society is steeped in the Judaeo-Christian moral culture. In a 1988 article on Aids the Chief Rabbi Lord Jakobovits cited parts of the Old Testament, among them Deuteronomy 23. This includes the following moral rules:

he that hath his privy member cut off, shall not enter into the congregation of the Lord. A bastard shall not enter into the congregation of the Lord; even to his tenth generation shall he not enter into the congregation of the Lord.

No one today would accept these rules. The presence in it of such plainly evil prescriptions must however deprive the whole text of any authority.

The New Testament is little better. Paul made it clear that sexual fulfilment even within marriage is disapproved of by the Church. It is, he said, good for a man not to touch a woman. Wishing everyone could be celibate as he was, but grudgingly accepting that this is impossible if the human race is to continue, Paul said: 'But if they cannot contain, let them marry; for it is better to marry than to burn'. Adding that what our human nature wants in the sexual realm is opposed to what the spirit wants, he said that the two are 'enemies'. The *Good News Bible* translates Paul's reasoning as: 'What human nature does is quite plain. It shows itself in immoral, filthy and indecent actions.'

Secular morality rejects the idea that human nature is immoral, filthy or indecent.

Some modern Christians try to wriggle out of the implications of Paul's clear statements on sex, just as they try to wriggle out of the equally clear New Testament doctrine of Hell, with its sinners seared (but never mercifully consumed) by torments of eternal fire. But it is a cheat for believers to deny the plainly sex-negative attitude of the Judaeo-Christian religion, about which more will be said in the discussion at the end of this chapter on the advent of Aids.

5

What are the manifestations of sex negation? They are numerous, and poison all our lives. Secrecy, prudery, guilt, shame and hypocrisy accompany them. They centre on the genital organs, and on other anatomical features that remind us of our sexuality (such as female breasts). They bid us conceal these features, or pretend we do not possess them. We must not own to the natural promptings of sexual desire. Unless respectably married, we must pass as eunuchs.

These preposterous restrictions are not observed, even by many of the religious: the sexual forces are too strong for that. But the restrictions do distort the effect of those natural forces. Bottled up desire, granted no socially acceptable outlet, breaks forth in rape or indecent exposure. Or, more commonly, it does not break forth at all but festers within. Repressed sexuality leads to personality disorders of a nature all too familiar.

A further alternative, for most robust or liberated individuals, is illicit indulgence coupled with guilt and the social disapproval of 'permissiveness'. Social disapproval can be crippling, as many homosexuals have found even after their activities ceased to be proscribed by the criminal law. On top of that comes the sniggering, furtive innuendo; the dirty joke that cheapens and degrades what should be wonderful; page three in the chronicle of our titillating society.

The religious attempt to push sexuality underground leads to fearsome evils. Human nature insistently demands sexual fulfilment. History shows that to ban anything for which there is an insistent demand results inevitably in unwholesome consequences. If honest people are prevented from supplying sexual services then crooks will do so. There will be racketeering, extortion and crime. Consumers will be overcharged and duped. Employment protection and quality control will be absent. Police will be bribed, and criminal lawyers will thrive. There will be a flourishing illicit market in prostitution, pornography and all forms of perversion. Such are the evil fruits of sex negation.

Sex must be moral, but Judaeo-Christian dogma teaches us it is irredeemably immoral. While people increasingly reject this dogma as incorrect or doubtful, no coherent set of secular moral principles has emerged to replace it. Being human, we must live by moral principles. We feel however that any moral principle we decide to adopt must be capable of reasonable explanation, and a convincing demonstration of its validity. In the realm of sex, this calls for a secular code capable of being taught convincingly to our youngsters.

No one has given us that. Lack of such acceptable teaching is productive of unhappiness. It strikes at the root of human nature. The time has come to place sexuality on its proper moral pinnacle. The Bible and the Church have laid down their code of sexual ethics. It is now necessary to lay down a code for those people who, in good faith, and often with heartfelt regret, find themselves unable to accept the teaching of the

6

Bible and the Church, in this if not in other matters. This does not mean wholesale rejection of the religious approach to sex, far from it. We must learn from the history of the Church as we learn from every other aspect of human history.

In a survey entitled *Sexuality and its Discontents*, published in 1985, Jeffrey Weeks asserted that we do not need a new sexual morality. Rather, he said, we should seek ways of living which recognise different beliefs, desires and moralities. This book rejects that view. While there are different beliefs, and sexual desire does manifest itself in different ways, a human morality of sex should be of universal validity – at least for non-believers. This is because, despite the erudite arguments to the contrary deployed by academics such as Weeks, human sexual needs are universal. So our code of secular sexual ethics must be valid for all, unless we are to settle for a weak relativism – or reject the whole idea of ethical principle.

We may sum up the argument for the existence of a code of secular sexual ethics in the following precept.

In the sexual field we all have a duty to be good, that is to act morally. This is part of our general duty, laid down by the ethical code, to act morally in every area of our life. Because the ethical code requires us to strive at all times and in all ways to be virtuous, it follows that we should strive to be virtuous in our sexual life. Indeed, since sexual wickedness can cause untold harm and distress, the duty to be good is particularly strong in this area.

The Duty of Ethical Understanding

For morality to be effective its precepts must be known by those bound by them. The suggested code therefore continues with a statement of this duty, which may be called the duty of ethical understanding. It would be presumptuous to assert or even hint that the duty applies to the particular version of the ethical code offered here. So far as possible we should each think out its principles for ourselves. The book's more modest aim is to help readers do this.

No one can be sure of acting morally in a given situation, or responding with moral correctness to the act of another, unless they know and understand what is called for by the ethical code. Therefore we should try to absorb its principles to the fullest extent of our capacity. This we may call the duty of ethical understanding.

The Duty of Ethical Action

It is of the essence of valid ethical precepts that they require to be followed. Here again we may look to Aristotle, who held that a moral virtue is no mere mood or feeling. It is he said a permanent *state* of the person's self or will, and consists in a steady self-imposed obedience to a rule of action in certain situations that recur in human life. For many of us, serious acceptance of this duty will require us to alter our outlook and behaviour. If there is indeed such a thing as right and wrong, there will always be some who need to mend their ways.

Does not the conscious adoption of a new morality require the exercise of free will? This book assumes, without attempting proof, that free will is available to its readers for this purpose. If any have doubts, let them act as if they did indeed possess this power. They will then find that this is one case where pretence is as effective as actuality.

Are there not psychological problems when trying to adapt one's personal moral system in response to intellectual argument? The book does not enter upon these. It assumes that if it is shown to be worth their while readers will be able to make this adjustment.

Is the ethical system here adumbrated correct? Readers may find that on this point their emotions will accept the lead of their mind. Even if they do not, it is surely of advantage to know clearly where the mind does lead.

We should comply with the ethical code not only directly but indirectly. It guides our own sexual acts and also our response to the sexual acts of others. What we must not do ourselves, we must not countenance others doing. What it is our duty to do, it is our duty to help others do also. All this may be called the duty of ethical action.

The Present Code

We have so far collected four moral precepts. It is time to say something of the entire formulation of which these constitute the opening propositions (referred to from now on as the Code).

The purpose of the Code is to express in verbal form the ideal or notional secular code of morality, so far as it relates to sex. To present in this way a set of principles of recycled sexual ethics is a bold, even presumptuous, enterprise. It is bound to be controversial, and can be justified only by the obvious need that exists for it. Technical works of moral philosophy are practically and intellectually inaccessible to most people, and in any case are suffused with disabling doubt and confounding qualification. We need to take a lesson, in this respect if no other, from those self-confident religious manuals addressed to the humble faithful. If their authors can be so sure of knowing what God requires, cannot the secular moralist pluck up courage enough to say what men, women and children require?

The Code is put forward as a universal prescription, ignoring religious and cultural differentiation. This again is controversial but is based on the contention that human morality is objective, not subjective, and that its essence is true to the absolutes of human nature. For those who cannot bring themselves to accept this contention the Code's status must be left to rest on the plausibility of the arguments supporting it, an unsatisfactory but not entirely worthless alternative. These arguments seem most likely to command agreement among persons living within the modern western secular culture, though this is not to accept that they lack universality.

Because the ethical code cannot be known in precise detail its prescriptions may be unclear in particular cases, and cannot be free from dispute. The present text (referred to in this book as 'the Code') attempts to formulate the ethical code, so far as it relates specifically to human sexuality, in a form most likely to produce certainty and command agreement in the modern western secular culture.

A word needs to be said at this point on the problem of coercion. Primarily, the ethical code is concerned to guide the acts and omissions of persons whose will is free, that is not overborne by pressure from another person or an artificial factor such as the effect of a drug. We do not consider that the will has ceased to be free merely because it is under pressure from a normal innate source such as sexual desire or lust, even though the subject is what we call over-sexed.

Therefore when the Code suggests that a particular act is immoral it is assuming that the act is done by a person exercising free will. Where this is not the case, different considerations may arise. It is beyond the scope of this book to enter at length into familiar problems of moral philosophy connected with the unfree or coerced will. By an immoral act we mean an act which is immoral when done freely. If such an act is done under the influence of a drug freely taken, the moral blameworthiness is much the same. If it is done under the coercion of a stronger person the degree of immorality may be lessened, depending on the degree and nature of the coercion.

Akin to coercion is medical disability. Can a psychotic be said to act immorally? Probably not. Does morality therefore apply only to those who are mentally intact? Certainly not. The moral problems created by the existence in the subject of a sexual dysfunction or disorder are complex. Therefore a separate chapter is devoted to them in this book (see chapter 5).

Interpreting the Code

The Code is intended to be coherent, but not repetitive. It is designed to be read as a whole, so that a particular statement cannot safely be taken in isolation. For example, the rule that it is not immoral to pay for sexual services does not validate child prostitution; elsewhere the Code lays down the principles applicable to sexual acts involving children.

The Code pays no regard to *legal* rules. That many acts declared not immoral by the code are proscribed by the current law merely indicates the need for law reform. When the social consensus changes, this will follow (though we need to remember Maugham's apothegm that however harmless a thing is, if the law forbids it most people will think it wrong). On the other hand an act declared by the Code to be immoral should not necessarily be made illegal. Harm is done by launching criminal prosecutions over relatively minor sexual misdemeanours.

The Code is incomplete in that it does not state *general* moral principles, such as our duty to be honest with one another, which apply in the sexual field as elsewhere. The Code concentrates on ethical principles which are limited to the sexual field because directly related to sexuality, such as the morality of masturbation or a woman's right to control her fertility. This distinction is worth bearing constantly in mind during a discussion of sexual ethics because it means that many moral problems encountered in the sexual field are not essentially sexual at all. By understanding this we can free our assessment, at least in certain areas, from the special difficulty that the sex-negating approach has brought to questions of private and public conduct.

Another distinction that needs to be remembered, in sex as in art, is that between aesthetics and ethics. The fact that I dislike a thing does not make it immoral. Your opinion that another's preferred sexual act is disgusting, repulsive or absurd in itself gives you no right to brand it as ethically wrong. It may merely be in bad taste (perhaps, as with some varieties of oral sex, in more senses than one). Conversely, to say that a sexual act is morally neutral, or even morally good, does not mean that you or I approve it, or that to commit it in particular circumstances is tasteful, wise or kind. One person's sexual meat is another's poison. The universality we are after here is solely moral, so the Code avoids pronouncing on subjective and variable criteria.

It is important to bear in mind when reading the Code that its effect is intended to be cumulative. Each precept is subject to limitations stated elsewhere in the Code, and also by precepts of the ethical code not specific to sexual matters. The Code is concerned only with morality, and pays no regard to law or aesthetics. In the Code references to acts include omissions.

The Need for Love

Though it does not belong in the Code, a little space must be found in this book on sexual morality for the statement that goodness is not enough, and love too is needed. Margaret Knight said warm-hearted and generous natures are developed not by training and discipline but by love, adding:

There is abundant evidence that if a child is brought up in a warm, happy, confident, affectionate home atmosphere, he has the best chance of developing into a well-balanced, secure, affectionate and generous-minded person. Whereas the child who has not got this background – the child who feels unloved, or who can never feel sure he is loved – is the potential problem case.

Another witness is Bhagwan Shree Rajneesh, known to his devotees as Osho. This eastern advocate of sexual freedom, who died in 1990, left us the message that sex should be accepted, explored, celebrated – and transcended. That transcendency is love.

People have little patience with one who, though moral, is unloving. Since, however, this is a book on morality rather than love, we can say no more on the subject here, but must leave it for students of morality to ponder on.

The Advent of Aids

Finally, space must also be found to address the question of what difference (if any) the advent of the HIV virus has made to the principles of secular morality. In the late twentieth century one cannot know whether Aids will be a quickly passing or a lasting threat, though it is likely to be the former. On either view, does the arrival of this fell disease alter the principles of positive sex morality?

The answer is no. A system of morality could not be valid if it required adjustment because of sudden changes in the medical *milieu*. Moreover there is no evidence that the existence, as opposed to the propagation, of the HIV virus is in the slightest degree attributable to human sexual activity. It is something God has sent us, if you believe in God. Otherwise it may be looked on as a blind natural development.

Aids has certainly brought forth moral confusion of a high order, particularly manifested in comments by various ecclesiastical dignitaries. At the root of this confusion are two linked propositions, invariably stated or assumed by such commentators. One is that only religious people are sexually moral. The other is that the only sexual ethics is religious sexual ethics. These propositions, though widely accepted, are transparently false and highly dangerous to our society. We have long known that religious people are not necessarily moral. It is now opportune to point out that moral people are not necessarily religious.

Aids, says Cardinal Hume, head of the Roman Catholic Church in Britain, is but one of the many disastrous consequences of promiscuous sexual behaviour. Promiscuity, he adds, has always been sinful, and is now suicidal as well. In this respect morality, he goes on, is not the exclusive concern of the Church and the clergy (a remark that subtly conveys the message that in general morality *is* the exclusive concern of the Church and the clergy). To be fully human and self-giving, the Cardinal continues, sexual intercourse must permit the possibility of conception. Once conception occurs it must never, for any cause, be terminated. That is the classic sexual morality of the Judaeo-Christian religion, but it is not the only sexual morality available to mankind.

The tone for religious condemnation in relation to Aids was set by an announcement issued in December 1986 by the former Nonconformist, now Catholic convert, Chief Constable of Greater Manchester James Anderton. God, he informed us, had, as happened on a previous occasion with Moses, spoken privately to him. This time there was no burning bush, but otherwise the scenario was similar to that described in Exodus 3. God told the Chief Constable, as He had earlier told Moses, that He had seen the affliction of His people, and heard their cry, and knew their sorrows. Nevertheless it had to be pointed out that they were, as the Chief Constable put it (acting as God's trumpet), swirling in a cesspit of their own making.

In similar vein was the first pronouncement on Aids made by the Chief Rabbi, Sir Immanuel (now Lord) Jakobovits. It appeared in *The Times* of 27 December 1986 under the heading 'Only a moral revolution can contain this scourge.' The Jewish rabbinical head began by pointing out that the earliest sources of Hebrew law and morality are unambiguous, branding sexual freedom as an abomination. He reminded us of the stern warnings of national doom consequent on any defiance of these injunctions. The land itself will 'vomit out' peoples violating the divine principle of sex negation. The Chief Rabbi went on:

Aids is the price we pay for the 'benefits' of the permissive society which, helped by the pill, liberal legislation and more 'enlightened' attitudes, has demolished the last defences of sexual restraint and self-discipline, leading to a collapse of nature's self-defence against degeneracy.

Prophylactic measures suggested to reduce the spread of Aids include the provision without charge of condoms. Clean needles, it is said, should be supplied for drug-abusers. The Chief Rabbi distinguished between the respective morality of these measures. Free condoms, he says, would merely encourage indecent conduct, condoning and facilitating sexual irresponsiblity and increasing the ravages of personal degradation and social disintegration. Clean needles for drug-abusers, on the other hand, might without moral offence be regarded as acceptable.

Let Aids prompt us towards morality, as the religious commentators urge. But let it be the right (which does not mean right-wing) morality. In truth Aids, like any other sexually-transmissible disease, is morally neutral. It is how we respond to it, as to any other such threat, that is moral or immoral. For a person who knows they have syphilis to engage in sexual intercourse without first informing the partner and giving them an opportunity of refusal has been immoral for as long as syphilis has existed. Now the same can be said in relation to Aids, except that the immorality is greater because the possible consequences are graver. The arrival of Aids may in a particular case transform what was a morally acceptable (because remote) risk of disease into a morally unacceptable (because present and fearsome) risk of disease. If and when Aids is brought under medical control, this will change accordingly.

The new risk of contracting the HIV virus has rendered many sexual acts which are morally good, because tender and other-regarding, for the present unwise and even immoral. The use of condoms may help in this situation by reducing the risk to an acceptable level. We cannot expel risk totally from our lives. It is part of morality to judge dangers sensibly, and reduce them by appropriate methods. Sometimes it is part of morality to elect to forgo an otherwise permissible sexual experience because it involves unacceptable risk to oneself or another. That is not a sex-negating attitude, but one that shows respect for the self, for the other, and for the marvellous human attribute of sexuality.

We see that Aids is a coercive, not an ethical, factor. I do not change my ethics because I am coerced. Human ethical values are seen as absolute, which means timeless and unchanging. They are not to be distorted by current medical anxieties, however demanding. So sexual ethics after Aids is what sexual ethics used to be before Aids. The crucial difference made by the advent of this disease is that the practicalities, not the moralities, are altered. It has always been an ethical principle to respect one's own body. It has always been an ethical principle for one who knows that he or she is or may be diseased not to risk infecting the other's body. The rules are sharpened when the invading organism is an HIV virus, but the principle remains the same.

Aids raises another question, which is one more of taste than ethics. How should one regard and refer to an Aids victim? Even the phrasing of this question is open to challenge, since some well-meaning people think we are now meant to avoid any suggestion that Aids is a thing that victimises people. The correct phrase, we are told, is 'person with Aids'. Here the strange connotation is that to call a person a victim is to impute blame. Thus is the language turned upside down.

The truth is that some people infected by the HIV virus (such as drug-takers who share needles) may be morally blameworthy, while others (such as haemophiliacs given contaminated blood) are clearly not. So the mere fact that a person is infected carries no moral message, and should never be assumed to. We should respect the wishes of relatives and others who prefer it not to be known that their loved one was a victim of Aids. The same may apply to other questionable reasons for fatality, such as cirrhosis of the liver. Until recently, cancer was unmentionable as a cause of death.

Conclusion

The final word on Aids is that it must never be allowed to strengthen the already strong sex-negative bias within the countries of the west. Nor must it impede us in finding what we need, namely a sex-positive bias. This need was recognised long before the advent of Aids, as long ago as 1975, by the World Health Organisation. It quietly said (Technical Report Series No. 572): 'There is a need to change the existing attitudes toward human sexuality among the general public.' This desired principle of *sex acceptance* is the subject of the next four chapters.

2
Sex-acceptance and the Origins of Sex-negativism

The Duty of Sex-acceptance

Since we are all sexual beings we should look upon our own or another's sexual organs, functions and desires positively, with welcoming acceptance that they exist and work (the duty of sex-acceptance). We should never look on them negatively, with dislike, regret or contempt. This does not mean that remediable sexual disorders ought to be accepted as they are, or that immoral sexual behaviour should be tolerated.

This and the next three chapters are devoted to the important duty of sex-acceptance, defined in the precept of the Code set out above. The principle is of basic importance because sex-negativism, or the rejection of human sexuality, is deeply ingrained in our culture. It is part of the general rejection of the body (in favour of the spirit) which as we saw in the opening chapter has been fostered over nearly two millennia by the teachings of the Judaeo-Christian religion. In a review of Michael Gill's book *Images of the Body* Jonathan Keates brilliantly described the deleterious effect this has had:

Birds and beasts are at ease with their own bodies, we are not. Our deepest springs of self-hatred, of shame and unease, derive from our imprisoning framework of mortal flesh and bone. We inflate and reduce it, mutilate and deform it, we cover it in paints, oils, powders and creams, and suppress it almost entirely under layers of clothing. Ours is an enduring rage against the facts of physical form, outline and identity. [*Independent*, 26 May 1990]

We are under a duty somehow to overcome this negative conditioning, and train ourselves and our children to accept and welcome to the full the wholesome sexual nature of humanity. The conditioning has many aspects, and to be successful in uprooting it we need to understand all of these. Therefore this chapter is necessarily long and detailed.

We begin by looking once more at the religious origins.

Religious Origins of Sex-negativism

Under our Church-conditioned ethos, sexuality is only grudgingly admitted to be part of the human condition. All other areas of our bodily equipment are, the Church agrees, to be looked upon positively. The

15

current 'respectable' moral system, still struggling to free itself from Victorian and earlier religious constraints, views sex alone negatively. It was not after all liberated by the forays earlier this century of such innovative thinkers as Freud, Krafft-Ebing, and Havelock Ellis. These sought to make sex respectable by discussing it in terms of science. They overlooked the fact that most people are unwilling to accord science much respectability.

Roger Scruton says of these innovators in his 1986 book *Sexual Desire*:

Such was the prestige of science that any investigation conducted in its name could call upon powerful currents of social approval, which were sufficient to overcome the otherwise crippling reluctance to face the realities of sexual experience.

Unhappily, this is overstated. Though science may have been thought prestigious, it did not prove in this context sufficiently so. The social tide favouring science proved too weak to overwhelm the contrary currents of sex-negation.

Even Freud, though no evangelist, exhibited to some degree this negative impulse. He baldly described the aim of sexual desire as 'union of the genitals in the act known as copulation . . . a satisfaction analogous to the sating of hunger'. Scruton comments that such language expresses a certain hatred of the sexual act and all that pertains to it. He remarks that there is something strange and even a little pathological in a person who feel that his sexual parts and functions are in themselves contemptible or evil.

All other human parts and functions are welcomed, or at least accepted.

Take the intellect. No one (except possibly a hapless egalitarian) would tell a bright child that it was right for it to suppress its intellectual powers. No sensible person would suggest the child should cover up these natural assets, or exhibit shame when attention was drawn to them, or shrink from using them to the full at all times.

Again, consider human beauty. If a face is beautiful we rejoice. If it is supremely beautiful, we expect some artist to get its configuration and colouring down on canvas for the benefit of posterity. There can be no shame in any of this. Manual skill is another instance. A man or woman may be an elegant wood-carver, or a craftsman in metal, or merely a competent bricklayer. In each case we admire the work, and rejoice in the skill of the worker.

Take the opposite extreme. A child is a spastic, and we feel compassion. A young woman lacks imagination, or suffers nervous tremors, or is repulsively ugly, and we are sympathetic. A man is illiterate or in-numerate, or both, and we show our understanding of his plight (while blaming his supposed educators).

At either pole, in such cases (or any other outside the sexual field) we do not shrink from viewing the facts as they are. We may out of pity refrain from stressing the unfortunate side. If the case is one of triumph and achievement, we might wish to play things down a little so that the subject does not get carried away. For the unfortunate handicapped, our praise may be a little too loud. On the whole however we wish to treat all aspects of the human condition (always excepting sexuality) in a positive way. We seek to enhance whatever human qualities and attributes are brought to our attention, not diminish them. If there are defects, we want to see them removed.

So it ought to be with people's erotic natures. They should, as natural features, be viewed as morally good – or at least morally neutral. We ought to want each person to achieve his or her potential in the sexual field, as we do in any other field. Since sex is undoubtedly important to every one of us, we should give this positive aim a high priority. Yet we are all conditioned in the opposite direction.

Here is a trivial yet revealing example. In July 1988 the *Sun* reported the case of a young husband whose friend suggested he could improve marital love-making by persuading his wife to engage in sexual fantasies. So that night he solemnly asked that lady to pretend to be a strict schoolmistress. Whereupon she rose from the connubial bed and went downstairs. A few minutes later she handed him a piece of paper on which was written 'Write out 500 lines: "I must not be filthy".'

The opposite of hate is love, and similarly the opposite of negativism is positivism. Understanding its opposite helps us understand what sex-negation is. A person imbued with love of sexuality is not the same as a sex-fiend, obsessed by lust. Such people have a balanced, though basically positive, attitude to their inmost being, and that of others.

We can't love other people unless we first love ourselves. Loving ourselves requires a welcoming acceptance of every human attribute we possess, which includes sexual desire. Yet modern society denies this acceptance, and thereby turns us into emotional cripples. An erect penis or moist vagina is non-existent. The sex ache is an aberration. Desire equals lust, and lust is no more elevated than an itch. All such manifestations must be concealed, and so rendered into nothing, by the damnable veil of prudery.

We sense, indeed are sure, that we should strive to develop each human attribute and learn to use it better. In order to live as human beings, we need to know ourselves and accept the nature and quality of every faculty we are blessed with. Yet religion does not preach acceptance of the nature or quality of what it is pleased to call our carnal (that is fleshly) attributes. It does the opposite.

Paul viewed the flesh as contemptible, for it 'lusteth against the spirit.' The gnostic Manichean tradition of the inherent sinfulness of the flesh, though formally disowned by the Church, proved persistent (we return to this below). St Barnabas of Siena regarded it as a mortal sin not to abstain from sex before taking communion, and the medieval framers of canon law engaged in protracted debates on whether even connubial intercourse should for a time disqualify the 'unclean' couple from participation in the eucharist. References to women in early canon law were mainly concerned with excluding them from the sanctuary as 'unclean', and denying them contact with priests. In *Embracing the Chaos* Kenneth Leech says: 'as representatives of the lower, carnal nature, they were sources of contamination to those identified as holy.'

Religious sex-negation wishes to put down sex, but biology makes the achievement of this aim impossible. If the semen of men or boys is not voided voluntarily then it will be voided, through nocturnal emissions, involuntarily. What is more those emissions are likely to be accompanied by vivid images of a regrettably libidinous character, usually known as wet dreams. This applies whether the hapless subject welcomes it or not. Even holy popes are subjected by their bodies to wet dreams.

Chaste women too experience orgasms while they sleep. Among believers these may be attributed to religious ecstasy. According to Dr Desmond Morris in his book *The Human Zoo*, St Theresa of Lisieux innocently described her vision of an angel in terms indicating that not even saints are immune from erotic desire:

In his hands I saw a long golden spear and at the end of the iron tip I seemed to see a point of fire. With this he seemed to pierce my heart several times so that it penetrated to my entrails. When he drew it out I thought he was drawing them out with it and he left me completely afire with the great love of God. The pain was so acute that it made me utter several sharp moans; and so excessive was the sweetness caused by the intense pain that one can never wish to lose it.

Such is the power of sexuality, which exists even when unrecognised. Solemn treatises have been written by theologians debating whether sexual dreams encompass mortal sin or merely venial sin – or no sin at all. Such is the absurdity of the religious rejection of sex.

Believers are asked to accept that despite being a religion of incarnation Christianity despises our poor body, bidding us renounce all sinful lusts of the flesh. The doctrine of original sin makes every one of us inescapably wicked from our birth to our death, unless 'redeemed' by the Saviour. A punishment of Adam and Eve at the Fall was thereafter to feel they must keep hidden their sexual parts. E. M. Forster was one of many who have given up a desired refuge in Christianity, saying that those who base their conduct upon what they are, rather than what they supposedly ought to be, always must throw it over in the end.

The religious impulse is valuable. Spirituality can be a potent force for good. Whether founders of the church like Paul were mistaken, or whether subsequent church leaders misinterpreted their message, we do not know. But it is evident that we must take ourselves as we really are. We ought not to feel shame at attributes embedded deep within us by nature. We should accept them – and love them because we love (or ought to love) our whole selves. A prominent attribute of human nature is sexuality, so we should love that. We should be sex lovers.

What does this involve? Loving any human attribute involves obvious responses. We accept it fully, not stifling it or feeling apologetic about it (that does not mean giving it unbridled rein). We seek ways of achieving its fulfilment: according to its nature. We realise that if within our own peculiar habitation it is stunted or twisted then inevitably we shall be stunted or twisted too. We defend it against ignorant attack. Above all we welcome it in our children.

Sex-positivism is the happy acceptance of human sexuality, seeking its fulfilment: wholeness is all. But all the time the sex lover is aware of other values, such as tenderness and fidelity. He or she constantly reflects that we should never fulfil any emotional impulses of our own at the cost of casting another person as victim.

Sex-negaters feel the opposite. The pay no regard to the other, and seek to dismiss sexuality all round the compass. Far from accepting this quality as a vital element in the human make-up, they wish sex away. They would prefer human beings to be without such a messy attribute. That is arrogant: you fancy yourselves as designers of the universe?

Such negative aims are seen, even by the stupid, to be impossible of total fulfilment if the race is to be carried on (and we all complacently believe it *should* be carried on). So the sex-negative purpose becomes an endeavour to confine our sexual impulse to its narrowest limits. The boundaries are drawn by such false precepts as the following.

1. Sexuality is not possessed by children, since its messiness would pollute their innocence. (Childhood is extended well beyond puberty for this purpose.)

2. Inescapably, and for some regrettably, innocent childhood gives way to adolescence. Equally inescapably, adolescents are sex-conscious creatures. This too is regrettable. Their attention must be distracted, and they must be taught earnestly to save themselves for marriage.

3. Being a status requiring economic self-sufficiency, marriage has to be postponed well beyond the age of maximum sexual potency. Never mind, it does youngsters good to go without. It helps to teach them that life is full of hardships.

4. Next comes maturity, when sexuality may legitimately be indulged. But only by those who first manage to get themselves safely tied up in the estate of holy matrimony. Even then, in the eyes of the stricter religions (such as Roman Catholicism), legitimate sex is available only when conception is truly desired and no man-contrived obstacle is placed in the way of the thrusting spermatozoa.

5. Finally comes the time of life when childbearing is past. The argument about carrying on the race no longer applies. Sex-negaters prefer there to be now no sexual activity. Bodies are past the trim neatness of youth. It is seemly for their owners to recognise this, and behave with fleshly decorum until at last the undertaker beckons.

6. For those (notably lesbians and male homosexuals) whose sexual orientation altogether precludes procreation, there is no mercy at any time of life. Always, they must be chaste or be sinners.

These then are the age-old postures of sex-negation. They would do little harm if not enforced and reinforced by the whole apparatus of the state. The established Church is prominent here – along with the Church-based morality of many schools. Priests say: give us a child for its first five years and it is our's for ever. Early indoctrination is life-long indoctrination.

Also dominant is the law, again Church-based. Christianity, it used to be said, is part of the law of England. The trace lingers. Other common-law countries follow suit. Law reinforces sex-negation by fine or imprisonment for breach of the code. In former days (not so long ago) torture and death were also numbered among legal punishments for sexual crime. Politicians uphold the sex-negative attitude, mainly because it is their function to reflect the views of their electorate. That electorate is you and me, and nearly all of us are suborned.

Since SEX IS BAD, overt manifestations of this blood-reliant pulsating human attribute must be reduced to a minimum. That conviction, flowing weakly overtly, though rejected strongly covertly, is what feeds the springs of sex-negation. In Freudian terms it may be described as a component of the superego. For the Manichees, once a widespread Judaeo-Christian sect, it was a basic religious tenet. As Professor Parrinder tells us in his 1980 book *Sex in the World's Religions*, the Manichees held sexual intercourse to be sinful, polluting and inferior.

We need to look more closely at that tell-tale word *polluting*. Rational beings, we strive to convince ourselves that we should not dislike a thing unless there were reasonable justification. Being conditioned to dislike sex, we dutifully search for this. Eventually we come up with a number of reasons *why* SEX IS BAD.

One whole segment of the explicit and implied justification for the rejection of human sexuality is summed up in the proposition that *sex is dirty*.

The Proposition that Sex is Dirty

The Judaeo-Christian is far from being alone among the world's religious systems in propagating sex-negativism. Parrinder cites, as one instance among many, what was said of sexual desire in one of the Sanskrit religious texts known as the Upanishads.

In this ill-smelling, unsubstantial body, which is a conglomerate of bone, skin, muscle, marrow, flesh, semen, blood, mucus, tears, rheum, faeces, urine, wind, bile, and phlegm, what is the good of enjoyment of desires?

To which one can only answer, what indeed?

Our refined culture dislikes the idea that men, women and especially children are animals with bowels, bladders and continually discharging glands. We worship beauty, and that does not go with such things. We rather wish our bodies were constructed to do without elimination. That would be our choice, had we been consulted on the matter at the design stage. Public occasions reflect this sentiment. The airs and dignities put on by the human animal at the opening of a parliament, or in a law court, or at the laying of a foundation stone, are unconvincing – even pathetic. The beautiful figures gyrating in the ballet or stalking the fashion catwalk ought not, we feel, to have been urinating or defecating a bare few minutes ago.

The tangles of nomenclature we get into over sex are echoed in relation to excretion. There is still no satisfactory term to denote the place wherein we perform this essential function. Urinal is an honest word, but insufficient. Lavatory is acceptable, but inaccurate (it means a place where you wash). WC is accurate but cryptic (the initials stand for water closet). Toilet properly describes a process, not a place. Loo, now widely used, is truly an eighteenth-century card game. In the excretory context this word is morever class-conscious (not to say snobbish) and arch.

Like problems attend the eliminatory act itself. 'I must powder my nose' is a little more insufferable, and only a little less widespread, than 'I must spend a penny.' Jolly upper-class males will condescend to go for a pee but the person who, in any company, announces an intention to piss or shit will be looked at askance. A 'lady' who did so would promptly forfeit that title. Yet those two simple onomatopoeic terms are surely the most fitting. Why can we not use them without constraint or embarrassment?

Excretion has much to do with sex. The Great Architect of the Universe has chosen to saddle us with an anatomy where the two are inextricably mixed; for He (or possibly She) has placed the sexual orifices *inter urinam et faeces*.

Take the penis, whether flaccid or erect. For the adult or adolescent male this one organ forms the seat of his deepest sensual feeling, the fleshly tube by which he daily and casually eliminates liquid waste, and the stiff connector for initiating human life. The clever economy secured by this three-in-one arrangement is purchased at the cost of mental and emotional confusion. That this would be the result might have occurred to an apprentice plumber, never mind the Great Architect of the Universe.

The designer of the female did do better, but not much. At least she has separate orifices for micturition and fecundation, and a third bit of anatomy (the clitoris) for sexual feeling. But these organs are all placed depressingly close together, and are likely to get mixed up by the uninitiated or clumsy. In addition, both sexes have the anus lurking near.

All this has led to the cheapening of sex by equating it with excretion. Because the latter's products are 'dirty' the process naturally forms a basis in language for terms of abuse or aggression. But why should we do the same thing in relation to sexuality? To call a man a cunt or a prick is more or less equivalent to calling him a shit or (in American English) an asshole. The principle of sex respect, discussed in the next chapter, demands that we eschew such usages.

Biology decrees that excretory and genital organs shall emit discharges, and they insist on doing so whether we like it or not. The chastest priest or nun will from time to time find evidence of precisely the same effluent from his or her interior as the grossest libertine. It is something to be suffered and endured, part of the human lot. That doesn't stop punishment being handed out.

Take menstruation, a discharge with inevitable sexual overtones. The *monthly blood* has been looked on as ritually unclean by most human societies, including our own. The Kgatla of Bechuanaland (now Botswana), to take one instance at random, have a very low opinion of it. A girl of twenty told Professor Isaac Schapera of her mother's warning:

My daughter, you see many girls hurt boys by clutching them when menstruating. If a boy clutches such a girl, and she clutches him, it is a dangerous thing. The boy will die, and you will remain alive, so you must be careful never to clutch a boy when you are in this unclean condition.

The Hua tribe of New Guinea believe that *men* can become pregnant if they eat food that has been touched by a menstruating woman. The New Testament speaks of 'hating even the garment spotted by the flesh' (Jude 23) and of those women who 'defile' their garments (Revelation 3:4).

We are scarcely more enlightened today. Jewish married couples are still enjoined to refrain from sexual intercourse during a period of twelve days in each month when the wife is deemed ritually 'unclean'. Countless girls, of all religions and none, have suffered the shock of a first menstrual flow without the slightest warning from their embarrassed mothers (or anyone else). Even that most advanced of feminists Germaine Greer forced herself to admit in *The Female Eunuch* that:

Despite my own proselytising attitude, I must confess to a thrill of shock when one of the ladies to whom this book is dedicated told me that she had tasted her own menstrual blood on the penis of her lover. There are no horrors present in that blood, no poisons; I would suck, a bleeding finger, I would not scruple to kiss a bleeding lip, and yet . . . The only cure for such superstitions is base empiricism, innocently undertaken.

The vulva suffers from a general conviction that it is dark and unclean. Another ardent feminist, Eleanor Stephens, asks for release from the prejudices against oral sex, 'like the myth that our genitals are "bad" and "dirty" parts of our bodies'. Kate Millett, yet another activist in the women's movement, describes an interview with a prostitute who confided:

I think that the conviction that females are dirty, that their genitals are dirty, really sticks to us. I think that's why I don't like men to go down on me. Because I think I'm dirty . . . and I think they're not . . . A lot comes from this belief in our dirt – like I was douching all the time. Some of them like you to be dirty. One guy said to me, 'I would like it if you didn't douche for a week.'

Irving Bieber, the American psychoanalyst, tells of a young male patient who felt a woman's sexual areas to be very messy in contrast to the neat and clean male genital. Yet the male genital is not always so neat and clean. A smelly encrustation known as smegma accumulates beneath the foreskin of the uncircumcised penis when its owner washes it too rarely. Even the devoted homosexual J. R. Ackerley (devoted mainly to young guardsmen) confessed in *My Father and Myself* to his dislike of what he described as 'unwashed cocks'.

It is true some people find this dirtiness attractive, but society classes them as deviants. Christopher Isherwood in *Christopher and his Kind* tells of a homosexual who paid a young man not to wash himself for a month. 'At the end of the month he came to see me, and he smelt exactly like a fox. Delicious!' We recoil at this, as we are conditioned to do. Yet some liberationists have taught themselves to revel in such things. The gay activist Charles Shively wrote in 1980 of what it means to be 'good' at sex.

being 'good' is giving a good blow job or rim job, being 'good' is being hot and hard, being 'good' is letting it all come out: sweat, shit, piss, spit, cum; being 'good' is being able to take it all, take it all the way.

Smell is nowadays one more stick for the respectable to beat sex with. In the past, attitudes were different. J. A. C. Brown remarks of Victorian child-bearing:

Little attempt was made at bowel-training until the second or third year, and the child was often wrapped in swaddling-clothes; for bad smells, in those days of poor sanitation, and in particular faecal and urinary smells, were simply ignored.

We don't like the sound of this today, when bad smells are outlawed and most lovers expect their partners, with the aid of expensive, unnecessary and possibly dangerous deodorants and sweat-inhibitors, to make themselves 'squeaky-clean'. This sentiment can be, and often is, made a subterfuge by wives disinclined for sex. The Danish doctors Inge and Sten Hegeler put the matter in this way:

Is it perverse that some women ask their husbands to have a bath before coming to bed with them? No, it's only very natural. But sometimes it is used as an excuse for avoiding sexual intercourse. In which case it is only a pretext. We human beings do tend to smell a little. But *old* dirt and sweat is more than one should be allowed to subject one's partner to.

If women were able to sniff at their sexual organs they would discover that they can never become so thoroughly clean as to be completely free of smell. It is unnatural and over-romantic to attempt to quell one's own body odour – and the smell of one's sexual organs – with perfumes and other strange smells. Inge and Stan Hegeler go on:

We are not suggesting that this can be used as an excuse for anyone to refrain from washing themselves. But it is meant as a kind of kick in the pants to those women who examine their newly washed husbands, wrinkle their noses and say: 'You still smell.' It is a human being's right to smell like a human being.

Humans are evolving, developing, changing. We can't go back to being dirty and unwashed. We can't even accept natural odours. If the animal smell of the tumescent female offends us we need to do something about it. Vaginal deodorants have, after all, been invented – and are widely used. Sex *can* be dirty. But it need not be.

Anyway, whatever turns you on . . . A man or woman can be so carried away by passion as to care nothing for the state of cleanliness of the beloved. If it were not so, few of us would be here today. Dirt, like beauty, sits in the eye (or nostril) of the beholder. True love is blind, and without any awareness of offensive smells emanating from the beloved. Or is it?

No, however things may have been in the past most of us today want sex without smells, without dirt. Visual attraction is strong, and oral response often desired. Unless carried away, we are fussy about what goes into our mouths. Elaborate regulations, backed by strict enforcement systems, govern food hygiene. Additives are restricted. Restaurants are put out of business for having dirty kitchens. Wrapping and storing of food are controlled. Furthermore, we have become much more particular about personal cleanliness. The days are long gone when lawyer Grump lived in the Temple, that barristers' retreat in central London. Here is how, in his novel *Pendennis*, Thackeray depicts the personal hygiene of a professional man of the mid-nineteenth century:

Old Grump, of the Norfolk Circuit, who had lived for more than thirty years in the chambers under those occupied by Warrington and Pendennis, and who used to be awakened by the roaring of shower-baths which these young gentlemen had erected in their apartments – part of the contents of which occasionally trickled through the roof into Mr Grump's room – declared that the practice of washing was an absurd, new-fangled, dandyfied folly, and daily cursed the laundress who slopped the staircase by which he had to pass. Grump, now much more than half a century old, had indeed never used the luxury in question. He had done without water very well, and so had our fathers before him.

Would anyone today fancy oral sex with old Grump? In the past, people's bodies were filthy. Men and women chewed cachous to disguise the fact that, emerging past dirty and rotting teeth, their breath stank. In the theatre one evening Dr Johnson was rebuked by a lady who said: 'Sir, you smell!' The great lexicographer, a stickler for the accurate use of words, replied: 'Madam, you are mistaken. *You* smell. *I* stink!'

Nowadays we do not stink. Some prevent it by a daily bath. Others, still carrying on the ancient practice of drowning bodily odours by more powerful olfactory agents, use anti-perspirants, deodorants, after-shave lotions or other disguises. Some fearful souls use all of these. We are, in short, fastidious. Being fastidious, we find it difficult to come to terms with the animal nature of sex. The height of sexual action is orgasm, but this involves effluvia. Under Judaic law coitus, because of bodily discharge, renders husband and wife ritually unclean.

It takes considerable effort for the modern sex-citizen (if so we may call one who subscribes to orthodox tenets) to take within his or her body, however much inspired by passion, the dirt or other natural discharge of a fellow sexual creature. Even simple kissing fills some with doubt about the transfer of bacteria from one mouth to another.

At the other extreme R. A. Wilson in his book *Sex and Drugs* describes an ancient gnostic rite still in occasional use. It is inscribed in allegorical language, which Wilson translates:

it means that the man should obtain some of his own semen by performing cunnilingus after coitus has been completed. Some of this he himself swallows and some he transmits to the lady, who swallows it via a kiss. This curious rite, which goes back to the Gnostics *c.* 300 AD, has always been highly regarded by European occultists. Modern psychology might suggest that it is a particularly vivid way of communicating a love that forcibly transcends the sex disgust and loathing of the orthodox Christian.

We find it hard to accept this rite, and prefer to think of all bodily excretion as 'unclean'. Like the criminal described by Professor D. C. Gordon, we acknowledge the psychic link, conforming after all to the biological link, between excretion and sex:

Many criminals . . . urinate, defecate, masturbate or have an orgasm at the scene of the crime after its commission. Sometimes the evacuation is unpremeditated, involuntary and spontaneous and a result of the over-all relaxation of physical as well as mental tension, and at other times it is deliberate or mechanically and voluntarily induced, but, nevertheless, it is a result of the same great tension for which relief is sought.

Perhaps our culture is not so far removed from that of the savages after all. We, like them, link sex not only with dirt but with cruelty and violence. Here is Malinowski's account of a strange custom still existing in the Trobriand Islands:

The man is the fair game of the woman for all that sexual violence, obscene cruelty, filthy pollution, and rough handling can do to him. Thus first they pull off and tear up his pubic leaf, the protection of his modesty and, to a native, the symbol of his manly dignity. Then, by masturbatory practices and exhibitionism, they try and produce an erection in the victim, and, when their manoeuvres have brought about the desired result, one of them squats over him and inserts his penis

25

into her vagina. After the first ejaculation he may be treated in the same manner by another woman. Worse things are to follow. Some of the women will defecate and micturate all over his body, paying special attention to his face which they pollute as thoroughly as they can.

How sad it is, this contrast between our civilised, clean and sterile view of the whole of life, including sex, and the animal working of our bodies. We cannot accept our animal nature. Sex is dirty. We hate it. This hate has a hundred million horrid consequences. Here is just one, the case of a child-molester described by Dr Frank Caprio in his *Variations in Sexual Behaviour*. The young man, highly sexed, has a wife who finds it difficult to respond to his caresses. He develops a strong desire for cunnilingus:

I remember that I started having a strong desire to want to have mouth contact with a woman's privates. I was twenty-four years old at the time. I used to play around with my wife exciting her before we had intercourse. I used to suck her breasts for probably half an hour at a time while playing with her privates at the same time. I seemed to enjoy trying to get her intensely excited. I wanted to excite her in every possible way. I remember my wife expressing a definite distaste about the subject of a man putting his mouth on a woman's privates. It seemed sickening to her.

Being blocked from carrying out his wishes to perform cunnilingus on his wife, and inhibited by his own belief that to do so would be unclean, he decides to find an immaculate little girl.

I seemed to be repulsed at the thought of doing this with some other woman because of the uncleanliness of the privates and the smell. I analysed this and thought that if I could get a girl who hadn't even menstruated yet it wouldn't be so dirty and I could try this thing. I just seemed to have to try. That's what was going through my mind when I picked up the little girl I told you about.

Human attributes are reflected strongly in human vocabulary. Books on sex, however mild, are widely referred to as *dirty* books. Photographs of naked girls found in a schoolboy's drawer are described by outraged parents or teachers as *dirty* pictures. Honest sexual desire is characterised as *filthy* lust.

So, in every way they can think of, sex-negators assert that SEX IS BAD because sex is dirty. They use an inescapable attribute of sexuality to put down the whole thing. What is the resolution of this dichotomy between, on the one hand, our evolving desire to banish dirt, bad smells and all uncleanliness and, on the other, the primeval pull of sex?

A clearly framed question, but the answer does not match it. There is no clear answer. We are evolving, and our sexuality is evolving with us. Everyone, according to the old saying, will eat a peck of dirt before he dies. Some of that dirt will have sexual connotations. We cannot hurry evolution. Our glands will go on secreting, and our bodies discharging, for some time yet. That must not be allowed to interfere with our sexual fulfilment.

For his survey of young people's views on sex and marriage anthropologist Geoffrey Gorer carried out a number of interviews. (young man, a practising Roman Catholic, dismissed sex without love as 'too animal'. A twenty-nine-year-old Post Office engineer said of a man who indulged in casual adultery: 'I sympathise with him; he is satisfying his baser instincts, but I pity that he hasn't more self-control.' So the deeply ingrained attitudes reveal themselves, even among young people. Sex, they feel, is animal and base.

In truth sex is no more animal than the rest of ourselves, and no more base. If sex is animal, we are animal. If sex is base, we are base. For sex is just one element of the living, breathing creature that is a human being. Obedience to its prompting leads to actions some would describe as unseemly. That is only because of the dignity we humans unwarrantably assume. We have no right to assume any dignity which is incompatible with our nature. If sexual expression betrays our dignity, it is not sex that is wrong but our dignity.

Primitive peoples know this. In their barbarous state they give due weight to the reality of sex. Only when contaminated by the false values of so-called civilisation do they betray their innate knowledge of the truth. In her 1928 book *Coming of Age in Samoa*, the American anthropologist Margaret Mead gives us an example:

The adult attitude towards all the details of sex is characterised by this view that they are unseemly, not that they are wrong. Thus a youth would think nothing of shouting the length of the village, 'Ho, maiden, wait for me in your bed tonight', but public comment upon the details of sex or evacuation was considered to be in bad taste. All the words which are thus banished from polite conversation are cherished by the children, who roll the salacious morsels under their tongues with great relish. The children of seven and eight get as much illicit satisfaction out of the other function of the body as out of sex. This is interesting in view of the different attitude in Samoa towards the normal process of evacuation. There is no privacy and no shame. Nevertheless the brand of bad taste seems to be as effective in interesting the young children as is the brand of indecency among us. It is also curious that in theory and in fact boys and men take a more active interest in the salacious than do women and girls.

It seems difficult to account for a salacious attitude among a people where so little is mysterious, so little forbidden. The precepts of the missionaries may have modified the native attitude more than the native practice.

There is a clue to the whole problem in that last sentence. So-called civilisation changes *attitudes*; but *practices*, being basic, tend to endure. So arises conflict and guilt. Some modern movements, such as that promoting sado-masochism, attempt to sweep this away by brute force. In 1979 Par Califia wrote of this movement:

We select the most frightening, disgusting or unacceptable activities and transmute them into pleasure. We make use of all the forbidden symbols and all the disowned emotions . . . The basic dynamic of S/M is the power dichotomy, not pain. Handcuffs, dog collars, whips, kneeling, being bound, tit clamps, hot wax, enemas, and giving sexual service are all metaphors for the power imbalance.

Commenting on this passage, Jeffrey Weeks remarks:

Sado-masochism becomes a theatre of sex, where the consenting partners freely engage in extreme activities, from bondage to fist fucking, mixing 'shit, and cum and spit and piss with earthiness', all on the borderlines of endurance, to attain an intensified sense of release and pleasure.

Later Weeks says that such practices 'are more a question of aesthetics than morals', but this is untrue. Such a perverse use of sexuality contravenes the moral requirement of sex-respect, a concept developed in chapter 6.

Fear of Conception

In some societies, at some periods of history, sexuality has been reviled as the source of unwanted pregnancy. Unless there is a miscarriage, this necessarily means either that a child is brought into a world which is unprepared and unwilling to receive it or that the pregnant woman suffers the trauma of an abortion, with possible risk to her health and even her life. Where contraceptives are not available, or for some other reason are not used, the wife or mate may understandably come to dread an annual pregnancy inflicted on her by what she may view as the insatiable sexual appetite of her partner. This attitude is especially likely to develop when, as has too often happened, the woman's own sexual needs are ignored or otherwise not adequately catered for.

In some circumstances, conception may be unwanted for economic reasons. Throughout human history the birth of children has usually been welcomed as providing what will in time be strong arms or earning power to assist the parents in their declining years. This has not always been the case, however, and first there is an interval of time during which the infant must be reared, and raised from its initial state of helplessness. Young families are a heavy drain on resources, particularly when the parents are economically under-endowed. Where the mother is very young preg-nancy may also be undesirable, as we shall see in chapter 11, for health reasons.

It is difficult to be sure how far these factors are truly responsible for current sex-negativism. Certainly there is no need for them to play any operative part in modern western society. Even in the past a correct approach to sexuality would have enabled people to attain sexual fulfilment without risk of unwanted conception. That unhappy conse-quences can flow from a thing does not mean it is intrinsically bad. Much unhappiness is caused by unrequited love, but no one would say love is bad. It is easier to prevent unwanted pregnancies than unwanted love.

Education in the use of contraceptives, moral training in the irresponsibility of male/female intercourse without contraceptive precautions, research to improve contraceptive methods, adequate availability of contraceptive drugs and apparatus – all these add up to a complete answer, which is further explored elsewhere in this book.

Other Supposed Reasons why SEX IS BAD

The sex-negaters who need to feel that sex is bad invent many reasons. We have gone at length into the argument that SEX IS BAD because it is dirty. We have seen that this reasoning is false, and that sex must be fairly equated with the biological nature of men and women.

Clearly we ought not to reject or put down our own nature or any part of it, though many try. Lord Devlin, in words most of his judicial colleagues would dutifully echo, contrasts the human faculty of reason with what he calls the *baser* faculties of feeling and emotion. Sex, Lord Devlin would say, is the basest of all the 'baser faculties'. This is self-evidently mistaken. Natural human attributes cannot sensibly be placed in some pecking order of moral worth. We are born as a package. Every ingredient in the package is of equal moral value. We are blessed with them all, and all are equally blessed.

Many other arguments are advanced why sex is bad. It would take too long to investigate them fully and all we can do is consider lines of thought leading to their rejection.

Some pundits say sexual acts are bad because they are weakening and 'wear out the body'. Don Revie, the disgraced manager of the England football team, defined professionalism as not having sex on Thursday and Friday: players in the weekly match on Saturday afternoon will display more energy if they have not dissipated it by sexual indulgence. It is to be the weekly match, not the weakly match.

In truth sexual activity, though it uses up energy, does so in no greater proportion than any other physical exercise. There is a hoary myth that one can use oneself up sexually. This, says Dr Isadore Rubin, is connected with the primitive belief that emission of semen weakens and debilitates a man or youth. Many people, he adds, still believe that each drop emitted in ejaculation is equivalent to the loss of forty drops of blood. He goes on:

Actually, it is well recognised today that the emission of semen is no more of a loss than the expectoration of saliva. Both are quickly replaced by the body.

Equally foolish is the notion that the genitals (especially those of young people) are in some way worn out by sexual activity. In *Sound Sex Education* Dr Margaret White, a lecturer and writer on sex education, discourages adolescent sex with the admonition: 'Your body is a vital present to give to your wife or husband on your wedding day, so don't let it become used and worn.' *Used and worn?* This is a physiological

29

travesty. Does the arm with which an enthusiastic schoolboy cricketer bowls a ball become 'used and worn' from his incessant practice at the nets? Does his brain become 'used and worn' from conscientious wrestling with algebra or Latin? Why then should his youthful penis become 'used and worn' from the activity its nature leads him to practise?

More serious is the argument that sex is bad because sexual activity can lead to infection by sexually transmissible disease. The advent of Aids has sharpened this objection. A leading medical expert on such diseases, Dr D. Llewellyn-Jones, maintains however that the conquering of them, and the cure of infected persons, is severely hampered by sex-negative attitudes. In his book *Sex and VD*, published just before the advent of Aids but doubly relevant in the present era, he wrote:

In Western society, sexual intercourse is not discussed openly, and infection acquired during it is thought by society, and the infected person, to be disgusting, indecent, and something to be concealed . . . This disapproving attitude to the sexually transmitted diseases extends to the type of clinic where advice and treatment is given. All too often it is an ugly building, difficult to find, unpleasant to attend, uncomfortable to wait in, dirty and dingy. As venereal diseases have a marked social stigma, many patients are reluctant to attend for treatment, and many an anxious patient is deterred when he or she sees the inadequate facilities.

As Dr Llewellyn-Jones says, prejudicial attitudes have always prevented sufficient money being devoted to the research needed to stamp out sexually transmissible disease. It has long been urged that vaccines against gonorrhoea and syphilis could quickly be developed were sufficient funds made available. An antidote to the HIV virus is not within sight of discovery. No one doubts that the only way to find it is through generous funding of the necessary research.

Some think sex is bad because it can endanger relationships. Friendship, whether between persons of the same sex or opposite sexes, is a valuable element in our culture. Except where it is an intended prelude to courtship, friendship does not go with sex. If sex rears its ugly head (a revealing phrase) the friends may occasionally become lovers. More likely the relationship will end. We do not expect our friends to project their sexuality in our direction, and tend to be affronted if they do. They should stay crouched in the niche we have consigned them to occupy. Here the true analysis is not that sex is bad when it damages friendship but that the friends' treatment of it may be faulty.

Another stick used to beat sex with is the prevalence of rape and other crimes of which it is an ingredient. Many murders are committed for sexual reasons, but does that mean that sex is bad? No. These crimes spring not from anything evil in the nature of sexuality but from society's rejection of it. This sets up conflicts which lead to many varieties of antisocial conduct. The sexual crime is the bitter fruit of sex-hate.

Then there is the aesthetic objection. Ideally, we are prone to feel, sex should be confined to a handsome youth and a fair maiden disporting themselves gracefully in a sun-dappled, daisy-strewn meadow. Even then we desire a fig-leaf or two. When the old, the ugly or the damaged essay sensual embrace we feel uncomfortable. Again, this attitude results from a false idea of the nature of sex.

A powerful reason why the world holds that SEX IS BAD is that it is unspiritual. It is of the flesh, and its delights are carnal. We are taught to mistrust the flesh. The legal term for vaginal intercourse is *carnal knowledge*. This sort of knowledge we do not want to possess, for officially we admire the spirit far, far more than the flesh. As the Bible says: it is the spirit that quickeneth; the flesh profiteth nothing. Officially we rate very highly concepts like celibacy, chastity, purity, modesty, innocence, virginity . . . How meek and good those terms look, set out on the page! In fact those terms are disguises for sex-hate. Every one puts sex down.

So at last in this catalogue of reasons why sex is bad comes the most potent reason of all. Sex is bad because God hates it. We know that from the Bible, and from teachings based thereon. If you have ever been a church-goer you will remember hearing the line in Genesis about Adam and Eve: 'And they were both naked, the man and his wife, and were not ashamed.' It may have occurred to you to wonder why on earth this prototypical married couple should be ashamed. There has just been an elaborate (if unconvincing) account of how their bodies were created by God. It would have been very presumptuous of them to think any bit of that divine fabrication was a matter for shame; and clearly they were not created to be presumptuous.

Look what happened when, at Eve's instigation, Adam ate the fruit of the peculiar tree God had created, the Tree of the Knowledge of Good and Evil. The eyes of them both were opened, and they knew that they were naked. Then what did they do? Why, they sewed fig leaves together and made themselves aprons. Their newly acquired knowledge of what God regarded as good and evil taught Adam and Eve that their genitals were evil, and so unfit to be seen. So God was the first sex-hater.

Jesus was a sex-hater too. Even to *think* of sexual intercourse is described by Jesus as evil and defiling – sex is dirty. Sexual desire is 'lasciviousness', and that too is evil and defiling. The only reason allowed by Jesus for divorce was sexual intercourse with a person other than the spouse, sex being the one thing so bad that it could burst the divine marriage bond. The attitude has persisted right up to the present day. When in 1988 it became known that the Martin Scorsese film *The Last Temptation of Christ* was to be given public exhibition in Britain objections centred on the scene where Christ is shown as being tempted to have sexual intercourse with Mary Magdalene. 'We believe there is a lot of filth in this film', declared the leader of the United Kingdom Asian Christian Fellowship, when presenting a petition for the banning of the film based on this scene.

So there we are. Our culture says no to sex because our culture is sex-negative. It is sex-negative because it believes that SEX IS BAD. It is bad because it is dirty, animal, base and unseemly. Submission to it is weakening, and wears out the body. It produces unwanted children or unpleasant abortions. It spreads disease. It endangers relationships. It is unaesthetic. It is unspiritual. God hates it.

To those who truly believe in a God who hates sex, we here bid a courteous farewell. We do likewise to those who, while not subscribing to so crude a formulation, believe in a God who has a special purpose for sex that limits its expression to some of the people, some of the time.

Sex is for all of the people, all of the time.

3
Sex-acceptance and the Defeating of Sex-negativism

Sex-negation operates against the sex anatomy both by physical mutilation and psychic mutilation. The latter often amounts to complete obliteration. Since even this is never enough to extirpate the sex anatomy, sex-negation then proceeds by various devices to belittle almost every aspect of sexual functioning. We now examine these processes in turn.

Holes in our Anatomy: the Henry Moore Syndrome

The crudest and most certain way to put down sex is by surgical removal of the organs that create sexual desire and pleasure in female or male. The clitoris, described by physiologists as a rudimentary penis, is an obvious target. Unlike its male comparable, this organ has no saving reproductive function. It has no function at all, except to give sexual pleasure. Clitoridectomy (sometimes called clitorectomy), the excision or cutting out of the engorgable clitoris, is a practice in many cultures. As Elizabeth Draper put it in her book *Birth Control in the Modern World*:

In some communities clitorectomy was and still sometimes is performed to reduce sexual sensation as a safeguard against premarital relations and loss of virginity, without regard to reduction of enjoyment in marriage subsequently.

The practice is common in Africa, as Professor Parrinder tells us in his book *Sex in the World's Religions*:

Female circumcision, or more properly clitoridectomy, is practised in many parts of Africa, though not in all. It involves cutting off the clitoris, and sometimes removal of part of the labia minora, with the apparent aim of making sexual penetration easier for the man and removing any opposition or rivalry in intercourse from the woman ... It purpose seems to aim at ensuring male pleasure and dominance, without considering the woman ... The effect was to subdue women, and certainly to make them suffer unnecessarily ...

Early in the twentieth century some American doctors are reported to have carried out clitorectomy as a 'cure' for female masturbation.

Mutilation of the natural penis by surgical removal of the prepuce or foreskin is still widely executed. For Jews it is obligatory, being carried out on or near the eighth day after birth so as to initiate the baby boy into the covenant of Abraham. Muslims also insist on this form of purposeless mutilation.

Such religious prescriptions are remarkably resistant to reform. In his book *Judiasm* Isidore Epstein records the devastating effect of the new civilisation of Hellenism upon the religious and moral life in pre-Christian Judea, as indicated in the Book of Jubilees (written around 180 BC). The bibical ordinances were disregarded, the Sabbath was desecrated, the rite of circumcision was neglected. Jewish youths would strip themselves naked for Greek athletic games. The rabbis soon regained the upper hand, however. In modern times an attempt to abolish the barbarous practice of male circumcision by the 1892 Central Conference of Jews did not succeed any better, and it remains an axiom of orthodox Jewish observance to this day.

Male circumcision is still generally popular in the Unites States, despite the fact that it reduces sexual sensitivity, hinders masturbation and deforms the unclothed male figure. The ostensible excuse is hygiene. In an autobiography entitled *Me and the Orgone*, the American actor Orson Bean describes the fight by him and his wife Carolyn to save their baby son from circumcision in the New York hospital where the child was born in the late 1960s:

One after another, the nurses and doctors of this modern enlightened up-to-date hospital came into Carolyn's room, smiled at her, inquired how she felt, and then asked why the baby had not been put down for a circumcision. Carolyn explained that the baby's father was not circumcised, that she was aware of all the arguments in favour of it and knew that most people believed in it these days, but that she simply preferred not to have it done.

'But aren't you aware that there is a higher incidence of cancer of the penis among non-circumcised men?' the staff people would say.

'The statistics are questionable', she would answer, 'but if it is true, it probably has to do with the lack of cleanliness and we have indoor plumbing and don't expect that to be a problem.'

'Well', said one daring nurse, looking round to make sure no one was listening, 'there is the question of sexual prowess. It's well known that circumcised men have greater staying power than uncircumcised men.' She smiled knowingly at Carolyn, who resisted the temptation to ask how extensively she had researched the point herself. Instead she replied, 'My husband isn't circumcised and I have no complaints.'

'Well you don't know what you're missing', said the nurse.

When the staff realised that reason was not going to prevail, they became increasingly insistent and almost hostile, issuing implicit warnings that we would live to regret our actions. The obvious depth of feeling on the subject startled me. Nature's purpose in creating the foreskin is to protect the sensitive head of the penis so that it will be capable of providing as much pleasure as possible to its owner. If the foreskin is removed, the sensitive head of the penis, exposed over the years to jockey shorts . . . will toughen up and be less sensitive. In a culture oriented to 'successful performance' of the sex act this may seem an asset. Basically it represents an anti-pleasure attitude, despite all the spurious health claims which are used to cover this up.

Another form of physical mutilation is infibulation. We have progressed since the days when the chastity of youths was secured by cutting holes in the foreskin and placing a metal ring through them. Weinhold, a nineteenth-century Prussian, proposed that until a youth was pronounced wealthy enough to marry he should be fitted with such a ring, secured by a seal which by law would be subject to public inspection at regular intervals. This interesting suggestion was never carried out, however. Female infibulation, effected by sewing up the entrance to the vagina, has been a common feature of many primitive societies. Fortunately for us, it is a little too crude for the modern western mind to accept.

Although (apart from male circumcision) organised physical mutilation of the sex anatomy is rare in modern society, private mutilation by deranged persons is not unknown. A horrifying instance where a girl cut off her lover's penis inspired Nagisha Oshima to make the film *L'Empire des Sens* in 1976. The film is described below (pp. 262–3).

If most forms of physical mutilation are now ruled out as an expression of sex-negativism, the same does not apply to psychic mutilation. This goes far beyond the mental equivalent of clitorectomy, circumcision or infibulation. It achieves in psychological terms the removal of the entire genital apparatus.

The sculptor Henry Moore became famous for his depiction of the human figure in abstract shapes frequently containing holes in place of vital parts of the anatomy. So apt is this as an image of psychic sexual mutilation that we may conveniently refer to that phenomenon as the Henry Moore syndrome.

The Henry Moore syndrome is the determined pretence that the sex anatomy *does not exist*. It is not a pretence in express terms, for that would require mention of the very thing desired to be suppressed. The syndrome works obliquely, in a manner reminiscent of Hans Andersen's tale of the emperor who wore no clothes. It operates in relation to the way living human bodies appear in the presence of other living people, but also in relation to photographs, paintings, sculptures and other depictions of the human body, and in relation to the language used about that body. It even has some effect as respects the bodies of animals.

If one human being is naked in the presence of another, it is difficult for that other to convince himself or herself that the sex anatomy is non-existent. Even the word 'naked' is an awkward reminder, as Lady Fidget showed in Wycherley's *The Country Wife*. When her husband spoke of telling her 'the naked truth' about some household matter she rebuked him: 'Fye, Sir Jasper, do not use that word *naked*.' Even in modern times the term 'naked' has been felt too extreme for public use. In 1936 a woman removed her clothes in St Paul's Cathedral (whose patron saint was no doubt highly affronted). London newspapers, when reporting the incident, chastely described the unfortunate creature as appearing 'unclothed' or 'unclad'.

We are a little more relaxed today, but the tremendous weight of past attitudes still has its effect. Dean Swift unsuccessfully sought to puncture these some two centuries ago. In *Gulliver's Travels* he has Gulliver offering to explain the nature of clothes by undressing himself before his audience – asking to be excused 'if I did not expose those parts that nature has taught us to conceal'. The Houyhnhym, to whom this remark was primarily addressed, found it a strange asseveration: 'for he could not understand why nature should teach us to conceal what nature had given'.

This desire for concealment may be traced to the Judaeo-Christian tradition, though it is shared by other religions also. Only the Catholic church has carried it to the ultimate point of requiring people to conceal their nakedness *from themselves*. The problems of nuns seeking to wash the dirt from their bodies without risking visual or tactile contact with their sex anatomy have been fully documented.

The spectacle of unclothed animals, even when not engaged in sexual congress, can be an inconvenient reminder that sex exists. Peter Fryer in *Mrs Grundy*, his excellent book on prudery, tells of the Society *for* Indecency to Naked Animals (it should, he explains, have been against, but the founder was stricken in years when he drew up his will). In 1963 the Society is said to have designed bikinis for stallions, petticoats for cows, knickers for bulldogs and boxer shorts for smaller animals, all so as to shield the eyes of Americans from the sight of these creatures' genitalia.

In order to sustain the effectiveness of the Henry Moore syndrome, it is not enough to forbid the nudity of living people. Accordingly our culture has gone further and sought to prevent any depiction of the naked human form, whether in paintings, photographs, sculpture or other media. One impressive medium is the vast chalk down in Dorset whereon the Cerne Abbas giant was long ago painfully inscribed. Stone-age men, being honest fellows, gave him a twenty-five-foot erect penis in due proportion to his overall height of 180 feet. In 1764 the *Gentleman's Magazine* published a drawing which did full justice to the giant's genital endowment. By 1842, as portrayed in John Sydenham's *Baal Durotrigenis*, his phallus is so reduced in size as to be lost in the undergrowth. Five years earlier the virginal Victoria had ascended the throne. Virgins are expected to fear phalluses.

On the ground, the Cerne Abbas giant still keeps his erect chalky penis – though not without grumbles from the public. A Home Office file reveals that, on receiving a complaint of the figure's 'impassioned obscenity', a departmental official minuted: 'What does the complainant want us to do? Plant a small grove of fig trees (on measurement, hardly less would suffice)?' The complainant was informed that the Giant of Cerne is a national monument, which there is a statutory duty to preserve, not conceal. That was one rare case where sex-negation suffered defeat at governmental hands.

The period beginning around 1960 shows marked relaxation of the long repression of nudity in art and the media. Family magazines now freely print unretouched photographs of naked bodies – pubic hair, male genitals (in a detumescent state) and all. We have moved on from the position where, as the Commissioner of Police for the Metropolis solemnly told an Arts Council working party in 1958, 'the courts usually adopt the view that a photograph of a male or female showing pubic hair is obscene.'

Absence of pubic hair might be just as bad. The photographer Jean Straker told the same working party, on the subject of his attacked book of nude female images: 'We had published a photograph in the book of a Chinese-Malay girl, Shanzie Laine, showing her hairless pubis in clear labial detail'. Straker went on to say that because of this hairless detail the book was banned in Australia and Ireland. In enlightened England the Board of Trade passed the buck by referring the issue to the Director of Public Prosecutions, who decided not to prosecute.

A prime sufferer from the ban on depicting the innocent naked human form has been Jesus Christ, though that is no doubt his own fault for being a sex-negater. All portrayals of Christ throughout the ages have shown his genitals draped. Drapes are as effective as a Henry Moore hole. Hiding is as good as eliding . . .

Yet we cannot doubt that Jesus Christ possessed a sex anatomy. He came 'in the flesh'. God made man in his own image, and Jesus was hailed as the Son of Man. The Church has always maintained that Jesus was in every respect a complete man. No complete man lacks a penis. No complete man has ever lived for whom sex was not a vital concern. The shame-faced denial of this in the case of Jesus is a fundamental flaw in Christian dogma.

Christians have never felt able to contemplate, even in imagination, what lurked beneath the drapes which in all holy portrayals are chastely placed around Christ's middle. Yet if Christ was truly a man he was created, like Adam, in the image of God. We know Adam possessed genitals because he made an apron of figleaves to hide them. Where was God when a penis first became erect? What happened to Jesus at puberty? When did the Son of Man obtain His first erection? Did that august being receive any sex education? Precisely how old was Christ when He first ejaculated? How often, as a boy, did He masturbate? What sexual fantasies did this celestial being experience? The Bible answers none of these questions, yet they are of obvious importance to Christian believers or would-be believers. How can one imitate Christ, as believers are bidden to do, when one does not know how Christ behaved in a matter so vital as his sexuality?

If, despite an earlier farewell, any religious readers are still with us, and are shocked by that last passage, we can only reply in the words of John Quainton's poem 'The Impudent Creator':

37

> I created a two-legged toy
> only for fun, just for joy
> gave him his orders, then to annoy
> told him to wish away
> ignore, abhor, say nay
> whenever a certain part of him
> reached for the light of day
> a part I had bestowed on him
> that I meant to have its say
> but later changed my mind about
> – don't look at me that way!

The most telling impact of psychic mutilation comes not from the fact that all the people one encounters have their sex anatomy hidden, nor from the fact that pictures of people are likewise draped, but from the behaviour of people – particularly that of parents to their children. The young child is conditioned to see reality reflected in parental attitudes. Coming hot-foot from an earlier world of truth, it expects to see that.

Everything that is important to the child must be important to his parents also. If the child cuts a finger, the parent reflects the pain and shock by his or her reaction of sympathy and aid-provision. If the child wakes screaming from a nightmare, the parent is instantly on hand to administer comfort and understanding. With considerable anxiety, the young child slowly begins to perceive one exception to this supportive parental regime. Consciously or not, he or she comes to realise the basic importance of the genital apparatus. To this carefree creature's dismay it finds parents conspiring to pretend this is not so. The pretence often extends to a psychic obliteration of the genitalia.

Here once again we recognise the Henry Moore syndrome. The infant may find it alarming. It may even destroy him or her. Such alarm can permanently undermine the reality of life to an intelligent child, who for ever thereafter, but vainly, seeks to plug that psychic hole. To his or her everlasting sorrow the child finds that, once made in the psyche, such a Henry Moore hole can never be filled in.

The pretended non-existence of the sex anatomy extends throughout life. It is possible for a victim of sex-negation to keep up the pretence most of the time. Except in their own company, healthy persons living alone may for years on end succeed in never dropping their guard, never for one moment admitting to others (either expressly or tacitly) the existence of their sex anatomy. It is a pretence doomed to ultimate failure, but that may be continuously postponed while health endures.

A potent aid in this pretence is our medium of explicit communication, language. Language accurately reflects our attributes and desires. If we wish to avoid directness, language gives us tools of circumlocution. If we wish to make our hearer understand that we find it necessary to refer to a matter which inevitably postulates the existence of genitalia, we can do so without using scatological terms or even medical terms. We can do it by indirect allusion. Nevertheless many cultures have conceived it necessary to go further, and *doctor* the language in order to promote psychic mutilation of the sex anatomy.

This was common among nineteenth-century Americans. When wishing to refer to a male chicken, they felt obliged to say rooster rather than cock. They called cockroaches *roaches*, so fearful were they of the sexual connotation. Cox-swain became rooster-swain. Instead of a cock and bull story, these simple folk spoke of a rooster and ox story. They said *limb* instead of leg (even of a table), and *bosom* instead of breast (even of a turkey). Marryat, in his novel *Peter Simple*, gives the following description of a dinner his hero attended in Carolina.

It was my fate to sit opposite to a fine turkey, and I asked my partner if I should have the pleasure of helping her to a piece of the breast. She looked at me very indignantly and said, 'Curse your impudence Sar, I wonder where you larn manners, Sar. I take a lilly turkey *bosom* if you please. Talk of *breast* to a lady, Sar; really quite *horrid*.'

'Nipple' shared the fate of 'breast', even when used in a technical sense as respects guns. An 1863 edition by Sir Richard Burton of an American travel book has the footnote: 'The American "cone" is the English "nipple". Beg pardon for the indelicacy!' In Kansas in the 1920s 'bag' was banned, for 'when they hear it . . . they always think of *scrotum*'.

The English are by no means immune. As recently as 1962 an English national newspaper, the *People*, coyly, described a woman's navel as her 'waist-dimple'.

Garments used for covering embarrassing parts of the sex anatomy have shared the same embarrassment. Peter Fryer lists some wonderful euphemisms for trousers. These include inexpressibles, indescribables, unspeakables, ineffables, unmentionables, inexplicables, unwhisperables, unutterables and unthinkables. Similar words have been coined and used for many other suspect articles of clothing. As Fryer points out, to the sex-negater the sexuality of others is at the same time both inflammatory and disgusting. It is detected in a thousand innuendoes, in inanimate as well as animate forms. Fryer says:

It is a constant and fascinating reminder of their own frustration and unhappiness; it perpetually awakens feelings whose existence they spend their lives denying and trying to suppress; it impels them to punish both their tormentors and themselves.

The zoologist Desmond Morris makes the same point.

Even in the most puritanical cultures, sex has played a major role, if only because it was constantly on people's minds as something that needed suppressing. It is probably true to say that no one is so frantically obsessed by sex as a fanatical puritan.

Finding that mutilation, whether physical or psychic, is insufficient to do away with the sex anatomy, sex-negaters turn to *minimising* it.

Before the 1960s, male clothing was designed to make the genital bulge appear as small as possible. Male statues and pictures, where they did not sport figleaves, were equipped with a penis considerably smaller than life-size. Even that male lover of males Michelangelo felt obliged to depict Adam, in the Sistine Chapel fresco of the creation of Man, with scaled-down genitals. The great artist was abashed by his young hero's close proximity to that archetypal sex-hater the Old Testament God.

Belittlement has been adopted as the guiding principle. Pretend this gross male equipment does not exist, and perhaps it will go away. Many an unsuspecting virgin has been astounded on her wedding night by the contours of an erect organ of whose appearance, size or even very existence she had received no familial or other forewarning. Perhaps this chaste maiden had been encouraged to be a frequenter of art galleries, for what could be more suitable? There she would have been conditioned quite falsely. No paintings or sculptures placed on public view would have given the poor child any knowledge of the force and earthiness of tumescent sex. In our respectable culture galleries and the flesh, though attempting conjunction, walk on opposite sides of life's road. To do otherwise would be to venture within the closed garden of *pornography*. Galleries are usually official, and officialdom, by its nature, can have no truck with eroticism.

Despite setbacks, we are emerging from the fond denial of imperious male sexuality. Our youths wear clothing that reveals their bodies, in place of the shapeless sports coats and flannel bags wished upon their predecessors. Youths have wrenched free also from the short haircuts that denied their vigour, though many have chosen to revert to these. At least they now have the choice.

Another way of belittling the sex anatomy is by jeering at its appearance. Ascetic writers commonly deride the shape and configuration of organs even they reluctantly bear. The male genitals are held to be ugly and shapeless, without aesthetic appeal. In the female, these accoutrements are fortunately placed mostly out of sight.

The sex anatomy, either explicitly or in more subtle ways, is further belittled by damning it with all the attributes which establish, as we saw earlier, that SEX IS BAD. Nevertheless, everyone possesses a sex anatomy, and sometimes, like other parts of the anatomy, it gets out of order. This can be embarrassing. Even when the disorder has nothing to do with sexual functioning, the patient required to undress still feels awkward in the doctor's presence. For in order to obtain medical help it is necessary to acknowledge to the professional consultant the existence of what we have been taught to deny. Worse, it may be necessary for the consultant to examine some part of it. This can be traumatic indeed, and truly finds out the Henry Moore syndrome.

Our medical profession has had its share of sex-negaters – some would say more than its share. An American doctor, Eugene Scheimann, went so far as to say of his colleagues: 'Medicine is for all practical purposes as antisex as religion.' Germaine Greer contends that doctors feel disgust for the vulva and seldom investigate its disorders properly. Itching, for example, is associated by the medical profession with excessive sexual desire, and not taken seriously. In truth it may have a simple physiological cause.

The long struggle to put down the sex anatomy has failed, as it was bound in the end to fail. Sex is far too important for that strange, perverted attempt to have had the slightest hope of success. Sex is designed by nature, whom there is no gainsaying.

So the sex-negaters perforce adopted another method.

Compulsory Marriage

If the river of sex persists in flowing, even flooding, it must be channelled underground. It must be confined within the concrete culvert that Freud's follower Wilhelm Reich described in *The Invasion of Compulsory Sex-Morality* as life-long compulsory monogamous marriage. Sexual intercourse outside this hallowed state was, still is, and presumably always will be given by the Christian church the rude name of *fornication*. This pejorative term means no more than sexual intercourse between unmarried consenting adults, an innocent enough thing. Yet the Bible aims at it the most fearsome diatribes.

And Jesus said, Are ye also yet without understanding? Do not ye yet understand that whatsoever entereth in at the mouth goeth into the belly, and is cast out into the draught? But those things which proceed out of the mouth come forth from the heart; and they defile the man. For out of the heart proceed evil thoughts, murders, adulteries, fornications, thefts, false witness, blasphemies. These are the things which defile a man. [Matthew 15: 17–20]

Paul placed simple sexual intercourse first in the list of proscribed acts:

Neither fornicators, nor idolators, nor adulterers, nor effeminate, nor abusers of themselves with mankind, nor thieves, not covetous, nor drunkards, nor revilers, nor extortioners, shall inherit the kingdom of God. [1 Corinthians 6: 9–10]

Though sex-negaters were grudgingly prepared to accept sexual intercourse within licensed marriage, they insisted on imposing terms. There is to be no nonsense about the husband and wife *enjoying* this regrettable activity. The arrangement must be recognised and accepted as being strictly for procreation. In tune with this, the respected philosopher Fichte called it the abnegation of authentic human and manly honour to make man's capacity to produce out of himself new men into a means of sensual pleasure.

No way could be found of denying the male his sexual pleasure entirely, but the female was to have none. She is fertile in its absence, so here sex-negation could operate without check. One leading physician sagely remarked towards the end of the nineteenth century that any woman who feels pleasure in the sexual relationship is no better than a prostitute.

That sentiment has been inwardly echoed down to our own day, yet is thought of as typically Victorian. There is some truth in this. Dr William Acton, in the 1880s a leading authority on sexual matters in England, condemned the idea that women have sexual feelings. It was, he said, a 'vile aspersion'. J. A. and Olive Banks, in *Feminism and Family Planning in Victorian England*, explain that a married woman, if she had any pretensions to virtue, was required to be a passive recipient of her husband's necessarily brutal sexual thrusts. A lady does not move. Instead she grits her teeth and thinks of England. The husband's demands, say these authors, were seen not as a natural and necessary biological drive but as an unhappy indication of the beast in human nature.

The historic formula of compulsory marriage therefore requires sexual intercourse to be limited to procreation, so ruling out contraceptive devices and techniques. Also ruled out are variant postures for intercourse. It is most convenient for the wife to lie inert on her back with her thrusting husband face down on top her. Let that therefore be the invariable position for this unseemly rite, lest suspicion arise of a seeking after lascivious pleasure and titillating variety. Stimulation of the wife is unthinkable, still more such horrors as fellatio or cunnilingus. Dr Frank Caprio records a female patient who wished to divorce her husband because he was a 'pervert': the sex-crazed brute wanted to kiss her breasts! When marital intercourse does regrettably take place, the spouses must be decently clad in night attire. The act of darkness must be accomplished, as its title indicates, with the lights out.

We have progressed some way from this in a comparatively short time. Nowadays many young couples think it normal to live together without benefit of wedlock. Some consider it fashionable or smart to do so. But let us not forget that sex-negation runs deep, and licensed marriage in its classic shape is the utmost concession this sentiment willingly allows. In that shape it is to this day steadfastly preserved by the Pope and his cohorts in the Roman Catholic Church. Many non-Catholics also feel in their hearts that the doctrine is right, and that any departure from it wrong. The accepted view is that marriage is necessarily and of its nature life-long. By the devout it can never be regarded, however ill things turn out, as no more than what Robert Louis Stevenson called a sort of friendship recognised by the police. On this view even a deserted spouse must continue to live in fidelity to the marriage, eschewing any extraneous sexual fulfilment. Otherwise, as one earnest writer put it, an expedient will have destroyed a vital principle.

Legitimate sexual activity is thus confined to marriage, and even there must not be unbridled. In his book entitled *The Physiology of Marriage*, written in 1866, the American physican William A. Acott warned married couples against excessive frequency of coitus, suggesting it be restricted to once a month. In England at the same time the Dr Acton who thought female sexuality a vile aspersion told in a book on marriage of how he had been consulted by a man suffering from loss of semen, weakness, inaptitude for work and deprivation of sight in one eye. The doctor asked how often the patient had sexual intercourse with his wife. When the muttered answer was two or three times a week, Dr Acton's diagnosis came quick and brief: 'this one fact, I was obliged to tell him, accounted for all his troubles.' Apart from restricting frequency of intercourse, Victorian doctors placed other embargoes on amorous husbands. Coitus during menstruation is unthinkable. It is most undesirable also during pregnancy, or for a protracted period after confinement. A foetus subjected to the indignity of nearby penile penetration during its growth period will probably be born diseased or malformed.

The effect of this antique teaching lingers. Even if thrown off for a time, as during the 1960s, it returns. The truth is however that the effect of intercourse (with or without orgasm) on the foetus, or on the vagina and uterus during the post-natal period, was totally unknown until the Masters and Johnson reasearch was conducted in those same liberated 1960s. Until very recently, doctors have confidently given advice on matters of sexual conduct from a condition of total ignorance. Many still do.

The expert counselling administered to Victorian patients, swallowed as such and almost invariably negative and inhibiting, simply reflected the sex-negating attitudes of contemporary society. It reinforced the patients' prejudices. They would have been surprised and indignant if it had not. We are slow to shake off this dire restriction.

Also reflecting social and religious attitudes are the prescriptions of the law. These, as one would except, uphold the institution of marriage both positively and negatively. The civil law upholds it positively in numerous ways connected with the status of marriage and married persons. It regulates who may marry, the formalities required, the obligations of the parties and the status of their offspring. Up to 1857 English law rendered marriage indissoluble except by private Act of Parliament, a procedure so costly as to be beyond the reach of all but the rich. Until the Married Women's Property Acts were passed in the second half of the nineteenth century a woman's property necessarily passed to her husband on marriage. The common law (that is the law apart from parliamentary enactments) treats husband and wife as one, 'and the husband is that one'.

The civil law ensures that the powerful support for marriage given by the legal framework is not available to any other form of sexual union. It goes further than this. Any other form of union is 'illicit', and subject to as many penalties as judges have been able to devise. Thus a contract to provide maintenance for a mistress is void at common law on the ground of immorality. The old action for 'criminal conversation' enabled a wronged husband to recover damages against the adulterer. In substance this right survived till as recently as 1970, in the form of the archaic action for 'loss of services'. So too did the right of a father to compensation for the seduction of his daughter. Again this was for 'loss of services', or in the Latin *per quod servitium amisit*.

We should perhaps take comfort from the fact that the law has abandoned some of its more excessive reprisals for illicit sex. In one part of Devonshire a widow who was unchaste would in former times be evicted from her property by the steward of the manor. She could recover it only by entering the court-house riding backwards on a black ram, holding its tail in her hand and chanting:

> Here I am,
> Riding on a Black Ram,
> Like a Whore as I am;
> And for my Crincum Crancum,
> Have lost my Bincum Bancum;
> And for my Tail's Game,
> Am brought to this Worldly Shame,
> Therefore good Mr Steward
> Restore me my Lands again.

Until very recently, marriage settlements and separation deeds commonly included a 'dum casta' clause under which the widow or separated wife forfeited her maintenance allowance if she became unchaste. As so often in our history, sexual trangression was hit in the pocket.

Our criminal law also upholds marriage, and the catalogue of sex crimes outside it is enormous. A criminal sanction is justified where, as in rape, the moral requirement of consent to sexual activity is infringed. Often however the law renders a sexual act a crime even though the act is in private, the parties are adults, and each has given at least apparent consent. Here are some examples: bigamy, incest, intercourse with a woman of unsound mind, procuring a girl under twenty-one, brothel-keeping, causing a woman to become a common prostitute, living off the earnings of prostitution, soliciting or importuning for an immoral purpose, anal intercourse with a woman, group sex.

In 1961 the scope was enlarged by the judges in the famous 'Ladies Directory Case'. Here the House of Lords in its judicial capacity announced that the common law (that is, judge-made law) is the guardian of morality and should punish any act, even if not previously regarded as criminal, which has the intention of 'provoking libidinous desires'. This is the ultimate in sex-negativism, and is still English law today.

Sex-citizens and Sex-aliens

We have looked briefly at ways in which sex-negation operates, through the medium of health services and the law, against any sexual activity outside marriage. We find it operating similarly in other fields. Take for example the work field. Employers, particularly in relation to senior posts, are sensitive to any suggestion of sexual irregularity. Dr J. A. C. Brown, author of *The Social Psychology of Industry*, says that psychological testers for commercial appointments both in Britain and America are suspicious if a candidate reveals any interest at all in sex. They are still more suspicious if there is any indication that the candidate may not conform to the usual sexual pattern, for example where he or she has reached middle life without having married. Few employers want to risk finding they have taken a sex-alien into their service.

Here we preceive a fundamental distinction drawn by our culture. The majority of people, though some may wish to reject marriage as unsuited to them for various reasons, do not find their own sexual orientation is opposed to its requirements. They are primarily heterosexual, and have no strong psychosexual fixations preventing the libido or sex-drive finding an adequate outlet in marriage. Whether married or not at any particular time, they have been or will be married – or else reject marriage for reasons other than their sexual orientation. We may refer to members of this moral majority as *sex-citizens*. Society gives them its passport to acceptance within the community, and is organised to accommodate them.

It follows that the remainder of society, the excluded ones, can suitably be referred to as *sex-aliens*, whether they be gays, lesbians, bisexuals or members of smaller sexual minorities such as pederasts, transvestites, pedophiles, transsexuals, fetishists, sadists, masochists or others.

Few people are disposed to spend time trying to fathom what turns anyone into a sex-alien. They prefer to deal with the matter by a number of assumptions, mistaken as it happens. First, the alien has elected to be the way he or she is, and therefore can claim no sympathy. Second, the alien chooses by free will to commit sexual acts which are obviously sick, for example engaging in anal intercourse. Who but an evil monster would wish to thrust his organ of generation into a channel solely designed for passing shit? Third, the alien has perversely decided to eschew the propagation of children – which is the obvious aim of sexuality. There are other such doubtful assumptions.

The truth is that the alien had no choice whatever over what he or she has become. The product is the unforced, unchosen result of heredity and environment. As well blame the leopard for his spots or the wasp for its sting.

Anal intercourse has attracted the utmost obloquy. Even Swinburne, himself a sex-alien by reason of his masochistic love of being flogged, had no time for this. In a letter to his friend Theodore Watts-Dunton he spoke of one who indulges in it as 'besmeared by blood and dung by criminal lunacy'. For those minded to explain, if not excuse, anal relations this has an uncomfortable ring of truth. Youthful buttocks can possess a poignant beauty, urgently demanding from some an active response. Yet does not such a response indeed partake of 'blood and dung'? Is it not therefore repugnant, even wicked? Much the same might be said of oral sex involving the genitals or anus. What answer can the sex-lover give to this grave charge?

The only answer possible is that the response signalled by the erect penis demands its entry into some orifice of the beloved (the male desire for intromission). Only one orifice is appointed for the purpose by nature, namely the vagina. Where the beloved has no vagina some other orifice must be found, for it is necessary that the beloved be somehow *possessed* by this rampant organ, whose only purpose is connection. Connection is all when one loves, or so the phallus insists. So despite the obvious objections, some lovers feel forced to use orifices that are plainly unsuitable. They would say they cannot help themselves, so impelling is the need to respond. Even the hideous rape of a young child can be explained in this way. It is explained, not excused. Nevertheless the world should pause in its ready condemnation to acknowledge that the unacceptable act has a base in true emotion, even love. The child-abuser may often be an unhappy lover gone tragically wrong. He has the overwhelming need to *connect*. He may even imagine he loves the child, feeling constrained to demonstrate the fact in this unsuitable and repugnant way.

Clearly marriage has little or nothing to offer the sex-alien, a misfortune society is accustomed to bear with equanimity. It serves him or her right for being such a monstrous creature – one for whom the description sex-alien is really too polite. Nearer the mark is pervert, a term commonly employed by sex-citizens of the higher establishment, such as judges. Out of common courtesy we who are citizens of the whole world should avoid that epithet. Even judges have been found to be sex-aliens. Besides, we need to be charitable.

It is not only the sex-alien who suffers from the inadequacy of marriage as the sole vehicle for sexual activity. The sex-citizen finds many occasions when no sexual fulfilment is possible for him or her on these rigid terms. Some of these have been discussed already. Others include unwillingness or inability (perhaps through illness) of one of the spouses, and times when the spouses find themselves in different places – a not infrequent situation in most marriages. Sex-citizens who are not currently married find there are no legitimate sexual outlets at all. For the young whom society considers unfit for marriage on emotional or economic grounds, for adults who have for any reason not yet married, for the separated, for the divorced, for the widowed, marriage offers nothing except daydreams or memories.

All this means that at any one time a very large number of people have no legitimate sexual outlet. Current census figures show that in Great Britain the persons who have attained the age of fifteen and are single, widowed or divorced amount to some fourteen million. Add the married people who are separated either temporarily or permanently from their spouses and you have a very large number of sexually mature people deprived of the opportunity of legitimate sexual functioning. Society has been accustomed to put up a solid wall of sex-negation against these millions of its people, though recently there has been an attempt to resolve this by claiming the right to live in sin (as it has long been called). This claim is officially regarded as permissiveness, and rejected. It is thought, with some justification, to be particularly hard on the offspring of the illicit union.

To speak of the permissive society of today is a misnomer. Society is still steeped in the repression it has inherited. Here is one more real-life example.

A speaker gave an address to a local Humanist group supporting so-called 'permissiveness'. It was reported in the press, and a medical practitioner wrote objecting. The speaker's reply to the doctor's published letter accused him of sex-hate. He answered saying that he did not hate sex, only the abuse of it. But in the next breath he continued: 'Sex divorced from true human love and wedlock is not human. Whatever Humanists may say, it is bestial.' This doctor was saying that half his patients were 'bestial'. There are many like him. It is a frightening attitude for a healing profession.

To sum up, we may say that sex-negation operates by various means. It operates by physical mutilation of the sex anatomy (to a minor extent), by psychic obliteration of the sex anatomy (to a major extent), and by denial or severe restriction of sexual functioning. In our culture, as it has developed over centuries, the main device for limiting sexual functioning is to confine its approved occurrence to life-long compulsory monogamous marriage.

Sex-guilt

A dire consequence of all this sex-negativism is widespread guilt about almost every aspect of sexuality. It is our moral duty to combat this, both in ourselves and others.

Because of negative conditioning, guilt about the mere existence of sexuality (sex-guilt) is endemic in western culture. Yet the duty of sex acceptance means we should eschew this guilt in ourselves. Moreover we are under a duty not to implant or nurture guilt in another person, particularly a child, because of their sexual organs, functions or desires, or because of their sexual acts where these are not immoral. When we encounter such guilt we should where possible help to alleviate it.

47

We consider in chapter 7 the kinds of physical and mental harm caused by abstention from desired sexual orgasm. Prolonged abstention is scarcely possible for any human soul, so powerful is the force of sexuality. Yet many feel compelled by sex-negativism to pursue this abstention, or claim it if they have it not. Otherwise they will be engulfed by guilt. Our social conditioning ensures that sexual gratification without guilt is scarcely possible outside marriage, and not always then. Some of those responsible for that conditioning, the Margaret Whites of this world, go further and instil *fear*. In her pamphlet *Sound Sex Education*, as we saw in chapter 2, Dr White threatens youthful lovers with cancer. She tells them they risk enormous medical and emotional damage. A girl contemplating use of the contraceptive pill should be given various warnings, which Dr White specifies. She goes on:

Girls should also be told that the risks of taking the pill include infertility, high blood pressure, liver damage, loss of vision, coronary thrombosis, and possibly breast cancer, also a 10% chance that the user will experience depression, with irritability and headache, due to retention of fluid.

These risks, so far as they are real and not exaggerated, operate at any age. All of life involves risk. Insurance companies weight premiums against young motorists because they have accidents more often than older people. It would make just as much sense for Dr White to tell girls who contemplate accepting a lift in an eager boy's car or on the back of his motorbike that they risk 'enormous medical and emotional damage' if he has an accident, and to continue:

Girls should also be told that the risks of accepting such a lift include broken legs, broken arms, broken ribs and broken skulls, also loss of blood, contusions, unconsciousness, and even, in extreme cases, death.

The surgeon Dr Frank Slaughter, in his book *Medicine for Moderns*, comments that we strive to be healthy in order to be happy. But, he asks, how many of us strive to be happy in order to be healthy? Slaughter argues that achieving sexual happiness conduces to health, and that it is far more important that the sex impulse be recognised and treated fairly than that 'morality' be not offended. He continues:

A person who satisfies his sex impulse in what society likes to call immorality, and has no further trouble with it is far better off than the moral person who becomes obsessed with the ideas of cleanliness and godliness, in compensation for sex urges which he or she refuses to recognise, resulting in invalidism, and even insanity. Too much morality is probably worse, psychologically, than too much immorality.

The war waged by the sex-negaters constantly uses, or rather misuses, the concept of *morality*. To say something is immoral is effectively to damn it, since morality turns on the difference between right and wrong. We are all unhappy, and therefore guilty, at doing anything we believe to be wrong –

whether we admit that guilt or not. In the quotation given above Dr Slaughter is confused about this. It is a confusion shared by many people. Slaughter talks of too much morality being worse, psychologically, than too much immorality. But one cannot have *too much* morality, if it is true morality. One cannot have too much of anything that is right and good.

Neither, putting the converse, can one have too little of what is wrong and bad. Any wrong at all is undesirable. When Dr Slaughter talks of 'immorality', what he refers to is commonly accepted views about what is right and what is wrong which he considers to be erroneous. For *ex hypothesi*, as lawyers say, a correct principle of morality could not cause anyone psychological harm.

But is Dr Slaughter right anyway to speak of a person who satisfies his sex-impulse in what society likes to call immorality, *and has no further trouble* with it? Such a person would be wholly indifferent to society's opinion, wholly untroubled by guilt at contravening the dictates of his superego. Such people are rare. This is just as well, because they would need to be hard and unfeeling. Or (and this offers the only hope to those already conditioned in childhood by sex-negation) they would need to have arrived at and been able to accept true morality, disregarding the nonsense often talked by society. Apart from this acceptance, guilt is the lot of those who contravene society's false moral code.

There are plenty of people around to shovel on the guilt. We have considered Dr Margaret White. Another well-meaning lady intent on filling any natural, and therefore sexually conscious, youngster with guilt is Dr Louise Eickhoff. She was described by the self-appointed Longford Committee on Pornography as a well-known consultant child psychiatrist, and enthusiastically quoted by them as believing that there is no more need for sex education than for the induction of labour at childbirth. Dr Eickhoff laments what she calls the unhappy effects of sexual excitement on the immature. Contrast the approach of Dr Eustace Chesser in his 1972 book *Reich and Sexual Freedom*:

Intercourse can begin at adolescence, provided there is instruction about birth control, and Reich's experience with young people in his work in hygiene clinics convinced him that abstinence at this period – say, between the age of fifteen and eighteen – was positively harmful. It is very seldom complete since most young people practise masturbation, and this he regarded as decidedly inferior. It arouses a more intense guilt feeling than intercourse because it is often burdened with incest fantasies, whereas intercourse makes such fantasies superfluous.

Note that even the enlightened Dr Chesser assumes there will be guilt with masturbation – it's just a question of which guilt goes deeper!

Guilt leads to anxiety. Severe anxiety can induce neurotic states requiring psychiatric treatment. As Professor J. A. C. Brown puts it in *Freud and the Post-Freudians*, when the biological drives cannot be satisfied according to the culturally approved patterns there arises a feeling of being bad, and a sense of insecurity and discomfort. This state is what is generally described as anxiety. Sometimes it arises from the 'sex-trap', where strong sexual urges conflict with a strong superego, and there is no acceptable way out. This sex-trap can exist even within marriage, as Dr Donald W. Hastings shows in a discussion on the propensity of some wives to treat their sexual favours as a bargaining counter, to be withheld if the husband falls to comply with any of their domestic demands:

Sexual withholding is a frequent hostile act in a disrupted marriage. It is a particularly powerful weapon against the husband or wife who has relatively high sexual drives and equally high morals or ethical bars to extra-marital contacts, masturbation, or other sexual outlets. This person is 'trapped'. Mounting resentment and anger often result in symptoms ranging from insomnia, bitterness and irritability, and mild depression to psychosomatic disturbance. Often it gives rise to fantasised death wishes against the withholder, which in turn can produce feelings of guilt for entertaining such violent ideas.

The sex-trap catches many of us in one way or another, and often its victims retreat into neurosis. For a few, psychotic conditions lie in wait. Sex-aliens such as homosexuals are under particular pressure, because their rejection by society is the most determined. Ironically, their condition is often caused by the very attitudes that later lead others to condemn it.

Keeping Sex in its Place

Acceptance of sexuality does not mean we should get it out of proportion. The duty of sex-respect, to be discussed in chapter 6, requires us to confine sexual activity to appropriate times and places. It does not belong, for example, in the workplace.

If we have a job to do we should not let sex interfere with its proper execution. While accepting our sexuality, we should not therefore allow a sexual relationship with a fellow worker to become so demanding or stressful as to obstruct the work. If things do reach this stage, it may be our duty to seek other employment.

Sexual harassment is immoral. It is dealt with in chapter 9, as part of the discussion of sexual overtures.

4

Sex-acceptance and Nudity

The Western Nudity Taboo

Our society's nudity taboo applies to specific areas of the body only. In the female these are the labia majora and the mammae (vulgarly known as the cunt and tits). In the male they are the penis and scrotum (prick and balls). In addition the taboo applies, in relation to both sexes equally, to pubic hair and the gluteus area (bottom, bum, buttocks, arse or in American ass). Practically this means that for both sexes sight of the region extending from the waist to the knees is forbidden, while for females the prohibition extends also to the chest area. It operates with varying degrees of intensity in relation to different parts. In diminishing order, the classification is as follows:

> Male genitals
> Female genitals
> Female breasts
> Female buttocks
> Male buttocks

Another form of gradation relates to the age of the subject. The taboo operates most strongly in relation to adults, and only slightly less strongly for adolescents. It is still present where the subject is pre-pubescent, but fades into insignificance for infants.

Why does this particular pattern prevail? The following appear to be the reasons. The taboo applies most strongly in relation to mature male genitals because they convey the message of sexuality most directly. Besides, if allowed to be exposed in public the penis might through psychic factors be stimulated to tumescence. This would further emphasize its sexual purpose. (It would also give away rather too much about the state of mind of its proprietor.) A further consideration is related to the prevalent male fear of genital inadequacy. If every man's penis were freely open to inspection its length would become a matter of observation and comparison. Since most males consider themselves insufficiently endowed genitally (not 'well hung') the majority vote in our egalitarian society favours concealment. Better safe than sorry.

As there is not much to see when it comes to female external genitals, it might be supposed that the nudity taboo would apply to them with little

51

force. Here the ground of the taboo is different, however. For historical reasons, the concepts of virginity, chastity and purity operate with particular force in relation to the female. Accordingly the male gaze is averted even though there is virtually nothing to be seen. Just in case it is *not* averted, the area must be kept covered up.

Female breasts are regarded as mainly sexual objects though in reality their prime function is in relation to an aftermath or by-product of sexual activity, namely infant suckling. Furthermore our culture attaches importance to the size, regularity, muscular tone, and jut or angle of a woman's breasts. Like most men in relation to their genital endowment, most women are dissatisfied with their breasts. The majority vote is again for concealment.

The taboo regarding exposure of the bum is explicable only in terms of anal inhibition. In young people the curvature of the buttock, with the accompaniment of clear skin and good muscle tone, is aesthetically pleasing. It rounds off the appearance of the nude figure when seen from the side or rear. Yet the arse is a reminder of eliminatory functions we are accustomed to carry out in private and do not consider aesthetically pleasing. We prefer not to be reminded of them, for they are not truly 'civilised'. It is 'civilised' values, after all, that are intended to be served by the nudity taboo.

These various reasons for the taboo are understandable, even in some sense laudable. Yet the harm it does should be recognised. It gives rise to a consequence more damaging than any breach of it would cause. This may be expressed in what we may call the nudity rule: *To prohibit exposure of a particular area of the human anatomy leads to that area becoming the subject of unwholesome, even unhealthy, curiosity. For some this curiosity may become obsessive, or in rare cases pathological.*

Obsessions linked to nudity-prudery often originate in early youth, when humans are at their most inquisitive. Strangling of this natural curiosity may result in voyeurism, unhealthy absorption in pornography, and other familiar ills. Occasionally, as the following account shows, the consequences may be even direr.

An Incident in Fifeshire

It is spring, and this is a true story. A group of raucous boys are spending a day's holiday fishing on the banks of a lonely loch in Fifeshire. One is fourteen-year-old Timothy Wright. Tim is embarrassed at possessing genital organs, which have started being a positive nuisance to a lad who wishes above all to go fishing. Like the rest of his schoolboy contemporaries Tim believes, because he has been taught to believe, that these parts of his anatomy are shameful. So they must be kept hidden – particularly from girls. Poor Tim's delusion is doomed to have fatal consequences before the sunny April day is out.

At one point in the day Timothy, feeling the need to urinate, casually opens his flies and takes out his penis. Another boy is watching, but Timothy does not bother about him. Age-mates are exempt from the nudity-taboo – provided they are of one's own sex.

A few minutes later, young Tim discovers to his horror that the witness was not a boy after all but twelve year old Kathleen Penman. Kathleen is a tomboy, who likes to wear boyish clothes. That liking is about to end her life.

Tim convinces himself that Kathleen will tell her friends that she has laid eyes on the most secret part of any boy's anatomy. There is only one thing to do. Kathleen must be silenced. The affronted youth persuades her to accompany him into the trees that grow thickly on the shores of the loch. There without a word he strangles her.

Some weeks later, after a careful hearing, the High Court in Perth orders Timothy to be detained during Her Majesty's pleasure. The nudity taboo has taken its toll of two more young lives.

Childish Nudity

Opposition to human nakedness reached its height towards the end of the nineteenth century. Unlike their immediate predecessors the late Victorians were particularly censorious about male nudity, as when men or boys were innocently bathing in a public place (women and girls would not dream of doing such a thing). At Eton College, the premier English public school, the boys had for centuries been allowed without question to swim naked in the adjacent River Thames even though the bathing-place, known as Athens, was within view of the Windsor Castle grounds. Then, towards the end of the Victorian era, the following rule was introduced, perhaps in response to complaints from the monarch herself.

At Athens, boys who are undressed must either get at once into the water, or get behind the screens provided, when boats containing ladies come into sight.

Even this proved insufficient for the prudes. Shortly after, in 1893, the order went out that boys swimming at Athens must at all times wear 'bathing-drawers'.

Prudery was similarly introduced at the rival school, Harrow, though, since their bathing-place, known as 'Ducker', is not open to public view, this dismal event did not occur until the second half of the twentieth century. Daphne Rae, wife of one of the Harrow masters of that period (later headmaster of Westminister School), boasts in a book of reminiscences how she succeeded in effecting this change so that ladies such as herself would not be embarrassed by the hairy and spotty nudity of the school's large complement of adolescent youths. Mrs Rae goes on to suggest that hiding the genitalia of their fellows might save some boys from homosexuality. The reverse is likely to be the case. Evidently Mrs

Rae is unware of the corrosive power, within the sexual realm, of unsatisfied curiosity.

As so often, the origins of this folly lie in the Bible. In the extraordinary chapter eighteen of Leviticus a tirade against nudity goes on for fourteen consecutive verses, the first of which commands: 'None of you shall approach to any that is near of kin to him, to uncover their nakedness: I am the Lord.' In *An Analysis of Human Sexual Response*, R. and E. Brecher point out that in our culture the nudity taboo applies chiefly to nakedness in front of the opposite sex, but that there are exceptions. Schools and camps, they say, are accustomed to boys who feel shame in baring themselves before other boys, and who go to extreme lengths to avoid gym classes, swimming-pool lessons, and other occasions when nudity may be expected. A Responsible Society pamphlet complained that in one Devon school, after the introduction of a sex education scheme emphasising nudity, a headmaster snatched a towel from around a young boy who insisted on covering himself while waiting for a shower.

Why does a child behave like this? Some ascribe it to natural modesty, but it is clear there is nothing innate about it. Agony over nudity, like most childish attitudes beyond the first years, is solely the result of adult conditioning. One of the first things most children learn is that genitals must be kept concealed. This is illustrated by the case of Leonard McComb's statue, reported in the *Independent* of 24 July 1990. McComb is a sculptor, who was invited to include his nude life-size statue *Portrait of a Young Man Standing* in an exhibition in the nave of Lincoln Cathedral. The statue is of highly polished bronze covered with gold leaf, and the young man is not 'standing' in an aroused way. On the contrary, his penis is demurely flaccid. The sculptor explains that the work is concerned with the importance of the individual, adding: 'By using gold, which emanates light, I was symbolising an inner spiritual life; as gold is the most precious thing we have, it was meant to suggest the value of all living creatures.' The damage was done when, after being shown round the cathedral, a party of schoolchildren reported that the gold man was the most memorable part of their visit. It was promptly removed. McComb ruefully commented: 'It is only when adults take an adverse view of nudity that children realise there's something strange.'

Enlightened parents who seek to defy this cultural rule risk criticism, and even enlightenment has its limits. Dr Frank Caprio is one of the more relaxed American psychiatrists. In his *Variations in Sexual Behaviour*, Caprio asserts that sexual taboos have caused more unhappiness, including mental and physical suffering, than any other area of ignorance in the long life of the human race. Yet on the next page we find him specifying, as one of the hazards to a youngster's normal sexual development, 'carelessness about nudity before children'. Such carelessness, gravely warns Dr Caprio, is a cause of youthful sex shocks. In one way he is right. If there is an absolute ban on nudity in the family, but on one isolated occasion the young child sees father or mother in the raw, that may well give the kid a sex shock. But is it the parent's momentary carelessness that is the true cause of trauma, or is it the foolish ban that has kept little Johnny or Belinda in blank ignorance of the adult sex anatomy?

Nudity of Adults

The old taboo, derived from those figleaves we are taught were worn for modesty's sake in the Garden of Eden, is hard to kill off. Our generation has not outgrown the attitude shown by the respected Sir Sidney Harris. An ex-Home Office official, Sir Sidney was in 1947 appointed President of the British Board of Film Censors. He was then aged seventy-one. In his book of reminiscenes *What the Censor Saw*, John Trevelyan tells how Sir Sidney once said about a French film which had X-certificate bed-scenes: 'I suppose we shall have to pass it, but men and women don't go to bed together with no clothes on.'

At a well-known health farm, where the female staff tolerated nudity among male clients because they could scarcely carry out their duties otherwise, male domestic staff objected to lady clients bathing nude in the indoor swimming-pool. It embarrassed them, they said, to see naked women as part of the usual scene when they went about their duties.

Christians are still far from accepting the nudity of Jesus. Theology says he was a man, as well as a god. There are times when men are compelled to be naked. Did that not apply to the man who happened to be Christ? A young Florentine artist, Bona Baraldi, was commissioned to paint in a Siena church a fresco of Christ after the resurrection. She painted the man-god nude because, she stoutly said, to clothe him would be hypocrisy. The Roman Catholic archbishop of the province ruled that the addition of a modesty cloth was 'opportune and even necessary'. When Signora Baraldi refused to alter her painting, a necessary brick wall was opportunely built to conceal it.

Oh that brick wall! How often we run against it!

There is no need to multiply examples of the nudity taboo. What can be put forward in its defence?

Origins of Nudity-Prudery

When prehistoric man desired to copulate with his mate, the two withdrew to seek a hidden spot. Why? We surmise, with the hindsight provided by the skilled aid of professional palaeontologists and archaeologists, that it was for one reason. In the innocent trusting and thrusting act of copulation, the two are vulnerable to attack from an enemy. The male, whose function it is to defend, has no attention to spare for detecting possible foes. He is face-down. His weapons, save one, are necessarily laid aside. So is his shield.

The copulator is therefore compelled to find a secret place, where he and his mate can fulfil their urge without anxiety. Whether that is truly the origin of nudity-prudery we do not know. The matter is complex, and anyway what matters is the correct approach for modern men and women. The Longford Committee on Pornography said flatly that sex is essentially a private affair. Were they right? And if they were, does this justify a ban on simple nudity when divorced from sexual activity or even tumescence?

The first step is to separate these two questions, for the answers are not necessarily the same. Taking the first, we need to break it down still further. No one would argue that men and women should be *forced* to engage in sexual activity in the presence of other people if they do not wish to do so. We are not insisting on a return to the days when the bridal couple were required to consummate their union in public so as to provide evidence that this event had indeed taken place, that the bride was indeed a virgin, and that the bridegroom was indeed potent.

Sex liberation is about freedom, including the freedom to be prudish. The problems arise over the right to restrict the freedom of others to reject prudery for themselves, and over the upbringing of children.

When in 1967 Parliament abrogated the law that made it a crime for adult males (but not adult females) to engage in homosexual acts it limited this relaxation to acts done *in private*. What is more Parliament provided that an act is not to be treated as done in private if more than two persons take part or are present. Sex, as we so often hear, is for two people and not more than two.

There is perhaps greater justification for laws penalising sexual activity in a place which is genuinely public, especially where it is aimed against a specific non-consenting person. This occurs where for example a 'flasher' exposes his erect penis to a woman or girl, obtaining sexual gratification from her alarmed response. But such aberrant acts fall into the category of positive interference with the freedom of others, which the law is right to restrain. Does that mean the law is right to restrain two exhilarated but consenting adults from having sex in a remote field where strangers *might* see them? Society's current view is that legal restraint here is also justified, but liberationists doubt that this is right.

The Law Commission recently published a report recommending the creation of a new criminal offence of engaging in public sexual behaviour. Under this, the participants would be guilty if they knew or ought to have known that their behaviour was likely to be seen by other persons to whom it was likely to cause 'serious offence'. The Law Commission did not consider it necessary even to debate the question of whether people are justified in taking offence at sexual conduct not aimed at them. They said:

The crucial element in the conduct to be penalised is, in our view, the disgust with which most people would react if confronted by a person or persons publicly indulging in these activities. The activities themselves may well, as we have said, become disgusting or indecent only by reason of the circumstances in which they take place.

So, on the usual sex-negating level, it is assumed without argument that people seeing an enthusiastic young couple engaged in sexual intercourse will be disgusted by the sight. Sex is dirty; sex is disgusting. We try to pretend it does not exist. Punish its manifestations with the crude might of the criminal law whenever opportunity offers. Never think you might be privileged if you chance to witness a human act of happiness and joy.

A more relaxed approach might justify the creation of a somewhat different offence of this kind, for which after all the Law Commission propose as a maximum penalty only a fine of £100. If instead of using terms like 'disgust' and 'cause serious offence' the Commission had considered the matter from the point of view of arousing sexual desire at inopportune moments there might have been some merit in their proposal. It may even be that this factor is really what the opposition to sex in public places, to pornographic displays in newsagents' shops, and to nudity on beaches is really all about. Disgust is a euphemism for undesired arousal.

Should people be protected by law from being sexually aroused when they do not wish to be? This may largely be a male problem, for it is usually said that women are not aroused by the sight of nudity. The popularity of male strippers and magazines like *Playgirl* suggests the contrary, however (as do recent research findings). The naturist movement has always fought against the idea that nudism is what has been called 'a bizarre branch of neo-puritanism'. In *The Erotic Minorities* Dr Lars Ullerstam says of nudist or naturist enthusiasm:

This movement aims at curing mankind of the disgusting vice that consists of enjoying the sight of another naked body by making nakedness a commonplace affair. It seems to be a successful enterprise: one never sees any male person with an erection in their publications.

This satirical observation points to the answer. Arousal is not a serious problem, because those who do not wish to be aroused can avoid it by moving on or averting the gaze. The blunderbuss of the law is uncalled for.

So we should say, in response to the Longford Committees's statement that sex is essentially a private affair: let the participants themselves be the judge of this. Sexual activity should not be thrust on those who have not consented to take part, as it is by the exhibitionist on his victim. On the other hand those for whom the sight of sexual intercourse by others is unwelcome should learn to look away and fight down disgust, contempt or panic. Sex is natural, and sexual activity is natural. No one should be surprised or shocked at a reminder that natural things go on. Sex out of doors brings people closer to nature, and to themselves. A youth accused of having sexual intercourse with a willing girl in the open defended himself by saying: 'Making love outside makes me feel united with everything in the world. You can feel the love-vibrations around you.'

Whether a ban on sex in public can ever be justified, and if so when, is a separate question from whether a ban on simple nudity can be justified. Questions of taste and good manners enter here. What is suitable for the beach is unsuitable for the cocktail party or formal dinner; but that is no business of the criminal law. Nudity in itself should never be a crime. Yet even now that view is not accepted, nor even it seems taken into account, by those responsible for framing our laws.

Recently a Home Office committee produced a report recommending the creation of a new offence of indecent exposure. They proposed that, for the first time in our history, it should be made criminal for a *woman* to appear naked in public, 'given the volatile state of social *mores* and the number of people still likely to be offended by such conduct'. The committee argued that it would be absurd, where a couple were sunbathing nude in a public place and thereby causing offence to others, if the man could be prosecuted while the woman was immune. That absurdity has existed for many years in our law. To cure it by widening the prohibition instead of removing it is symptomatic of an over-regulated and sex-negating society.

Another symptom is the exorbitant interest aroused by the phenomenon of 'streaking'. When a naked young man ran from one side of Lord's cricket ground to the other during a Test match, perilously leaping the stumps in the process, the TV cameras recorded the incident. It was rerun during each news broadcast that day, and was clearly regarded as much more interesting than the cricket. It was shown on various pretexts during the days following, even getting included in more than one broadcast of a well-known comedy show.

On this occasion the young streaker was not punished. Some youngsters escape less lightly. Thomas Douglas of Belfast, aged seventeen, streaked in that city for a bet. After being chased for 200 yards by police officers he was caught and brought before the magistrate, whose verdict was three months' imprisonment. The newspaper report does not reveal whether there was any special reason for his savage sentence. On the face of it, locking a youth of seventeen up with convicted criminals for a prank of this sort was barbaric folly. If Thomas Douglas's life is not wrecked as a result, it will be no thanks to the Belfast magistrate. Thomas seems likely to join the Fifeshire Timothy and Kathleen (see pages 52–3) as a total victim of nudity-prudery.

Back to the Child

There are very many such youthful sufferers. Usually, the toll begins early in life with the young child being denied the easy learning and acceptance of human anatomy that comes from untroubled nudity in the home. The alternatives are clear-cut. The child's natural curiosity will endanger the concealment policy unless that policy is bolstered by *positive misrepresentation*. The child must be led to believe that the sex anatomy simply does not exist. Sir Walter Scott might have been thinking of this situation when he observed:

> Oh what a tangled web we weave
> when first we practise to deceive.

The unfortunate child becomes ensnared in a tangled web of deception. No such web can be strong enough to hold back the truth indefinitely. The child, sensing that it is being deceived, may feel chronic anxiety. When, as well may happen, the modesty cloth accidentally slips and the true anatomy is revealed, the child experiences intense interest, followed by guilt.

In some people, anxiety and guilt are recipes for neurosis. The psychologist Dr Charlotte Wolff includes in her book *Love Between Women* the autobiography of a lesbian who ascribes her aversion from the usual feminine role to her first sight of the male anatomy at the age of five. For her it was 'the dreadful discovery that I had been born into the wrong body'. She had never seen a naked male, and sexual differentiation had never entered her head. 'Now suddenly the basic difference between my own body and that of a male was thrust upon me . . . I was appalled, affronted.'

We have seen that Dr Frank Caprio diagnoses sex-shock in certain cases of children who have been kept in ignorance of adult sex anatomy. Assessing the development of a homosexual patient of his, Caprio describes how as a boy he was never allowed to see his father in the nude. When at the age of eleven he perceived his father's genitals for the first time, they excited him to the point of getting an erection. The argument was summed up by Dr G. B. Barker, consultant psychiatrist at a large London hospital, when in evidence to a 1969 Arts Council working party on the obscenity laws he said:

I would state dogmatically that if nudity was accepted completely from the earliest age, there would be far less neurotic unhappiness, and less need for vicarious enjoyments of alternatives to sexuality (i.e. pornography). It is likely also that there would be less promiscuity, because promiscuity is based upon the neurotic inability to find or to form an adult relationship.

The neurotic harm caused to young people by the nudity taboo is amply documented, and we need not labour it here. It is unfair however to throw all the blame on parents and the home. The blame belongs to society generally for making it much easier for young parents to conform to the nudity taboo than fight against it. Nudity in the home needs to be accompanied by publicly accepted nudity outside the home – in the school swimming-bath, in public parks, on the beach, and wherever else it is natural. Otherwise the child will look on its naturist parents as abnormal, and that can set up stresses of another kind.

Being True to Humanity

Mental health is important, but the plea for nudity should not be based entirely on this. There is too the positive joy in observing the beauty of the human form. The ancient Greeks, despised by Christians as pagan, welcomed that joy. Greek athletes wrestled and ran naked, and were admired for their looks as well as their prowess. The Christian put-down of the body brought condemnation of all this. Beauty, freedom, naturalness are on one side of that coin which on its obverse is inscribed with terms such as guilt, anxiety and neurosis.

But, the defender of nudity taboos quickly points out, not all bodies are beautiful. Are we to be affronted in public by sagging breasts, bloated bellies, wrinkled buttocks, and other such unlovely sights?

The answer is twofold. First, there would be fewer unattractive bodies if it were the custom to display bodies openly. The puritan put-down leads many people to despise their bodies. They stuff them with unnecessary food, exercise them inadequately, poison them with excessive alcohol and tobacco, and thankfully conceal the resulting mess under layers of clothing. Second, there is dignity even in an aged and wrinkled human body, and there is dignity in truth. Clothes make the man, says the proverb. The man they make is not the true man, but a being manufactured. We live our lives too much by appearances.

In a last-ditch defence of the nudity taboo, sex-negaters will assert nudity to be immoral and claim that as a sufficient answer. It is not sufficient. Modern anthropological studies have shown that taboos vary greatly from society to society. Professor J. A. C. Brown, in his *Freud and the Post-Freudians*, shows that even Freud himself was largely ignorant of this important fact.

The 'culture concept', which implies that human societies may differ from each other in quite radical and striking ways, is of recent origin, and the prevailing trend at an earlier period was to ascribe the peculiarities of one's own culture to human nature in general. Freud seems to have assumed that 'human nature is the same the whole world over', and in his theories cultural phenomena are regarded as having developed from essentially biological and instinctual origins.

Karen Horney, the American psychoanalytic theorist, states categorically that there is no such thing as a universal normal psychology. Behaviour regarded as abnormal in one culture may be quite normal elsewhere. What constitutes normality or abnormality, says Horney, can be decided only when we consider the culture within which the individual is functioning. Thus even nudity taboos vary as to what parts of the body must be concealed. In some primitive tribes it is the anal region that is regarded as most private. A young woman surprised without clothing will throw herself down on her back to hide her buttocks. In Saudi Arabia women are uninhibited about their bodies but will not take off their masks. 'Their face is for them what our private parts are for us', one commentator remarked.

When it comes to *actions* regarded as taboo there are similar variations not only between different countries but between different periods in the same country. In Victorian England a lady would not walk in the evening with a man to whom she was not related. In Samoa, on the other hand, husbands and wives never walked side by side through the village; they would be 'ashamed' to do so. Kissing in public was until recently frowned on in Britain and America. The famous Dr Alfred C. Kinsey, author of the mould-breaking reports *Sexual Behaviour in the Human Male* (1948) and *Sexual Behaviour in the Human Female* (1953), was himself brought up in strict sexual puritanism. He has told how the reaction of a cinema audience to kissing was one of two incidents which opened his eyes to the narrowness of his early sexual attitudes. Here is Kinsey's account of those crucial incidents, as recalled by Wardell Pomeroy in Ruth and Edward Brecher's collection entitled *An Analysis of Human Sexual Response*:

The first was on an expedition to Mexico, where he happened to attend an American movie in a run-down old theatre. When the hero and heroine kissed, the audience hissed and booed. Suddenly it was borne in on him that attitudes towards such sexual activities as kissing can vary from culture to culture. This concept of cultural variability became one of the keys to his later research success. His initial lack of sexual sophistication helped him to perceive more clearly, and to be more sharply impressed by, differences in behaviour and attitude among people of different backgrounds.

The second eye-opener incident occurred on Dr Kinsey's trip to Guatemala with two graduate students. On a miserably hot day they visited a Guatemalan official in their shirt sleeves and hiking shorts, and were criticised rather sharply for appearing in his office with bare arms. That afternoon Dr Kinsey and his students went down to the local river for a swim. Most of the town were gathered there, all completely naked. Dr Kinsey was so embarrassed that he and his students walked upstream to find a bit more privacy. But the official who had chided him earlier spotted him, and accompanied by his wife and fifteen-year-old daughter, all without bathing suits, he followed Kinsey upstream to pass the time of day.

Later Dr Kinsey was surprised to observe how quickly the most ingrained attitudes to nudity can be altered. At first he and his students shied away from the beaches where people were nude – afraid, he said, that they might show signs of being sexually aroused. Soon they were able to accept nudity as a matter of course. Others with similar cultural inhibitions have had the same experience of rapid adjustment.

The variability of taboos is not of course confined to sexual behaviour. In the Trobriand Islands Malinowski noted that it was taboo for members of opposite sexes to eat together. 'Thus it was all right for a boy to take a girl into the bush for sexual intercourse, but people would be shocked if he asked her for lunch.' Among the Arapesh people of New Guinea *aggression* is so distasteful that, says Professor J. A. C. Brown, it appears to hold an equivalent position to that of sex in Victorian society. The sight of anyone in a temper shocks the Arapesh profoundly.

We are now concerned, however, with nudity. We want to reach a state where people are at all times, and not just when swimming, 'able to accept nudity as a matter of course'. We want this because we believe it is one of the attitudes that will help us achieve emotional happiness. We were long ago ejected from the Garden of Eden, but we glimpse in the distance another garden, perhaps more desirable for human beings. It might be called the Garden of Happy Emotions. Here no one is afraid of the body, and no one seeks to hide it. The value of clothing for warmth and adornment is acknowledged, but subject to that nudity is accepted without question. From the earliest age children become familiar with human anatomy by freely observing their own, their parents' and that of other people. Sex is not thought to require mystery for its full expression. In this area as in others, truth is valued highly and deception rejected as a basis for any aspect of human existence.

Fortunately we have progressed some way towards this objective in recent-years. Nowadays when the plot of a film or play calls for nudity the general public is permitted to witness what is required – at least in some measure. In many countries (though not in England) there are public resorts where normal family life can be led openly and easily by naked people. One such is Cap d'Agde, a resort on the Mediterranean coast of the Languedoc in southern France. This is a new holiday area, built in the 1970s under the auspices of the French government on what were formerly swamps and marshes infested with malaria-carrying mosquitoes. There are several naturist resorts in the area, of which one of the most striking is Heliopolis. This is a structure in the form of two-thirds of a circle beginning and ending on the sea-shore. There are apartments for several thousand people, each with its own paved patio. Each floor-level is set back, so that sunshine floods every apartment. Within the circle are gardens and swimming-pools. The complex includes shops, cafés, restaurants and night-clubs. There is a marina for 300 boats. And of course there is a long sandy beach and the blue Mediterranean sea. Whether lounging or playing on the beach, doing the shopping, sailing in the harbour or sipping an aperitif at a café, people rarely wear any clothing before the evening chill descends. There are holiday visitors of all ages, for the area is very popular with French and German families. Unlike an older French resort, the Île de Levant, Heliopolis does not *insist* on nudity. People can dress or not dress as they wish. There are no entrance formalities – the place is freely open to anyone who wishes to enjoy it.

The reaction of any healthy male on first arriving at Heliopolis is to gaze his fill at the beautiful young bodies, taking care to avoid any obvious sign of sexual arousal. This is a corrective response to the covered-body syndrome of the society he normally inhabits. Females may experience a similar reaction. What is clear is that everyone speedily adjusts to the situation and begins to enjoy an exhilarating sense of freedom. Only by living in such a community, for however short a time, can one grasp how stifling, and how monumentally unnecessary, the nudity taboo of our society is.*

We need to grasp that human nudity is innocent because honest, and that its converse is unhealthy and therefore immoral.

The duty of sex-acceptance requires us to tolerate the sight of the nude human body, even where because of the subject's advanced age or other factors it seems to us aesthetically unpleasing. We should refuse to countenance prudishness about the body or its functions, which can be harmful psychologically. On the other hand we need to recognise the effects of past negative conditioning, and not knowingly outrage another person by the sight or sound of any extreme sexual activity or display.

---

*As a final example of the absurdities we get into over nudity-prudery consider the case of the Watergate special prosecutor and the Cincinnati Bengals, an American football team. In the United States it has long been customary for sports reporters to enter team locker-rooms after a football match in order to interview star players. These are places where naked young men are commonly seen, but in the past this did not matter. Sports reporters were always men, and therefore had no interest whatever in such sights. So the proprieties were not infringed. (The fact that some male reporters are gay, and therefore sexually interested in gazing at nude youths, did not seem to occur to the authorities concerned.) Nowadays, however, we have equal opportunities in employment. Women reporters insisting on their constitutional right to interview naked football players in locker-rooms have caused problems. On 6 October 1990 Sam Wyce, head coach of the Cincinnati Bengals, was fined nearly $30,000 for excluding a woman reporter from his team's locker-room. An earlier case concerned the New England Patriots. This is a football teamed owned by Mr Victor Kiam, the man who liked the Remington electric shaver so much that, as he is fond of telling us in television commercials, he bought the company. Lisa Olson, a twenty-six-year-old reporter for *The Boston Herald*, said on a television programme (these details are taken from *The Independent on Sunday* of 7 October 1990) that she was sitting on a bench in the locker-room after a Patriots game when five naked players came up, positioned their genitals close to her face, and made lewd suggestions. She went on: 'A couple of players had decided to teach me a lesson. That if I was going to be in their locker-room, they were going to give me what they thought I was in there for.'
These incidents caused such a stir that Philip Heymann, a former Watergate special prosecutor, was appointed to investigate what is referred to as 'sexual harassment' of women reporters in such circumstances. One wonders what would happen if male reporters claimed the right to penetrate dressing-rooms reserved for female athletes.
It would be better for everyone concerned in such matters if males and females were thoroughly accustomed to see each other naked from the earliest age, so that by adulthood the human body was a sight as common as a sunset. 'Common' here does not mean commonplace. We find sunsets wonderful however often we view them.

5
Sex-acceptance and Sexual Disorders

The ethical code, being general, prescribes what we are morally obliged to do when able to act freely, that is without being coerced by another person, or influenced by a drug, or affected by some dysfunction or disorder within our own makeup. Coercion and drugs were briefly discussed in chapter 1. This chapter deals with the more complex questions of the effect of a dysfunction or disorder on what is normally our moral duty.

Sex Dysfunctions

We shall see in chapter 7 that for normal adults the basic emotional or psychic need is for periodic orgasm in the right setting, which is preferably a settled loving setting. Surrounding this need are ethical values and obligations, which the Code attempts to formulate. Can we expect a person who is fundamentally 'normal', but is suffering from some sex dysfunction, to comply with these obligations?

In relation to sex, the term 'dysfunction' is used for a hiccup in normal functioning (chiefly considered to be vaginal intercourse between a heterosexual man and woman). An example is vaginismus, when the muscles surrounding the vaginal entrance go into spasm if penetration is attempted (described by the Relate spokeswoman Zelda West-Meads as often due to an authoritarian or religious upbringing in which sex is something 'nice girls' don't do).

The parallel in men is impotence, where for some psychological reason the man is unable, either in all circumstances or in certain circumstances only, to achieve and sustain an erection. In his 1965 book *Fact and Fiction in Psychology* H. J. Eysenck presents what he calls 'the case of the wallpaper man'. The patient, a dutiful husband, was impotent only in his own home. When he and his wife were on their travels no erection problem was experienced. The psychologist found that the couple's bedroom wallpaper resembled that in a room where, as an adolescent, the patient had been beaten up by an outraged husband who discovered him commiting adultery with his wife. When the wallpaper was changed the dysfunction vanished. (Inadvertently revealing his own sex-negativism, Eysenck says: 'It should be noted that the patient was in the habit of making love while the lights were on; he was, of course, French!')

Can the presence of such a dysfunction in one of two spouses or other sex partners alter the moral duty each owes the other? The answer is clear. Anyone suffering from a sex dysfunction is under a moral duty to seek medical help to get it put right. The duty is accentuated when a spouse or lover is suffering from the effects of the dysfunction. All this is so obvious that it would be otiose to insert it expressly in the Code. (Sex dysfunctions are discussed further in chapter 7.)

The position is different when it comes to sex disorders. These are not so easily got rid of.

Sex Disorders

The term 'disorder' is reserved for more severe sexual malfunctions, for example sado-masochism, exhibitionism or pedophilia. Does secular morality admit exceptions or modifications of its code for persons afflicted in this way?

Civilisation is about minorities. More specifically, it is about the protection of minorities. What feels right to me may not feel right to you. If what feels right to me also feels right to the majority of people (though not you), I may feel vindicated. I choose to disregard the fact, well known to me, that this majority vote gives my feeling no moral authority over what feels right to you. Might is not right. Morality is an absolute, not decided by numbers. You have an equal claim to your own point of view. You may think it right, because prompted to do so by inner emotional forces, to expend your sexual impulse in what is generally regarded as a deviant activity. Who am I to deny you? Who is anybody else? Yet if morality is an absolute, we cannot say that every inclination is moral. Some human doings are morally right; others wrong. That is the meaning of morality, as compared to relativism. The moralist rejects relativism: it puts him out of business.

So let us consider those people whose sexual inclinations are indeed directed to solitary fulfilment, or to other practices deemed by the moral majority to be aberrant. We are about to look at forms of what is called deviation, often practised by those whose preference is to operate without a human partner. For convenience of reference we may describe these, without any wish to form a judgement, as *solo deviants*. Since sexuality is generally regarded as a social quality, this preference for acting alone attracts condemnation. Its adherents are branded as sex-aliens. For persons of this particular kind, emotional satisfaction is achieved alone. Solo deviancy is not a choice but a compulsion. They are not experimenting, or playfully cultivating variety. They are into solo sex for earnest, because they have no choice.

It is argued in chapter 9 that merely because a sex act is solitary it is not therefore deviant. The masturbator is not a sex-alien unless masturbation is his or her preferred form of release. As explained in chapter 9 (page 131), the primary sexual act is heterosexual vaginal intercourse. This means that sex is for partners, and those who are healthy always desire a partner. Damaged persons, such as the professional masturbator Jean Genet, who have retired from life's interchange and prefer to be alone, do not set us a worthy example. That should not prevent us from pitying them. Here it is necessary to point out that pity is not, as modern sentiment would have it, a patronising put-down. It is akin to mercy, a humble acknowledgment of a state of misfortune any one of us could have fallen into.

The Voyeur

Instead of fantasy or erotica, the sex-alien masturbator may rely for his or her psychic stimulation on perverted pornography or on the secret witnessing of sexual activity by others. In the latter case the masturbator becomes a voyeur or skoptophiliac. Then his patron is peeping Tom; who in the middle ages spied on Godiva, wife of the Earl of Mercia, as she rode naked through the streets of Coventry. Legend says Tom's punishment was to be struck blind, a fitting symbol of the negater's attitude to those who delight in the sex anatomy of others. Society has had little mercy on later peeping Toms. Admittedly they may infringe other people's right to privacy, and in that respect act immorally. Furthermore a male who discovers that he is being spied on may become violent. Otherwise the peeping Tom is harmless enough. Knowledge of being spied on may even add to the pleasures of arousal.

Skoptophilia is a widespread condition. There are few people who do not (if they are honest) admit to taking pleasure in the sight of naked bodies – at least if they are beautiful. There are also few who would not be absorbed by watching those beautiful bodies engaged in sexual activity. The observers can feel, if their existence is unknown to the lovers, that they are partaking of an erotic feast to which they would not otherwise be admitted. This is no matter of shame, but of the nobility of sexual congress.

Even where the element of secret peeping is absent, there may well be heightened emotion felt by the spectators. When in the early 1970s the film *The Body* was shown in public cinemas in the London area this public, even communal, emotion was noted by observers. The film was quasi-educational, and not pornographic in intent. Its object was to portray the workings of the human body. In the extended sexual scenes the main roles were played by a handsome young man and an attractive girl. An intense communal excitement gripped the cinema audience as the nude couple were shown making love to climax.

Is this voyeuristic delight perverted, or even unhealthy? It is fashionable among clinicians to say so. The psychoanalyst Stekel describes it as 'psychosexual infantilism'. In his book *Variations of Sexual Behaviour*

Dr Frank Caprio, when discussing skoptophilia, uses the phrase 'sexual immaturity'. He tells of a young married man who became a patient of his after being arrested for peeping into ladies' toilets. Caprio traced the patient's voyeurism to sexual excitement experienced in early adolescence when he formed the habit of peeping through the keyhole as his sister took a bath. What Caprio strangely calls 'this premature sex stimulation' became a fixation. The patient was cured of what he agreed was a senseless game of satisfying a sex urge that began in childhood. He wished his marriage to be successful, and became convinced that for any husband to consider himself sexually adequate he first had to achieve sexual maturity. What this case shows (but Caprio does not mention) is the harm done to a growing child by prudery in the family. If as a pubescent boy the patient had become familiar with seeing his sister undressed he would never have felt the slightest urge to spy on her when she took a bath. Malinowski tells us that under the conditions of freedom prevailing in the Trobriands voyeurism as a perversion does not occur.

No doubt if people can be cured of such inconvenient habits as peeping at women in toilets they should be. No doubt, too, the privacy of lovers should be respected (if only to prevent breaches of the peace). Subject to that we leave the last word on skoptophilia to Dr Lars Ullerstam (he spells it slightly differently):

No, my dear scopophiles! Believe in the legitimacy and respectability of your sexual needs, express them without fear, and, above, all, never believe what the superstitious authorities – even if they are doctors – try to insinuate into your minds!

The Exhibitionist

The converse of the voyeur is the exhibitionist. Rather than watch others, and obtain self-satisfaction from that (coupled with self-stimulation), the exhibitionist desires others to watch him. Typically, he wishes to surprise a female when she is least expecting sexual activity. His trigger is her shock and disgust, which in itself can induce ejaculation. It shows that in some sense she cares.

The exhibitionist approaches nearer than the voyeur to having a relationship. At least he makes a difference to the other.

As with skoptophilia, the tendency is to equate exhibitionism with immaturity. Both Freud and Stekel refer to it as psychosexual infantilism. It is rarely found in women. R. D. Laing, in his book *Self and Others*, ascribes it to a person's inability to reveal his true self, his feeling that the true self is not 'seen' by others.

The exhibitionist shows off his body, or part of his body, or some highly prized function or skill trying to overcome that haunting isolation and loneliness of one who feels his 'real' or 'true' self has never been disclosed to and confirmed by others. The man who compulsively exhibits his penis substitutes disclosure through this 'thing' rather than through living . . . instead of making patent his latent self and thereby 'intensifying' his being, he holds himself in (inhibits himself) and holds out (exhibits) his penis.

A powerful reinforcement of this perverse process, indeed in many cases its origin, is the fact that society teaches a man *not* to exhibit his penis. He must not even reveal that he possesses such a piece of equipment. Society does not wish to know about or witness male genitalia. This is the psychic obliteration of the sex anatomy discussed in chapter 3: the Henry Moore syndrome. The consequence of this conditioning is to give a man a weapon (significantly, a word often used to describe the phallus) which he would not otherwise possess. If the penis, even in erection, were a familiar sight the exhibitionist would be deprived of his weapon, and with it his deviation.

Meanwhile, self-exposure is for some the only means for adequate discharge of their sexual energy. Exhibitionism vanishes with taboo, but the taboo is still with us. Is society justified in its scornful rejection of the 'flasher'?

Assuming there is no attempt at physical contact or threatening behaviour (and this is the usual situation), it does not seem too much to ask people to put up with a minor nuisance. Life is full of shocks. As Edward de Bonò told the *Oz* trial, the mental shock of being told by the church that you are going to be burned for eternity is at least as damaging as seeing a man expose his penis. The 'victim' can surely regard the exhibitionist as merely an inadequate demonstrating his inadequacy. Again we may cite the charitable words of Dr Lars Ullerstam:

I want to appeal to my readers: should you see an exhibitionist in action, do regard him as a fellow human being, not as a leper! Try to understand the touching and pathetic element in his behaviour. Above all, do not report him to the police – nothing but harm can come of that. We ought to allow our fellow human beings the beneficial magic of the exhibitionist rite.

Unfortunately, exhibitionists usually *are* reported to the police. Whereupon the state apparatus is likely to perform its trick of locking inadequates up together so as to compound each other's inadequacy. Prison has long been known as the breeding-ground of crime. Young lags, taught by older lags, steadily progress through the University of Crime. On graduation day they receive their ten-year sentence. Then they embark on the post-graduate course.

Occasionally, more enlightened treatment is given. The mental health journal *Mind Out* has reported on a scheme for teenage boys run by a probation officer at Farnham in Surrey. Jean-Ann Mead thought up the scheme when she realised that many youths in the area convicted of 'flashing' had common backgrounds and problems. They came from strict homes with over-protective mothers, where sex was never discussed. The boys were introverted, had no real friends and tended to stay at home rather than go out to clubs and discos. They failed to meet girls and knew little about sex, let alone its expression within an emotional relationship.

Jean-Ann's solution was to hold weekly group meetings for the boys. This gave an opportunity for counselling, and enabled each youth to discuss his problems with contemporaries in a way he never could at home. The atmosphere was informal, and sometimes the group met in a pub (or in summer in the park). Convicted boys were required to attend the group as a condition of probation. For others, attendance was voluntary. *Mind Out* reported that none had chosen to drop out, and the scheme was regarded by the authorities as successful.

The Transvestite

Akin to exhibitionism is *transvestism*, or cross-dressing. The desire for this may have diverse origins, but as a sexual deviation it is marked by arousal of the subject when wearing garments appropriate to the opposite sex. As such it is prohibited by the Old Testament: 'The woman shall not wear that which pertaineth to a man, neither shall a man put on a woman's garment; for all that do so are abomination unto the Lord thy God' (Deuteronomy 22:5). The transvestite is not necessarily homosexual, although resembling a person of the opposite sex he or she comes to resemble a natural erotic target for heterosexual persons of his or her own sex. This leads to confusion of gender-roles, a thing abhorred by the sexist establishment.

A typical origin for the male transvestite is to have an over-fond mother who, when she was carrying him in her womb, truly desired to give birth to a girl. Irving Bieber gives an example in his book *Homosexuality*. The mother, in her middle thirties, was married to a professional man and had three sons. The eldest, aged thirteen, was a transvestite. His mother had wanted her first child to be a girl and was deeply disappointed when it turned out to be a boy. She raised the lad as a girl, taking great pleasure in dressing him in pretty clothes. She slept in the same bed with him, stating that it gave her great pleasure to do this. She became very involved emotionally with the child, being frigid with her husband. By the time he reached puberty the boy's status as a transvestite was established.

As commanded by the Bible, our law has made cross-dressing illegal. Despite the rise of the unisex fashion in the 1960s, somewhat in retreat by the 1990s, society maintains the general rule that the sexes dress differently, and are thus identifiable at a glance. Those who infringe this rule encounter society's displeasure, unless they are professional entertainers like Barry Humphries (Dame Edna Everage) who confine their cross-dressing to stage or screen. The commercial success of male and female impersonators suggests that people derive satisfaction from witnessing performances by persons in wrong-sex attire.

The Fetishist

Not far removed from transvestism is *fetishism*. This is akin to exhibitionism and similar deviations in being motivated by a compulsion. The sufferer's libido, or sex drive, is fixated awry. It yearns not for a suitable human love-object, that is an accessible mature person of the opposite sex. Its longing, pitiable but real, is for an inappropriate inanimate object. The fact that this object, which may be something like a glove or a shoe, is or was once connected with a suitable love-object does not help the victim. He or she (it is usually he) has inadvertently, perhaps disastrously, drifted off the true focus of sexual attention.

The sought-after inanimate object may or may not have an obvious sexual connotation. If it does, being perhaps a pair of knickers, a jockstrap or a bra, the suffering is likely to be more acute. Many an unfortunate youth has found himself in prison through stealing lingerie from a washing-line, or shoplifting in the wrong department.

The fetish object is commonly used as a focus in solo masturbation. If, which sometimes happens, it forms an essential accompaniment to coitus the partner is likely to go through such common sexual emotions as embarrassment, shame or tearful bewilderment. Either way, outsiders discovering the fixation are likely to observe it with ridicule or aversion, or both. Yet the origins invariably lie in sex-negation.

The Partialist

It is possible for the libido to become fixated on a specific part of the human anatomy, rather than the whole person. A man may reach maximum potency only when caressing a woman's buttocks, and may therefore prefer anal to vaginal intercourse. This deviation is called partialism.

Partialism is objectionable because it reveals at once to the sexual partner that he or she is being loved not for the whole nature (which is required by true love) but for conformity to some ideal target related to the angle of a breast, the cut of a buttock, or even the outline of a hand, knee or ear.

The message is clear. Some incident in his or her formative past has fixed my lover's erotic attention on an irrelevant feature. I feel cheated, and am forced to struggle not to despise my poor deluded lover. I may take comfort from the fact that this vagary is not positively harmful. If I am wise, I will accept it and seek to administer comfort. In time, if my love is strong enough, it may fade and even disappear. The power of love is tremendous. It can move mountains of false conditioning.

Other Deviations

Some unfortunate sex-aliens are conditioned to prefer activities that almost anyone, whether a sex-negator or not, would find disgusting or nauseating. For completeness, we need to take a brief look at these.

Animal bodies, among which our's are numbered, are constructed to excrete the waste product. This, by definition, is matter the body has no use for. Having taken what it needs from the nourishment it receives, the animal body naturally expels the remainder. So that remainder, on any sane view, must be the last thing the body's owner should want to readmit. The body has already rejected it as useless, rich though it may be in fertilising agents.

Such a common-sense conclusion does not always hold sway. An Indian prime minister in the 1980s admitted to drinking, every day, a pint of his own urine. That was supposedly on health grounds. Other people in less exalted positions find a sexual attraction, to most people inexplicable, in their body's waste products. Instead of getting rid of them as expeditiously and cleanly as possible, as most people want to do, these find them attractive to ingest. Some few among us are sexually excited by faeces or urine (vulgarly known as shit and piss). Other bodily discharges such as sweat or menstrual blood can arouse sexual stimulation. Such aberrations are associated with psychosexual infantilism. The libido may be fixed for some reason at the anal stage. The arrival of a younger, competitive sibling may in the instructed infant focus attention on the paraphernalia of birth. Consoling hugs in infancy may fix in the nostrils a longing for the aroma of human sweat. A young child's sight of a man or woman pissing or shitting, accidental and forbidden in our culture, may out of psychic shock fix an erotic trigger for life.

All this talk is revolting to most of those brought up in an age which is taught, particularly by advertisers, to look on hygiene as imperative. Yet we must deal with the factual situation. If it is a fact that for a given person the only, or best, sexual release obtainable is with the accompaniment of what to us seem disgusting elements we are obliged on humanitarian grounds to accept the position. Let us draw once again on the wisdom of Lars Ullerstam:

Ukrophiles (literally, piss lovers) like to frequent urinals, and their greatest wish is to meet someone who will be kind enough to urinate into their hats or pockets. They rarely experience this joy, and they often get beaten up instead. To want one's garments soaked in urine may be a legitimate desire, based on need, and it is revolting to hear people boasting of how they have given such individuals a rough time.

The Morality of Deviation

Ullerstam points out that a strongly antagonistic attitude to some kinds of sexual behaviour may well be a defence against very strong unadmitted inclinations to practise that behaviour. The censure with which sex-aliens are regarded may not be wholly due to sex-negativism. As we have seen, some sex-lovers also view these aberrations adversely. Why is this?

Perhaps it is because sex-lovers have an idealised view of sex. Maybe they have been fortunate enough to experience a perfect sexual relationship with another person. If so, they know that when true human love and compatibility enter, sexual expression rises to a loftier plane. Then the cruel urgency, the ugliness, the obsessive guilt are transmuted. Magic, beauty and tenderness come flooding in. Sexuality is transformed. It becomes a vital element in a *full* human relationship, where the lovers feel unbounded concern and sympathy for one another. They partake of each other on an equal basis, committing their whole lives. The lovers may be of opposite sexes or of the same sex. To them it does not matter – except in the ways it may affect their treatment by other people.

For a person who has once been on this plane, anything else is second rate. That does not mean censure is justified. Rather, those who are so fortunate should turn with redoubled sympathy to those who are not. Sympathy, not censure, is the true human response. This becomes incontrovertible when we consider that the solitary deviant is a victim unable to help or avoid his or her condition. The exact cause of the condition is unknown; but it is clear that it is not voluntarily assumed. Who, properly informed, would choose to be what the world unjustly calls a pervert?

Freud did most to cast light here. It is hard to resist his conclusion that sexual preferences of the kind we are discussing are due to an *arrestment* in the maturing development of the human sexual impulse. Some extraneous factor, often a specific event in early childhood, fixes the libido in a particular pattern. Instead of the discriminating behaviour necessary to the higher mental functions, there is little else but a conditioned reflex.

The fixation may be on a person (often one of the child's parents), or on an animal, or on a specific type of event or activity. Where the fixation is on a parent, the subject is unable to treat strangers as other than parent-figures. In later life he or she behaves accordingly, as a fixated child. A typical (and very frequent) example is the boy with the over-attached mother and the inadequate or absent father. If the boy becomes fixed on his mother he may throughout life display childlike characteristics, seeking even from strangers some form of maternal protection and cosseting. As Erich Fromm put it in *The Art of Loving*: 'He may try to find "mothers" in everybody, sometimes in women and sometimes in men in a position of authority and power.' When such a fixated man becomes senior enough to assume authority and power over others, he finds himself unable to do this convincingly.

The solitary deviant frequently owes his condition to an event occurring once only, or repeated. The following examples from case histories illustrate how an event in childhood can operate to 'fix' the libido.

At the age of five a boy had his first sexual experience. An older playmate enticed him to a wood and induced him to undress completely and fondle his own penis. The experience was very pleasurable, especially the act of being naked out in the open and in broad daylight. The little boy was discovered and scolded by his mother. In the course of time he became an exhibitionist.

Also at the age of five, a boy was given an enema by his mother. This event acted as a psychic trauma. The boy developed a lidido-fixation to the anus, reinforced by numerous subsequent enemas also administered by his mother.

At the age of nine, a boy was on a picnic with his mother and a man of thirty-five. The boy tore his trousers while climbing a tree. The mother told him to take them off so she could mend them. Clad in a towel, he walked with the man in a wood. The man exposed his erect penis and asked the boy to suck it. He did so. The act was repeated later, and the boy became fixed on fellatio.

At the age of eleven, a boy was shown by another boy a working model of a girl acrobat. When a string was pulled the girl did the splits. On having this demonstrated, the boy received a strange erotic sensation. Thereafter his masturbation fantasies were of women dancers who performed this feat. As an adult he made a point of going to circuses just to see acrobats doing the splits.

At the age of twelve, a boy was told by a girl about an incident when she kissed and licked a hunchback's hump while the hunchback played with her genitals. This image haunted the boy for life. Regularly, he searched for a prostitute or any other woman who would perform similarly with him.

At the age of fourteen, a boy experienced an ejaculation while playfully wrestling with his sister. Thereafter he made frequent attempts to excite himself sexually by rubbing against his sister's buttocks. After marriage he preferred to masturbate by rubbing his penis against his wife's buttocks rather than engage in the act of coitus. (This rubbing deviation is known as *frottage*.)

The above are illustrations of an event causing a psychic shock sufficient to arrest or divert the natural development of the libido. Often, such traumas are compounded by the violence of a shocked parental response on discovery. Their effect is to *multiply* the erotic force of any later incident corresponding to the fixation.

A similar multiplying effect is found whenever a person who for one reason or another is constitutionally predisposed to a particular type of stimulus experiences that stimulus. The predisposition is invariably due to some kind of fixation, not necessarily caused by the sort of specific incident just described. It may arise from a multiplicity of less dramatic factors. Either way, the victim sooner or later becomes aware of what stimulus corresponds to his or her fix. A vivid example is given in an account of an interview by Charlotte Wolff with a lesbian girl. The child described how the first friend she ever had was an older girl at her grammar school.

We used to walk to school together every day, and come home together too. And we also met at the weekends. Once, when we went out for a picnic, she put her arms round me. I was then about thirteen. I had never experienced anything like what went through my body at that moment and afterwards. I was all tingling with excitement and almost shivering. And I felt quite breathless. It changed my life, and I couldn't think of anything except that wonderful moment and the look in her eyes.

This is not a field where reason holds sway. The intellect has little influence. The intellect and the will may seek to reject what the emotions impose, but they are not likely to succeed. We do not have emotions: they have us. Recognising that, society should have mercy on the sex-alien. Civilisation is about minorities. There but for the grace of God go I: so runs the humble acceptance of the religious. The atheist or agnostic should be no less humble, and no less accepting. If there is a way of remedying a sexual disorder then of course we should assist in this wherever possible. Otherwise we should make allowances.

The duty of sex-acceptance requires us to tolerate the sexual disorders of others, except where they give rise to immoral acts. If however such a disorder is remediable we should where practicable assist in its cure.

Conclusion

At the beginning of this chapter the question was posed: whether to be subject to a sexual disorder or dysfunction alters the moral imperative. We see that the answer broadly depends on whether the defect is remediable. If it is, then the sufferer's duty is to seek a remedy. If it is not, then this sufferer is to a greater or lesser extent under coercion. An act is not immoral if we are compelled to do it by some force beyond our control. But before claiming immunity on this ground we had better make very sure that we have done everything in our power to avoid or resist the temptation to do what in a normal person we know to be wrong.

6
The Duty of Sex-respect

The nature of human beings suggests the ethical principle that we should at all times respect, even reverence, our sexual impulse. This we may call the duty of sex-respect.

Since sexuality is the source of all human life, and is of profound emotional concern to all human beings in the living of their lives, we should treat our own or another's sexual organs, functions and desires with respect, even reverence (the duty of sex-respect). We should therefore not commit any act that degrades or trivialises them.

The Reason for Sex-respect

The prime reason for respecting sex is that sexual desire drives the creation of new human life, an awesome process still not fully understood by scientists. Why is sex so fascinating? Mainly for this reason. Procreation is our one link with the past of the human race, and with its future. That is the awesome quality which sex possesses. Moreover it is a quality invested, unlike religious feeling, with knowledge and certainty. We can never be certain of religious truths, but we are reasonably well informed as to the nature and quality of our sexual attributes, even though there is much that remains mysterious.

Ancient religious movements over the globe acknowledged the duty of sex-respect. What other purpose has universal phallic worship? We see its potent traces in such remnants as the Cerne Abbas giant, described in chapter 3. Also universal are fertility cults, and the religious use of sex in holy places. The widespread employment of so-called temple prostitutes demonstrates that mankind has long respected sexuality, and revered the now so often despised sex anatomy.

People would not worship the phallus if it were truly no more than an uninstructed Martian would consider it to be: a stiff tube of tissue and blood. Other vital organs, such as the vagina, testicles and ovaries, are less accustomed to worship, being less obvious. Without them, however, the phallus has no meaning. So in considering phallic worship as a clue to sex-respect we must include all the organs of generation.

The gay man, forced by circumstances to adore an organ whose main purpose he rejects, is at the same time led to admit (if he is candid) that without its power of fecundation the phallus would hold no interest for him. That staggering potential commands reverence from all people. It is impossible to escape this duty of sex-respect, even if we would. Those who try to ignore it are quickly made to pay. They lose the central purpose of the human gift of sex, which is its wonder, mystery and awesomeness. They cheapen it, and forever thereafter mourn its loss.

Some might object that they would find it difficult to observe this duty. How can a person reconcile it with, say, persistent masochistic fantasies? The answer must be along the following lines.

1. Many disorders such as masochism are due to sex-negativism, which we must surely try to bring to an end.

2. The principle of sex-respect means that one who suffers from a remediable sex disorder should seek to remedy it.

3. If the disorder is not remediable the sufferer is a victim, who should nevertheless try to behave morally.

So the cardinal ethical principle with regard to human sexuality is that it should at all times be accorded, *in every one of its aspects*, the deepest respect. Only by recognising this truth can secular morality validly claim preference over religious morality.

The Bible does not teach this duty of sex-respect. On the contrary, it teaches what might be called the duty of sex-disrespect. The Bible calls desire a lust of the flesh, and bids us despise it. It comes not from God:

For all that is in the world, the lust of the flesh, and the lust of the eyes, and the pride of life, is not of the Father, but is of the world. [I John 2:16]

So lust is classed by the Bible among the seven deadly sins. This perverse ruling, the *fons et origo* of sex-negativism in our society, must be firmly rejected. Even to the blinkered believer, it is obvious nonsense. If we are indeed created by God, then He cannot escape responsibility for implanting our sexual impulse. Those who truly believe in Him will respect it accordingly. Those who do not will form their own judgement, and still respect it.

The principle of sex-respect applies to every aspect of sex. It may here be useful to remind ourselves what those aspects comprise.

First they comprise the human sexual organs or genitalia, in this book referred to as the sex anatomy. Because we think particularly of what we can see and touch, this means honour should be accorded to a woman's vulva and breasts, a man's penis and testicles, and even a child's immature reproductive equipment (which we think it polite to ignore). These are the icons of the body where sex-respect is concerned.

The second aspect of sex is the feature called sexual desire (or lust). We know that without the psychic drive imparted by this compelling impulse the race would not be continued. It is notorious that a person currently

76

suffused by lust takes an intellectual view of the use for its designed purpose of his or her sex anatomy (or that of another) which is very different to that of a person who is sated following recent performance, when sex for a brief times ceases to interest. If we were always in that condition of uninterest, copulation would be a chore we would seek to avoid.

Thirdly we must include more diffuse elements connected with the sexual impulse, and here the boundary may not be so clear. The instinct for pair-bonding, the instinct for nesting or home-making, parenting instincts in their various forms, qualities such as affection and tenderness, even the capacity to fall in love, are all relevant when we seek to number the aspects of sex deserving of respect.

An obvious example of disrespect is to treat our sexuality as if it had been designed solely for pleasure. This is a reversion to Onanism (in this sense justifiably called self-abuse). Sex is never for mere pleasure, but always for psychic release and fulfilment.

Sex is primarily designed for continuing the race. It cannot at all times be deployed in that way, so its secondary purpose is to accentuate dual human relationships. Only when we are forced to be alone is it legitimate to practise solitary sex. Even then we do it not for pleasure but for fulfilment, or at least release. It completes something important we would otherwise forfeit.

Such things as sado-masochistic practices engaged in for 'kicks' are therefore immoral. We reject the statement made by Jeffrey Weeks in his book *Sexuality and its Discontents* that these are 'more a question of aesthetics than of morals'. Sex for kicks is degraded sex, and therefore immoral when voluntary. For those who feel themselves coerced into pursuing this form of sexual activity we have pity. Maybe they cannot help themselves, and for that we are inclined to blame sex-negativism. If they can remedy their condition we hope they will try.

The Right to Sexual Privacy

We are conditioned to believe that sex is a private matter. Peeping Tom is an unpopular character, even where his excuse is that he suffers from the sex dysfunction known as voyeurism. It is generally felt to be wrong, and a breach of the principle of sex-respect, to spy on other people's sexual doings.

One distant origin of this sentiment, namely that the sex act renders a warrior defenceless, has been mentioned. We still often feel defenceless when in this posture. Perhaps we are in some way at the mercy of the other party. We feel our equipment is inadequate, or our technique open to criticism. Sex-guilt may, for one reason or another, have its part to play.

We may also demand privacy because the richness of true sexual intercourse requires the participants to abandon various things. They

77

abandon restraint, and caution. Controls are loosened. Sounds may be uttered or otherwise emitted which are not our usual thoughtful considered sounds. We are off guard. Accordingly we may think it right to adopt the following precept.

It is immoral, as contravening the right to privacy and the duty of sex-respect, for anyone, without the consent of the person in question, to gaze at or listen to the sexual activity of another person, whether directly or by means of a recording or listening device.

The Ethics of Promiscuity

Many would say that promiscuity plainly contravenes the principle of sex-respect, and is therefore always immoral. It is not that simple, however. In fact the concept of promiscuity is really quite complicated. Can we be promiscuous, and yet show sex-respect? To answer this question we need to know the difference, which certainly exists, between virtuous and vicious promiscuity. As we saw in chapter 1, religious moralists pronouncing on the Aids crisis pin the blame for it on promiscuity and permissiveness. These are terms of deep opprobrium, but it was not always so.

Promiscuity, from the Latin *promiscuus*, properly means no more than 'mixed at random', without order. Permissiveness denotes a state of being absolved from certain rules, and is in itself morally neutral. If the rules are good, it is wrong to depart from them. But if they are bad then 'permissiveness' is a virtue. A growing number of caring, responsible people in our society are sincerely of the view that the Judaeo-Christian rules on sex are bad, since they arise from a stance that negates and dismisses the natural sexuality of human beings.

Promiscuity is passing like a bee between flowers. It is never being satisified. It is the everlasting vain hope, the constant fond titillation. It is the mood of Don Juan, the sexual athlete and insincere wooer. Surely it is to be condemned?

Promiscuity is indeed roundly condemned, and with great frequency. The second chapter of Michael Schofield's book *Promiscuity* is entirely devoted to showing the various ways this condemnation manifests itself in our society. Sex education is to be discouraged because it leads to promiscuity. Contraception and abortion are to be discouraged for the same reason. Sexually transmissible disease is not to be fought too vigorously because it is after all a fit punishment for promiscuity (Schofield was writing before the advent of Aids).

Even the liberal Lord Soper does not hesitate to attack promiscuity. In *Does Pornography Matter?* edited by C. H. Rolph, he wickedly writes:

A boy who takes sex because he wants it will tend to take somebody else's goods for precisely the same reason. The girl who is encouraged to see nothing wrong in pleasing herself with somebody else's body will be unlikely to see any objection in pleasing herself with somebody else's money.

This is wicked because it brazenly disregards, in the hope the hearer will not notice, the fundamental difference between sex with consent and theft (which is always without consent).

The promiscuous lover displays the human virtue of expectation, stronger even than the Christian virtue of hope. There is always, round the corner, something better. Or at any rate there is something just as good. This is optimism, a quality not to be derided. Promiscuity can sometimes be regarded as the simple wish to relate closely and warmly to as many people as practicable. Is that truly to be condemned? As Schofield says, sex, like most leisure activities, is usually more enjoyable when done with someone else. Maybe there is after all a positive side even to promiscuity. It treats sex as an added means of relating, instead of insisting that usually when we relate to another person in the everyday sense, for friendship or companionship, the operation must be colourless, bloodless and sexless.

Many would say, with Lord Soper, that the ethics of sexual promiscuity are obvious. *Do not be promiscuous*. It stands to reason. Or does it? No, after all it does not. Not when you look more closely. Reason demands a closer examination of this area. Things are not quite as simple as all that. Promiscuity may be vicious, but it may also be virtuous.

So when is one viciously promiscuous, and when is one legitimately fulfilling sexual purposes? We need to begin, as so often in argument, by asking what the term in question really signifies. The dictionary meaning of promiscuity as mixing in a way that is disorderly, without discrimination or method has been stated. It gives us a start. Promiscuity is casual, careless, irregular.

So those who condemn promiscuity are saying : 'Do not employ your sexuality, which is an integral portion of your being, casually. Do not cast it about indiscriminately, careless of the consequences. Do not imagine you are entitled simply to *use* the sexual parts of others in order to enjoy a slightly superior form of masturbation.'

In some quarters the business tycoon Sir Ralph Halpern has a reputation for being promiscuous in this sense. So the *Sun*, like the Devil citing scripture, takes it upon itself to rebuke him for it. In its edition of 29 July 1988 this newspaper alleged that Sir Ralph dated a 'bimbo' named Fiona Wright because 'the best way I could satisfy my urges was to pick on somebody who wouldn't be a threat to my wife'. It quotes him as saying he met Fiona Wright about ten times for carnal reasons, and adds: 'Translated, that means he met her for sex. Like an animal. As a human being she didn't exist at all.' Well, of course that statement can be criticised. To meet someone for sex is not necessarily immoral. It is not derogatory to be likened to an animal, for in truth we are all animals. But it is wrong to forget the humanity of any sexual partner, even on a one-night stand. Whether or not Sir Ralph really did forget the humanity of his 'bimbo' we do not know. One suspects he did not.

Cyril Connolly wrote in *The Unquiet Grave*: 'Like the bee its sting, the promiscuous leave behind them in each encounter something of themselves by which they are made to suffer.' The first part of this is true. The second is true sometimes, but not always. In any close encounter we leave behind something of ourselves. That is a rule of human life. We do not always suffer by it; sometimes we are greatly enriched. Many a person on their deathbed has mused over some isolated illicit conjunction that somehow, however unreasonably, has for ever after dominated in memory. They bless the passing one who gave them that lasting memory.

Connolly's epigram fails to point the distinction between caring and uncaring promiscuity, or in other words virtuous and vicious promiscuity. We should not blame Connolly for that. It is a distinction which, though undoubtedly valid, is very rarely drawn. Promiscuity is virtuous when appropriate ethical conditions are fulfilled; otherwise it is vicious. That is a statement of the obvious applying to any sexual activity. Since promiscuity is so widely maligned, let us stress five ethical requirements that apply to it with particular force.

1. The promiscuous must always remember that it is immoral for a person who knows or suspects they are infected by a sexually transmissible disease to have sex with another person without first informing them of the fact and taking adequate precautions against infecting them.

2. They must remember that it is also immoral for either party to sexual intercourse to deceive the other on the question whether adequate contraceptive precautions are being taken.

3. There must be observance of sex-respect. That this concept can go very wide is illustrated by the young American gay writer Arnie Kantrowitz who, when describing the impact on his hitherto abandoned sexual behaviour of the new threat of Aids, signed off promiscuity unrepentantly:

> My experiment in sexual anarchy was a rare delight, a laboratory lesson in license, an opportunity to see both flesh and spirit gloriously naked. I will never apologise to anyone for my promiscuity. I practised it with high ideals. But if I endanger my own mental or physical health, then I am myself an apology.

4. Force must not be employed, nor unfair exploitation of the other's innocence or weakness. The sexual partner of the moment must not be *used*, without regard for his or her humanity.

5. There must be no breach of any duty of fidelity to a third person. It is the impulse to pair-bonding which creates this duty. If I am

bonded to you, then I have a moral duty not to be sexually promiscuous. Given loyalty to one person requires *all* sexual power to be expended on them. For a person who is not within such a pair-bond promiscuity is morally permissible, even good, provided the other requisite conditions are met. In such circumstances sexual response can be looked on as a joyous form of social recognition.

A so-called dirty joke which, like many such, contains a kernel of truth tells of a man who boasted to a friend that his practice was to go up to any pretty woman and say 'Do you fuck?' His friend replied 'I bet you get an awful lot of face-slapping.' The answer was 'Yes, but I also get an awful lot of fucking!' Some moralists would say that this type of promiscuity manifests an excessive regard for the stranger's sexuality, at the expense of his or her other human attributes. Others would argue that it marks a refreshing change from the usual social attitude, which displays an inadequate, often non-existent, regard for the sexual nature of other people.

This book sides with the latter view, since our thesis is that people have a moral duty not to go on politely disregarding the sexual needs of relations, friends, acquaintances – even strangers. A sexual response, even though isolated, can be a mark of respect. Or it could be if our culture allowed it to be so.

Sex-negativism, and lack of respect for sex, drive many of us into the arms of commercial sex-providers. They do not provide what we want, though they offer to do so. They take our money and leave us feeling unsatisfied and degraded. They titillate then fail to deliver. Their badge is the goggling unclothed beauty on page three of the tabloid newspaper.

The Page Three Syndrome: Our Titillating Society

Human emotions can be compared to flowing streams. Like an insistent river, sexuality demands its outlet. If not offered a channel, it may burst its banks. Then it seeps through countless chinks and cracks in the neighbouring countryside. The whole of society becomes permeated with thwarted, debased sexual emotion. As Marcuse said in *One Dimensional Man* (as paraphrased by Professor Alasdair MacIntyre in his *Marcuse*), frustrated eroticism saturates the surface of social life.

There comes into existence, as a result of sex-negativism, what the Longford Committee on Pornography graphically described as 'the sex-laden atmosphere'. Or as John Mortimer put it in his final speech for the defendants in the *Oz* trial, every citizen is bombarded by diffused sexuality. Mortimer added that thwarted sex 'rears from every hoarding, beckons from every advertisement, shouts and murmurs from every television commercial . . .'.

The titillating society is not limited to the exploitation of sex for selling products and services. The entertainment industry depends heavily on it.

During their period of popularity the comedians Morecambe and Wise, beloved of our royal family, did not tell dirty jokes on television: their's was a family show. But consider the following interchange:

Eric: I'm going to watch *Upstairs and Upstairs*.
Ernie: What's that?
Eric: It's a series about a honeymoon couple . . .

A mild and harmless joke? Of course. Even Lord Longford's committee of self-appointed busybodies would have stopped short of trying to get such jokes banned. But that joke, and a million like it, operates within a particular frame of reference. One cannot imagine it being greeted with gales of laughter in Samoa or the Trobriand islands. Its required setting is *sex-suppression*. It depends for its effect on the fact that the audience largely consists of people who either are sex-starved currently or remember only too well, because it was their fate for long stretches of their life, what it is to be sex-starved.

To be sex-starved is to be in a state of emotional tension in which the mention of a honeymoon couple is like the twanging of a tense string. That is why we have to realise that the titillating society is a product of sex-negation and not, as some would have it, a product of laxity and permissiveness. In the words of the American professor of psychiatry Dr Harold Lief, the blame must be fixed on our culture and its institutions: it is not that the official culture is too slack, but rather that it is too taut.

Our culture breeds and feeds hypocrisy, a thriving product of sex-negation. In 1951, when John Trevelyan joined the British Board of Film Censors as an examiner, there was a clear policy under which nudity was never allowed in a film, with the possible exception of naked little children. This was changed two years later, when the board decided to grant 'A' certificates (limiting films to adults only) to documentary-type nudist films so long as no pubic hair or genitals were shown. Otherwise they would be banned altogether. In his book *What the Censor Saw*, Trevelyan highlights a typical piece of hypocrisy.

The Board's decision to pass these films was . . . strongly criticised in the *Daily Mirror*. An article in heavy type on the centre pages referred to it as 'an outrage on public decency' and said that the Board ought to be ashamed of its decision. Accompanying this denunciation were four 'stills' from nudist films which, I was told, increased the sales of the newspaper!

This remains a frequent ploy of tabloid editors. For many years the *Sun* published every day its page-three nude, always a girl staring defiantly into the camera lens. One typical page three caption said that the displayed photograph was designed 'to put the lads in a lather'. Another read: 'Gloria Gooseflesh [or some such name] is the particular favourite of a group of schoolboys in Essex.' The tabloids love to play in this way on the throttled sexuality of youths. It exploits the model by making her body a synthetic sex-object. It exploits the audience too, since it twangs the taut string of their unsatisfied sexuality. The sales of the *Sun* go up, and our titillating society hums merrily on.

But there are evil consequences. Sometimes these are extreme. In January 1986 the father of nineteen-year-old Tessa Howden, who lived with her parents at Selsdon in Surrey, took in his daughter's morning cup of tea. He found Tessa propped up in bed. During the night, without her parents being awakened, she had been sexually assaulted, slashed eleven times, and strangled. The murderer was a youth named Gary Taken, an unemployed scaffolder. *The Times*, reporting his conviction, said:

Detectives who searched Taken's home in Weather Way, Selsden, found more than 90 items of women's underwear, which he had stolen from washing lines in his area. They also found a black and white swimsuit taken from the bedroom of the murdered girl. The court was told that since childhood Taken had spied on his parents having sexual intercourse, through a hole he had bored in the loft floor. He had drilled another spy hole in the toilet wall.

The report went on to explain that the youth had shown severe symptoms of sexual frustration since puberty. This was because, while society offered Taken no acknowledged outlet for his strong sex drive, it subjected him to constant titillation. That is a recipe for disaster, and many such disasters occur.

Where would our tabloid press be if nudity were generally accepted? The page three girl would lose her pulling-power, because there would be nothing out of the ordinary about her. Manufacturers of provocative swimsuits would be deprived of their market. Bikinis are designed to titillate, being far more arousing than simple nudity. Which is truly 'indecent', a simple bare bosom or an enticing display of cleavage with a shrewdly designed minimum covering?

The same applies to male near-nudity, which the *Sun* now exploits on its page seven. Genitalia of young men are a useful circulation booster, provided they remain generally hidden. Only then can the rare escape of this equipment, described by the *Sun* as wedding tackle, be exploited for money or money's worth. Consider the following item in the *Sun* of 31 May 1988, published under the heading 'Pop Goes A Willy':

A group of nude males dancers were blacked out by Telethon bosses yesterday when one of their cover-up balloons burst – revealing a fella's willy to millions of TV viewers. The four-strong group, called the Oddballs, danced around juggling ballons to hide their tackle. But one went pop – leaving Danny Bamford, 30, displaying his manhood. The cameras quickly cut to co-host Michael Aspel, who apologised.

Why apologise for what nature has provided as necessary equipment for half the population? It would make as much sense to apologise for a naked elbow.

How foolish we are to allow ourselves to be thus manipulated. It leads to the sort of nonsense seen at the 1988 Derby horse race, when police officers chased a deranged male stripper all over the course, determined to place a concealing helmet over his pathetic pudenda.

The same applies to the female body. In July 1988 the *Sun* had a small item elegantly headed 'Boobs come out in the wash!' It read:

Busty girls trying out a fun park's new 70ft water slide ended up topless yesterday when the waves washed away their bikinis. A spokesman at the park in Paignton, Devon, explained: 'The water pressure was too high, but we've adjusted it.'

Adjusted it! Would that we could adjust our ridiculous attitudes to what we all possess – the human body.

The entertainment industry also makes commercial use of the ban on general nudity. Girls' bodies are painted and decorated to create sexual arousal among males in the audience, with no offer of satisfaction. As Dr Desmond Morris has pointed out in *The Human Zoo*, these are ritualised performances of what are truly the early stages of the mating sequence.

Compensating for the incompleteness of their sexual patterns, they frequently exaggerate and elaborate the preliminaries that they offer. Their sexual postures and movements, their sexual personality and anatomy, all tend to become magnified in an attempt to make up for the strict limitations of the sexual services they provide.

Since what customers want is orgasm, such titillation quickly palls. The commercial response is to step it up, while still refusing to satisfy the real demand. Strip-*tease* is an accurate name.

In San Francisco in 1964 a bar hostess named Carol Doda appeared bare-breasted, and began the topless craze. Soon waitresses in bars and restaurants all over the city were topless, but after a while this ceased to be enough to attract custom. Therefore some went 'bottomless' as well, till the police stepped in. Others tried offering so-called encounter studios, where frustrated clients found the 'encounters' were strictly limited to conversation. One tourist who, having spent several hundred dollars on watered drinks and tepid chat, made advances he felt he had paid for, quickly found himself beaten up and thrown outside. This is a common pattern of exploitation.

As a further stage in the 'stepping-up', Sam Conti, owner of 'The Garden of Eden' in San Francisco, put on a 'gorilla act'. One topless native girl will, it is announced, sacrifice another to a ravenous gorilla. The victim gyrates round the floor for ten minutes and is then thrust into a cage. With the help of mirrors, she seems to change into a sexy gorilla. The *Los Angeles Times*, reporting this, quoted Mr Conti as saying that he had no sympathy with any male customer of 'The Garden of Eden'. After five minutes any such customer knew real sex was not on offer, but kept paying and paying because 'he has an ego so big he thinks he is the one who is going to seduce the girl despite the house rules'. Conti takes a high moral line. When a man lets his sexual desire get the better of him, says the proprietor of 'The Garden of Eden', 'he isn't a man any more and isn't entitled to that money in his pocket'.

Inadequate though commercial striptease may be, it is clear that some people prefer it to nothing to all. Our sex-negating society readily segregates young men at the height of their potency in environments offering no provision whatever for acceptable sexual fulfilment. This happens particularly in the armed forces. Here is another United States example.

The crew of the nuclear submarine USS Finback, about to leave for a lengthy North Atlantic patrol, asked their captain if they could arrange for a performance to be given on the ship by a go-go dancer, Miss Cat Futch of the Evil People's Lounge at Cocoa Beach, Florida. Thinking it would boost morale, the captain agreed. The performance was given, Miss Cat Futch was put ashore, and the ship sailed. That was not, however, the end of the matter. Word reached the Pentagon, and they recalled the ship. After an investigation the captain was relieved of his command. He had broken an unwritten law by proceeding on the basis that his crew-members were sexual creatures. Perhaps the Pentagon were equipped with superior wisdom, though. All Miss Cat Futch's performance could have given the young sailors of the USS *Finback* was titillated desire without possibility of fulfilment, the basis of almost every sex-crime.

Desmond Morris cites a savagely satirical drawing on the subject of striptease, captioned simply 'tripes-tease'. A naked girl, having removed all her clothes before the audience and still being faced with shouts of 'more', makes an incision in her belly and, with a seductive smile, starts to pull out her entrails to the beat of the music. The 'more' the audience wants is love-making culminating in orgasm. Rather than give them that society prefers mutilation even unto death.

As we saw when discussing the Henry Moore syndrome in chapter 3, it is by mutilation (psychic if not actual) that sex-negation mainly operates. Wholeness is out. That is why more honest sex shows such as the late Ken Tynan's *Oh Calcutta!* which, though commercial, make a genuine attempt to convey the wholeness of sexuality, are condemned by the 'moral majority'. Such shows commit the unforgivable sin of venturing beyond impotent titillation into the realm of actuality.

The frame of reference created by sex-suppression is universal in our society. It applies to every one of us. When we communicate with each other, we do so within this cramped frame. Consciously or not, everyone old enough to talk knows that his or her sexuality is denied.

As again we have seen, language, the most advanced means of communication between people, reflects this denial in its vocabulary, its idiom and its use. We are conditioned to distance ourselves from our sexuality, and how we use language conforms to this. Indeed language is a powerful tool of the distancing process. The World Health Organization has pointed out that medical students in many parts of the world 'grow up in cultures that evade direct confrontation with sexuality; sex acts are private and secret, and are only referred to by indirect suggestion or by "joking"'. That tells us, as if we didn't know already, that the titillating society is worldwide. In his *Psychology of Personality* Professor Notcutt points out that so-called dirty jokes have an important psychological symbolism, playing their part in the conspiracy of sex-suppression. Of this saloon-bar humour he says:

With the leer in the voice and the gleam of glasses to define the context, it is not difficult to interpret most of the symbols which at other times would be deeply hidden.

Many of these are Freudian sex-symbols, as described in Freud's book *The Interpretation of Dreams*. The dirty jokes are signals, most often of distress. The man who feels insecure about his sexuality attempts to convey an impression of confidence by telling strings of aggressive dirty jokes. But an obsessive, persistent dirty-joke teller arouses suspicion. Hearers begin to sense the real cause of his obsession. So his expedient fails in its object. As he begins to realise its failure, the entertainer falls silent. He remembers that the clown is sad at heart.

The moral standard imposed by a sex-negating society is not truly moral, and the discrepancy shows. Dirty jokes, and most other manifestations of the titillating society, reflect it. Whatever they actually say, people are signalling that something vitally important to them is stifled and crushed within. They are not allowed to be true to themselves. Though they use words, they speak like one who is gagged and forced to communicate by pointing. The clumsy words point to one thing: the sex anatomy denied by the culture. How much better it would be if the culture ceased to deny the sex anatomy and instead recognised it openly while insisting it be respected.

Unlike another great human problem, that of malnutrition in the third world, the sexual revolution needs no economic resources but only a change of attitude. Unlike political revolutions, it can be accomplished without bloodshed – though not without aggression. The overthrow of sex-negativism will not lead to vicious promiscuity and the cheapening of sex. On the contrary, it will uphold respect for sex. The titillating society will fade into history.

We pass now to quite a different aspect of the need to respect our sexuality. This is sex with animals, or what English common law calls *bestiality*.

Sex with Animals

It is contrary to the duty of sex-respect for a human being to have sex with an animal.

To call a sexual deviation 'bestiality', as English law does, gives it no chance. When we say that any conduct is bestial we condemn it out of

86

hand. So let us, in a mood of indulgence, call this recourse to a non-human response 'animal sex'. It is not an appropriate name, because we are all animals. But it will do, since most of us refuse to admit the fact.

Many condemn animal sex as being cruel to the animal. It has also been suggested that it infringes the animal's rights, since it is incapable of giving or withholding consent (though if the animal truly objects it can make things rather unpleasant). These sentiments should not surprise us. In a country where the honorific 'Royal' is granted to the national animals' charity but not to the national children's charity it is only to be expected. In his book *What the Censor Saw* the film-censor John Trevelyan records how, as a trustee of the National Society for the Prevention of Cruelty to Children, he was distressed to find that the legacies it received amounted to substantially less than those bequeathed to the Royal Society for the Prevention of Cruelty to Animals.

It does not appear that the latter body has ever protested about animal sex. That may be because its members are too prudish to raise the subject. Let us charitably assume otherwise, and take it that the general rejection of animal sex is on the ground not of cruelty to the animals but of disrespect to the human sexual impulse.

In their book *Prostitution and Morality* Harry Benjamin and R. E. L. Masters report that animals trained to copulate or have other sexual relations with humans have been provided as a facility in brothels throughout history. Dogs, donkeys, goats, baboons and monkeys have commonly been used for this purpose, and also for stage performances. These authors mention *avisodomy* as a service provided in some French brothels. The client sodomizes the bird, cutting its throat as his climax approaches. This act raises the bird's body temperature, while provoking it to violently convulsive movements, triggering the patron's orgasm. One does not know whether to be sorrier for the client or the bird.

It is not only in brothels that animals trained to provide sex-services are found. They also appear in some religious temples. Here male animals are taught to copulate with women worshippers, have anal intercourse with men worshippers, and (in the case of monkeys and baboons) manipulate the genitals of both sexes. The payment extracted from the human client is devoted to temple funds.

Throughout the ages, animal sex has been the norm in agricultural communities. Deprived of female company, yokels turn to the livestock within their reach. In his 1957 book *Variations in Sexual Behaviour* the American psychiatrist Dr Frank Caprio records the story of a patient of his:

I was thirteen years old when I had my first animal contact. I had seen cows of our's in heat, chasing each other around the pasture and jumping on their backs. It excited me. So one time I decided to try and put my penis in the cow's privates. I stood on a stool and did this, having intercourse with the cow. I remember the cow's privates were all wet and hot and I got an ejaculation real quick.

I did this for about three or four months and then I stopped. I think the reason was my step-mother nearly caught me . . . Another time, I put my penis in a calf's mouth and it sucked on my penis exciting me so that I got an ejaculation. I did this several times and one time the calf started to butt me, which discouraged my doing it any more.

The same year, at the age of thirteen, I started masturbating my dog. It started when one day a female dog had been around and my dog had an erection so I decided to see if my dog could have an ejaculation like I did. I did this for about a year at the rate of once or twice a month. I don't remember getting an erection from doing this to my dog. It just sort of fascinated me somehow.

This is straightforward sexual experimentation, of a kind that this poor boy would have happily carried out with human age-mates had opportunity allowed.

When opportunity does not allow, there is danger. At the time of sexual awakening the peasant child may become fixated, through propinquity, on animal sex. Later he may experience anxiety. Caprio mentions a young male patient who developed an ulcer because of such guilt. He believed he had done himself permanent damage by having sexual contact with cows.

Such guilt feelings are encouraged by religious taboos. The Bible hands down its usual savage prohibition: 'Whosoever lieth with a beast shall surely be put to death' (Exodus 22:19). There is an afterthought: 'and ye shall slay the beast' (Leviticus 20:15). This is clearly unfair to the beast, but the the Old Testament is not noted for fairness. English law is more merciful: buggery with an animal is punishable merely with life imprisonment.

The bitter universal antagonism to animal sex is one more illustration of the hatred of that human attribute we call sexuality. It is socially acceptable for lonely people to use pets as substitute friends. They coddle (and cuddle) their pets because they lack human friends, or because their human friends do not give them enough love. We understand that. We even approve when a childless couple use a dog or cat as a child-substitute.

Canine faeces befoul our streets and parks. Despite the obvious health hazard, we shrug our shoulders. In a world where millions of human beings starve, money and resources are squandered on pets. Still our shoulders shrug. Love is lavished on domestic animals, and we approve of that too. When baby-talk is talked at these brute creatures, we smile indulgently.

Let it however be bruited abroad that some woman who cannot find a lover is gaining sexual comfort from her pet dog's tongue, and ostracism is immediate. The new additional factor is sex. Sex-hate turns indulgence to censure. Animals are permitted to be a substitute for any human function except sexual fulfilment.

This is the right result, though for the wrong reasons. The tincture of sex should not turn innocent acts into those that are condemned. We should have sympathy for poor souls who feel driven to turn to animals for the sexual solace they need, like the drunken young man arrested in 1990 for committing a sex act with a cat in a compartment on the London underground railway. Yet we feel bound to insist that the principle of sex-respect forbids humans to seek fulfilment elsewhere than with other humans.

7
The Duty of Sex-fulfilment

Previous chapters have argued that we should *accept* and *respect* our sexual nature. Now we proceed to the third basic proposition of the system of secular sexual morality suggested by this book, that we should *fulfil* that nature.

Because sexuality is an essential and vital part of the human constitution, we should develop and fulfil our sexual nature throughout life (the duty of sex-fulfilment). This does not mean that remediable sexual disorders ought to be accepted as they are, or that immoral sexual behaviour should be tolerated. However it does follow that we should help and encourage others, particularly the young, to achieve fulfilment in the sexual field as in any other area of life. Equally we should not deny old people sexual fulfilment or denigrate their pursuit of it. We should not condemn any sexual relationship on the ground of a disparity in the ages of the partners.

Sexual Need

The main basis for the duty of sex-fulfilment is the need people have for periodic sexual release, illustrated by the following true story.

It is dark at the bus stop. We are in Ballards Lane, Finchley. No one is about on this early spring evening except Maria, a twenty-year-old language student who has travelled to Ballards Lane from distant Venezuela. A devout Catholic virgin, Maria stands quietly waiting for her bus. She has not been in England long, and so far has made little progress with the language. The desired vehicle is a long time coming. Feeling chilled, Maria restlessly adjusts her petite South American feet.

Instead of the bus, an English youth slowly riding a bicycle appears. He spots the solitary Maria and calls out, as he wobbles past: 'Hello, Sexy!'.

Maria does not understand. She fails to decipher this message so powerfully transmitted by a sex-starved young male. Out of politeness and desire to please she responds with a pale slight smile.

Emboldened, for he seldom receives encouragement, Ronald Jones halts and looks back. He gets down from his machine. Just seventeen, he is filled through almost all his waking hours with erotic desire. This might be the moment of fulfilment.

'Like to come for a walk, Sexy?'

A walk is not what he has in mind. Maria, beginning to get the drift, shakes her head. Ronald replaces his haunches on his saddle, and shakily rides off. Maria looks back up the road to see if her bus is coming. It isn't.

Ronald, who had turned and cycled back unobserved, later dragged Maria into a nearby car-park and began to tear at her blouse. She screamed, and fought him. He produced a cut-throat razor, opening the blade. Then he lunged at Maria's neck, inflicting a two-and-a-half-inch gash. Frightened by the blood, he threw the girl to the ground and punched her in the face. Still she screamed, whereupon Ronald tossed away his razor and fled.

The newspaper report mentions that when police arrested the boy he began to cry. Then he said 'I wanted her but she wouldn't have it; I really fancied her.' At the time of the offence he was living in an aftercare hostel for Borstal boys. By a Home Office decree, this provided the inmates with no facility for entertaining the opposite sex.

Ronald carried the razor, he explained to the Old Bailey judge, for protection in case he got into a fight. His Lordship was unimpressed.

Ronald Jones was convicted by due legal process of attempted rape, and sent back to Borstal. Our sympathies are with Maria, and rightly so. Yet Ronald deserves a little sympathy too. He had a pressing need, for which society offered him no means of satisfaction. To understand the duty of sex-fulfilment we must understand sexual need.

The basic sexual need of the female is for impregnation and parturition, but only within a secure setting. A woman loves the man who will get her a child, and protect them both for ever after. Her sexual need is for a begetter and a guardian. Fleshly thrills are a bonus.

The male on the other hand is programmed instantly to fecundate every woman within his grasp. From puberty onwards, his testicles produce non-stop the fluid called semen. His body is designed to void this fluid at frequent intervals. If it is not able to do so, mental pressures build up.

The above may be dismissed as describing sexual stereotypes of female and male. Today's reader often revolts from these. The stereotypical view of a woman's sexual needs is likely now to be viewed as old-fashioned, patronising and discredited. Civilised man takes a similar view of such purely physiological descriptions of his functioning. So culture has overlaid origins, let that be admitted. Yet to forget origins, or worse despise them, is to invite the sort of catastrophes that fill our newspapers. Our primitive nature still affects many of our responses, and we should not feel unhappy about that. Indeed it is our surest guide to conduct (though often we need other guides in addition).

Since, far more frequently than women, males crash the boundaries with their erotic needs, society feels itself obliged to pay them more attention. Fully to understand the male erotic pattern we need to go to the one sort of woman who really knows the sexuality of men – a brothel-keeper. Cynthia Payne, of luncheon-voucher fame, tells it as it is in Paul Bailey's *An English Madam*. She learnt the truths of sex at first hand. Here is what she tells us about Sam, her boyfriend of early days.

I remember crying once while he was doing it because I didn't want to and said so, it was that time of the month. He took no bloody notice. When the prick is hard, the brain is in the balls – and that's where his was. I used to get into bed with Sam and want him to cuddle me, show me affection, but of course a man like Sam couldn't cuddle for long without having a hard-on . . . Anyway, I learned early on in our relationship that the best thing to do was get him despunked. Sam was marvellous company as soon as he'd come – when his cock was soft he was a carnival bloke. With his brain in his balls, though, he was a bloody pest.

Sexual Categories

Help in understanding the nature of sexual need can be obtained from the way specialists categorise sexual function. The American psychoanalyst Harry Stack Sullivan divides innate human aims into the pursuit of satisfactions and the pursuit of security. The satisfactions he lists are those of food, drink, sleep and sexual fulfilment. Satisfaction of the first three is essential to life. We can remain alive without sexual fulfilment, but at what cost!

In his 1975 book *Sex Can Save Your Heart . . . and Life* the American physician Eugene Schiemann says sex involves more than producing babies, having fun or expressing love. He lists *duty sex* (typically that engaged in by the unloving wife carrying out her matrimonial obligations), *revenge sex* (the wife, discovering her husband's infidelity, goes out and finds a lover of her own), *promotional sex* (the casting couch), and *ritual sex* (the temple prostitute). These however are more examples of the way human sexuality is used than indications of its true nature.

The zoologist Desmond Morris may be thought nearer the mark with his ten functional categories given in his book *The Human Zoo*.

1. *Procreation sex*, engaged in for the purpose of rendering the woman pregnant.

2. *Pair-formation sex*, a vigorous activity which (intentionally or not) works towards the formation of a new pair-bond.

3. *Pair-maintenance sex*, a less vigorous activity directed to maintaining a pair-bond already established.

4. *Physiological sex*, culminating in an orgasm designed to give relief from the periodic buildup of sexual tension, particularly in the male.

5. *Exploratory sex*, satisfying mankind's inventiveness, and desire for new forms of erotic experience.

6. *Self-rewarding sex*, or eroticism for its own sake. It is, says Dr Morris, inconsistent to sing the praises of exquisite gastronomic experiences, or sublime aesthetic experiences, while condemning as obscene beautiful erotic experiences.

7. *Occupational sex*, an antidote to boredom or a therapeutic remedy for the negative condition produced by a monotonous lifestyle.

8. *Tranquillizing sex*, a respite from emotional turmoil such as is endured by an examination candidate or a soldier awaiting battle.

9. *Commercial sex*. The prostitute is the typical case, but Dr Morris widens this category to include such persons as those who marry for money or security.

10. *Status sex*, used to assert dominance – as where a man pays a prostitute so that he can perform acts that degrade her as a woman or hireling.

Dr Morris's grouping reminds us of the great variety of human sexual expression. This goes wider than even his ten categories. Any deliberate touching by one person of the body of another has sexual overtones, which accounts (by way of sex-negativism) for the powerful tactile taboos now operating in our society. Many bodily functions not directly sexual are *related* to sexuality more or less closely. This includes anything involving bodily orifices, such as eating, drinking, excreting, sneezing or suckling. Freud noted that in the anal and oral behaviour of infants actions are traceable which resemble those of adult sex-deviates, suggesting that those we call deviates may in truth may be the only ones who are in touch with reality. Reminders of the sexuality of animals or even plants can arouse erotic response in humans, as Dr Eustace Chesser illustrated with an account in *Sex Without Fear* of a pubescent boy who experienced his first penile erection while watching a time-lapse film of a flower bud unfolding.

Human sexuality is labile, and capable of taking any form to which, intentionally or not, it is conditioned. In their book *Patterns of Sexual Behaviour* the anthropologists Ford and Beach assert that it is possible, by a process of cultural and individual conditioning, to make a person an exclusive homosexual. Most homosexuals indeed become such in this way, rather than from congenital causes; though their conditioning is seldom deliberately directed to that end. If conditioning is so effective, it seems that what the human race really needs is conditioning designed to be conducive of sexual happiness.

The Orgasm

Despite the all-pervasive nature of human sexuality, it has a focal point.

This is the orgasm, about which more is known since the Masters-Johnson research in the 1960s. The physiological structure of the orgasm, with its triggering of acute pleasure-sensations, release of muscular and nervous tension, and freeing of engorged blood in tumescent organs, links powerfully with deep emotional responses. Usually orgasm, taken in all its aspects, is an event of significance to the person experiencing it. Often it is of considerable significance. On rare occasions in a person's life, the significance may be overwhelming. Such experiences are never forgotten, even though their intrinsic value may appear small. The emotions refuse to be measured by scales thought appropriate in other connections.

Masters and Johnson showed that the response cycle of the orgasm, in both males and females, has four phases. First there is the *excitement* phase, which is entered upon whenever erotic arousal begins. Often it does not result in orgasm, but is discontinued before that point arrives. The arousal may be caused by bodily contact, visual or olfactory stimulus, or erotic fantasising. The primary physical reaction is engorgement of the genitals caused by a locking device by which more blood flows into the organ than is allowed to escape. The secondary physical reaction is the contraction of various voluntary and involuntary muscles. In males the first sign of excitement is stiffening and enlargement of the penis; in females it is lubrication of the vagina. Clearly the first is due to engorgement of blood. Surprisingly, Masters and Johnson attribute the second to the same cause also. There is a 'sweating reaction' on the walls of the vagina caused by moisture seeping out of congested blood-vessels. The clitoris and labia also become engorged with blood, while in both sexes the nipples become wholly or partly erect. Muscular tenseness occurs in various parts of the body, the pulse rate speeds up and blood pressure rises. Often a measles-like rash (the 'sex flush') appears on the breast and abdomen. In the male the skin of the scrotum tenses and thickens, and the scrotal sac is lifted and flattened.

The second orgasmic phase is the *plateau* phase, though there is no clear dividing line. Features of the first or excitement phase grow in intensity as the orgasmic peak draws near. The testes increase in diameter, and are pulled even higher by further shortening of the spermatic cords. The coronal ridge at the base of the glans or head of the penis swells. In both sexes the rate of breathing increases and muscular contractions become tighter. In women the 'orgasmic platform', the swelling of tissues surrounding the outer third of the vagina, appears – together with secretions from the Bartholin's glands in the outer labia. The uterus is elevated and increases in size. The clitoris too becomes elevated, and also retracts into the folds of the labia. All these reactions mark the fact that during the plateau phase the female gathers psychological and physiological strength from the stockpile of mounting sexual tension, until she can direct all her physical and mental forces toward a leap into the third, or orgasmic, phase of sexual tension expression. In heterosexual vaginal intercourse the couple will now be linked by the phallus or erect penis. Penile thrusts in the vagina will be adding to the heightening tension. Masters and Johnson stress, however, what is one of the most significant facts to emerge from their research. *The same responses occur, in very much the same order, regardless of the type of stimulation that evokes them.* Whether the orgasm is produced by vaginal intercourse, masturbation, fellatio, cunnilingus, or anal intercourse, the complex physiological processes are virtually identical.

After the plateau phase comes the third phase, the *orgasmic* phase itself. In the female this takes the form of muscular contractions of the orgasmic platform, beginning at intervals of four-fifths of a second. The uterus contracts in a similar rhythmic way, and this rhythm may be shared by the sphincter muscles of the anus. The male orgasm follows the same pattern. In both, the pleasure sensations reach maximum intensity at this stage, in line with the peaking pulse rate, blood pressure and breathing cycle. Involuntary exclamations (verbal or non-verbal) may be uttered. The face may be contorted in a grimace, while other muscles similarly tighten. The hands may grip the partner in a spasm of intense feeling. (Frequently the muscular tightening in various parts of the body is so marked that aching is later experienced.) The climax is reached, with an ejaculation of semen from the male.

Finally comes the *resolution* phase, when muscular tension is eased and blood released from the engorged vessels. The body gradually returns to normal, the time differing according to the degree of psychic engagement. Many women are by now covered all over with a thin film of perspiration. Males find the erect penis returns to its normal flaccid state in two distinct stages. The first follows rapidly on ejaculation, but still leaves the organ considerably enlarged. It then gradually returns to its normal size and angle of projection from the body. The man or youth goes on to experience a refractory stage, during which renewed erection is not possible. Female orgasm however can be repeated without need for an interval.

This brief account is enough to show the inadequacy of the bibical description of sexuality as a mere 'lust of the flesh'. It is on the contrary a subtle and elaborate process. Humans have no part in its devising, though many are still inclined to seek its diminution. Roger Scruton in his book *Sexual Desire*, published in 1986, speaks of orgasm in itself (that is when divorced from a pair-bond relationship) as the curious pleasure of a palpitating gland. Equally dismissively, he calls the sexual act a spasm of the flesh. Yet this spasm, however achieved, is something wonderful. Orgasm, on the physiological level alone, involves complex, delicate and multifarious changes which the bodily mechanism is equipped to undergo regardless of the initial stimulus. The human body is constructed to do this as it is constructed to breathe, digest or walk. Orgasm, with all its processes, is as 'natural' as any other bodily activity. It has its dignity, even when brought about in solitude.

However, says the critic, it is a natural bodily activity for the muscles of the hand to tighten and for the muscles of the shoulder to contract and raise the arm. If the hand tightens round an iron bar and the arm is raised for the purpose of hitting a mugger's victim, we are unimpressed by the plea that these actions are 'natural'. We would be similarly unimpressed by an account of a rapist's excitement phase, sex flush and so on. There are limits to where detailed knowledge of the fact that orgasms are natural takes us. Just as Paul was wrong to assert that sexual functioning is inherently evil, so we would be wrong to assert that it is inherently good. Morally, like other bodily functioning, it is in itself neutral. Morality resides in intention, and nowhere else. Here we may get help from a maxim of the criminal law: the act is not criminal unless the mind is criminal. No orgasm, and no act involved in producing an orgasm, can be either criminal or immoral unless the *mind* is guilty.

As we look down upon a new-born child, what do we think? We hope to see it grow and develop according to its nature. We wish it to fulfil its potential in every way (except the sexual). If a medical examination revealed that this babe was endowed with an unusually large brain, we would hope to see it grow up to use that asset to the full. But what would we think if the maternity nurse told us that the babe had a penis of remarkable size, or a clitoris promising much in the way of future sexual excitement? Would we rejoice for it then? If not, why not? When informed that a baby has the capacity for a full and active erotic life we should rejoice. Furthermore we should resolve to help it, in every reasonable way, to fulfil that capacity. Such a sentiment reflects sex-love, and rejects sex-hate. We should all wish to be sex-lovers, which is only to accept and welcome this among our many human attributes.

Yet the sex act is traditionally called the act of darkness. Couples who engage in it are told they form *the beast with two backs*. Each new generation finds itself engulfed in the filth that is not sex, but our evangelistically conditioned putting-down of sex. The way to release from this is pointed by Scruton, in his helpful concept of 'intentionality'. This is a mental or intellectual state. The intellect lies midway between flesh and spirit. But all three qualities are equally human, and equally valid in human terms.

Every human sexual act has its intentionality, which may be moral, immoral or morally neutral. What we now need to grasp, and most urgently, is the significance of the intentionality behind each erotic response. For in truth the erotic response is for most of us in the present age the ultimate human response. Perhaps it is not as spiritual as we would like (though we reject the idea that the flesh lusteth against the spirit). In quiet moments we may cherish the thought of being, like Friar Lawrence or a thousand other bloodless clerical figures of literature, all grace and wholly spiritual. Within a monastic cell or hermit's grotto we feel we too might manage this. But not in the electronic hurly-burly of today's world.

So the next best thing is our sexual impulse. Its response is for us, here and today, the ultimate response. To stimuli we feel and register, but do not understand, this is the utmost we can offer. Far from being the act of darkness, sexual intercourse is the act of light. When we perform sexually, we care and are moved. This applies to all people, varying in detail only according to the nature of their sexual nature. Should they happen to be gay or lesbian, rather than heterosexual, it applies to them just as legitimately – in their own legitimate way.

Humans refuse to accept any limitation on behaviour which is based on purposes they were 'designed' to fulfil. We will not limit orgasm to reproduction because that limitation conflicts with the need arising from our true pyhsiological and emotional nature. In modern conditions, only a tiny proportion of our immense reproductive capacity is required to replenish the planet with its needed complement of people. So we infer that our sexuality is to be developed, refined and accepted as also available for ends other than reproduction. Vital though that end is, we must grasp that it is not the sole sexual purpose. Alternatives beckon. They must be taught to our young, and accepted by our society.

In a famous phrase, the seventeenth-century philosopher Thomas Hobbes described the life of primitive man as solitary, poor, nasty, brutish and short. Our ancestors, Hobbes reminded us, lived in continual fear and danger of violent death, famine and disease. It was to meet such primitive conditions that our complex sexuality evolved. The brief expectation of life, and the difficulties and dangers of rearing offspring, made powerful reproductive equipment imperative for carrying on the human race. Hence the fact that in humans the breeding season is continuous and not limited to periods of oestrus or heat, that one billion spermatozoa are contained in a single ejaculation of semen, and that throughout life the sex drive is powerful and insistent.

The Need for Orgasm

Despite our adaptability, biological urges respond very slowly to environmental changes. The time-scale of evolution is measured in millions of years, not hundreds. We now find ourselves equipped with primeval reproductive drives in an age of overpopulation resulting from better food production, medical advances and comparative safety from violent slaughter. The human race no longer needs powerful sexual impulses for its continuance, but the drives won't go away or diminish. They can be subdued by drugs such as Androcur. Attempts can be made to repress or sublimate them. Or they can be allowed full expression, consonant with the right of others to freedom from unwanted involvement. What does such full expression require? *The basic need is for orgasm.*

At all times when the human being is capable of orgasm, he or she usually has a physiological need to experience it frequently. The required frequency varies according to age, temperament and other factors. This physiological need corresponds to the way the human body is 'designed' to operate. It is linked however to psychological need, arising out of the emotional importance to the individual of his or her sexual functioning. There are innumerable reported instances of this combined need. Here are just three.

The ethnographer Raymond Firth, in his book *We, the Tikopia*, describes how in the country of the primitive Tikopia peoples brother and sister may live together in close (non-sexual) intimacy. Although incest between them is abhorred it can nevertheless occur simply because of the sexual needs of the male:

Sometimes . . . an informant will admit that the temptation may be too much for a man, and that he may yield to an overwhelming urge for sexual satisfaction. Such conduct is always represented as the fruit of his momentary sex passion, not the attainment of a long-cherished desire. It is the presence of an accessible female that is held to be the cause of the incest, not the wish to embrace the sister as such.

This degree of understanding and tolerance in a so-called primitive community contrasts markedly with the way such conduct would be condemned as 'yielding to filthy lust' in western evangelised societies.

For another example we may go to Sigmund Freud. In *The Psycho-pathology of Everyday Life* he tells of the Turks in Bosnia who in the event of sexual disorder are plunged in a despair which contrasts strangely with their resignation towards the threat of death. A Turkish patient of one of Freud's colleagues remarked: '*Herr*, you must know if *that* comes to an end then life is of no value.'

The third example is given by Gunnel Enby who, in her book on sex for the handicapped entitled *Let There Be Love*, says:

To be able to retain one's sexual capacity is of enormous psychological importance to even the most severely disabled person. A young man I know who had broken his neck in a diving accident was offered an operation which would relieve him of painful spasms and bladder trouble. At first he gradually accepted the suggestion, but when he learned that he would lose his capacity to have an erection in the future, he categorically refused. It was psychologically more important to him to retain his sexual capacity, although he was almost totally paralysed, than to be relieved of his physical pain.

For the male, virility and fertility are literally vital. This is why many instinctively turn away from the very idea of vasectomy, and despise *castrati*. Women have an equal respect for their reproductive function. They get depressed when the menopause ends their ability to conceive (even though their capacity for orgasm continues). To possess, and to have functioning, intact sexual equipment is of great psychological importance to human beings – though few of them could explain why.

Nietzsche said that the degree and essential nature of any human being's sexuality extends into the highest pinnacle of his spirit. This does not refer to disguised or sublimated sexuality, but sexuality functioning as it is 'designed' to function both physiologically and emotionally. That is why a sex-negater like the retired judge Lord Devlin is wrong to speak, in his book *The Enforcement of Morals*, of sexual desire as 'lust' and the yearning for its satisfaction as 'human weakness'. Even for believers this is a form of blasphemy, for how can a feeling supposedly implanted by God be said to constitute a 'weakness' except blasphemously?

Our need for orgasm is not solely, or even mainly, physiological. If it were, a hasty act of solitary masturbation, with no mental accompaniment, would suffice. It does not suffice, except perhaps in the case of those who accept payment as semen donors for AID. Strictly, an act without a mental element is not a sexual act at all. The human need is for physical release with appropriate psychological and emotional accompaniment. Here we approach the heart of the matter, in more senses than one.

First, the sex act must not be accompanied by any feeling of guilt or shame. On the contrary there needs to be a feeling that the activity is socially acceptable and morally right. Unfortunately for most us, guilt feelings spring from the nature of the superego arising from our childhood conditioning. That we can do little about in our own case, but we can no longer presumptuously assume that a child must learn from us and be sexless. It would be more humble, probably more productive and certainly more sensible if we would consent to learn from the child. We can change the conditioning for children of the future, and we can fight our own guilt feelings by reference to the positive morality we now consciously adopt.

Next there is the *nature* of the orgasmic activity. Here we recognise the need for a sexual partner, while accepting that in many cases this need cannot be met. The pair-bonding function of sexual activity requires solitary orgasm to be less satisfying than orgasm with the right partner. Ideally the partner is one who is *loved*. Ideally again, the partnership is seen as permanent. At least there should be sympathy, if not some degree of affection, between the two. R. D. Laing says in his book *Self and Others*:

Two basic intentions in sexuality are pleasurable relief from tension, and change in the other. Sex may be felt to be empty if the other is not dancing as well. The pure self-gratification of rise and fall of tension can be eminently frustrating. Any theory of sexuality which makes the 'aim' of the sexual 'instinct' the achievement of orgasmic potency alone, while the other, however selectively chosen, is a mere object, a means to this end, ignores the erotic desire to make a difference to the other. When Blake suggested that what is most required is 'the lineaments of gratified desire' *in the other*, he indicated that one of the most frustrating possible experiences is full discharge of one's energy or libido, however pleasurable, without making any difference to the other.

Laing slightly overstates the case. More frustrating than pleasurable discharge of the libido with an indifferent partner is inability to discharge the libido at all.

Orgasm may be on a basis of actuality or substitution. It is on a basis of actuality where it takes place with a partner fully adequate to satisfy erotic needs. It is on a basis of substitution where it is accompanied by *fantasies* of actuality, or visual equivalents provided by voyeurism or pornography. Substitution may occur either where the orgasm is solitary or where the relationship between the partners is erotically inadequate. The latter case involves mixed actuality and substitution unless the relationship is minimal, as in the case of pubescent boys masturbating together each with his own private fantasy.

Substitution is not always inferior. Where the sexual orientation is immoral, or at least socially unacceptable, as in pedophilia, necrophilia or bestiality, substitution is preferable to realism.

As we saw in considering the categories of sexual function, there is more to orgasm than libidinal release. Orgasm may seem an appropriate response to a powerful emotional stimulus. Any person strongly moved by an actual or imaginary experience or relationship feels the need to do something important to mark the fact. To achieve its object, this 'doing' must be commensurate with the stimulus. If no commensurate response is available, the stimulated person has no means of resolving the crisis induced by the stimulus. He or she suffers frustration.

Orgasm may void, or at least terminate, this frustration. Properly viewed, it provides through its connection with the vital core of sexuality an episode of appropriate significance. Often it is the only response open which is on the required plane. While the stimulus may be an erotic one, as in the typical case of love and attraction, equally it may not. Masturbation is a frequent response to emotional stress of a non-erotic order, such as fear, anxiety or insecurity.

So this is sexual need. In its basic erotic form it was the need felt by seventeen-year-old Ronald Jones when he attacked Maria in the incident related at the beginning of this chapter. Ronald had been conditioned to regard masturbation (or 'wanking' as he would call it) with contempt. In his environment no provision was made for orgasm with a partner. His pent-up need for acceptable orgasm finally asserted itself in an alarming and disastrous manner. Society blames him, and many like him, for that. The blame truly belongs to our cruel, hypocritical society. Out of innumerable available examples, we give just one more.

Georgette Floyd is a syndicated agony aunt. In her column in July 1988 she included, under the headline 'Shocked by a shy son's sexy secret', a mother's letter about difficulties relating to her son of fifteen, described as shy and withdrawn. Following advice from the boy's teacher, she and her husband had begun to 'encourage our son as much as possible'. This led to severe disappointment, as the mother's letter goes on to explain:

I thought we were getting somewhere with him as he seemed more relaxed. Now we are back to square one. My husband found our son reading sexy magazines that are nothing but filthy pornography . . . My husband burned the lot and my son and his father have not spoken to each other since. I feel sorry for my son because I know he is unhappy, but I also feel sorry for my husband because he is so disappointed in his only son.

A suitable answer to this rubbish would have been on the following lines:

Your husband is a hypocrite, and you are not much better. He knows perfectly well from his own youth that most fifteen-year-old boys are very highly sexed. Indeed at that age males reach their maximum potency, as other cultures (and previous eras in own culture) have openly recognised. Your son's current, and harmless, sexual outlet is likely to be through masturbation. So-called pornographic books are a help and comfort in this, and the parents need to be understanding about their use. This particularly applies because of the unjustified denigration by our society of the universal practice of masturbation.

This was not of course what the agony aunt, syndicated in dozens of 'family' newspapers, said. Her reply was:

A shy and lonely boy is quite likely to read pornographic magazines, but this does not mean he is depraved or a son of whom you need to feel ashamed. It could mean that he is finding out about sex in the only way available to him.

This is good as far as it goes, but it does not go nearly far enough. A frequent cop-out by adults is to say that adolescents are 'finding out' about sex, when what is really meant is that they are engaging in activities directed solely to sexual *fulfilment*. It is not a matter of 'finding out' but of doing. Our society stubbornly refuses to accept that young adolescents, even children, are sexual creatures with a need for some form of sexual fulfilment. The very thought is shocking.

However, it is not only fifteen-year-old boys whose sexual need is not met by society. It is a large proportion of the population. Moreover sex is more than a need. It can also be a joy.

Sexual Joy

In his introduction to the renowned liberating manual *Ideal Marriage*, the English version of which first appeared in 1928, the Dutch physician T. Van de Velde accepted that publication of a book treating sex more frankly than the British public were used to would have unpleasant results for him. Explaining that he nevertheless felt it his professional duty to go ahead, Van de Velde said:

There is need of this knowledge; there is too much *suffering endured* which might well be avoided, too much *joy untasted* which could enhance life's worth [Emphasis added].

In discussing the human need for orgasm in the previous section we covered briely the first aspect of Van de Velde's twofold formulation. A need which is not met causes suffering. Meeting the need avoids that suffering. But there is more to sexuality than that. Properly used, it offers mankind opportunities for boundless joy. As Van de Velde courageously proclaimed, much of this available joy goes untasted. It is poisoned by unjustified guilt, or wrongly induced shame. It is chased away by ridicule, cheapened by the false values of that titillating society engendered by sex-negation. Or it is untasted because sexual fulfilment is, for one false reason or another, forsworn.

As the American psychologist Harry Stack Sullivan pointed out, the hunger for orgasm has something in common with the hunger for food and drink. Both arise from physiological need directed to preservation of the individual and the race. Both have a wide range. Both have links with orality. Both are significant from the social aspect, for eating or drinking alone is in its way akin to solitary masturbation. When the body has taken sufficient food and drink for its age, state of health and work rate, it requires no more. To put in more is to risk an accusation of gluttony. Is there an equivalent with sexual activity? The answer is probably yes, though psychiatrists now would be more likely to look for neurotic causes in over-indulgence of either kind.

Human intake of food can involve anything from an ice-cream in the back row of the stalls to an Etuvée de Volaille Albufera in a fashionable restaurant of the Boulevard de la Faubourg St Honoré. Drink can range from a glass of tap-water to a glass of Montrachet. Sex varies from the schoolboy's casual wank to the high passion of an Abelard and Heloise. With any of these, religion may enter.

For many Christians, the summit experience of eating and drinking is Holy Communion, with its sip of consecrated wine and sanctified wafer melting on the tongue. Equally, sex has played a part in many religious rites. In her reminiscences of running a brothel, Marise Choisy says that the difference between a sacred courtesan and a call girl can be likened to that between a priestess who offers holy wine and a bartender. Though that may be a harsh judgement, many would insist that the schoolboy's casual wank and the cinema ice-cream are not truly on the same level, and that the heroic lovers of legend are far removed from even an Etuvée de Volaille Albufera. Sexuality occupies, except for one who is starving, a level placed far above food and drink. It is on the mysterious dimension that leads to new existence. Sex is the unique factor which, suffering through the ages the utmost contempt, leads us nevertheless to the highest pinnacle.

Some human beings there have been, and indeed still are, who think that pinnacle more surely gained by renouncing the flesh. They are wrong, just as on this point the Bible is wrong. The flesh is part of man, and man is part of the flesh. No part of the flesh of man is to be renounced, least of all any sexual part. Sexuality links a man or woman with the human generations that have gone before, and the human generations yet to come. This link, among many other attributes, gives sexuality an importance in the life of humans which is second to none, deny it though we may.

There are many who do wish to deny it. Typically they are men, putting down women just after they have had their way with them. Roger Scruton thus expresses this crude male view of life after orgasm: 'Suddenly everything seems flat, arbitrary and mundane; what was for a moment a glowing body, offered and accepted as an individual life, is now only a piece of human flesh, to be rewrapped and set aside for another occasion.' Into so low a view of sexuality seep other gross human attributes, such as selfishness, egotism and mental obtuseness. We who defend sex cannot guard against all that. Even sublime sex is not proof against human weakness of another order.

What we must reject, with utmost vigour, is the philistine concept of shame in sexuality. This is exposed in the definition of modesty laid down by Camille Melinaud in her essay 'Le Psychologie de la Pudeur': *la pudeur c'est la honte de l'animalité qui est en nous* (modesty is our shame at the animality that is within us). The last thing we humans must do is feel shame at being what we are. There is a very long way to go before the human race can realistically expect to be wholly spiritual. It will not happen in our time, and those to whom it does happen will have ceased to be human.

Where then is the pinnacle of sexual joy? Perhaps it is found by the virgin bride and groom contemplating happily the future offspring of their wedding-night coupling. That is the evangelist's view. But we suspect that more often than not on these occasions the looked-for joy escapes, especially where the bride was not prepared for sex. Frequently the inexperienced couple, weary after the day's events, suffer disappointment. The guilt the evangelist has conditioned them to associate with sexual indulgence is not easily chased away, and is by this sad experience reinforced.

We have our private idea of where the pinnacle of sexual joy is to be found. Some of us have found it, only to lose it again. For others it is all along glimpsed at a distance. The very young approach it as a promised certainty. This is the thing we all long for constantly, and enjoy seldom. It is the constant theme of artists, rarely untouched by sadness. Browning gave it a poet's expression in *De Gustibus*:

> Hark those two in the hazel coppice –
> A boy and girl, if the good fates please,
>
> Making love, say –
> The happier they!

> Draw yourself up from the light of the moon,
> And let them pass, as they will too soon,

With the bean-flowers' boon,
And the blackbird's tune,
And May; and June!

Browning did not pause to enquire whether the ecstatic boy and girl were married, and it seems they were not. Even this eminent Victorian was concerned only to celebrate sexual joy. Sexuality is indeed the key to human joy. But that joy is the birthright of every human being. If a man or woman has not linked with a soulmate because the right person has not come along, or diffidence or shyness has conquered, or life with another has seemed a huge step, or the responsibility to serve has prevailed, that joy is still not to be denied. It is to be taken as best it may – freely, openly and in good heart.

In the end we see that the evangelists of Christianity, and of any other cult that exalts man's spirit above the flesh, are in fundamental error. We refute the evangelists. No solution is right for a human being which denies his or her sexuality. No puritan straitjacket clamped on the free flesh of man is to be worn unscathed, or endured without protest. So let every man and every woman, every boy and every girl, unhesitatingly reject restrictions that deny their birthright. Otherwise we will lose joy. Keats discerned:

Joy, whose hand is ever at his lips
Bidding adieu . . .

The secular moralist has a high opinion of joy, and considers its pursuit a moral duty. Obviously this extends to the learning of what we need to know for its attainment, and the acquiring of the necessary skills.

As with most things in human life, satisfaction in sexual intercourse depends on knowledge and improves with practice. It is our duty to our partner and ourself to learn and practise the techniques needed to make the best of our sexual natures.

Celibacy and Chastity

Celibacy is pursued by religious people who wish for freedom from the torments of desire. It is an understandable wish. The hungry person wishes to be freed from the torments of a clamouring belly. The thirsty person wishes to be freed from the torments of a parched throat. The costive person desires the congested bowel to yield. The pregnant woman on the point of delivery longs for that delivery. The injured or diseased person wished to be freed from the torments of agonising pain. We are not surprised to find that those who yearn to convert themselves into spiritual creatures find sexual desire otiose.

The person who would be celibate often thinks sexual renunciation will bring him or her nearer to God. This is very strange when one thinks that for the believer it is certain that God and no one else planted sexual desire in every creature. Yet we find the Dominican Donald Goergan boldly saying in his book *The Sexual Celibate*:

Celibacy also means freedom . . . it is the freedom to be with God, for God, and to do the work of God. At the end of a celibate formation process, a person should be more free. I speak here of interior freedom, the freedom of the sons and daughters of God, which comes from prayer as well as from a well-integrated personality.

In an early classic of feminism, *Woman*, the nineteenth-century socialist August Bébel said that unquestionably the neglected satisfaction of the sexual impulse exerted the most detrimental influence on the mental and bodily condition of men and women. He argued that no social institutions could be regarded as healthy which prevent the normal gratification of the sexual instincts. Unexpectedly, Bébel was able to cite Martin Luther in support of his views. Luther, a former monk, was strongly opposed to priestly celibacy. His church experience had convinced him that the lives of monks and nuns were contrary to nature and therefore wrong. He held that a woman could as little dispense with a man as with eating, drinking and sleeping. Neither could a man dispense with a woman. Luther said of those who rob the sexual organs of their function: 'what do they else seek but to restrain Nature from being Nature; fire from burning; water from wetting.. . . '. His words have been echoed (to little effect) by many subsequent observers.

Luther, a deeply religious man, asserted that God may so sanctify a person as to enable him or her to dispense with sexual indulgence; yet he regarded such cases as rare and exceptional. For ordinary people, even those in holy orders, sex deprivation is unnatural and cruel. We may express this in the following precept.

Because they contravene the duty of sex-fulfilment, enduring celibacy and chastity are undesirable in the way that any other failure to fulfil one's human potential is undesirable. This does not mean that young persons should be hurried into sexual experience before they are physically or emotionally ready.

Celibates are seeking to be inhuman, and inevitably fail in their object. They cannot avoid involuntary orgasm, since biology refuses to be altogether denied. But is there any force in the argument that spiritual power can be enhanced by forgoing *voluntary* orgasm?

Freud thought that high features of civilisation, such as great art, were due to repression of the sex-drive. This has been denied by such followers of Freud as Fromm and Reich. The latter argues in *The Invasion of Compulsory Sex-Morality* that the relation between sexual gratification and sublimation is not a mechanical one (the more sexual suppression, the more social achievement) but a functional one. To a certain degree, says Reich, sexual energy can be sublimated. He adds: 'However, if the

diversion goes too far, sublimation changes into its opposite, a disturbance of work capacity.'

Freud's contrast between sexuality and civilisation is also rejected by
Marcuse. As Professor MacIntyre puts it in his account of the latter's
work, Marcuse wishes to envisage a possible social order in which human
relationships are widely informed by that libidinal release and gratification which, according to Freud, would spell the destruction of any social
order.

While orgasm is an important need for almost everyone, there can be
no question of denying any individual the right to choose the way of
celibacy. It is just such denials of freedom by sex-negaters that we have to
fight. The sex-lover is not antagonistic to celibates who have freely chosen
that course, but will feel concern at any suspicion that it has been chosen
for motives induced by sex-negative conditioning. A positive view of sex
is incompatible with celibacy, or its equivalent for females, chastity.

August Bébel argued that, despite the protests of society, every human
being has both the right and the duty to satisfy his or her sexual
promptings. These promptings, Bébel said, are intimately connected with
the innermost being; indeed they form an integral part of it. If social
institutions or prejudices prevent the gratification by any person of these
instincts, the wise Bébel added, then the development of his or her being is
checked. It becomes crippled and stunted.

Also in the nineteenth century an enlightened reformer, Dr Elizabeth
Blackwell, wisely said in her book *The Moral Education of the Young in
Relation to Sex*:

The sexual impulse exists, as an indispensable condition of life, and as the basis of
society. It is the greatest force in human nature. Whatever else disappears, this
remains.

The restriction of legitimate sexual expression to marriage has always
meant that abstaining from orgasm is officially expected of some people
all of their lives, of all people some of their lives, and of many people most
of their lives. Society is still geared to this principle of at least part-time
celibacy, even though it is often ignored. To ignore it is to court censure
and sometimes punishment. Yet medical and other authorities hold that
sexual abstinence can be positively harmful to the abstainer.

So we lay down an official pattern of behaviour that we are bound to
acknowledge may be damaging. In any other field of human concern, this
discrepancy would not be tolerated. What then has sex done to be the
target for social abuse? It is not as though we had no wise teachers.

Dr Frank Caprio, psychiatric consultant to the Department of
Correction, Washington, remarks in *Variations in Sexual Behaviour* that
it is a common fallacy that the best health is achieved through sexual
abstinence. If anything, he says, psychiatrists have discovered that
abstinence in many instances precipitates a neurosis or psychosis. Dr

Caprio adds that urologists are convinced that sexual abstinence can produce disorders of the prostate gland.

Dr Wendy Greengross, in her book *Entitled to Love*, writes of the sexual needs of the disabled. Are there such needs? Society does not seem to think so. Yet Dr Greengross observes, even of the physically incapacitated, that 'sex is undeniably good for you'.

Benjamin and Masters, in their book *Prostitution and Morality*, say of the need for sexual outlets among youths in the armed forces: 'A young man who could actually live for any long period without any kind of sex expression, not even masturbation, would be a grave neurotic and most likely have been rejected as 4F.'

Psychoanalysts stress that sex-starvation can cause a high level of anxiety. Freud himself found this. One of his early collaborators Wilhelm Reich went so far as to say that sexual abstinence is dangerous and absolutely harmful to health. In his book *The Sexual Revolution* Reich asserts that in adolescence a tendency to protracted sexual abstinence is a pathological symptom liable to produce damaging social results, such as reduced achievement in work. In *The Invasion of Compulsory Sex-Morality* Reich wrote that pathological neurosis originated in the conflict between sexuality and the denying outside world, particularly the family. Their upbringing, he said, destroyed the sexuality of infants, inflicted 'this misery of puberty' on twelve-year-old boys, and altogether created sexual repression akin to a mass plague.

Dr Isadore Rubin said sexual deprivation can place strain on the heart, while another Freudian, Wilhelm Stekel, wrote of the value of masturbation as an outlet. He found that some patients develop suicidal ideas after renouncing masturbation, especially when it is associated with incestuous fantasies. In his experience, the neurosis breaks out only *after* the subjects give up this form of relief. He adds: 'The disease is afterwards falsely regarded as the consequence of the habit, instead of being properly recognised as due to abstinence from masturbation.'

To show that the view of sexual abstinence as positively harmful is not confined to modern authorities here is an extract from a book first published near the beginning of the nineteenth century, Drysdale's *The Elements of Social Science*. The author, a medical graduate, was clearly ahead of his time. He wrote, in somewhat exaggerated language:

The ignorance of the necessity of sexual intercourse to the health and virtue of both men and women is the most fundamental error in medical and moral philosophy. A society in which all men and women should restrain their sexual desires till the age of thirty or upwards would be a scene of such horrible restraint, such absence of manliness and nature, such widespread genital disease, spermatorrhoea, chlorosis, hysteria, and all the allied signs of enfeeblement and morbidity, that it would be next to impossible to find a single healthy or natural individual.

Dr Hegerisch, the nineteenth-century physician who translated into

English Malthus's *Essay on Population*, held that chastity in women was a crime against nature not infrequently revenging itself by the cruellest form of disease. He considered it led to morbid processes in the breasts, the ovaries and the uterus. This is a reference to cancer, though even today the causes of cancer are not fully known. That makes it all the more irresponsible for a leading modern authority on sex education, Dr Margaret White, in *Sound Sex Education*, a pamphlet published by the Order of Christian Unity, to warn teenagers that premature sexual intercourse can cause cancer of the cervix. Dr White quotes a lecturer in obstetrics as saying the boy is the carrier of the disease, which is manifest nonsense. Not enough is known about cancer to justify any such statement. What *is* known renders it most unlikely that cancer is 'carried' by anybody. If the human body shows itself biologically ready for full vaginal intercourse it is unthinkable that such an activity could give rise to pathological conditions in the absence of some predisposing factor special to the individual.

Sexual Techniques and Services: the Sleaze Syndrome

Fully and successfully to implement the principle of sexual fulfilment requires the availability of adequate services. One of the consequences of sex-negation is that these are often denied.

As we have seen the noted Victorian analyst Dr Elizabeth Blackwell, echoing other commentators, described the sex impulse as the greatest force in human nature and the basis of society. Once hunger and thirst are satisfied, and protection from the elements secured, we may take hers as a true assessment of the human condition. It must follow that the arrangements made for the welfare of citizens should recognise their sexual needs and respectfully and efficiently accommodate them. Yet in our society, as in past human societies, this does not happen. Next in importance to the damage to individual health caused by sex-negation, which we have examined, comes the denial of much-needed amenities and services. With us, arrangements for servicing sexual needs are not made at all or are grossly inadequate. Either way, such services as are provided are generally frowned on as unfortunate, regrettable, unnecessary and dirty. Often they are treated as wholly contemptible. The result is that these services, in so far as they are available at all, are squalid, scorned, over-priced and little enjoyed. Their ambience can only be called sleazy. We may therefore call this societal lack the sleaze syndrome.

The sleaze syndrome is immoral. It is inhuman, even obscene, to regard the servicing of natural needs as dirty, since dirt is no more than matter situated in places we do not wish it to be. If human sexuality is to be looked on positively, society must make available sufficient health and advisory services to counter ignorance and disease. The accent must be on helping people get the greatest fulfilment from their sexuality, so far as medical science can assist in this. Rather than concentrating on clearing away the wreckage of physical or mental sexual mishap, medical professionalism should take a wider view. This means openly treating the child from birth as a person whose sexuality, like its other attributes, is to be nurtured and encouraged by adequate treatment of disease and dysfunction, by the skills of preventive medicine, and above all by the giving of advice, counselling and assistance towards achieving maximum sexual fulfilment throughout life. Sexual potential must be realised, not inhibited. We see that there are broadly three sexual provisions humans require from their society: disease prevention or prophylaxis, clinical response to disease when contracted, and sex-positive nurture.

There has been particular failure in the treatment of sex dysfunctions, a necessary part of nurture. If you deny sexuality *in toto* you are not likely to be very interested in obstacles to the proper functioning of the human sexual process. As we have seen, a bodily condition caused by such an obstacle is nowadays called a sex dysfunction. Often the cause of such a dysfunction lies in the childhood conditioning that sex-negation produces. In themselves therefore sex dysfunctions are largely a consequence of this negative emotion. So too is society's failure to make proper arrangements for treating such common traumas. Consider the following case history, based on an example in K. A. Menninger's book *Impotence and Frigidity*.

A physician is called to a young woman, who has developed fits of compulsive weeping. She will not go out, and lies all day in her bedroom crying. Her worried parents explain this to the doctor, who carries out a thorough physical examination. When this is completed he says:

Your daughter is suffering from paroxymal lacrimation. I recommend treatment of the eyes with belladonna and astringents, locally applied. To reduce discharge from the tear glands her intake of fluids should be restricted. If these measures fail, surgical removal of the tear glands will become necessary.

We see at once the absurdity of this imaginary physician. It is obvious that if a girl is weeping and you want to help her you must find out why she is sad, not apply physical treatment to her eyes and tear-ducts. What is only just coming to be realised, however, is that this kind of absurdity is actually practised. Weeping is far from being the sole physical response commonly made to psychological stress. Many sexual dysfunctions spring from this very cause. Instead of treating the physical manifestations directly (as it still frequently does), the medical art must seek out the underlying psychological factors.

In their book *Psychosomatic Medicine*, published in 1949, Weiss and English criticised physicians of the time who assumed an organic basis for frigidity in women. They instanced a case where a young bride developed abdominal pains which were diagnosed as symptoms of appendicitis. An appendectomy failed to cure the trouble. At short intervals other abdominal operations were performed. Finally, the ovaries, fallopian tubes and uterus were removed. Only then was it discovered (on a change of medical advice no doubt) that the bride's problems were psychological.

Things are slowly improving. At the Cornell-New York Hospital, for example, a sex therapy clinic has been opened – an unheard-of departure for a large metropolitan hospital. This, known as the Payne Whitney Psychiatric Clinic, was first headed by Dr Helen Kaplan, who claimed to have made a major advance in the treatment of sex dysfunctions. She pointed out that in men these are principally *impotence* (failure to achieve or maintain an erection), *premature ejaculation* (lack of control over timing, formerly known as *ejaculatio praecox*), and *retarded orgasm* (where the man cannot release his orgasm, or can release it only after intense stimulation, or does not feel it when it happens, or feels it in so faint a way that he thinks himself robbed). Corresponding distresses in women are *vaginismus* (involuntary contraction of vaginal muscles, rendering entry of the penis impossible), *frigidity* (inability to begin the excitement phase of orgasm through lack of physiological response), and *orgasmic phase disorders* (various difficulties in achieving climax).

Hitherto, treatment of these common conditions has scarcely been considered feasible by the generality of the medical profession. This was not surprising when the very existence of the conditions could not be openly acknowledged, only a dysfunction that wholly prevented vaginal intercourse being recognised. That solitary exception was a result not of any concern for the emotional welfare of the dysfunction's victims, but to the law's insistence, based on the social requirements of property and succession, that a marriage incapable of consummation was voidable at the suit of either party. In nullity suits medical evidence of incapacity was required, so doctors were forced to become involved to that extent. It was not realised that, since most cases of impotence or vaginismus are due to psychological factors capable of resolution, the law's demand for proof of *permanent* incapacity could rarely in truth be met.

The first serious attempts to treat sex dysfunctions came from Sigmund Freud and his followers. Psychoanalysis is, however, open to the objection that it requires a length of time, and corresponding cost, that puts it beyond the reach of most sufferers. Dr Kaplan claims to meet this drawback by treatment which is partly behavioural and partly psycho-analytic. Since in her view sex dysfunctions are among the most common medical complaints ('more common than the common cold'), this advantage is to be welcomed. She considers, surely rightly, that people have as much right to sexual health as to any other kind of bodily wellbeing.

Sex therapists of Dr Kaplan's persuasion, while not disputing the Freudian view that a patient's sexual disorder is frequently a manifesta-tion of psychological problems embedded in childhood experiences, nevertheless treat only the *immediate* causes of the problem – together with the defences the patient has put up against accepting the true strength of his or her sexuality. The remoter determinants are dealt with only to the extent necessary to abolish the symptoms of the dysfunctions and prevent their recurrence.

Although progress on these lines is being made, it is very recent and not in general operation. The standard of the services available to treat sex dysfunctions remains abysmally low. As the World Health Organization said in a report published in 1975, and still not generally accepted, there is need for a change in attitudes of most doctors and other health workers, and for acceptance of sexuality as a *positive component of health.*

Health workers at all levels share the same beliefs, myths and superstitions that exist in the society to which they belong, and they may themselves have unresolved sexual problems. Their training generally does little to dispel these attitudes, because of the current emphasis on curative rather than preventive services; for example physicians are better prepared to cope with pain and disease than with the establishment of pleasure and sexual wellbeing. The attitudes of health workers can present an important obstacle to their effective functioning as educators and counsellors in the field of sexuality, and it is not surprising that they are often reluctant to become involved in this area. This reluctance may be manifested in unconscious denial of the sexuality of their patients, or a mechanical and impersonal approach to the examination and prescription of contraceptive methods. To the extent that people with sexual problems look to health professionals for guidance and advice, punitive or negative attitudes, careless statements, and inappropriate methods regarding sexual matters may seriously damage the patient's sense of the importance of his or her own personal sexual life.

Since society's recognised arrangements for treating sex dysfunctions have been grossly inadequate we need not be surprised to find that over the years quack doctors and quack remedies have arisen instead. Where there is human need, for the relief of which people are prepared to pay, entrepreneurs will always be found to meet that need to their own profit. This has been the case throughout the world's history. Quacks are impervious to notions of respectability. They exist to serve human demand, in whatever channel that may lie.

In 1844 *The Economist* published an advertisement it would be unlikely to accept today.

MANLY VIGOUR: A Popular Inquiry into the CAUSES of its PREMATURE DECLINE with instructions for its COMPLETE RESTORATION . . . Illustrated with cases, etc by C. J. LUCAS & CO, Consulting Surgeons, London . . . Messrs Lucas & Co are to be consulted from ten until two, and from five until eight in the evening at their residence, No. 60, Newman Street, Oxford Street, London, and country patients may be successfully treated on minutely describing their case, and enclosing the usual fee of £1 for advice.

Dr Helen Kaplan complains of present-day sex therapy quacks, calling them 'despicable'. Often, she says, 'It's just an excuse to show dirty movies and have sex with patients.' We note without much surprise that even an enlightened sex therapist of the late twentieth century, perfectly willing (indeed anxious) to show erotically stimulating films to patients as part of their medical treatment by herself, yet brands these as 'dirty movies' when exhibited by medically unqualified therapists openly out to make a profit. Having sex with patients is similarly put down, notwithstanding the fact that surrogate partners are an accepted feature of clinical therapy for sex dysfunctions. Even to the enlightened (at least in an unguarded moment) therapeutic sex is still within the SEX IS BAD proscription unless hedged about with the respectability of degrees, diplomas and regular medical practice.

We have looked at what are perhaps the most serious consequences of sex-negation: damage to general health, the causing of specifically *sexual* dysfunctions, and society's failure to provide adequately for the treatment of these. That is but one aspect of the pitifully poor service which, because of the sleaze syndrome, is provided for our sexual needs. Another aspect concerns the sexual requirements for those who are in good health. Here we can indentify the following six categories of needed services.

1. *Education and training.* Services dealing will all aspects of sex education, and training in sexual techniques. The former continues to be the subject of fierce battles, and is discussed at length in chapter 12 of this book. Training in sexual techniques continues to be generally unavailable.

2. *Provision of orgasm.* Comforts offered by what the sleaze syndrome calls courtesans, madams, prostitutes, strumpets, harlots, whores, models, callgirls, gigolos, hostesses, rentboys, escorts, relief masseuses or masseurs, toyboys and others. We may prefer to call these by a kinder name, say erotic Samaritans. They are dealt with below in this chapter and in chapter 15.

3. *Enhancement of the orgasm.* Practical aids, such as porno magazines, vibrators, lubricants and sex videos, which help to ensure (for those who need them) that the orgasm, whether within or outside marriage, and whether solo or accompanied, is as rewarding and fulfilling as it can be made. So far as the orgasm is substitutional, there is need to improve the fantasies of actuality and their visual equivalents. The potential for improving the orgasm by physical assistance is largely unexplored.

4. *Introduction services.* Where a person lacks a suitable sex partner, introduction services help him or her to find one. Often the law prevents this, however. Approaching anyone with an invitation to engage in sexual activity, if done by a man on more than one occasion, is punishable by up to two years' imprisonment. Matchmakers are an ancient institution, and their modern equivalent the

matrimonial agency is tolerated within strict limits. Other forms of contact agency have recently sprung up, though many are branded as illegal. It is one of life's tragedies that for almost every person deprived of sexual fulfilment there is, somewhere unknown, another person in similar condition who if discoverable would be a perfect match.

5. *Services to deal with unwanted pregnancy.* Provision of moral forms of contraception, sterilisation and abortion. This is discussed in chapter 11.

6. *Information services.* Information on the availability, quality price, etc, of the above.

Although there have been marked improvements in some respects, no one would deny that the present quality and availability of these services in our society is greatly inferior to that of other vital services. Moreover recent efforts to improve sex services have been subjected to a backlash from the 'moral majority' and have had to yield ground they had freshly gained. The welcome innovation of so-called sex shops (more properly sex-equipment shops), which began to spread throughout Britain in the 1960s has been checked. In response to clamour from the sex-negativists, Parliament stepped in and passed a restrictive licensing Act in 1982. This has led to a marked reduction in sex shops, and deterioration in the quality of those few that remain.

Compare the situation with regard to another vital service, the supply of food and drink. In western countries this is provided and consumed on a scale far exceeding what is needed to sustain life. Food shops, cafés and restaurants abound, as do recipe books, good food handbooks, wine and beer guides, and other information sources. Complex legislation, backed by an active inspectorate, enforces standards of quality, hygiene and trade description. The growing of foodstuffs is subsidised and closely regulated. A large and expert advertising industry promotes food and drink products of bewildering number and variety, giving the public widespread choice.

As we have seen, once hunger and thirst are satisfied, and shelter secured, sexuality is on a plane of human importance far above any other. A sensibly ordered society would first ensure that everyone had enough to eat and drink, and sufficient shelter, and then would turn its attention to promoting sexual happiness. It would not countenance for one moment the sleaze syndrome. Yet inhabitants of western countries, while consuming in food and drink far more than their bodies need or is good for them, contemplate with equanimity (or avert their gaze from) the sexual malnutrition suffered by many. As an organised society, we do very little to promote our sexual happiness, and one must insistently ask why this should be. It makes no sense.

On the official, or establishment, level our society simply does not accept the need for sex services, and punishes in various ways people who seek to provide them. In 1877 those pioneers of family planning Charles Bradlaugh and Annie Besant found themselves consigned to the dock, at London's criminal court known as the Old Bailey, for publishing Dr Charles Knowlton's medical pamphlet on birth control entitled *Fruits of Philosophy*. Designed only to help in the provision of a needed sex service, this sober work was, as we learn from the defendants' account of the trial, branded by the indictment as an 'indecent, lewd, filthy, bawdy and obscene book'. The two were duly convicted and sentenced to terms of imprisonment.

Throughout history many would-be providers of sex services have landed in the dock, and still do. But it is not only the criminal law that is employed against human sexuality; the whole powerful apparatus of social disapproval is brought into play, as this book illustrates all through. One argument used by the sex-negaters is that sex should not be commercialised. Yet the objection that money is being made out of sex is false. It is levelled not only against prostitutes but against other providers of sexual services, for example sex-shop owners and pornographers. A moment's clear thought will show that there is nothing whatever in this pecuniary objection, unless one is a Marxist believing all private profit to be wrong. The rest of us *expect* commercial interests to provide for our wants, and feel aggrieved when they fail to do so. Our society is based on that principle. Commercial demand is demand that can suitably be met by commercial means. All that illicit commercial exploitation of sex proves is that there is widespread commercial demand. Why should it not be supplied by licit (that is lawful and acceptable) means?

It is irrelevant that the demand concerns an intensely intimate and personal part of our lives. All such intimate areas are commonly served by commercial interests. Commercial interests supply the bride with her trousseau and ring, and the clergyman who marries her with his cassock and surplice. If the wedding is followed by Holy Communion, commercial interests supply the wafers and communion wine. Commercial interests supply the happy couple with contraceptives (provided they know where to go for them). If these fail, other commercial interests supply the unwilling parents with a pram, a cot and baby clothes. All through life we are constantly served by commercial interests, and when we die commercial interests arrange the funeral, supply the coffin, incinerate the remains, furnish the funeral feast and publish the obituaries. From cradle to grave, we are in the hands of commercial interests.

Why then should commercial interests not help to satisfy our need for sexual services? What ought to concern us is not that commercial interests supply any of our sexual wants (and make a profit out of it), but that they are prevented by legal rules and social attitudes from supplying more of them – and that at a reasonable price and to an adequate standard. In trying to stifle needed sex services, society makes us victims of an ineluctable social law, which may be called the sleaze law: *prohibition of a strongly demanded service merely ensures its provision at a debased level and high social cost.*

Sex therapy, sex-enhancing equipment, contact services, so-called prostitution, so-called pornography, provision for contraception, sterilisation, and abortion, sex-information − all these and more are supplied somehow because the demand is irresistible. But society pays a bitter price for its coy reluctance to accept the truth about sex. Poor-quality services, excessive charges, diminished lifestyles, endangered health, criminality, police corruption and other ills are the result of the irresistible sleaze law.

8
Sex-fulfilment in Special Cases

The duty of sex-fulfilment applies not only to our own fulfilment. It also requires us to help and encourage other people to achieve fulfilment in this field as in any other area of life. Yet often the institutions of society are so organised as to *deny* such fulfilment, rather than facilitating it. Since our society is run on democratic lines we should feel a personal responsibility for this. It is often our own attitudes that reinforce the pressure organised society brings to bear on our neighbours' sexual natures. In this chapter we look at some of the most glaring examples of this anomaly, beginning with the negative treatment of attempts to achieve sexual fulfilment by the elderly.

Sex in Old Age

The precept of the Code set out at the beginning of the previous chapter suggested that we should not deny old people sexual fulfilment or denigrate their pursuit of it. Nor should we condemn any sexual relationship on the ground of a disparity in the ages of the partners. That there is no sex in Sunsetville is a false notion wished on the old, too often successfully, by the impatient young.

Of any old person (and of some who are not that old) one might helpfully enquire: are you still competing sexually, or have you given up? Usually it is not necessary even to ask this impertinent question, for appearance gives the answer. The person who dresses attractively, and is always well turned out, proclaims they are still in contention. Admittedly the contention may be in fields other than the sexual, for example business or politics. But of one thing we can be sure. The person who lets their appearance go is signalling that they have given up sexually. This is sad for a lone person, since it appears to signify that they have renounced the hope of sex-fulfilment with another. It is also sad for a person who is within a pair-bond, for it means the partner is being taken for granted.

Even for the old however, clothes do not always make the man (or woman). Consider the following.

The lovers lie bronzed and naked in warm sunshine. They are on their backs in the sand, side by side, hands clasped, half asleep. On each elderly face a half-smile plays. Is it an expression of satisfaction, of remembered embraces and current tenderness? Passers-by on this naturist beach in the south of France glance casually, then catch something of beauty in the abandoned attitude and happy relaxation of this pair – both in their eighties and white-haired. The beauty is scarcely of the body, for the years have done their work. There is a defencelessness about them, and an innocence; also a pride that they can still share physical love and not be ashamed. Many others on the sun-drenched *plage* lack for one reason or another bodily perfection. This does not bother them. Face-lifts and wrinkle-removers are not within their compass. Nor do these trivialities bother our ancient couple. In nudity they are able to be themselves, honest and without pretence. They are not ashamed of genitals, breasts, or buttocks that lack the size or contour held needful by the values of our titillating society. These two know that sexuality, properly regarded, is concerned with other things as well as the perfection of youthful beauty, important though that is.

> Will you still need me
> Will you still feed me
> When I'm sixty-four?

So sang the Beatles in the exuberance of their youth, when sixty-four seemed an age impossibly distant. They didn't dare or think to add: Will you still have sex with me? To their age-group the question would have been ludicrous. There is no sex in Sunsetville.

Not only the young, who may be forgiven, take this negative view of sex and the elderly. Many of the elderly are inclined to share it.

Miss Margaret Tucker, a retired civil servant living in Cheltenham, gave evidence before the Chancery Court in 1977. The case concerned the will of her wealthy cousin, Mrs Violet Salmon. Just before she died at the age of seventy-eight, Mrs Salmon found herself suddenly in love. The lucky man was a police sergeant aged fifty-one.

Miss Margaret Tucker heartily disapproved. Her elderly cousin, she told the court, behaved like a sixteen-year-old when the sergeant was about.

'They held hands, and he stroked her hands. He called her "Vi" and she called him "Darling". Nobody else in the family called her anything but Violet. Only her late husband called her "Vi".'

Miss Tucker enlarged on the enormities of this: 'My cousin said she *lived* for Sergeant Davies. She was desperately in love with him. From the very beginning I said I didn't like the sound of it.'

Then came the ultimate objection. Mrs Salmon had shyly confided that she and the sergeant were having sexual intercourse. Miss Tucker remonstrated.

'Violet! At your age! And in your state of health! That *must* be bad for you.'

The outcome of the case does not matter. Its sole purpose here is to furnish an illustration of the widespread prejudice against sexual activity by the elderly. This is one more aspect of sex-negation. The negaters dislike sex and long to eradicate it. They can't achieve that, so they do the next best thing and reduce to the minimum legitimate occasions for its exercise. The old cannot procreate, or if (in the case of males) they can do so they should not because of genetic risks. So, as with young people within the maturity gap, the old lack the one respectable reason for sexual activity.

Besides, it is unseemly. At their age they should know better. Here we see one more success for the form of improper discrimination nowadays known as ageism.

It is worse when an old person fancies a young one: even enlightened people let their prejudice show then. And heaven help us if a youth or maiden should perversely lust (as they occasionally do) for someone much older than they. The dirty old man is a common target of scorn. Even when, like Sheridan's Sir Peter Teazle, he goes through the procedures of lawful matrimony before embracing the girl, he is not forgiven. Yet it is no more blameable to be attracted by a pretty maid when you are sixty than when you are sixteen, and certainly it is just as natural.

Society still condemns such cavortings however, as Mr John Clemence, a Welsh magistrate aged fifty-nine, found at the end of his four-day trial for indecent assault in 1988. As it was put by a tabloid newspaper reporting the case, Mr Clemence was jailed for fondling the breasts of his son's teenage girlfriend Donna. The girl shyly told the court how she was wearing only a pink bathrobe when Mr Clemence JP approached and hoarsely said 'You are bloody gorgeous.' He then nibbled her ear, stroked her thigh, and committed the act complained of. The elderly magistrate's accompanying words were 'I am a naughty boy, aren't I?' The judge sternly told the accused that there was only one way he could deal with the offence, and that was by a custodial sentence. For a brief caress that conveyed affection, and perhaps even traces of love, the old man was not merely ruined socially but also locked up. His fault was momentarily to slacken the control we are required to exercise over natural prompting. Donna may have felt gratified at this confirmation of her charms. Society felt itself obliged to view the matter otherwise.

Dislike of the very idea of an old man pawing the body of a nubile girl is one manifestation of the general hostility to the old having sex at all. Because of this attitude the elderly lecher, as he would properly be called, is stricken by guilt. Betjeman wrote of this in his poem *Senex*.

> Oh would I could subdue the flesh
> Which sadly troubles me! . . .
>
> To see the golden hiking girl
> With wind about her hair,
> The tennis-playing, biking girl,

> The wholly-to-my-liking girl,
> To see and not to care.

Why should he not care? And if he cares (and she cares), why not do something about it?

If *she* cares. There we come to the most frowned-on area of all. There is even a Greek-based medical term for it: gerontophilia, or sexual love for the elderly. Even quite advanced thinkers balk at that. Take Lars Ullerstam, whom we have met before. Giving what he calls 'a Swedish view' in his book *The Erotic Minorities*, Ullerstam points out that gerontophilia, which can have either a heterosexual or homosexual tendency, is common among adolescents, and usually disappears as they grow up. He pitilessly adds: 'This is of course due to the fact that the sexual urge is sometimes so strong in those years that almost *any* sexual object is acceptable – it is the same age group that engages in sodomy.'

Lars Ullerstam, who pleads throughout his book for compassion towards sex-aliens, clearly has little compassion for the old. He equates a youth's desire for an older sexual partner with a youth's desperate desire to penetrate, as the only available target, a sheep or cow (for animal sex is what Ullerstam means by sodomy in this context). Gerontophilia, according to this advanced writer, is 'anomalous'. Through it old people are mysteriously preferred to 'fresher partners'. Things are not much better when we come to Benjamin and Masters, who would also lay claim to advanced views. In *Prostitution and Morality* they describe geronto-philia as 'a not uncommon aberration', adding that probably in most cases it attests to incestuous cravings.

Several years ago in Italy a 'ring' of grandmother prostitutes was uncovered by the police. The 'ring's' clientele consisted almost exclusively of young men. It is such elderly females, trading on their age and on the aberrant desires of young males, that we have in mind when mentioning a category of 'elderly prostitutes' . . . We might add that it is singularly fortunate for some of these grandmother types that such a deviation exists. Otherwise most of them would long since have had to go out of business.

This jaundiced view of the sexual attractiveness of the elderly is one more example of the propensity to condemn what is not sexually beguiling to oneself. Benjamin and Masters should have learnt, as a result of their exhaustive researches, that the only reliable motto as regards sexual tastes is *whatever turns you on . . .*

A striking example of the truth of this motto, and of the fact that not all elderly people lust after the young, is given by Beverly Nichols in his autobiography *The Unforgiving Minute*. As a young man in the 1930s Berlin beloved of Christopher Isherwood, Nichols was walking one night with a young German friend, Peter Class. Tired and in need of a drink, the two youths saw a discreet-looking bar, dimly lit. They went in, and sat down in a quiet corner. A waiter approached, and surveyed them with an unfriendly expression. They ordered Schnapps.

As they waited for their drinks, Nichols looked round the bar. It struck him that they had wandered into a very curious establishment. All the clients were male, and well over sixty. Moreover, every single one was bearded. Without exception, they were staring at Nichols and his friend with undisguised hostility.

The waiter returned, without the drinks. There was a rapid interchange in German between him and Class. One white-bearded ancient, who appeared to be nearly eighty, rose and shook his fist. Hastily the two youths left.

Nichols gives the explanation.

By chance we had wandered into one of Berlin's most exclusive brothels, which was reserved for the use of elderly gentlemen who happened to find their pleasure only in the arms of other elderly gentlemen, and could only express their endearments if their beards were closely entangled. And when we had entered, young and sprightly and clean-shaven, they must have felt a sense of outrage, as though we had come to violate their sad and secret world.

The current disdainful view of the sexual attractiveness of the elderly, whether or not face-lifted, was not always so strongly held. The seventeenth-century writer John Webster remarks in his *Westward Hoe* that old wives are wholesomest and old lovers soundest. John Cleland has Fanny Hill, the woman of pleasure, describing in glowing terms the advantages of her connection with a much older lover. This man, with whom the teenage girl lived for eight months, was a bachelor turned sixty. He had a fresh vigorous complexion, having never racked his constitution by permitting his desires to overtax his ability. What he lacked in the bewitching charms of youth he atoned for with the advantages of experience, the sweetness of his manners and his ability to touch the heart by the use of his understanding. The elderly gentleman taught Fanny Hill many things, not least that the pleasures of the mind, far from being incompatible with those of the body, serve to exalt and perfect them.

If we grasp what sexuality is truly about, we understand that its expression is as important to the old as to the young. Humans are sexual creatures all life through, from cradle to grave. To be happy and well adjusted they need life-long fulfilment of their sexuality. If they presume to despise that quality, they despise their own nature. In his article 'Sex After Forty – And After Seventy', Dr Isadore Rubin comments that Masters and Johnson, through their detailed laboratory study of the sexual responses of older persons, have helped to destroy the stereotype of sexless old age which has done such serious harm to the health and happiness of the elderly. They studied sixty-one women between the ages of forty and seventy-eight, together with thirty-nine men aged from fifty-one to eighty-nine. While the rapidity, intensity and duration of anatomical response in the women declined with advancing years, the researchers found their female subjects fully capable of adequate and meaningful orgasms. Results were similar for the men. After sixty, erection is achieved more slowly, and ejaculation loses force and duration. This in no way lessens the importance of orgasm as physical release and, with the right partner, emotional fulfilment.

As Rubin points out, other researchers, such as Kinsey, agree with these findings. Erections on waking drop from an average of 4.9 a week in youth to 1.8 at the age of sixty-five and 0.9 at seventy-five. But there are exceptional cases where a high level of sexual activity has continued throughout life. Kinsey reports one married couple who conducted a constantly active sex life though the man was eighty-eight and his wife ninety. Masters and Johnson stress the importance of *regularity* in preserving a high level of sexual performance, particularly in women. Reduced hormone production after the menopause results in decreased lubrication and thinning of the vaginal walls. This can cause discomfort and even pain on infrequent intercourse.

For the male too, regularity is valuable. Masters and Johnson, who clearly regarded sexual activity as desirable, found that the most important factor in the maintenance of life-long fulfilment is *continuous* exercise of the sexual function: 'It does not appear to matter what manner of sexual expression has been employed, so long as high levels of activity were maintained . . .' In other words, if you believe in sex then practise sex – even to your life's end.

Some think this does not apply to the physically unfit. Elderly sufferers from heart disease often assume that their condition precludes sexual activity. They may be reinforced in this view by their medical consultants, yet research shows that sexual intercourse is beneficial in most medical conditions. An American physician, Dr Eugene Scheimann, wrote a book on this theme called *Sex Can Save Your Heart . . . And Life*. He points out that coronary risk factors are most dangerous when accompanied by stress. Sex, he says, is an antidote to stress. It can therefore play a major part in the prevention of cardiac arrest.

Elderly married couples often find their sex-life diminishing through boredom. They are advised to try variant positions and artificial assistance. The helpful vibrator carries no moral stigma. Sex is worth an effort. An ageing wife should strive to keep herself mysterious, entrancing and seductive. The husband should treat his spouse of forty years as ardently as his fresh young bride, for that is what in the truest sense she still is.

Yet we are fallible, and deserve indulgence. If the marriage has sunk to unredeemable erotic levels why not let in, if only as a last resort, the hope of extraneous romance? A long-married couple civilised enough to recognise and accept the place in their lives for sexual experience with other, younger, creatures are unusual but perhaps wise. If this thorny problem can be rightly handled the marriage may even be strengthened. The old couple might rediscover each other's bodies with renewed joy, after a brief holiday with someone else.

Many will not agree with this, and their attitude must be respected. What can never be respected or accepted is the view that sex is not for the elderly, and in some way degrades them. In this area of life, as in most others, there is need for the rehabilitation of sex. We should no more speak of a dirty old man than of a dirty young man. To do so is called *ageism*.

We should respect the right of an older woman to take to her bed the glowing body of what is sneeringly called a 'toyboy'. For this she is not to be dismissed as a nymphomaniac, any more than he is to be dismissed as a gigolo or lounge lizard. All such as these are cruel words, putting down the tender joy of sex. Its emotions are for all of us, old and young. The beauty of young bodies is to be respectfully shared, and ardently enjoyed. It is never to be wasted, through hiding and disuse, until it fleets away.

Sex for the Disabled

The duty of sex-fulfilment applies to those suffering from mental or physical disability, as it applies to everyone else. We consider now some special problems that arise in their case.

By and large society has contrived that there should be *no* sex for those with serious mental handicap who require institutional care. If they do manage to obtain scraps of sensual comfort, these are officially frowned upon: the regime does not allow for it. As we shall see in chapter 13, the sexuality of youthful sufferers has always been looked upon with horrified repudiation. Marriage is likely to be impracticable for those who are severely handicapped, yet they often have as great an interest in sex as anyone else. Indeed this may be one of the few joys left to them. For less grave cases marriage can be rewarding and beneficial, bringing out the best in each.

Consent can be a problem with the mentally disabled. As we shall see in the next chapter, consent is in general a requisite for sexual acts. But what if a person's mental condition precludes the formation of any genuine decision to give or withhold consent? The law is unequivocal here. It is a criminal offence, punishable with up to two years' imprisonment, for a man to have sexual intercourse with an apparently consenting woman to whom he is not married and who is severely subnormal mentally. There is an escape clause for the man who can prove he did not know, and had no reason to suspect, that his sexual partner was in this unfortunate condition. But there is no excuse for the man who pleads that his aim was philanthropic, namely to take pity on, and give some fleeting joy to, a poor deranged creature who has little else in life to hope for. Society seeks to condemn such women, unnecessarily and for no fault of their own, to life-long sexual deprivation. Because a medical expert will testify that theirs is not a 'true' consent, their factual agreement to a harmless act that gives simple pleasure is overruled.

It does not console the mentally backward woman or girl to be told that this negative treatment is administered with the best motives. The aim may be to protect her from 'exploitation', a heinous sin in our present culture. Even Dr Wendy Greengross, no friend of sex-negativism, sympathises with what she describes as the fear of exploitation that bothers many people involved with the handicapped. And of course there always are heartless males prepared at the slightest opportunity to exploit vulnerable females. Yet this talk of exploitation reveals one of the most subtle and insidious weapons of sex-negativism: the idea that to gain enjoyment from a sexual act with another person is necessarily to exploit or 'use' that person.

Here is another anti-sex crime in our calendar. The law makes it an offence, punishable with up to two years' imprisonment, for a man on the staff of a mental hospital to have sexual intercourse with a consenting in-patient or out-patient, even though her mental disability is comparatively trivial. David Shotbolt (his real name) was employed at Darlington Memorial Hospital as a male nurse in the psychiatric unit. He became friendly with Dora, a married out-patient with four children. She asked David to give her extra treatment at her home. He did so, paying frequent visits and administering relaxation therapy. After a while the couple began to have sex during these visits. The affair went on for more than six years, during which time Dora's husband left her. One Christmas, halfway through this period, Dora, as the law permitted, voluntarily discharged herself from the hospital. More than four years later David was retrospectively charged with committing the criminal offence just described. He was convicted, and sent to prison for nine months. Note that Dora, though a psychiatric patient, was classified as a sane adult. Clearly she knew perfectly well what she was doing with David Shotbolt. Why was he put in jail? We may wish to condemn him morally for breaking up Dora's marriage. We would do so on insufficient evidence, for reports of the case give no details about this aspect. Moreover breaking up a marriage does not land a man in jail in any other circumstances.

A way needs to be found of releasing people with mental disabilities from sex-negating restrictions, whether imposed by law or culture. It is suggested that the following moral precept would be appropriate.

Apparent consent by a mentally incapacitated person to a sexual act cannot be taken as true consent where the incapacity is too great to permit the person to understand the full emotional and ethical significance of the act. Where however such a person would otherwise be condemned to involuntary celibacy or chastity it is not immoral to afford them sexual fulfilment with no more than their apparent consent, since in such circumstances the usual requirement of true consent is prevented from applying.

It is necessary for those having care of a mentally incapacitated person to ensure that compliance is made with other requirements of the ethical code, for example regarding protection against disease and the need for contraceptive precautions.

When we turn from the mentally handicapped to those with severe physical disabilities we find the same sex-negative stance. The proportion of such people in the population is growing. Medical progress ensures that more babies with congenital disabilities such as spina bifida or cerebral palsy now survive to adulthood. Development of new drugs produces novel victims like the thalidomide children. Crippling diseases such as muscular dystrophy emerge during early life but do not now cause infant death. Then there are the familiar disabilities suffered by the deaf, the blind, epileptics and others. Finally there are the victims of modern plagues such as accidents in the home, in the factory, or on the road.

Where the physical handicap is severe, marriage is sensibly ruled out: it is a difficult enough condition without superimposing the trials of bodily incapacity. Out therefore goes sexuality. Largely from embarrassment, the physically disabled are treated as sexless. If sex does insist on rearing its head it is regarded as an awkward nuisance – or even a matter for punishment. Here we may seek information from two recent books, one written by a medical expert and the other by a victim. Significantly they have similar titles: *Entitled to Love* by Dr Wendy Greengross and *Let There Be Love* by the severely handicapped Swedish girl Gunnel Enby. Both plead movingly for more enlightened attitudes.

Dr Greengross points out that for too long society has not credited the physically handicapped with even the capacity of falling in and out of love, of feeling sexual urges, of needing emotional satisfaction. Here the Henry Moore syndrome operates to an acute degree. The parents of the handicapped child, as soon as the extent of the disability is recognised, unconsiously resolve to keep their stricken offspring neuter or sexless. We may sympathise with this, for even to rear such progeny presents problems enough, without the added complication of sex. The disabled one is powerless to escape from this deadly trap. Requiring help and supervision at all times, he or she is necessarily deprived of the opportunities for free exploration open to, and required by, normal youngsters. The latter are supervised at school, and supervised at home. There remain occasions when they are neither in the school nor in the home, but free in the wide world. Here, as Dr Greengross says,

they manage to be exclusively among their contemporaries, testing out their strengths and their weaknesses with passionate friendships and violent feuds. They fight and tease and touch each other, groping and feeling each others' bodies and beginning to recognize the signals of pleasure and indifference and animosity. As they grow older they hold hands, dance together, sit close on chairs, push and shove and generally indulge in the socially acceptable exploration of feelings and reactions which is their early introduction to sexual excitement and awareness.

123

Not so the severely handicapped child, under watchful adult eyes all the time. Here the damaged body, washed, dressed and tended always by others and never by its owner, becomes almost a public thing. Attempts at genital manipulation are observed and put down. Gunnel Enby reports being reprimanded: 'Don't touch yourself dear; nice girls don't do nasty things like that.' Her whole experience as a handicapped child was of what she calls the anti-sexual brainwashing practised by hospitals and other institutions. And these were in modern Sweden, usually thought of as sexually emancipated.

The truth is that those having the care of a handicapped child should not merely tolerate auto-erotic activity by the child; they should encourage it. Dr Greengross records the case of a mother who for the first time 'caught' (as the mother put it) her disabled teenage son masturbating. She was horrified and ran to her husband. He told her quietly to turn her back 'because our son is learning a skill'. He wisely added that all she should do was make sure paper tissues were within reach so that the boy could clean up for himself. Elsewhere Dr Greengross contemplates that parents might go further. She tells of the father of a thalidomide boy who told her that he had taught his son to masturbate. She says that masturbation should figure in parents' teaching of handicapped children 'because with less emotive attitudes it can help the handicapped to get the physical release they may otherwise be denied'. She adds:

Many parents find it an embarrassing and fraught subject, and some view it with disgust and abhorrence; but with open discussion, perhaps more reading on the subject, they might be able to see that masturbation is not 'dirty' and that it is just part of growing up. Some parents may want to help their handicapped children to masturbate where hands are limited in their movements.

That last sentence could be a trap for unwary parents. Any adult who masturbates a child under the age of consent is guilty under English criminal law of indecent assault. It makes no difference that the child is the adult's own. Indeed the judge is likely to regard that fact as exacerbating the offence. Also treated as exacerbating the offence (so perverse is our society) would be the handicapped condition of the child. The parent would be fortunate to escape a prison sentence.

As severely handicapped children grow up to sexual maturity, their deprived state becomes ever more acute. Parents who have struggled to look after a child may understandably give up the struggle when the child comes of age. The young adult then enters an institution, to join others whose parents gave up sooner, or who never enjoyed parental care. Lars Ullerstam criticises the way, even in enlightened countries like present-day Sweden, long-term patients suffer deprivation from the fact that the staff do not minister to their sexual needs. He blames this on the fact that hospitals carry on the work of convents, where sexuality was seen as an invention of Satan. He adds: 'Sexual charity is a blasphemous idea in the eyes of Christianity – except when it is practised within a marriage, that blanket excuse for everything.' Ullerstam goes on to cite approvingly a recent Swedish novel in which a nurse helped out a seriously stricken polio patient by masturbating him. How far this is removed from reality is revealed in pitiless detail by Gunnel Enby. Although she is writing about Sweden, what she says applies with equal force to Britain.

Some patients in Gunnel's institution sought to form a patients' group which would appoint an ombudsman to represent patients at meetings of the hospital board. In particular the ombudsman would fight the restrictions against sexual contact of any kind. 'We felt very strongly that the staff ought not to devote so much of their time trying to prevent the patients from finding some sort of sexual happiness together.' The authorities dismissed the suggestion. They were not even prepared to consider allowing those young people who were capable of having sexual relationships freedom to do so. The principle was rigidly adhered to, so that those discovered engaging in sexual activity would be immediately sent home, whether or not there was anyone there capable of looking after them. Even the husband of a married patient with a private room was not allowed to spend the night with her when visiting. Instead, he was consigned to an attic. When an engaged couple who were both disabled asked to share a room they were refused on the ground that the matron had threatened to leave if their request was granted. She openly declared that she found the thought of handicapped people having sex together intolerable.

Gunnel Enby comments on the disastrous effect these attitudes have on the patient's rehabilitation. If a person's faith in their own lovableness is denied by ignoring or dismissing the sexual part of their personality, the whole process of rehabilitation is undermined. Yet doctors regard this as unimportant.

What seems to me so horrible is that sex is not only disregarded but that efforts are made to actually prevent any kind of sexual activity among the patients. I should have thought that it would be regarded as progress when a physically handicapped person stops thinking of himself as a sexual failure and begins instead to devote himself to a life-enriching sexual relationship with another human being. All his rehabilitation prospects will improve. For isn't it true that we all use our sexuality to boost our ego? Don't we all like to imagine that if we wanted to, we could easily have a sexual relationship?

An obvious problem with the severely handicapped is how to manage the operational side. Gunnel Enby records the case of a friend of hers, a single man in his early thirties who 'loved fast cars and women'. He broke his neck in an accident, and became paralysed. The doctors considered a rehabilitation centre useless, so the patient remained at home. He lay in bed all day staring at the ceiling. He refused to see visitors, but a girlfriend was insistent. The couple then discovered that the man was capable of a reflex erection. If the girl helped him, and was very active herself, he could sustain the erection until she had an orgasm. He could feel nothing himself, but was happy to know he could still have a sexual relationship with a girl and make her happy too.

Vibrators and other mechanical aids can assist the disabled to reach orgasm, but institutions frown on these. Gunnel Enby relates the story of a girl in a home who had been courageous enough to buy a vibrator by post.

In spite of partial paralysis of the arms she had found a way of satisfying herself when she went to the lavatory, the only place in the hospital, needless to say, which had a key in the door, and where she had a natural reason to ask for help with her underclothes. The vibrator produced a high pitched note which could be heard in the corridor. On one occasion the sound was heard by the sister, who immediately demanded that the door be opened – and there the girl sat, exposed in her misery and degradation.

The girl was suitably reprimanded. Her vibrator was confiscated. It was stored with the rest of her belongings – to be returned to her only if and when she ever left the hospital.

We must get these attitudes changed, deep-rooted though they are. Sometimes, in order for a disabled person, or a disabled couple, to enjoy sexual release the positive intervention of another person is necessary. If the scene is a hospital this helper may have to be a staff member. Should we aim to change attitudes so that nursing staff are expected to perform such services? We have seen something of the obstacles the law erects. Clearly a nurse should not be asked or expected to break the law. While these laws remain they present a barrier that only devoted and dedicated nurses will surmount, because they consider it to be in the highest traditions of their calling to do so.

What of the cases where there is no legal barrier? To begin with, it should be said that it is by no means certain what these cases are. The elderly gentlemen who sit as judges in our highest appellate courts are perfectly capable of deciding that sexual conduct not hitherto treated as criminal shall in future be so regarded. We may think that fairly safe from this treatment is the rare case of a *married* couple whose physical disabilities are so great that they cannot copulate without the active assistance of at least one other person. If they are patients, should it be part of the duties of hospital staff to provide such assistance?

Dr Wendy Greengross in the final chapter of her book tells of residental homes with humane staff who consider it their nursing duty to give such help 'because they know their charges need the sexual release'. In other cases patients give relief to fellow-patients. She says nevertheless that it may be better to allow a couple to find their own level of satisfaction, rather than accept a standard they have difficulty in achieving and for which they need the help of a third party. 'Many of course would be so turned off by such an intrusion that the question does not arise.'

A social worker contacted Dr Greengross about a very severely disabled young man who masturbated himself with physical (but little emotional) release. He desperately wanted to make love, or try to make love, to a real woman. Dr Greengross visited the youth and talked about his problem.

I was not convinced that he really would find the satisfaction he wanted merely by intercourse – even if he could manage. I was sure that what he really wanted was the warmth and love and caring of a heterosexual relationship. If he had been able-bodied, he would have worked this out for himself; as he was disabled, did I or anyone else have the right to prevent him testing out his own needs?

This raises the question of surrogate sex partners. These give sexual services on a caring basis (whether for payment or not). They are not 'lovers' but they are 'carers'; and their own pleasurable enjoyment is not ruled out. Usually they work in conjuction with sex therapists, but, as we saw above, such useful services are still regarded by our society as questionable.

Gunnel Enby reminds us of another dimension when she says: 'The sexually deviant among the physically disabled have a heavy burden to carry, for theirs is a *double handicap*.'

We may sum up the discussion on sex for the disabled in the following precept.

The duty of sex-fulfilment indicates that it is immoral to deny people a full sex-life merely on the ground of their mental or physical incapacity. Those having charge of such people therefore have a duty to ensure so far as practicable that they are afforded suitable opportunities for such fulfilment, provided necessary contraceptive and other precautions are taken.

Closed Institutions

Sex-negativism flourishes in closed institutions, sometimes called total institutions. These include hospitals, army barracks, state prisons, government hostels and other establishments where the regime is under control of administrators rather than inmates. The key feature is impaired autonomy, particularly impaired privacy, for the inmates. Without privacy sex-negativism tends to rage unchecked. So let us take a look at what privacy really is.

Privacy means many things; above all control over the immediate environment. Where one is, whom one is with, how one is interfered with by others, are things the individual desires to control. We all wish for personal autonomy, and this is an aspect of it. We have our social roles to play, and we resent interference.

In his *The Presentation of Self in Everyday Life*, roles are divided by the sociologist Erving Goffman into front-region and back-region roles, with corresponding onstage and offstage behaviours. Clothes and other personal physical characteristics are used as props. Hair-style and makeup are manipulated to support a role, or show its rejection. With many people it may be difficult to determine where acting ends and truth begins. If a waiter puts on one performance for the diners and quite a different one for the kitchen staff, when is he ever himself? Has he even got a self, or are his successive performances all he is?

Goffman speaks of 'personal space' to describe the area surrounding an individual, anywhere within which an entering other causes a feeling of being encroached upon. You may not stand close to me in a lift unless it is very crowded. You may not intrude into a conversation. Complex signals indicate resistance. The woman signals 'Don't come closer', and the man heeds the sign. Two parties to a dialogue ignore a third person and he goes away.

Role-playing and personal space signals need to be distinguished from other signals which are involuntary and drive people away against the wishes of the signaller. These can give the disabled much more privacy that they want (and make them lonely). People's inability to cope with their feelings about the maimed or disfigured leads to avoidance. So does any defect that makes a person look or sound odd or different, or hinders mobility, or renders social intercourse difficult or troublesome. The deaf suffer deeply from this.

Among both normal and disabled people, individuality is expressed through personal possessions. A car-owner identifies with a mass-produced car 'personalized' by fancy wheels at a fancy price. A pet animal or favourite pipe is regarded as intensely personal, fully private. It is as if a person vests an element of the self in personal belongings. They are part of who he or she is.

Interference with any of these complex and delicate patterns is a fundamental breach of privacy. Total institutions interfere totally. There are council children's homes which allow no personal belongings and allocate all clothing daily from a communal pile. Denial of privacy to prisoners has been found to cause irritability and resentment, revealed in excessive fault-finding and boasting. A claim by mental patients for a degree of privacy, or territorial behaviour such as liking for a particular chair or corner, is interpreted by staff as a symptom of their illness. A convicted criminal cannot be left alone with his private identity; the institution has a responsibility to change him. (It may change a neat and clean young man by banging him up with an old lag who is dirty and careless in matters of hygiene, or with a powerful homosexual who rapes him.) Even good citizens serving in the armed forces, the police or the prison service are denied privacy in their living quarters. At the end of life, the terminal patient may suffer from conditions in the open hospital ward. One such kept his eyes closed all the time. Asked why, he said: 'I'd prefer an ordinary life.'

In conditions like these it is not surprising that sexuality, often the first victim of difficult circumstances, suffers. It is given no place in the regime.

No allowance is made for it. More by default than deliberate policy, it is deemed not to exist. If an inmate insists on belying this fiction he or she is likely to suffer punishment in some form.

It follows that one of the unadmitted consequences of committal to a closed institution is a regime of sex-starvation. The judge who sentences a young convict says: 'You will go to prison for a term of so many years.' He ought to add (but of course never does): 'During that time you will be denied any opportunity of legitimate sexual fulfilment.' If the man is married the judge ought then to turn to his wife and say: 'That goes for you too.' Yet if the upholders of compulsory marriage really respected that social institution they would insist that a married prisoner should be afforded opportunities for sexual intercourse with his wife. On a less humanitarian, and more practical, level conjugal visiting in prisons would ease the difficulties of administrators by reducing tension. In his evidence to the Home Office inquiry on the 1976 riots at Hull prison, the Labour MP John Prescott commented on how the abundance of obscene graffiti on prison walls indicated obsession with unsatisfied sex-impulses. He added: 'Sexual deprivation must surely constitute one of the worst and potentially most harmful aspects of loss of liberty. These are powers that produce frustrations and tensions.'

In his book *Conjugal Visits in Britain* (published in 1977) Jules Quentin-Burstein reports that many foreign governments do now make arrangements for prisoners to have occasional sexual intercourse with their wives. These enlightened regimes are not found in the Anglo-Saxon countries – with the limited exception of two of the American states, Mississippi and California. The book gives a detailed account of arrangements in the notorious Soledad prison. Conjugal visits are a privilege limited to prisoners with a good security rating (though not necessarily with a record of good prison behaviour). They last forty-eight hours, and are permitted every few weeks. The privileged prisoners express great satisfaction with the arrangements, which involve setting aside apartments and trailers outside the perimeter fence. The subsequent records of the prisoners show them to have fewer parole difficulties than prisoners not so favoured.

Even conjugal visiting would be of no use to the unmarried prisoner. Why not put male and female prisoners in the same building, and encourage them to form sexual relationships if they wish? That has actually been tried at the Fort Worth Co-Correctional Prison in Texas, and has worked well. Another expedient is suggested by the Swedish doctor Lars Ullerstam. There ought, he says, to be mobile brothels to provide for acute hospitals, mental hospitals and similar institutions. Similar facilities should, he adds, be available for the paralysed or housebound, and for old people. All these would be grateful for the straightforward manipulations offered, such as masturbation or a striptease performance. The employees of these mobile brothels might, says Ullarstam, be called *erotic Samaritans* and should be held in great esteem. 'One would wish that cheerful, generous, talented, and morally advanced persons with a knowledge of the joys of giving would feel attracted to this humanitarian profession.'

At various periods of history brothels have been officially provided for service personnel. R. S. Morton, in his book *Sexual Freedom and Venereal Disease*, describes army brothels used by British troops in the Great War. Separate facilities were arranged for officers and enlisted men, and standing orders laid down clear rules as to hygiene. Morton says that after intercourse men were required, as a drill, 'to urinate, wash, douche and apply a freely provided ointment'. This enlightened regime is a rarity for British forces, and when discovered has invariably been greeted by a chorus of outraged attack from sex-negativists.

We may sum up the arguments in the present section of the discussion in two further precepts.

The duty of sex-fulfilment indicates that it is immoral to deny people a full sex-life merely on the ground of their service in the armed forces or other state services. Those having charge of such people therefore have a duty to ensure so far as practicable that they are afforded suitable opportunities for such fulfilment.

A sentence of imprisonment inevitably restricts the prisoner's freedom of activity; indeed that is its social purpose. However the duties of sex-fulfilment and sex-respect indicate that we ought not to deny people a full sex-life merely on the ground that they are state prisoners, just as we do not deny them food, drink and rest. Those having charge of such people therefore have a duty to ensure so far as practicable that they are afforded suitable opportunities for sexual fulfilment.

9
Sexual Acts

On a strict religious view, a sexual act is immoral unless consisting of vaginal intercourse with the possibility of conception. Even then it is immoral unless performed within wedlock. Such a view lays stress on the precise nature of the physical act, but secular moralists regard this as generally unimportant.

On the other hand in both religious and secular ethics the mental state of the participants is crucial.

Types of Sexual Act

The secular moralist acknowledges that human genital organs are designed, or have emerged through evolution, for the reproduction of the species. This is their 'purpose', or primary function. However, as we saw in the description of the response cycle of the orgasm in chapter 7, the same physiological responses occur, in the same order, regardless of the type of sexual stimulation that evokes them. Whether the orgasm is induced by vaginal intercourse, or by solo or plural masturbation, or by frottage, fellatio or cunnilingus, or by anal connection, or by fantasy (dreamt or waking), or by accidental collision with the sheets, the complex bodily processes are identical.

It follows that the type of stimulation leading to orgasm is irrelevant from a moral viewpoint. Moreover it is clear that humans need sex in many situations where reproduction is inappropriate or impossible. If a baby was born every time a human had felt sexy the planet would now be crowded beyond bearing. So we can put forward the following precept.

Since the primary purpose of our sexual organs, functions and desires is reproduction of the species, contraceptive-free vaginal intercourse between a fertile male and female may be regarded as the primary sexual act. However, healthy sexuality goes much wider than this, and no type of sexual act is to be condemned on the ground that it departs from the primary act.

In the present chapter we briefly explore the ethical factors involved in the commission of sexual acts generally, or of particular sexual acts. We begin with a basic factor in any civilised society, the need for consent to a sexual act performed with another person.

Consent to Sex

The principle of sex-respect acknowledges that the sexual activity of any person is of intense individual concern to that person, and ought therefore to be regarded as exclusively within his or her control. We may say it is or should be private, a concept echoed in the description of genital organs as 'privates'. So we must accord each person the right to decide whether or not a proposed sexual act is to be undertaken by or with him or her. A sex act is immoral unless committed with the consent of each participant. This means an *informed* consent, a concept fraught with difficulty – as Carolyn Faulder has shown in her 1985 book *Whose Body Is It?* One difficulty concerns the application of this principle to people who are not in a position to give or withhold true consent, notably those with mental incapacity or deficiency and the immature. Problems concerning the former were discussed in the previous chapter, while those concerning the latter are dealt with in chapter 13. The overall principle, applicable to people without incapacity, can be expressed in the following precept.

We ought not to touch another person sexually without their consent, whether explicit or reasonably inferred. Nor should we do any other act towards a person sexually (such as showing them a pornographic picture or exposing their nakedness) which is out of scale with any indication they have given regarding their willingness for this. Special considerations apply where the person is too young, or is otherwise unable, to give informed consent.

Sexual Harassment

Withholding of consent to a sex act can be signified in a number of ways. In our society people are often unwilling to come out with their true wishes, for fear of giving offence or appearing prudish or otherwise out of step. So we cannot rely on the absence of outright refusal.

Instead, approached people give out signals. These may be of greater or less subtlety. We ought to observe these signals, and act in accordance with them. When one person has sexual designs on another, the other is either willing or unwilling. A willing person may give out signals of reluctance, but this can be construed as 'playing hard to get'. An unwilling person may give out negative signals that are faint. This may be due to weakness of will, or a sense of physical inferiority, or reluctance to offend, or a feeling of subservience or obligation, or fear of losing a valued position or simple indecision. It is the moral duty of the pursuer to take trouble to decipher the signals, and bend his or her actions accordingly.

Sexual harassment is immoral. Yet in defining it we have to recognise that some degree of pressure may be necessary to overcome natural or feigned reluctance. That is what courtship is about. Where it becomes clear that the reluctance is genuine, the wooer must however desist. In cases where one party is in a position of superiority over the other, as with employer and employee or senior and junior in any hierarchy, it constitutes immoral harassment to use the superiority in order to gain sexual favours that would not otherwise be granted.

We should not make sexual overtures to any person beyond a point where the recipient indicates refusal, disapproval or distress. If for any reason the other is or may feel coerced or otherwise subservient, we need to realise that the signs of rejection may be faint. That does not mean they are to be disregarded.

Solitary Sex

A headmaster, giving evidence to the Longford Committee on Pornography, testified that sexual activity always affects at least two people. The truth is the opposite. Most sexual activity involves one person only. The headmaster was more accurate when he went on to say that sex comes good only when self comes last.

It is true that the primary sex act demands the presence of a partner. For this reason we are inclined to feel that solitary sex is inadequate. That does not make it immoral. When good sex is not available, half a loaf may be better than no bread.

Adolescents, particularly males, are ready for sex long before they are ready for a sexual relationship. Therefore solo masturbation provides a suitable outlet. It relieves sexual tension, while enabling the young person to avoid premature entanglement. This is the sensible moral view. In the past it was not held, and many reject it in the present.

One of the most devilish, yet revealing, terms invented by the sex-negaters is 'self-abuse'. It was still defined in the 1972 edition of the *Shorter Oxford English Dictionary* as 'self-pollution'. Pollution is defined as 'uncleanness or impurity' and 'seminal emission apart from coition'. To masturbate is defined as 'to practise self-abuse'. Thus is the vicious circle completed. It is true that in the completely revised 1976 edition of the smaller version of this leading dictionary, the *Concise Oxford*, 'masturbate' is defined as 'produce sexual orgasm . . . by manual stimulation of genitals etc., not by sexual intercourse'. That is better, but yet this edition, whose editors pride themselves on having excised all words not in current use, still retains 'self-abuse'.

It is a relief to turn to the wisdom of the Danish doctors Inge and Sten Hegeler. In their book *Living is Loving* they say:

Sex is one of the things which to a very high degree makes our lives richer. So it is almost our duty to look after it, refine it and generally care for it imaginatively and with the will to train and practise.

Masturbation quite simply helps to keep one's sex life going. It is important to young and old alike, to single as well as married persons, to happy as well as unhappy ones.

It is important to know that masturbation is *in no way wrong*. Many letters which we receive from elderly people reveal that they have had bad consciences because masturbation is a big problem for them. It shouldn't be at all.

It is healthy, instructive and lovely to masturbate; it also helps to develop our sex lives . . . In other words, masturbation forms a natural part of a natural sex life.

Mrs Whitehouse would purse her lips and dismiss this as Danish extremism. After all it was she who badgered the BBC in 1974 to ban Chuck Berry's hit song 'My Ding-a-Ling' on the ground that it was an encouragement to masturbation. This was because it included a youthful choir exuberantly singing the repeated refrain:

> My Ding-a-Ling, my Ding-a-Ling
> I want to play with my Ding-a-Ling

Let it be noted with gratitude that there is respectable British medical support for the Hegelers. In its 'Family Doctor' booklet *Teenage Living and Loving*, published in 1976, the British Medical Association said:

Masturbation – the stroking of one's own sexual organs – is a common substitute for sexual relationships when these are not desirable or possible. Masturbation provides a pleasant and convenient way of relaxing sexual feelings, and is entirely harmless. Masturbation may just be quietly comforting or it may lead to the spasm of pleasure and excitement called orgasm (or climax).

The most sensitive part of the girl's sexual equipment is the clitoris, which is like a small penis and is situated where the flaps of skin that fold over the entrance to the girl's vagina come together at the top. Investigations have shown that, whereas almost all males masturbate at some time, masturbation in females is not so common, possibly because the build-up of sperm ready for ejaculation does not occur in their bodies. But for females, as for males, masturbation is a harmless substitute outlet for sexual feelings.

Where now are the dreadful Victorian schoolmasters who threatened their hapless charges that 'self-abuse' would make them blind, or stunt their growth, or ruin their marriage prospects? Unhappily, their descendants are still with us, as Marjorie Proops confirms. In her career as a lonely-hearts columnist, Miss Proops claims that close to a million people have written for her advice. In her book *Dear Marje* (1976) she describes the anxiety girls feel about sex, and then continues:

Boys are equally anxious. They actually send me penis measurements, flaccid and erect, hoping for reassurance that their size is comparably up to standard. They worry, too, if their chests are narrow, or if hair on their faces and bodies is slow to appear. But far and away the most dominant anxiety among boys is what they believe to be the dangers of masturbation. Ignorance about this practice brings more guilt and depression and insecurity than any other problem which boys – and some girls – face. The astonishing myths still abound: 'Will hair grow on the palms of my hands?' 'Will the habit damage my penis?' 'Will I ever be able to have normal sex if I don't stop doing it?' 'Will it make me impotent?' 'Will it stop me having babies?' 'Will it give me heart disease?' 'Is it, as my mother says it is, a sin against God?'

Writing from the enormous range of her experience, Miss Proops says that masturbation is seen by youngsters as an evil practice for which due guilt must be endured. Young people count the days of abstinence 'like giving up smoking'. She continues:

Parents are largely to blame for the deep misery and fear from which their masturbating children suffer, for mothers still smack toddlers found doing it, tell them it's a filthy habit and perpetuate the myths. And fathers, their sons have reported to me, have actually taken the belt to masturbating offspring.

Solitary sex is widely condemned. Even the liberationist Dr Charlotte Wolff commits herself to the statement that the sexual act is a loss unless it originates from a deep-seated emotion for another person. The truth is that it is a loss unless performed with awareness of the meaning of the act, which involves sex-acceptance and sex-respect. Sex should never be perfunctory.

Dr Wolff's remark tells us that in defending solo sex we are not merely fighting sex-negating upholders of compulsory marriage. We expect them to oppose auto-eroticism, and of course they do. Opposition to going solo spreads much wider than that. Flowing from the pair-bonding impulse there is a strong human belief that sex must never be solitary, since it is about procreation. It takes two to tango. It also takes two to make three.

Auto-eroticism in its simplest and commonest form consists in solo masturbation accompanied by fantasy. An early treatise described this as an activity to produce a gross form of sensory pleasure, bought at the expense of high moral tone. That view has been held ever since, and is still held. It is false.

The masturbator is not seeking a gross form of sensory pleasure, quite the reverse. The masturbator seeks natural fulfilment. What he or she does is rehearse the profoundly significant act of procreation in circumstances where that act is not practicable. Nature, being necessarily abundant, multiplies the possibilities of fecundation as a form of insurance. Under modern conditions it has become over-insurance to a considerable degree. The sexual impulse continues unabated.

Some medical authorities consider solitary masturbation more satisfying than intercourse with a partner. This is likely to be true in all cases except those where the partner is truly loving and also sexually competent. The purpose of fantasy is to compensate for the inadequacy of reality.

Inge and Sten Hegeler, basing their views on the Masters and Johnson research, state that orgasm produced through masturbation or in dreams is qualitatively better and more intense than the best orgasm produced during ordinary sexual intercourse. This places a lot of weight on the concept of ordinariness.

Adults too find they can gain solace and relief from masturbation. If we are within a pair-bond, however, we should realise that the other may be hurt by our solo enterprise, seeing it as indicating rejection. Furthermore it may signify too great a reliance on, and interest in, the self. We call this form of obsession narcissism. In Greek mythology the youth Narcissus was the son of a river god and a nymph, renowned for his beauty. Rejecting the love of the maiden named Echo, Narcissus withdrew into a state of adoration of his own physical self as reflected to his gazing eyes in the waters of a spring. So powerfully did this image affect Narcissus that he pined away for love of the beauteous reflection of his own lineaments, and died. In the place where this happened, the flower sprang up that bears his name. The beautiful white flower we call narcissus is a reminder of the need one has to get away from the self. Self-love is necessary, but self-adoration is a fatal fault.

A sexual act (such as masturbation) is not immoral because done in solitude. Since young people are often ready for sex before they are mature enough to enter a sexual relationship with another person, solitary sex may for them be the most suitable form of early sexual activity and should not be condemned by parents or others in authority. However, solitary sex may encourage narcissism, and lacks the richness that comes from a loving relationship with another. Where the subject is within a pair-bond, solitary sex may be immoral if it indicates a rejection of the partner.

Troilism and Orgies

The power and delight of sex is something that people may wish to share with each other on a group basis. Sex-negativism instilled in most of us from infancy inhibits this desire, and leads to its being looked upon with feelings of guilt. If the members of the group are unknown to one another there is a danger of going in at the deep end, though this can be exhilarating. Sex with a stranger, in the company of other strangers, is a risk in more senses than one. But life is full of risks.

The clue is furnished by the duty of sex-respect. To be offered access to the sexuality of a stranger can be regarded as a privilege. The idea of sex as a vast open sea, whereon we may sail to destinations exciting and unknown, is intoxicating. Yet it must be remembered that in offering oneself to a stranger one may be inviting cynical force, infection by disease, unwanted pregnancy or other degradation. Unhappily, strangers are not to be trusted.

Suppose the sexual partners are not strangers at all, but well known to each other? Could not this lead to a deepening of the ties of friendship? Certainly it could, and let us hope it does. But one needs to be aware that this is one rock upon which friendship may meet shipwreck. The risks of such actions are great, though there is the possibility of richness beyond measure. The height of friendship is to share all.

Of one thing we can be certain. The mere fact that more than two persons share in a sexual act does not of itself render the act immoral. So we can put forward the following precept.

The participation of more than two people does not render a sexual act immoral.

Sex between Persons of Different Race

Much prejudice exists over inter-racial sex acts. The subject of racism is outside the scope of this book, and so this prejudice cannot be gone into in detail here. Suffice it to say that, subject to what is said in chapter 11 about the propagation of mixed-race children, the secular approach to the morality of sexual relations finds no basis for distinctions based on racial difference. Accordingly we can put forward the following precept.

It is morally neutral for a person of one race to have sex with a person of a different race, and it is therefore wrong to condemn persons of different races merely because they have sex together.

Harmful Sexual Acts

There cannot be any argument about the immorality of a sex act of a kind that may inflict lasting harm. The most common example occurs when one of the partners is infected with a sexually transmissible disease such as the HIV virus or syphilis. Here we may put forward the following precept.

Where it is known or suspected by either party to a prospective sex-act that one or other is or may be infected with any sexually transmissible disease it is their duty to ensure that adequate precautions are taken against infection.

It often happens that after a sex act has been committed one of the parties finds that he or she has been infected. Here there is a moral duty to take appropriate steps to ensure that the person from whom the infection was contracted does not go on to infect others. This may require the medical authorities to be informed, so that treatment may be given.

If a person knows that an infected person is likely to contravene the previous rule (for example because they have themselves contracted disease from that person) it is their duty to help ensure that the infected person does not transmit the disease to others.

It is clearly immoral for a diseased person to have sex with another without informing them of the fact, so that they have an opportunity to decline.

It is immoral for a person who knows or suspects that they are infected with any sexually transmissible disease to have sex with another person without first informing them of the fact.

Apart from the question of disease, it is clearly immoral, even with the actual or apparent consent of the other person, to commit a sex act that may cause physical or psychological injury. On this ground alone, for a man to thrust his penis into the vagina of a child is wicked. Some would say that anal intercourse, even when willingly entered into, is always wrong on this ground since it is likely to cause lasting injury to the anus and sphincter. The male desire for intromission leads many gay men to argue, however, that this means of expressing their passion or affection ought to be considered allowable. The answer to this and similar questions (such as the morality of sado-masochism) must turn on the precise meaning one attaches to the term 'injury'. Obviously it excludes merely trivial injuries, such as love-bites.

It is immoral to have sex with another person by a method or technique that may cause either party physical or mental injury.

In the 1990 *Genital Torture Case* eight members of a sado-masochistic group of 'masters and slaves' were jailed at the Old Bailey. Among them were John Lofthouse, a fire-station officer whose delight was having his penis nailed to a board, and Saxon Lucas, a restaurateur and lay preacher convicted of cutting the genitals of another group member with a scalpel. The fifteen accused men were found guilty of genital torture with such instruments as nails, canes, branding irons, nettles and electric wires. None had gone so far as to make hospital treatment necessary; indeed most of the willing victims' wounds healed overnight. Judge Rant commented: 'Much has been said about individual liberty, but the courts must draw a line between what is acceptable in a civilised society and what is not.' Reporting the case (20 December 1990), the *Independent* asked: 'If a man wants his scrotum sandpapered in the privacy of his own home, is it anyone else's business?' Whether it is the law's business is not the concern of this book, but it is clearly the moralist's business. Such conduct not only contravenes the moral duty of sex-respect but also that of respect for human life and health.

10
Pair-bonding and Marriage

Fidelity

Where a man and a woman, whether married to each other or not, have with one another a sexual relationship demanding mutual loyalty, otherwise known as a pair-bond, then neither is entitled to be promiscuous. Some close sexual relationships do not demand this loyalty, as when each partner has agreed that the other may take lovers. This we call an open relationship, but it is exceptional. Many would say it contradicts the natural law of humanity. Normally the pair-bond precludes this type of arrangement, and the moral duty of fidelity prevails. This duty is basic to the Judaeo-Christian religion. It is embodied in the seventh commandment, which enjoins: 'Thou shalt not commit adultery'. Most people in the west would root it in the nature of sexual union, though some would argue that it is essentially cultural: other cultures may be polygynous or polyandrous, and such systems have their own standards of faithfulness.

The valuable pair-bonding concept requires that if two persons, impelled by this impulse, have joined in a trusting sexual relationship then it is one of the laws of the relationship that neither will deceive the other regarding that most basic factor, rooted in sex-respect, which is the sharing of either's sex anatomy with an outsider. We may express this in the following precept.

It is common for sexually mature humans, whether heterosexual or homosexual in orientation, to form themselves into pair-bonds, that is couples who choose to link exclusively by means of enduring emotional-erotic ties. This bonding originates with the need of the human young for settled parenting during their lengthy period of infancy, and now has a deep emotional significance for humans generally. Accordingly the parties should strive to make the relationship fulfilling and enduring, particularly where children are being nurtured within the bond. Except in the case of an open relationship, outsiders should respect a pair-bond and not intrude upon it with competing sexual demands.

The concept of fidelity in sexual relationships is fundamental. (Of course it applies in other matters also.) To be faithful is one of the most splendid, yet sometimes most difficult, human attributes. To be utterly trustworthy, despite all temptation to the contrary, marks one out as a rare and valuable human being. As is just, it has its rewards. Upon this rock, said Christ of Peter, I build my Church. We are fortunate if we manage to find a human rock of fidelity upon which to build our own particular church. One of the most telling lines in modern literature describes the emotions of the faithless Lady Brenda Last's faithful husband when she leaves him for a younger man in Evelyn Waugh's *Handful of Dust*: 'But it was several days before Tony fully realised what it meant. . . He had got into a habit of loving and trusting Brenda.'

A couple locked in sexual fidelity may miss out on variety. For those who believe human existence lies in collecting experiences, fidelity seems humdrum. It may even be called boring. This is shown in John Quainton's poem *Wedlocked*.

Seated opposite each other in the restaurant
they say nothing
since there is now
nothing they can say

Said already, all the words
are locked in their joint history

In return
for props they each provide
they have made mutual surrender
of the right to stand upright

And of the words
they once knew

Goodness often does appear boring to the superficial. Yet it is of the essence of human goodness to stand like a rock in the face of all temptations, to be there still when anyone else would have decamped, to say that I am yours and know with certainty that you are mine.

Pair-bonds give forth fruit, and there can be no argument that from its own viewpoint a baby is best brought up in a home run by *both* its natural parents, living together, loving each other at all times, and quarrelling in a way to upset the child seldom if ever. Whether this is always the happiest mode for the parents themselves is less certain, but (as the baby might say if it could) no one is forced to produce children.

Here we need to distinguish two issues: pair-bonding and propagation. Under the natural order the one usually leads to the other. Nowadays, however, we do not live under the natural order, and are able to address the two separately. The latter issue is discussed in the next chapter. Of the former we may add the following.

The basis of the pair-bond, apart from the needs of children, lies in the idea no one should live their life alone. The Old Testament story of the Creation puts it thus: 'And the Lord God said, It is not good that the man should be alone; I will make him an helpmeet' (Genesis 2:18). This word *helpmeet*, otherwise rendered *helpmate*, conveys the idea that in the journey through life each adult person needs another adult to serve as helper, companion, lover, parent of his or her children, defender and upholder. In return for such close services, fidelity is an obvious requirement. Indeed the Christian religion, closely followed by English common law, regards two spouses as in some sense one person. Hence marriage was for long regarded as indissoluble. The greatest immorality was, having embraced marriage, to turn to living as if single.

At the core of the pair-bond are twin human desires: the desire for sexual congress and the desire to propagate. Some people, as is their right, reject both of these and live as spinsters or bachelors. It is of perennial interest to discover why they have elected to do this, but the truth is seldom forthcoming. As an example at random we may take the *Independent on Sunday* of 4 November 1990. This carried an item headed 'Who has stayed single?' Eight well-known people were featured, and each purported to give their reasons for disdaining matrimony. Not one mentioned sex. Marcelle D'Argy-Smith, editor of *Cosmopolitan*, said she didn't want anyone to control her. Hilary Armstrong MP said marriage and her life in the House of Commons didn't seem compatible. Novelist and unmarried mother Celia Brayfield, aged 45, said marriage was what her prettier friends did, but she hadn't given up hope. Actress and unmarried mother Lisa Harrow said she preferred friendship, and pointed out that many married people don't have independent friendships. Cookery writer Jennifer Paterson, aged 62, said it never occurred to her that she needed 'that blessed state'. Among the men the Bishop of Wakefield said being single was for him a way of responding to God's call to service, and that he needed 'to respond to the solitary in me'. The disc jockey Sir Jimmy Savile said he did not want to be 'locked in some never-ending drama'. Imran Khan the cricketer thought one could be much lonelier in marriage than in solitude, and was not 100 per cent sure he could do justice to the institution. It is striking evidence that in our society sex-negativism still rigidly rules that every one of these sophisticated people felt that to touch on the sexual aspects of living single would somehow let the side down. Perhaps they felt it might put readers off their Sunday lunch.

The Social Institution of Marriage

The instinct of human societies is to acknowledge the pair-bond by public responses. Hence the social institution of marriage. This is claimed as their own by various religions, but is in truth an essentially human institution. The community wishes to see the couple publicly joined in matrimony by an institutional process. It then confers privileges upon them, as a mark of approval. It desires to see the additions to its number reared within the secure framework that marriage provides. It welcomes the social stability it brings.

The highest form of pair-bonding is secular marriage, whereby society formally recognises the tie and accords it special consideration in law and otherwise. Since married bonding is supported by social consensus and state institutions, since it increases the chances of happiness of any children of the union, and since it enhances the bond's prospects of permanence and success, it is morally preferable to unmarried bonding. The institution of marriage should not be withheld from homosexual couples or transsexuals.

A pair-bond may be formed by two people of the same sex, and this is not immoral. The final sentence of the above precept acknowledges that the community should recognise such a bond by providing for it a form of marriage. The reasons underlying this are the same as for heterosexual marriage, except that the rearing of children will only rarely enter into the equation.

Open Sexual Relationships

Secular morality must recognise the right of a couple to agree that theirs shall be an open relationship. However it is not fair to young children who are being reared by a pair-bonded couple to expose them to the stresses likely to ensue if the relationship is open.

An open marriage or other open sexual relationship is one where the partners agree that the relationship shall not be exclusive, so that a partner is free to have sex with outside persons. Because it can lead to their unhappiness, children should not be propagated or reared within an open sexual relationship.

Passing as Single

One of the commonest forms of fraud is for a man to pass himself off to a woman seeking a pair-bond as being single and unattached. This undermines the relationship from the start, and must be condemned as immoral.

It is immoral for a married person to enter into a sexual relationship without informing the other person that he or she is married. Similar considerations apply to an unmarried person who is within a pair-bond.

Adultery

As stated above, fidelity is of the essence of a pair-bond unless the partners have agreed that it shall be an open relationship or it has broken down. The test of marriage breakdown has been adopted by the current British divorce law, which uses (among others) the arbitrary criterion of physical separation or living apart. Separation for two years by consent, or for five years without consent, gives ground for divorce. This seems a reasonable criterion to adopt in the moral sphere also, where doubts may arise if one spouse considers the marriage to have broken down while the other does not. If without such a separation the two freely agree that their marriage has broken down, that may be treated as concluding the matter where the duty of fidelity is concerned. Similarly where one spouse has emphatically demonstrated an intention to treat the marriage as being at an end, as by inflicting gross violence on the other before departing permanently. This view assumes that people who have entered upon the state of civil marriage retain the moral right to end the marriage if they wish to do so. What they are not entitled to do is cheat on their partner while the marriage subsists.

Unless a marriage or other pair-bond is an open relationship or has broken down, it is immoral for one of the partners to have sex with anyone except the other.

Sterilisation of a Marriage Partner

Marriage is a moral contract under which the possibility of childbearing forms a central feature. One of its terms (written or unwritten) is therefore that one spouse will not without the consent of the other alter his or her capacity to perform this crucial function. This collides with the principle that a person should be regarded as in control of his or her body, but it is the nature of marriage that this principle should, as part of the consent marriage requires, be yielded to some extent.

One party to a marriage should not undergo sterilisation without the consent of the other, since this operation fundamentally alters the nature and significance of the relationship of marriage

Incest

To the secular moralist incest, or a sexual relationship between family members other than those who are pair-bonded together, is not of itself subject to special rules. If however it is established that the pair may, because of their near relationship to each other, produce defective children, then there is a clear moral duty to ensure that they do not propagate. Equally, if the sexual relationship is, or is likely to be, painfully disruptive (perhaps by giving rise to feelings of sexual jealousy on the part of others within the family group), it should be ended or avoided. Finally, as will be discussed in chapter 13, incest is immoral if it amounts to exploitation of a youngster by an older family member.

Incest may be morally objectionable on one or more of three grounds. It may (1) risk producing genetically defective offspring, or (2) grievously disrupt relationships within a family unit, or (3) constitute immoral exploitation of a younger person by an older relative. Where none of these conditions exist, incest is morally neutral.

11
Human Fertility

As we saw in chapter 6, the ethical duty of sex-respect is based on the fact that sexuality prompts all new human life. The sexual organs are known as the reproductive organs, for reproduction is their main purpose. In this chapter we consider the particular moral rules that surround human fertility, which may be called the heart of sexuality. We look first at various aspects of the regular cycle of conception, pregnancy and childbirth. Then we consider the case where vaginal intercourse is desired without its natural consequence, bringing us to the vexed questions of contraception and abortion.

The Decision to Propagate

Obviously we need to have ethical rules governing the easily taken but momentous decision so to conduct ourselves that in nine months or so a baby may be born. The following are suggested.

One of the most important decisions a person can take is the decision to propagate, that is to bring a new life into the world. It is an awesome responsibility. Accordingly the decision should be taken with great care, having due regard to the likely quality of life of the child and the effect of its arrival on other members of the family.

It is wrong deliberately to propagate a child unless it is wanted and the parents are able and willing to rear it properly. A child needs both parents, and therefore needs both parents to want it.

The moral significance of a decision to propagate, which is normally the decision to have vaginal intercourse without first taking contraceptive precautions, is obvious. We are acting in a way that may directly lead to the arrival on this planet of a new person, and therefore our first duty must be to that person. Is it fair to call him or her into existence? Are we prepared and able to be good parents to the possible baby? Are there any genetic or other factors that may wreck its life chances? What will be the effect of its arrival on existing members of the family? Are we just having a fling, and be damned to the consequences, or are we acting responsibly?

The ones who are just having a fling are most likely to be young teenagers. Here concern must mainly be for the girl, for it is she who will bear most of the burden. While it is desirable that teenagers should enjoy a full sex-life, it is preferable for many reasons that pregnancy (even within marriage) should be deferred until the girl's teenage years are over. Each year in Britain 3,500 schoolgirls become mothers. This is undesirable for obvious reasons. Early pregnancy cuts short childhood and deprives the girl of learning time at school. If she bears and rears the child her position as a parent usually means she must sacrifice the further education needed to fit her for employment suited to her abilities. If on the other hand her foetus is aborted, the consequent psychological and emotional traumas may scar her for life.

Moral responsibility for a teenage pregnancy lies principally with the couple concerned, but parents, teachers and friends must take their share. The girl may have been unprepared, and whose fault is that? The parents' fault may crystallise in the fact that the girl became pregnant in an attempt (probably subconscious) to compensate for low self-esteem, a state that her parents should have been aware of. It needs to be known that a girl who feels inadequate or unloved may decide to get herself pregnant in order (as she sees it) to remedy this unsatisfactory situation. Her condition as a prospective mother brings her attention, and appears to raise her importance in the eyes of the world. Ante-natal care sessions make her the centre of attention, and are more interesting than school lessons. Parents may secretly welcome the child's pregnancy because it means they will see more of her. When the baby is born it becomes someone for the girl to love, and who will (she hopes) love her. As a mother she attracts increased status, and can insist on less rigorous control by her parents. Sometimes these factors are seen as such benefits that the girl soon gets herself pregnant again, and may end up as a lone parent with a large brood. This tendency can be overcome only by giving such girls more satisfactory reasons for self-esteem, and educating them in the advantages of delaying pregnancy. The best contraceptive for teenage girls with a low opinion of themselves is realistic ambition and a future to look forward to.

If we are sex-lovers, rather than sex-negaters, why should we object to teenage pregnancies? The girl is physiologically ready, or she could not conceive. Why not let nature take its course?

There are many reasons why teenage pregnancy is undesirable, some of which have been given. Young girls are often slow to realise they have become pregnant. Because they fear the consequences, they are reluctant to admit it has happened, and slow to tell others, for example their mothers or the prospective father. This means that one who is scarcely more than a child is forced to bear a heavy load. For teenage girls pregnancy can present health problems, since the ability to conceive now often predates the body's true readiness to bear the child. The maturity gap between ability to conceive and full readiness to rear the child is a recent creation of enhanced nutrition and general health. In Europe this brought the average age of menarche down from seventeen in 1860 to a little over twelve at the present time. On the continent of Africa figures show a similar spread today between the most advanced and the most primitive areas.

The physical unreadiness of the young teenage girl shows in several ways. Her bone structure may not yet be firm, the pelvis being particularly vulnerable. If the pregnancy continues to its natural termination there may be difficult and obstructed labour. This may involve tearing of the womb, and rupture of tissue between the birth canal and urinary tract. Sometimes even the lining of the bowel may be punctured. Because the young girl is not physically ready for childbirth, her baby may be small and ailing.

Parents of Different Race

The decision to propagate gains a new dimension when the prospective parents are of different race. In chapter 9 we considered the ethics of sex acts between persons of different race and concluded that they were morally neutral. Where however contraceptive precautions are not being taken, so that there is a risk of pregnancy, the couple have a duty to consider the position of any future offspring.

Before a person has sex with a person of different race in a way that could produce a child it is their moral duty carefully to consider whether, having regard to the social difficulties often experienced by children of mixed race, and the genetic factors involved, it is morally right to do this in their case. If their sincere answer is yes, their propagation of the child is morally neutral, but they have a duty to recognise the difficulties the child may experience and help it to overcome them.

Artificially Induced Pregnancies

The recent development of methods of *in vitro* fertilisation is the latest in a series of medical advances in the field of human fertility. They pose ethical problems for which the following precepts are suggested.

If the natural parents, that is the man and woman from whose bodies the sperm and ovum respectively derive, are pair-bonded to each other, the fact that a pregnancy is caused by artificial insemination, or is otherwise artificially induced, is morally neutral.

Where parties to a pair-bond accept insemination or implantation from a donor, this carries the same duties with respect to the resulting child as if both were its natural parents.

A woman who is within a pair-bond ought not to accept insemination from a donor without the consent of her partner, and a man who is within a pair-bond ought not to donate his sperm for another woman without the consent of his partner.

A man who donates his sperm, for example through a sperm-bank, without knowing its destination, or a woman who similarly donates her ova, has no moral responsibility for the resulting child and is entitled to keep his or her identity secret from it.

The Defective Foetus

In natural conditions, a baby that is severely defective will not long survive its birth. In recent years medical science has reduced the impact of this beneficent safeguard. That is a price we pay for medical advance, but its results can be unfortunate. For one thing, it imposes grave problems on the pregnant woman, assuming she is kept informed of the position. That she should be so informed is a clear ethical principle, unless she is judged incapable of taking the necessary decisions regarding the blighted product of her womb.

The remedy lies in the hands of skilled obstetricians and gynaecologists. Only they can monitor and as appropriate offset this unwanted result of man's progress in medical knowledge and skill. The deformed foetus must have its existence terminated in the way nature intended. There is no kindness in struggling to preserve the life of a grossly defective baby. If it manages to survive through birth, such a child needs to be reared with great difficulty either in the bosom of its family or in an institution. Either course has grave drawbacks. It must be depressing in the extreme for a young growing child to find itself severely deformed. The distress is multiplied when the blighted child observes that its life is to be passed in an institution where the other inmates are severely deformed also. A few resilient spirits may overcome this handicap. For most the experience, day in, day out, week in, week out, of such misfortune in the mass is bound to cripple the spirit.

Nor is it any better for the severely defective child to be reared within the family. The stresses of modern life are difficult for healthy people to bear. Add the burden of bringing up an incapacitated child and the problems often become insupportable. They frequently cause emotional disorders among the healthy members of the family. Marriages break up in consequence. Whole people suffer through having gravely defective creatures brought up in their midst.

The fact that some geniuses have been crippled, and that occasionally a family rises magnificently to the challenge, does not alter the conclusion. An ethical principle looks to the usual situation. It bears upon the common condition. For every success among the rare heroic, there are a thousand commonplace failures. The chances are overwhelming that to bring to birth a seriously defective child will on balance add to, and not diminish, the world's misery. Accordingly we may put forward the following precept.

A person ought not to take the decision to begin a pregnancy, or continue it while the foetus is still non-viable, when believing that the resulting child's quality of life is likely to be poor because of injury, disease or genetic defect.

It is here necessary to mention the case of the defective foetus that manages to survive birth. Although this raises ethical questions, these are strictly beyond the scope of a book dealing only with *sexual* ethics. Nevertheless we need to address them. If it should be considered morally right to kill a baby because on being born it is found to be gravely defective then *a fortiori* it would be morally right to have aborted it for the same reason at an earlier stage.

There is indeed authority for this view. In a book entitled *Should the Baby Live?*, jointly written by Peter Singer, Director of the Centre for Human Bioethics at Monash University, and Dr Helga Kuhse, it is stated that 'some infants with severe disabilities should be killed'. As a basis for this bold proposition the authors refer to the celebrated case of Dr Arthur.

In 1981 Dr Leonard Arthur, a senior pediatrician at Derby General Hospital, was tried at Leicester Crown Court for the murder of a neonate named John Pearson. The baby suffered from Down's syndrome, but was in other respects healthy. In compliance with the wishes of the parents, Dr Arthur ensured that it did not survive by giving the coded medical instruction 'nursing care only' and prescribing strong doses of the pain-killing drug DF 118. A member of the hospital staff reported the incident to the anti-abortion pressure group Life, and the prosecution was launched. Singer and Kuhse comment that 'the evidence at the trial showed that letting handicapped infants die is common medical practice'. The jury acquitted. A BBC opinion poll held at the time found that 86 per cent of respondents believed a doctor should not be convicted of murder if, with the parents' agreement, 'he sees to it that a severely handicapped baby dies'.

The *Arthur* decision was followed in the case of *Baby J* (*The Independent*, 20 October 1990). The baby was thirteen weeks premature and had suffered brain damage at birth. If it survived it would almost certainly be blind, deaf, dumb and paralysed. A judge in the case, Lord Donaldson, said one of the few things Baby J was able to feel was pain. Another judge said that to prolong its life would be 'so cruel as to be intolerable'. The court held that medical treatment should be withheld. Jack Scarisbrick, national chairman of Life, attacked the decision in predictably emotive language: 'Give us that baby. Don't allow it to die. Don't reject it. We will look after him for the rest of his life . . .' Such attitudes are cruel and irresponsible. It was not Jack Scarisbrick who would have had to live that pain-stricken and inadequate life, but the hapless Baby J.

Such cases may be viewed as an application of the principle that the medical profession, backed by the law, is by common consent entrusted with the decision as to life or death in certain critical situations connected with birth, life-threatening injury or disease, senility, and other circumstances where it is impractical to arrive at a humane decision by any other means.

Adverse Actions during Pregnancy

It is a clear ethical principal that a pregnant woman who intends to bear her future child should act as its guardian while it is still only a foetus.

Subject to the rules regarding abortion, during pregnancy the prospective mother ought not to take harmful drugs or other deleterious substances, or engage in any other activity that might endanger the wellbeing of the foetus.

Breast-feeding in Public

Some foolish people object to the sight of a woman breast-feeding a child. This is one of the least appealing manifestations of sex-negativism, and should be resisted.

The duty of sex-respect forbids our objecting to breast-feeding in public. It is wrong to equate this, as some do, with the public performance of excretory functions.

Contraception

Life, even human life, is abundant. Human life threatens to become too abundant. Advances in the conquest of disease and the production of foodstuffs, coupled with a welcome increase in compassion, face us with overcrowding of the planet. An infinity of very nice people *could* appear on this earth, but there is just not room for every one of them. Any man must occasionally think with regret of the army of millions who would stand at his back if every spermatozoon his body has produced had only been given its licence to live. But that is not nature's way, and it cannot be our way. Every person has the right, indeed the duty, to use contraceptive methods where these are justified.

Services to safeguard against unwanted pregnancy have improved in recent decades, but are still inadequate. This is particularly true for adolescents, who are not supposed to need such services (yet in truth need them more than most). In order to reach even the present unsatisfactory position tremendous battles have been necessary, and these are still renewed from time to time. We note the usual consequences in the form of increased price and diminished service.

It is not immoral to use any type of medically approved contraceptive method, whether natural or artificial.

Another moral aspect arises here from the fact that it is possible to be deceived over whether contraceptive precautions are indeed being taken, or whether they are even necessary.

It is immoral for a person to deceive their sexual partner by falsely saying or implying that they are sterile or have taken adequate contraceptive precautions.

Abortion

Abortion, it can be said, is contraception practised late. So the ethical rules that support contraception also support the abortion of a non-viable foetus, that is one not yet capable of living indefinitely outside the mother's body. Abortion is always sad, and depressing for the aborting woman. It negates her nature, and for that we should have pity. Yet it is her choice.

Humanity means the living, that is the born. To become one of the born requires each prospective or actual embryo to pass through a formidable obstacle-course. That has always been so, and it is still so. The chances are heavily weighted against success, and there is no right to it. Only a few of us win through. The foetus is not one of the born, but only potentially one of the born. It is not yet, and may never be, a child. People who assert the contrary ignore the meaning of the word child.

A foetus cannot be murdered, for that is a fate reserved to human beings and a foetus is not yet, and may never be, a human being. People who assert the contrary ignore the meaning of the word murder.

By the laws of nature a foetus has formidable obstacles to surmount before it successfully emerges into the light of human life. Often it fails to graduate. The potential is not the actual, and may not become the actual. People who assert the contrary ignore the meaning of the word potential.

There are indeed people, actuated usually by religious zeal, who do foolishly equate the potential with the actual in this respect. They assert that because a woman has conceived she is morally obliged to bear. For them, the doubtful foetus is already the certain child. They jump the gun, and ignore the fact that human plans often miscarry. It is a profound mistake, productive of much unhappiness.

The pregnant woman, on the other hand, has long ago achieved this status of being a born creature. Moreover she has achieved the further graduation of arriving at maturity. She must therefore be accorded precedence over the foetus within her. It is *her* body the foetus, whether to her welcome or unwelcome, has the privilege of occupying. It is she who has, until the creature within her is immediately capable of independent existence, the right to choose whether to cut it short or permit it to flourish. For that particular foetus she is Mother Earth, the omnipotent.

That is the true moral rule. It is based on the self-evident right of a woman to govern her own body, which may be called the principle of female self-rule or a woman's hegemony. Not even the man or youth who is the begetter of the foetus can effectively challenge this right. A male becomes a father only by courtesy of the mother.

The moral right of a woman over her own body has already entitled her to decide if, when and with whom she will engage in sexual activity. It entitled her to determine whether or not to employ contraceptive measures, and if so which kind to use. It entitled her, if she wished, to use 'unnatural' methods to procure the fertilisation of her ova, such as artificial insemination or in-vitro fertilisation. Now conception has occurred, that same right entitles her to procure a miscarriage or abortion at any time up to the point at which the foetus has graduated as a human being by attaining viability.

There is a crucial advantage of the moral position here set out. If complied with it conforms to the maxim *every child a wanted child*. To the uttermost extent possible, it also produces the converse and equally desirable result that *every wanted child is born*. Many of the world's crimes and cruelties have been and are perpetrated in revenge by persons whose birth was unwelcome, and who grew up unwanted and rejected. Many of the victims of cruelty have been and are persons equally unwanted. On the other hand to want a child and not be able to produce it causes heartache, and may rob the world of a loving parent.

In relation to abortion the inadequancy of the service usually available in the sex field is particularly tragic. Apart from the high cost (in both money and human suffering) of back-street abortions, the health and even the life of the pregnant woman may be endangered. We need to apply the principle that any woman or girl of childbearing age is entitled to sexual fulfilment, within or outside marriage, on the conditions as to fertility that seem good to her, provided they conform to morality. This means she is entitled to the fullest information on birth control methods, to detailed advice, to provision of the necessary contraceptive equipment and to adequate abortion services where unhappily they prove necessary.

A woman is so constituted that her body and nature wish to go on and bear the babe quickening within her. So those having care of a woman contemplating abortion must ensure that she receives competent and sympathetic counselling both before and after the operation. This does not refer to *directed* counselling, whereby the counsellor seeks to persuade the counselled to follow a course of action preferred by the counsellor. Such preferences have no place in a true helping process. To press them on a hapless victim is an outrage. The woman who has decided on abortion is to be pitied and cherished. Hers was a most difficult choice, but she has made it. We salute her courage, and respect her right to reach this agonised decision. Now we will cherish her, and help her face the consequences of the choice she has made.

Arguably there is one exception to the principle of female self-rule. If the woman is married, or is within a pair-bond, should not the husband or partner be conceded right of veto over the abortion of the fruit of the union? The case is plausible, but the answer must be no. It is the woman who has to bear the foetus. In case of disagreement it is her decision that must be allowed to prevail. She ought however to consult with her husband or partner, and carefully consider any arguments he may advance.

It is not immoral for a pregnant woman who does not want the child to abort her foetus before it has become viable, provided no pain is inflicted on the foetus and the woman has carefully considered, and rejected as too distressing, the alternative of bearing the child and then offering it for adoption. Where the prospective mother and father are married to each other, or have a subsisting pair-bond together, the former should consult the latter before deciding on an abortion, and should carefully consider any arguments he may advance.

Quite different considerations apply when the foetus has grown to the point where, once delivered from the womb, it is already mature enough to survive indefinitely. Then, even though still within the womb, it has become an independent person. It has survived the hazards that successively lie in wait for the seed, the embryo and the foetus. It has gained the moral right to protection. Only to safeguard the life of the mother herself may it then be sacrificed.

It is immoral for a pregnant woman to abort her foetus after it has become viable, except where this is necessary to preserve her life or health, because by that time (though not before) the foetus has developed into a person in its own right.

As has been said, a foetus is not a person. It is not, as the anti-abortion campaigners foolishly proclaim, a *baby* who can be *murdered*. Such inflammatory words are an abuse of language. Common law has always resisted the notion that the foetus has a life of its own. It is humanity *in posse*, not (as some wish to treat it) *in esse*. It has the possibility of being a human child, but does not yet exist as a human child. It is of the nature of a foetus that it may never do so. We own our lives only when we have gained them. The foetus gains its life when and if it succeeds in surmounting the hurdles placed by nature (or God if you prefer) in the way of viable birth. The portal is the neck of the womb, seen from inside. The foetus must pass through that in a viable state in order to earn the title of a human being. Many an embryo, called into existence by fertilisation, fails to achieve this. Nature intended it so, and we have no claim to be above nature.

It is immoral to distress a woman who is considering the abortion of her

non-viable foetus by asserting that the abortion would be immoral, or by using dysphemisms such as 'baby' or 'child' for the foetus or 'murder' for the process of abortion.

To conclude this discussion of the ethics of abortion we consider briefly a further question which has become realistic only because of advances in medical science. Many people who might grant the right to abort a defective foetus jib at the right to abort a healthy foetus merely because it is of the wrong (that is undesired) gender.

We have now arrived at the stage where medical science can, by prenatal diagnostic tests, reveal the sex of the unborn foetus. The tests, usually reserved by doctors for pregnant women who are either over the age of thirty-five or risk foetus abnormality for other reasons, are given at the sixteenth week of pregnancy. However a prenatal test using placenta samples can give this information at eight weeks.

People use information. One result of these scientific developments is that thousands of women in India and China, where the sex of a baby is crucial, have voted for abortion of the healthy wrong-sex foetus. A woman there longs for a male child, and so aborts the prospective female. Some western women also long for a child of a particular sex. With them, the longing is more likely to be in the female direction. This has often had untoward consequences for the hapless unsought male.

Professor Ferguson-Smith of Glasgow University warned in 1990 that some pregnant females are giving false information so as to obtain the carrying out of a test that will reveal the sex of their future offspring. Is this immoral? On the other hand is it moral to withhold information of this kind from the person most closely affected?

Believers in the principle of female self-rule over their own bodies can have no doubt of the answer. Up to the stage of viability, a pregnant woman has a right to decide whether to bear the child or not. Whether this is located among God-given religious rights or secular-derived human rights we need not pause to enquire. It is a right the woman has. If she does not fancy a boy, or does not fancy a girl, she has the right to command the appropriate act. No clinical cytogeneticist or other medical busybody has any business to gainsay her. Let him or her do what he or she is paid to do, and leave the principal agent to take the crucial decision.

12
Sex and Child-rearing

Throughout human history it has been accepted as the duty of the natural parents to rear their offspring. Indeed this is the rule throughout the animal kingdom generally. Accordingly the first precept of the part of the Code dealing with sex and the young must be a statement of this principle.

The natural parents of a child should accept and discharge their responsibility to rear it unless circumstances render this impracticable.

It is beyond the scope of this book to enter into the details of proper parenting (except in relation to sex), so we merely go on to say that the next precept must be to give the child a secure and loving start to its life.

It is the duty of the persons rearing a child to give it a secure and loving upbringing till adulthood.

If the child cannot be reared by its natural parents it is best that it be reared by a couple who are as near as possible in age and characteristics to the natural parents. To be reared by a lone parent, or by two persons of the same sex, may succeed. It is more likely however to be less than the best, since the child needs a close and extended view of rearers of both sexes in order to make sense of its world.

Infant and Pubescent Sexuality

We have seen that parents ought to follow themselves, and teach their children how to follow, certain principles – namely those of ethical knowledge and ethical obedience, together with the duties of sex-acceptance, sex-respect and sex-fulfilment. Before examining the topic of sex education we pause to consider the nature of infant and pubescent sexuality. Many twentieth-century researchers, from Sigmund Freud onwards, have stressed the existence and importance of this, yet our society on the whole continues to reject it. This is strange. The sex-lives of adults are based on their sex-lives as children.

Freud insisted that human beings are sexual creatures from the outset. Dr John Gagnon of the Kinsey Institute points out that the general shock caused by Freud's discoveries was not because the public learnt that when left alone a young child will engage in sexual activities, but because they were forced to accept that such activities are universal and indeed essential. Ken Plummer, in *Perspectives on Paedophilia*, says that children are sexual creatures and that in the process of having their sexuality denied them by adults the foundations are firmly laid for them becoming in due course themselves neurotic, perverted or malfunctioning adults. Dr Mary Calderone, Director of the Sex Information and Education Council of the United States, confirms this by saying that despite Freud western adults still insist on pretending that the sexuality of children does not exist, when in actuality it is our relegation of it to non-existence that is the cause of distortion and difficulty in later years. G. R. Freedman, lecturer in family medicine at the University of Newcastle upon Tyne, says in his 1983 book *Sexual Medicine* that denial of childhood sexuality by parents 'may lead to the opposite of what was intended and thus sexual guilt, secretive and shameful sexual expression, and perhaps unwanted pregnancies'. He cites the case of Sarah, an eleven-year-old girl brought to the doctor by her mother. The girl had a swelling on her private parts but was too embarrassed to show her mother this. Freedman explains what happened when the girl was alone with the doctor:

Sarah's initial embarrassment soon evaporated and she readily revealed her slightly asymetrical vulval labia. Some simple health education, with encouragement to Sarah to talk about her fears and feelings followed, with evident relief and benefit. Unfortunately, it was not possible to have a similar productive discussion with Sarah's mother. Her prudery was such that she had to excuse herself, saying 'It was too difficult to talk about such things.'

Although young people often fail to identity their sexuality for what it is, this is not always the case. In a newspaper interview the popular film actor Michael Keaton said of his schooling in the United States (*Sun*, 8 June 1990): 'I have had a strong sex drive ever since I was eight and Mrs Morgan [a teacher] really turned me on.' Despite reading such statements by their heroes, the public still steadfastly refuse to accept the reality of infantile sexuality.

Wilhelm Reich bitterly attacked what he called our 'destroying' of the sexuality of infants. He was right to react in this way. Natural childish functions are to be regulated, never destroyed, by the processes of upbringing or what is nowadays called parenting. The infant's needs are for play, for the satisfaction of curiosity, for experiment, for obtaining pleasurable sensations, and for a positive rather than a negative reaction by those occupying the parent role. These needs exist in the sexual realm as they exist in other areas of the child's life.

To gain understanding we need to begin by considering what the young child does of its own accord if adults do not interfere. The infant explores and experiments with its own body, and with the bodies of its age-mates of either sex. If in doing this it happens upon an act that gives it pleasure or comfort, the child repeats the act as often as those welcome consequences continue to result. Adult supervision is needed, but should be directed to the right ends. Childish experimentation can become physically dangerous, as with Irving Bieber's young boy patient caught trying to push a lollipop stick up a little girl's anus. When correction has to be given it should be made clear that the reason for it is this kind of danger.

In our society, punishment springs more often from anger and shame over the sexual connotations of the child's act than fears about physical safety. If another child is involved, apprehension as to the likely reaction of its parents will compound these negative emotions. Yet it has to be admitted that, left to themselves, young children readily engage in sex-play. Why therefore do adults presume to interfere to prevent it? We had better be pretty sure that we really do have a moral right to react in this punitive way.

Kinsey found that nearly half his sample admitted to genital play with other children before puberty. The figure was forty-eight per cent for boys playing with the genitals of other boys, but only forty per cent for heterosexual sex-play. These high figures were recorded despite the strong parental ban on such activity. The disparity in favour of homosexual play probably does no more than reflect greater opportunity. Both figures are likely to be understatements, since people are reluctant to admit to this kind of activity.

Societies that allow unrestricted sex-play by pre-adolescent children have long been dismissed by western culturists as primitive, though in recent times doubts have crept in. Indeed a vociferous, and growing, minority of pundits are coming to insist that any culture, however undeveloped, is worthy of the same respect as any other culture, however advanced. This is obvious nonsense, yet we must never be so arrogant as to assume we have nothing at all to learn from so-called 'primitive' cultures.

Anthropologists have found free-sex children to be much healthier mentally than those reared in repressive societies. A famous example is the Trobriand Islands, where Malinowski discovered that young children were free to examine each other's bodies and play sexually together as much as they liked.

There are plenty of opportunities for both boys and girls to receive instruction in erotic matters from their companions. The children initiate each other into the mysteries of sexual life in a directly practical manner at a very early age. A premature amorous existence begins among them long before they are able really to carry out the act of sex. They indulge in plays and pastimes in which they satisfy their curiosity concerning the appearance and function of the organs of generation, and incidentally receive, it would seem, a certain amount of positive pleasure.

Malinowski reported that the attitude of Trobriand parents and other adults toward these activities was either indifference or tolerant and amused interest. One said:

It is their play to *kayta* (have intercourse). They give each other a coconut, a small piece of betel-nut, a few beads or some fruits from the bush, and they go and hide and *kayta*.

All sorts of dancing games, played by the children of both sexes in the central clearing of the village, had a more or less strongly marked flavour of sex. How healthy that seems, yet it was, as in so many other places, later destroyed by missionary influences.

Unconditioned infants of either sex, when behaving wholly naturally together, do not distinguish between sexual and other play. To them it is all play – and discovery.

In a primitive tropical (therefore warm) society such as that of the Tikopia young children are allowed great freedom of interaction. They remain nude, there being no taboos on bodily contact with each other. The natural result, as Sir Raymond Firth tells us in his book *We, the Tikopia*, is that even young brothers and sisters, though subject to the incest taboo, frequently simulate sexual intercourse. Its clasping, jerking and thrusting come naturally to these children, though their actions in play may owe something to imitation. Significantly, the play is not seen by adults as threatening. Therefore the infants are not discouraged in what is considered a healthy part of growing up.

Margaret Mead in *Sex and Temperament in Three Primitive Societies* wrote of similar conditions among the Arapesh.

Small children are not required to behave differently to children of their own sex and those of the opposite sex. Four-year-olds can roll and tumble on the floor together without anyone's worrying about how much bodily contact results. Thus there develops in the children an easy, happy-go-lucky familiarity with the bodies of both sexes, a familiarity uncomplicated by shame, coupled with a premium upon warm, all-over physical contact.

In a different part of the globe, West Africa, Meyer Fortes in *The Web of Kinship Among the Tallensi* notes the same phenomenon. Speaking of a boy of eleven and his sister aged nine, he writes:

The children, who were quite naked, stood embracing each other, the boy with his legs round his sister's and they twisted and wriggled about as if they were engaged in a mixture of an orgiastic dance and a wrestling match. They were both in a state of high excitement, panting and giggling and muttering to each other, with obvious sexual pleasure. They seemed oblivious of their surroundings. This game went on for about twenty minutes, after which they separated and lolled back as if exhausted.

In his book *The Red Lamp of Incest*, published in 1980, the anthropologist Robin Fox notes that intercourse between seven-year-olds is not unknown. He adds that the sexual attempt is rarely fully consummated, however, 'with some saying that it is simply not possible in children since the little boy's penis cannot achieve penetration'.

Nineteenth-century Christian missionaries introduced the concept that such attitudes were pagan and barbaric. This is now widely seen as racist, culturist and unacceptable. It follows that parents of today should accept the need to revert to nature. The idea of the infant as 'innocent', that is sexless, is an aberration we need to get rid of. True innocence embraces all knowledge, and all aspects of knowledge.

In our culture parental checks speedily inhibit childish sex-play. We have compared this with conditions in primitive societies. Now let us adopt another form of comparison, with children in our own culture who are mentally backward. Here we find that, since parental checks are necessarily less effective, sexuality asserts itself more prominently than with normal children.

Professer Warren Johnson, head of the Department of Health Education at the University of Maryland, has reported on experiences at his clinic, where nearly half the hundred or so children are retarded mentally. He finds that parents of these backward children have usually received all kinds of information and advice – except in matters of sex. He tries to fill this gap, 'first by talking about and illustrating our society's traditional, irrational attitude towards sex'. Then he goes on to specific topics as they affect normal children. On male erections, he points out that these occur from birth and should be viewed as entirely normal and natural –like any other bodily function. This does not mean they are always to be ignored. As with a non-sexual physical manifestation, over-frequent erections in a boy may convey a significant message to the observer, as with the following example given by Professor Johnson.

One mentally-retarded boy made a practice of stimulating his penis, literally pounding it black and blue so as to get erections intentionally. Among other things, this was an attention-getting device when with other boys. The approach used with him was to help him learn to function more adequately as a member of the group so that he would not have to resort to such extreme measures to gain attention.

On masturbation, Professor Johnson says that if the child is capable of distinguishing between privately-acceptable and publicly-acceptable behaviour, he or she should be taught to confine masturbation to places and times when it will not be disturbing to other people – just as it is learned that urinating is done in the privacy of the bathroom. Again, however, masturbation may be a signal requiring attention from the parent figure.

Sometimes, frequent masturbation and/or sexual self-stimulation are virtually forced on children. For example, an over-active as well as mentally retarded boy was regularly confined to his bedroom at an early hour in the evening. His mother became alarmed on discovering that instead of going to sleep, William 'played with himself'. She did not bother to wonder whether the boy's bedtime was realistic, whether he had sufficient opportunity to engage in physical play that would encourage fatigue, etc.

On sex-play with other children, Professor Johnson tells parents that if the opportunity exists this activity is to be expected, though parents tend to become very much upset and likely to administer punishment. Sex-play by mentally-retarded children is viewed with horror as 'abnormality added to abnormality'. In fact however it can be clearly beneficial, as the following example shows.

A mongoloid boy and girl, well within the mentally retarded range, were playing actively together. In the course of playing, they had considerable physical contact, and while resting their contact continued and included a certain amount of caressing, the chest area and lower abdomen not being omitted. Professional observers at first felt compelled to identify this as undesirable behaviour but were unable to convince themselves as to why. As a matter of fact, they finally decided that through physical play and contact the children were learning and demonstrating what was for them an exceptional level of communication ability and concern for each other's feelings and welfare.

Professor Johnson goes on to point out that communication skills and social awareness are two of the major objectives in the training and education of the mentally retarded, and that sex is often one of the few things the severely handicapped are capable of responding to. In time, he adds, we may realise that in attempting to eliminate sexuality we have been wasting a great resource in our educational and therapeutic efforts with people generally, including the subnormal. 'Perhaps', the Professor concludes, 'we will learn to use this energy of life and pleasure constructively in our rearing and education of the mentally retarded.'

Because mentally-handicapped children are less susceptible to the direct and indirect pressures society exerts in aid of sex-suppression, their behaviour is more honest. We can learn from it what ordinary children's real needs are.

What happens if these needs are not met? There is plenty of evidence, but it goes on being ignored. Many people with a life-long experience of children and their needs have pointed out the lesson. One of these is A. S. Neill, who wrote in the book named after his famous school *Summerhill* that childhood sex-play is the 'royal road' to a healthy and balanced adult sex-life. Everything, he said, is loaded against our young people. 'Circumstances compel them to convert what should be lovely and joyful into something sinister and sinful, into smut and leers, and shameful laughter.'

One consequence of this repression can be to sour the child–parent relationship. Dr Frank Caprio mentions in his book *Variations in Sexual Behaviour* a male patient who at the age of six had been caught by his mother 'playing with himself'. She scolded him and told his father, who also took him to task. The patient associated this incident with later feelings of hostility towards them: 'I thought I was being deprived of something pleasurable by the unreasonable attitude of my parents.'

Mistrust caused by dishonesty about the facts of sex also sours the child–parent relationship. Freud cites as an example the emotion aroused in children who are fobbed off with such explanations of childbirth as the universal tale that the new baby is brought by a stork: 'from the time of this first deception and rebuff they nourish a mistrust against adults'.

Even more serious is the fact that sex-suppression sows in the child seeds of chronic guilt and anxiety. As we saw in chapter 4, a ban on family nudity, for example, means that the child's natural curiosity remains unsatisfied and he or she becomes anxious about what lies beneath the concealing veil. By the time, as inevitably happens, the veil slips it may be too late for the child to escape emotional damage.

So negative is the adult's usual attitude to childish sexuality in our society that, as Harry Stack Sullivan pointed out, the child ceases to be able to admit that this quality is a part of its self. It is repressed, and relegated to the unconscious. There it is out of reach of the reflective processes of the conscious mind, and cannot be adjusted in the light of the child's ongoing experience. Psychic growth is inhibited. As Sullivan says:

If . . . a parent had a subpsychotic fear of the infant's becoming a lustful monster and has gone off the deep end whenever the child was discovered to be holding the penis or fondling the vulva – then we expect that the personality of the infant as it develops will show a sort of hole in that area, in the sense that any approach to the genitals will ultimately lead to the appearance of a feeling which has scarcely evolved beyond a sudden, intense, all-encompassing anxiety.

This psychic 'hole' is the ultimate manifestation of what in chapter 3 was described as the Henry Moore syndrome. It was unknown in societies like the Trobriand Islands (in their pre-missionary days). As A. S. Neill says in his book *Problem Family*, a child left to touch his or her genitals has every chance of growing up with a sincere happy attitude to sex. This implies that the touching is done with parental approval, and in a family context of loving care.

Reich stresses the importance of the conscious and unconscious attitudes that accompany genital play, adding:

From the beginning of a child's life it has a positive attitude towards sexuality, through the pleasure mechanism. The social surroundings alone determine whether this originally positive attitude can survive or whether it must give way to guilt feelings and genital anxiety . . .

Reich also stresses the importance of *affirmation* rather than mere *toleration* of infantile and pubertal sex-life, calling it decisive for the psychic structure-formation of the child. It is an affirmation our society finds it difficult if not impossible to give.

Reich's view is echoed by Lars Ullerstam in proposing sexual reforms. He argues that parents should be taught to *encourage* their children's sexual curiosity and to be *pleased* with their sexual activity. The Trobriand islanders thought there was something wrong with the child who held aloof from sex-play. They were concerned about him or her, and sought a remedy. We should be like that too. What we must always remember is that, whether we like it or not, all children live an active sexual life: in emotion, in imagination, and in terms of their bodies. It is natural for them to do so. We adults have it in our power to make it happy for them to do so as well. Yet in the continuing survey known as Youthscan UK, which studies a group of 15,000 people each born within one week in April 1970, it has been found that in adolescence over half the sample said they were miserable or depressed at least some of the time. On the other hand 81 per cent agreed with the view that there is nothing wrong with sex before marriage. One wonders how much of the admitted misery and depression is due to suppressing, or attempting to suppress, the sexual drive so powerful at this age.

Like any other aspect of developing human nature, youthful sexuality needs wise and sympathetic treatment from adults within and outside the family. Above all it must always be regarded *positively*, whatever problems this brings. That it can bring problems is illustrated by the following true story of the emancipated parents Eric and Sybil, and their little daughter Alice.

One summer night Eric, sleeping in the nude, was awakened by Alice's crying. He went to her room, picked her up, and administered comfort. As her tears subsided, Alice suddenly said: 'Daddy, what a funny bottom you've got!' Eric passed off the remark, and soothed the child to sleep again. Next morning she came into her parents' bedroom as Eric was dressing. He already had his trousers on, but Alice demanded that he lower them so that she could inspect his 'funny bottom'. Embarrassed, Eric refused. At this Alice became hysterical and Eric felt obliged to comply with her wishes. As the child curiously fingered his penis, Eric felt it begin to stiffen. He pulled up his pants and managed to distract Alice with a hastily-contrived game of bears.

A few days later, Alice again awoke in the night. Remembering the previous experience, Eric asked Sybil to go to the child. Alice noticed Sybil's bare breasts and commented on them. Sybil felt very hurt when Alice reacted strongly against being held in the natural position for administering comfort, against her mother's bosom. 'No, no', she yelled, pushing Sybil away. 'I don't want to touch it!'

These two incidents would have been avoided if Eric and Sybil had taken the coward's way out and hidden their sex anatomy in Alice's presence. They occurred because Alice, though accustomed to seeing her parents naked, had suddenly reached the stage of *observing* their sexual organs as separate objects. Sensing their importance, she felt intensely curious. A child's curiosity is a vital component in its growing-up process. It needs to be satisfied on sexual matters every bit as much as on any others.

Eric's embarrassment and Sybil's distress were each understandable. These young parents could take comfort from the fact that they were helping Alice to face important truths at the right age, that at which her curiosity was *naturally* aroused. If, under the usual sex-negative system, her parents had sought to keep these from her, they would have begun the conditioning that turns some people into sex-haters or perverts.

The incident also illustrates a point at the heart of our treatment of childhood sexuality, namely the kind of parental arousal that can lead on to incestuous child-abuse. Eric became sexually aroused when his young daughter's inquisitive fingers began to explore his penis. The matter then passed beyond the stage when enlightened parents coolly instruct their offspring, treating sex as no different from algebra.

The truth is that sex is different from algebra. The parent–child relationship (as Freud clearly showed) is in part a sexual one. So the conventionally negative treatment by parents of child sexuality may be seen as a defence mechanism. Thereby powerful emotional forces are left unstirred, and many think it is safer so. If a father allows his young daughter to arouse him, where will he stop? Incest beckons, and that is subject to powerful taboos. Almost certainly, the last thing the father wants is any real sexual relationship with his own daughter. Yet penile erection is the beginning of male sexual relations, and beyond the power of the subject to control. All he can do is remove the stimulus before harm ensues.

So however enlightened we may feel ourselves to be, we surely must, as members of a society which seeks to call itself civilised, cry halt at this point. If necessary the father will explain to his young daughter, as gently as he can, that one of the household rules is that she cannot be involved when he has an erection. With her young brother she may play and experiment but her father is mother's sexual partner. If this is taught with sympathy, the child will come to understand. All children want is clear boundaries, provided these do not deny their own needs and nature.

Here is the true story of a woman who chose not to inflict this denial. To the displeasure of society (as represented by the prosecuting authorities), she perceived and ministered to the sexual needs of a pubescent boy. The story reached its climax in a criminal trial that took place at Stafford Crown Court in June 1988. In the dock was the boy in question (let us call him John). At the age of fourteen, John suddenly convinced himself that the time had come for him to taste sexual joy. He felt strongly about this, and brought his nimble wits to bear on the matter. The result was that he now stood charged with rape and indecent assault. His alleged victim was a married woman of forty-eight, said by the prosecution to be simple-minded. Let us call her Elsie (true names were not revealed in reports of the trial).

The evidence showed that John somehow discovered that Elsie had just taken a smear test for cervical cancer. He telephoned her, pretending to be a doctor. Doctor John gravely informed Elsie that there was a possibility she might be infected, and it was desirable to perform a further test to make sure. What would this test involve? Elsie asked. The answer reassured her. Doctor John gruffly said he would send round his young male assistant, who would carry out intimate tests on her body. Thankfully Elsie agreed to receive him.

The 'assistant', in the person of John himself, duly came round and was admitted. Elsie, alone in the house, led him upstairs to her bedroom. If she was surprised by his youthful appearance and school uniform she did not let on. Hoarsely John commanded Elsie, so that the further test could be carried out, to remove her clothes and lie on her back on the bed. While she was complying, John rapidly removed his own clothes. His moment had arrived.

Clambering on top of the recumbent nude form of Elsie, John wondered what exactly he had to do. His means of doing it was in good shape, but still he felt doubt as to the practical side. He need not have worried. Elsie, who had been married for twenty-two years and given birth to three children, had plenty of practical experience. She guided his youthful penis to its proper destination, moving her body in time with his amateurish thrusts. She let out delighted chuckles. Having finished, John climbed down and began to put his school uniform back on. He had donned no more than his grey shirt and jersey when Elsie coyly beckoned him back on to the bed and began stroking the parts of him that were still unclothed. She pleasured herself by sucking the boy's penis and rousing him to a quick second climax. The prosecution described all this as a cruel and heartless trick on the part of the youthful defendant. Cross-examined in the witness box, Elsie admitted that she was 'a bit carried away when the youth was on top of me'. She confessed that she had enjoyed their romp.

On the second day of the trial the prosecution dropped the charges, whereupon the judge ordered the jury to acquit. John's conduct was reprehensible in a number of ways, yet the case was not suitable for a court normally reserved for the graver crimes such as murder and robbery. One suspects that the authorities responsible for bringing it to the Crown Court were displaying sex-negativism of a kind only too common. People who, because of age or disability, were not supposed to have a sex-life had by a ruse slipped through society's net. Severe punishment was felt to be called for.

Sex Education

It is the duty of the persons rearing a child to ensure that it undergoes whatever sex education may be necessary to enable it progressively to learn the facts about human sexuality, and eventually to carry out its duties of ethical understanding and ethical action. Subject to this, a child-rearer who has not been proved to lack a genuine intention to promote the welfare of the child has the right to decide what it is to be taught about sex.

Parents or other rearers of a child should try to teach the child certain basic truths about sexual morality from the earliest age. It is the parents', rather than the teachers', primary responsibility to undertake this, as children themselves say. In the continuing survey known as Youthscan UK, which studies a group of 15,000 people each born within one week in April 1970, it has been found that at the age of sixteen 69 per cent of the children say their parents should be the main source of their information about sex. On the other hand 77 per cent of the mothers of these children think such information should be given at school!

The following is an outline for parental teaching of infants.

Your sexual parts, like those of other people, are important and special.

Because of this they are to be treated with respect, and not as joking matters or casual playthings.

People do not caress one another sexually unless they have a special kind of loving relationship with each other.

Within the family, only Mummy and Daddy have this kind of relationship.

You may caress your own sexual parts if you feel like it (and it is natural to feel like it), but it is best to do this when you are alone or with a person outside the family who is around your own age.

Though there is nothing shameful about your sexual parts, most people think they should be treated as very private and kept covered unless you are alone with the family or with a person outside the family of around your own age. Although we disagree with this prudish attitude, we have to go along with it.

Some grown-ups may want to caress your sexual parts. They ought not to do this, so don't let them.

Be careful about being alone with grown-ups you don't know, in case they try to caress you sexually. Even a grown-up you do know may want to do this.

Always tell Mummy or Daddy if any grown-up tries to caress you sexually.

Repressed parents attack organised sex education in schools or else-where. It brings together all that is traditionally objected to in sex outside marriage. Sex is being spoken of to the *unmarried*, who are supposed not to be concerned with it. Sex is being spoken of to *children*, who are supposed to be sexless. Sex is being spoken of to *groups*, whereas it ought to be intensely private. Sex is being spoken of *truthfully*, thus showing up as dishonest parents who choose to give sexual explanations (if they give them at all) in terms of storks, fairies or gooseberry bushes. Such repression is still strong, though less so than in the sort of society depicted in E. M. Forster's novel *Maurice*, set in around 1913. Describing the wedding night of two of his young upper-middle-class characters, Forster writes:

When he arrived in her room after marriage, she did not know what he wanted. Despite an elaborate education, no one had told her about sex. Clive was as considerate as possible, but he scared her terribly, and left feeling she hated him. She did not. She welcomed him on future nights. But it was always without a word . . . He never saw her naked, nor she him. They ignored the reproductive and digestive functions.

These difficulties are largely due to religious teaching. The Roman Catholic church leads the way, closely followed by other Judaeo-Christian denominations. The message of even their most enlightened teachers is vitiated by dogma. A comparatively liberal Roman Catholic book on sex education is *Life and Our Children*, first published in 1961. The author, Audrey Kelly, is a physician and mother of three. She is a pleasure to read. Witty, concerned, knowledgeable, Dr Kelly suffers from only one fault. She is committed to the neat Catholic view of sex.

That view is neat because its answers spring ready-made from a given dogma. In Dr Kelly's words, a perfect example of a *non sequitur*, this is: 'Almighty God has given us the sexual act for the primary purpose of begetting children should it be His will. It is wrong therefore to use the gift solely for the pleasure which it gives us.' Once that facile view is rejected, as increasingly it is nowadays rejected, the whole set of easy answers is invalidated. We are obliged to begin the slow, difficult course of reworking the answers in terms of human nature, human need and rational speculation. Some Christian qualities necessarily remain, such as mercy, charity and compassion.

In a pamphlet by K. H. Kavanagh attacking sex education, published by a body calling itself The Responsible Society, it is asked:

Can the child from a home where sex and nudity are taboo take without stress larger-than-life films and slides of nudity, erection and childbirth? Does not this erode the natural modesty of the child?

Certainly it may erode the natural *ignorance* of the child, but that is the purpose of education. If its parents have failed to educate their child in any vital matter, then the school has a duty do so. That is the purpose of schools.

An expert who, as has been mentioned before, has written much on the subject of sex education is Dr Margaret White. Here are four of her aphorisms: set out in her pamphlet *Sound Sex Education*:

1. The period from birth to five years is the auto-erotic stage when the baby and toddler is interested in his own body. This is why small boys innocently masturbate, especially if they are bored. It is a stage

of growth and it is wise not to take it seriously. My advice is: give them a biscuit or a toy so they have something to do with their hands.

2. Adolescent girls should be advised not to indulge in petting. Instead they should be told: there are years of married life ahead of you for full sexual activity.

3. Premarital sex slowly destroys the ability to give natural affection, and can so desensitise the heart and emotions that one is no longer capable of ever giving total love.

4. Physical attraction to those of the same sex is a normal part of puberty. This is a phase not to worry about, but to grow out of. It is homosexual practice which is wrong.

That word *innocently* in maxim 1 implies that masturbation at a later age is far from innocent. The maxim also indicates that when little boys 'innocently' masturbate they must be stopped. It fails to warn parents that the magic biscuit must never be proffered in a way that might arouse lasting feelings of guilt in the child.

For many girls, who for one reason or another will never marry, maxim 2 is simply a lie. For all it is an attempt to deprive them of their birthright of sexual joy before, and possibly in the intervals of, licensed marriage. Maxim 3 is obvious rubbish. Maxim 4 denies sexual fulfilment to perhaps one-tenth of the human race, and is simply immoral.

These two sex-education pamphlets are typical of many Christian-based productions. Their purpose is to put children off sex, not to give them factual information.

In a counter-pamphlet by Maurice Hill and Michael Lloyd-Jones, published by the National Secular Society under the title *Sex Education – the Erroneous Zone*, it was found possible to recommend without reservation one only out of forty-two publications examined, namely *Boys and Sex* by W. B. Pomeroy. Many of the rest were found to be factually inaccurate. Often they contained 'moralising of the worst kind'. The effect was frequently to frighten or disgust the young reader, filling him or her with guilt. One pamphlet, published even before the advent of Aids, referred to promiscuous sex as a sign of mental illness. Another put down a loving boy and girl's natural desire for sex together by saying:

Many people do not find it at all difficult to wait until they love sincerely and completely and confidently enough to marry before they feel the need for sexual intercourse. There have also, on the other hand, always been people whose sexual characters were weak, and people who love themselves so intensely that they use other folk to feed their vanity or satisfy their shallow desires.

The counter-pamphlet discusses in turn various types of sexual activity, ending each treatment by saying 'if you feel like doing it, do it – and we hope you enjoy it'. This is the much-needed *positive* approach, echoed in the title of a 1978 sex-education manual by Jane Cousins entitled *Make it Happy* (since reissued under the title, modified for obvious reasons, of *Make It Happy: Make It Safe*). Alas, this manual has been strongly criticised by the sex-negaters. The following quotations from it indicate why:

Our sex-lives probably start even before we're born. It's known for certain that many boys are born with an erect penis . . . A slap on the hand to stop us from touching our sex organs when we're young can cause a lot of harm because it makes us feel guilty and scared about our sex organs and our sexual feelings. [p. 1]

There's no reason why someone who is having her period shouldn't have sex if she wants to – in fact it often helps to relieve the pain of cramps to have orgasms and having a period is nothing to feel ashamed about. [p. 17]

Many boys hate waking up to find semen all over their pyjamas and sheets. If you want to avoid this, try sleeping in underpants which can then be washed out next morning, or give yourself an ejaculation before you go to sleep, and use a paper handkerchief to absorb the semen. [p. 20]

For homosexuals, sex is as natural as it is for everyone else. What they do and how they give and get sexual pleasure is up to them as individuals. [p. 25]

The negative attitude to sex education remains strong, in both under-developed and developed countries.

In Ghana children are still taught that contraception is only for married couples, and that if you use it before marriage then, when the time does come for marriage, you will be childless. To be childless in Ghana is to be a second-class citizen, so this is a potent threat. The children there are also solemnly taught that under-age sex gives you disease, and that the baby too will be diseased.

Shirley LaHaye is President of an organisation called Concerned Women for America, which represents more than half a million Americans. It considers sex-education unnecessary. Moreover it is in the organisation's view harmful, because it desensitises children to sexuality. Mrs LaHaye said on television in 1990 that sex education makes otherwise inactive and uninterested teenagers want to dabble in sex rather than reading, which is the basic education. She added that teaching on contraception and abortion is not needed. In her view young men and women should be taught that there is only one way to avoid teenage pregnancy, and that is total abstention before marriage. Why in relation to sex alone do such people think ignorance a good thing? In every other area, knowledge is prized.

Less than one hundred miles from the American East Coast the communist state of Cuba shows how it should be done. A government programme of sex education is on the way to transforming the sex-negative attitudes formerly preached there by the Roman Catholic church. Sex clinics are provided, and supportive clubs established for adolescents. The aim is not to keep young people in ignorance about sex, nor to deprive them of sexual fulfilment. It is to ensure that this is not accompanied by teenage pregnancy or sexually transmitted disease.

When it comes to sex education, it is necessary to separate factual information from moral guidance. This marks its distinction from most forms of education. As pointed out above, sex is different from algebra. Algebra has no moral dimension.

It is inappropriate to teach children the facts of human reproduction in the way one might teach them the facts of crustacean reproduction. Neither the teacher nor the pupil are crustaceans. There needs to be an awareness on the part of the teacher that the one relates to matters of intense interest and concern to the child personally while the other is a matter of indifference save in the academic sense.

Nor do all children have the ability to grasp the distinction between facts and morals (even supposing the teacher is competent to pose it). When question-time arrives, the boundary is likely to be blurred. The teacher's task is to demonstrate that while facts are immutable morals are open to debate, and rule only where the intelligence is satisfied.

One undoubted moral duty exists, which so far we have not mentioned. It is wrong for the teacher to conceal the intense joy that sexual fulfilment is capable of bestowing. If the budding adolescent asks 'when can I begin to taste that joy?' the honest sex-education teacher is bound to answer 'Now!'

Teachers, and parents also, need to be aware of the importance of sympathy, tact and respect in dealing with children's sexuality. For many children in our society, particularly those who are naturally shy (as many are, despite shows of bravado), sex is an embarrassment. How things can go wrong is illustrated by the following letter in the *Sun* from a sixteen-year-old boy (30 January 1991):

My Dad stormed off when he came into my bedroom and caught me fondling myself. He has threatened to throw me out of the house and hardly talks to me now. I'm so unhappy. Dad is old-fashioned and set in his ways and I don't have anyone to talk to.

The newspaper's reply offered the hope that Dad's threat was the result of shock, and would be forgotten when he calmed down. It wisely added: 'Maybe this will have taught him not to barge into your room.'

13

Child Abuse and the Age of Consent

As we saw in chapter 9, morality is generally agreed to require consent to be given or indicated before a sexual act is done. The following precept suggests what the position is where one party is too young to give effective, that is informed, consent. Even where there is apparent consent, the position must be treated as being morally the same as if no consent at all had been given. In other words the act is immoral. An exception is allowed for sex between age-mates, since this is held to be both natural and (within reasonable limits) desirable.

Apparent consent by a youngster to a sexual act with an older person is morally ineffective, and therefore counts as no consent, where the youngster is too immature to understand the nature and quality of the act, that is its physiological, emotional and ethical significance. Apparent consent by a youngster to a sexual act with an age-mate is however to be treated as morally effective. A test for whether a youngster who apparently consents to a sexual act really understands its nature and quality is whether, when maturity is attained, he or she would be likely to regret having committed the act.

Sex and the Child

While the above precept is put forward here as indeed the correct ethical position, it has two serious problems which will now be explored at length. The first is how do you tell whether the young person does or does not understand the nature and quality of the sexual act in question? The second is how do you reconcile the ethical precept with the fact that, as stated above, children are sexual creatures? Is it really enough merely to countenance sex between age-mates?

Although this book is not generally concerned with legal as opposed to ethical prescriptions, it is helpful to consider the law's answer to the first question posed above.

Our criminal law bristles with sex offences related to age, nearly all punishable with imprisonment. Most serious are rape, vaginal intercourse by a male with a girl under thirteen, and anal intercourse with a female of any age or a male under twenty-one. All these carry life imprisonment. Apart from them, any touching by another person of the sex organs of a youngster under sixteen consitutes indecent assault and is punishable with imprisonment for two years or, if the act is by a man on a boy, ten years.

Under British law therefore the age of consent to vaginal intercourse is sixteen. The minimum age for marriage is also sixteen. So the law says you are not old enough for intercourse until the very moment when you are old enough for marriage. No time at all is allowed for the learning curve. If anyone, of any age, persuades a person of either sex under the age of sixteen to break this ban he or she is a criminal. Consent given by even a fifteen-year-old, however genuine in the eyes of common sense, is a nullity in the eyes of the law. It is treated as wholly non-existent. By a legal fiction, the lover of a willing youngster, even though they are age-mates, is regarded as hardly better than a rapist.

For certain sex acts less complete than vaginal intercourse a fifteen-year-old *is* considered old enough by the law. Consider the following true story.

In the spring of 1951 a Mr Whipp (that was really his name) got into sexual trouble in Clitheroe, Lancashire. It was not sado-masochism that landed Mr Whipp in the dock but, as the law genteelly put it, 'making water on a river bank'. Having completed this innocent operation, Mr Whipp invited a nearby small girl who he saw had watched his micturition with interest to touch what the law coyly described as his 'person'. This object was not in a state of tumescence. The girl duly touched it; whereupon Mr Whipp shook the drops of urine off it, put it away in his underpants, buttoned up his trousers, and strolled off. He was charged with indecent assault, but the court reluctantly held that even its legal fictions department could not quite see its way to holding that a man who never so much as laid a finger (or anything else) on a little girl had 'assaulted' her. Shortly afterwards, in consequence of this case, an Act of Parliament was passed making criminal any 'gross indecency' with a child under the age of fourteen. It was assumed that any stout British jury (all British juries are deemed to be 'stout') would unhesitatingly hold that for a child merely to touch a flaccid penis is not merely indecent but 'grossly' so.

So we have the ages of thirteen, fourteen, sixteen and twenty-one – all in their different ways significant for the criminal law of sex. Are they the right ages? Under modern conditions children mature at a lower age than they did in the past. This suggests that the age of consent should be lowered to correspond. In fact the growth of sex-negation has led to the opposite result.

Four centuries ago, Shakespeare wrote this interchange between Juliet's father Lord Capulet and her suitor Paris:

> *Capulet*: My child is yet a stranger in the world,
> She hath not seen the change of fourteen years;

> Let two more summers wither in their pride
> Ere we may think her ripe to be a bride.
> *Paris*:   Younger than she are happy mothers made.
> *Capulet*:   And too soon marr'd are those so early made!

Not an unnatural attitude for a father to take, but we know what Capulet's reluctance led to. The runaway Juliet became Romeo's thirteen-year-old bride: a wife in the eyes of both church and law.

Few nowadays would dispute that thirteen is on the young side for the responsibilities of marriage and motherhood, but in Shakespeare's time brides of thirteen were not unusual (though youthful marriages were sometimes entered into, with no intention of immediate consummation, for dynastic or property reasons). Until as recently as 1929, when marriageable age was raised to sixteen, boys of fourteen and girls of thirteen could lawfully marry in Britain. Nearly half a century earlier, in 1885, Parliament had passed the Criminal Law Amendment Act, raising the age of consent to sexual activity *outside* marriage. This had always been fourteen for boys and twelve for girls (until 1875, when it was raised to thirteen). Now it was raised to sixteen for both, where it has in general remained.

Why did the Parliament of 1885 make this change?

It was done to satisfy a then current public outcry over the use of young girls for prostitution. They loitered in hundreds in the London streets, and were sometimes shipped abroad in the course of what was known as the white slave traffic. The government spokesman in Parliament, defending the choice of sixteen as the crucial age, cited the drop in marriage figures below that age: during the previous five years only thirty-seven youngsters under sixteen had married, compared with one hundred sixteen-year-olds and two thousand seventeen-year-olds. He said it could therefore be assumed that girls under sixteen 'were looked on as immature, and as having not arrived at the age of puberty'. Another MP commented that a girl under sixteen was still a child, adding: 'We do not allow such a girl to part with her property, and I think we ought not to allow her to part with her person.'

There are several points to be made about this argument. First, it was not sensible to deal with child prostitutes, a tiny proportion of the population, by taking away the sexual rights of all young adolescents. Second, the average age of menarche (first menstruation) is certainly not sixteen today, even if it was in 1885: it is around twelve. Thirdly, enlightened people now reject the idea that a young girl willingly enjoying sexual intercourse, even for the very first time, is 'giving away her person'.

Any legal age of consent is artificial, since children differ widely in their rate of development. If there must be one, we should acknowledge the sexual wisdom of our ancestors and return to the position that prevailed throughout our history up to the late nineteenth century. The change made then was based on false reasoning. Many people have suffered bitterly for that error. It is time it was reversed. Let us go back to an age of consent of twelve for girls and fourteen for boys. That will more or less correspond to the age of puberty, nature's dividing-line between the child and the adult.

This brings us to the strange fact that under present law the age of consent for male homosexuals is not sixteen but twenty-one, though this difference does not apply to female homosexuals. This anomaly continues to exist notwithstanding that recently the age of majority for both sexes was lowered from twenty-one to eighteen.

The reason for the anomaly is given in the report of the Wolfenden Committee, which in 1957 recommended that homosexual acts between consenting male adults in private should cease to be punished by the criminal law (implemented by Parliament ten years later). The Committee was set up to consider the criminal law relating both to prostitution and homosexuality. First they asked themselves what the function of the criminal law *ought* to be, and came up with this answer:

In this field its function, as we see it, is to preserve public order and decency, to protect the citizen from what is offensive or injurious, and to provide sufficient safeguards against exploitation and corruption of others, particularly those who are specially vulnerable because they are young, weak in body or mind, inexperienced, or in a state of special physical, official or economic dependence.

This looks harmless enough, but underlying it are the usual sex-negative attitudes. The reference to 'decency' reminds us that sex is indecent. Its expression is likely to prove 'offensive' or 'injurious'. Where sex is concerned, the young are likely to be 'exploited' if not 'corrupted'. And so on.

The Wolfenden Committee found that at the very least there were half a million male homosexuals in Britain, and that the most likely figure was around five million. Even heterosexuals concede that's a lot of people.

The Committee also found that seduction by older persons did not *cause* homosexuality, and that the fact of being seduced often did less harm to the victim than subsequent court proceedings and the over-reaction of outraged parents.

A striking feature of the Wolfenden Report is that while the committee accepted that the sexual orientation of this very large group of people is in no way due to seduction or the individual's own choice or wish, and is unalterable, they never doubted that the heterosexual majority are right to victimise, terrorise and incarcerate homosexuals for acts which do no more than correspond to what heterosexuals can freely and acceptably do. This is indeed the tyranny of the majority.

Almost all writings about adolescent sexuality are written by adults trying with difficulty to remember their own youth. An exception is *The Hothouse Society*, a book published in 1968. This is a compilation of adolescents' previously unpublished writings gathered by the Cambridge University sociologist Dr Royston Lambert. It makes clear at first hand the sexual deprivation felt by adolescents, particularly when immured in boarding schools. A sixteen-year-old boy describes his day.

Wake up at 7.25 Aaah! Bloody morning run in 5 minutes . . . God will there be any of the pretty boys outside; if I look at the pretty boys I always blush. Am I queer? I ask myself this 1,000 times; I don't think so; I mean the thought of actually buggering a little boy is repulsive to me but they're just a substitute, something pretty to look at when there are no girls around. Collect up books and go outside yes there's Brightwell; quick avert eyes god he's *so* like a girl you're going red; don't don't don't screams your brain . . . [Finally, at the end of the school day] At last into bed. Shall I have a flog? No, too tired. Turn over thinking, wishing, frustrated – and then merciful release to sleep.

Another passage, this time from a seventeen-year-old boy, returns to the theme of adolescent homosexuality.

When one becomes of VI form status, of about 16-17 years of age, the pressure is greatest towards homosexuality. Some respond physically, others passively. Physical contact becomes even more passionate, and fairly frequent. Boys tend to get more of a relationship than the mechanical 'Wank me off' type of relationship that particularly prevailed amongst them earlier . . . In the passive line which most boys take, boys talk more freely, joke about, admire so and so's lovely botty, and so on . . .'

The Wolfenden Committee recommended that sexual acts by male homosexuals up to the age of twenty-one should be criminal in *all* cases, even when willingly done in private. They accepted the medical evidence that sexual orientation is fixed at a much earlier age, but arrived at twenty-one as the age of consent with the following reasoning:

While there are some grounds for fixing the age as low as sixteen, it is obvious that however 'mature' a boy of that age may be as regards physical development or psycho-sexual make-up, and whatever analogies may be drawn from the law relating to offences against young girls, a boy is incapable, at the age of sixteen, of forming a mature judgment about actions of a kind that might have the effect of setting him apart from the rest of society. The young man between eighteen and twenty-one may be expected to be rather more mature in this respect. We have, however, encountered several cases in which young men have been induced by means of gifts of money or hospitality to indulge in homosexual behaviour with older men . . . to fix it at eighteen would lay them open to attentions and pressures of an undesirable kind from which the adoption of the later age would help to protect them, and from which they ought, in view of their special vulnerability, to be protected.

The key to this passage lies in the pejorative reference to being set apart from the rest of society. The committee did not literally mean the rest of society (which would include fellow-homosexuals), but the majority of society. The phrase *set apart*, with its echoes of the ghetto, indicates that homosexuals are to be viewed as an objectionable minority.

In the years following publication of the Wolfenden Report the tyrannous majority first became more liberal and then became more censorious than at the time of its publication. Yet there appears to be an underlying trend towards accepting that every person is entitled to sexual fulfilment in accordance with his or her sexual orientation, subject only to the true consent of others directly affected. On this basis the age of consent should clearly be the same for male homosexuals as it is for heterosexuals of either sex and for lesbians.

The second question posed above regarding the ethical precept concerning consent by the young to sexual acts was, 'how do you reconcile it with the fact that children are sexual creatures?' Is it really enough merely to countenance sex between age-mates?

To answer this we need first to add to the discussion in the previous chapter of infant and pubescent sexuality by saying a little about the sexuality of the adolescent between the ages of say fourteen and eighteen.

Adolescent Sexuality

Youths and maidens are perhaps the greatest victims of our sex-negating society. These are the beautiful creatures, whose trim and pristine shapes and looks inspire too often the envy of the mature. So they must be, and are, kept down. During the most potent years, when new-budding sexuality could be a vivid joy, all sorts of sensible reasons are produced for *waiting*, for *saving* and for *deferring* the glorious transports that rightfully belong to the mid-teens. To illustrate this, here is an incident taken from a Scottish local newspaper of the 1970s (with the addition of a little imaginative detail).

'Come on, let's do it again' whispered Andrew, just sixteen. Susan, who had not quite attained that age, looked doubtful.
'You enjoyed it last time' he urged.
'Have you got another. . . ?'
'Course.'
The boy and girl, tanned from the summer sun, walked into the bedroom. The time was just after midnight. Andrew boldly switched on the bedside lamp. A rock band playing on the floor below filled the house with urgent sound. The party was going strong.
Andrew pulled off his tee shirt. Then, with sudden shyness, he slowly drew down his jeans. Susan gazed at him, suffused with loving feelings. Then she too undressed.
They had done all this before. Only once before, and but an hour ago. There was however a comforting sense of familiarity.
The boy stood facing Susan, clad only in his underpants. He still felt a little shy, though bold enough to allow the outline of his aroused masculine equipment to display itself beneath the cloth. He noted that his girl was by now quite naked.
'Where is it?'
'Where is. . . ? Oh it's in my pocket.'

Susan, having assisted in the obstructed removal of Andrew's underpants, now with some difficulty helped the boy place the condom in position. Being well instructed about such threats to a young girl's wellbeing as pregnancy and Aids, she was anxious this operation should be carried out correctly. Throughout it, Susan experienced a pleasurable combination of the warm loving feelings of mother, wife and concubine.

Susan's bare feet then walked over the thick pile of the bedroom carpet. She lay down on her back across the double bed, opened her legs, and extended her arms in joyous expectation. Andrew, clumsy but ardent, caressed her fully-developed breasts. He pressed his lips to hers, and struggled to put his slim young body in the right posture for fleshy communion. Susan, with an expertise she was unaware of possessing, guided the youth's amorous movements.

Minutes later, the bedroom door swung open. Susan's mother, returning early from an evening out, entered pulling her gloves off. She was closely followed by Susan's father.

The two beheld the interesting sight of Andrew's bare white bottom moving rhythmically up and down in the middle of their connubial bed. They instantly recognised the recipient of the naked boy's penile thrusts.

'You dirty little beasts!' Thus the perennial cry of the comfortable middle-aged.

The local paper reported the sequel:

A father handed out a good hiding to his sixteen-year-old son when he learned that the boy had taken part in sex games at a teenagers' party. The youngster had made love twice to a girl of fifteen during the all-night pop session at a house in Leuchars. The story of the father's anger was told at Fife Sheriff Court, when the boy admitted having intercourse with an under-age girl. He was bound over for a year. Sheriff William McKay told him: 'Your father was right to give you a hammering. I hope he hit you hard. You will be far safer running around on your motor-cycle than with under-age girls.'

What did Daddy really think as he 'hammered' his boy? Did he remember the time when he himself was sixteen? Perhaps, just as there was no pop music, there were then no nubile, willing girls around either. Was Daddy envious? Had his sex-life, now well into decline, proved disappointing? Did he get some unadmitted sexual joy from using the tawse on his teenage son's bare buttocks?

What of Sheriff William McKay, who thought sex far more dangerous to youths than motor-cycles? How did the girl feel as she braved her parents' wrath, told her story to the police, told it again to the Procurator-Fiscal, told it yet again in court to Sheriff William McKay, the press reporters, and the public gallery?

What's become of the night of joy now? What will future relationships be like between the boy and his parents, the girl and her family?

The questions are endless, just like the repercussions of that terrible night when the sex-negaters had their way and trampled all over youth and joy. They did so in the name of the law. Susan was, after all, a few weeks below the legal age of consent.

Before going further, we need to grasp one vital fact. What we might call the maturity gap is a new phenomenon. In all previous ages of mankind, and in the present age too in undeveloped countries, puberty and physical and intellectual maturity were or are one. It is as a consequence of greatly improved standards of nutrition in modern western society that with us the age of puberty or menarche has dropped by about five years, leaving adolescents to grapple with the maturity gap.

In a symposium held in 1976 by the Royal Society, R. V. Short, a Fellow of the Society, expressed this little-known fact as follows:

In developing countries, with a late age at puberty, the acquisition of fertility and intellectual maturity are almost coincident. In developed countries it seems we now acquire our sexuality well in advance of the intellectual maturity that enables us to cope with it. Early teenage pregnancies are something quite new in our evolutionary experience, since hitherto they were a biological impossibility.

Dr Short added that this development poses a dilemma for mankind. The importance, in terms of human happiness, of resolving it correctly can scarcely be exaggerated.

Those who run our society now have to ask themselves a critical question. Are we doing the best we can as respects the sexuality of our adolescents? The evidence suggests that we are very far from doing this. What we offer them is below what they have a moral right to expect. Here a typical young adolescent male might, if he had the courage, make three points to the adults who rule his society.

1. I am in a confused, uncertain physical and emotional condition. Have sympathy with that, and make allowances.

2. I am beautiful, with my slender build, fresh complexion, and vigorous new body. Don't let your envy of that overrule your understanding.

3. Sexually, I am at life's peak. My potency is at its maximum, my feelings at their most intense. Don't impose rules that require that to go to waste.

Of course one or more of these points may *not* apply in a particular case. Some youths in their mid-teens are self-assured and confident. Some are not beautiful and vigorous, but fat, spotty and perpetually tired. Some lack a strong sex drive. Adults must respond to the actual facts of the case, while being aware of all the possibilities.

Typical adolescent females may have a slightly different viewpoint, depending on the extent to which their sexuality has been awakened. Both sexes have the moral right to demand far more of sympathy and freedom, always coupled with responsibility, than our present society is prepared to give them. As we saw in the opening chapter, moral philosophers say society should be organised to make its citizens happy. Our tradition is to coerce and subdue adolescents. Cubs must be licked into shape. Elders must be betters. The enlightened now see that this is a mistake. As William Godwin said: 'The true object of education is the generation of happiness.' We should apply that saying to our entire treatment of the young. In particular we should organise society so as to ensure that youngsters are sexually happy. That would be a reversal of past practice. Hitherto western society has tried in every way to make its young people sexually miserable. By and large it has succeeded.

We have seen earlier in this chapter the freedom and indulgence with which so-called primitive societies treat infant and pubescent sexuality. What should happen at the next stage of growth is sketched by Malinowski in relation to the Trobriand islanders:

As the boy or girl enters upon adolescence the nature of his or her sexual activity becomes more serious. It ceases to be mere child's play and assumes a prominent place among life's interests. What was before an unstable relation culminating in an exchange of erotic manipulation or an immature sexual act becomes now an absorbing passion, and a matter for serious endeavour. An adolescent gets definitely attached to a given person, wishes to possess her, works purposefully towards this goal . . .

This stage in fact differs from the one before in that personal preference has now come into play and with it a tendency towards greater permanence in intrigue. The boy develops a desire to retain the fidelity and exclusive affection of the loved one, at least for a time. But this tendency is not associated with any idea of settling down to one exclusive relationship, nor do adolescents yet begin to think of marriage. A boy or girl wishes to pass through many more experiences; he or she still enjoys the prospect of complete freedom and has no desire to accept obligations . . .

Young people of this age, besides conducting their love affairs more seriously and intensely, widen and give a greater variety to the setting of their amours. Both sexes arrange picnics and excursions and thus their indulgence in intercourse becomes associated with an enjoyment of novel experiences and fine scenery.

Here is sex taking its rightful place alongside all the other interests in an adolescent's developing life. Sexuality is consummated, not with guilt or defiance but with full acceptance and approval from adults. The result is a happy adolescent now, and an adjusted and integrated adult later.

For a confirmation of this result we may turn to another anthropologist, Margaret Mead. In *Coming of Age in Samoa* she examines the question whether adolescence is inevitably a period of turbulence and stress, as we know it in our own society. For many chapters she has outlined the lives of Samoan girls:

watched them change from babies to baby-tenders, learn to make the oven and weave fine mats, forsake the life of the gang to become more active members of the household, defer marriage through as many years of casual love-making as possible, finally marry to settle down to rearing children who will repeat the same cycle.

At this point Margaret Mead asks herself whether, on the evidence she has seen, adolescence is a period of mental and emotional distress for the growing girl as inevitably as teething is a period of misery for the small baby. For Samoan girls the answer has to be an unqualified no. Growing up is easy and simple, sex a natural, pleasurable thing. The only dissenters are the missionaries. Margaret Mead sees their influence as 'the fore-runner of conflict'.

In poignant words Shakespeare reminds us that:

> Golden lads and girls all must
> As chimney-sweepers, come to dust.

He was but one of many poets to glory in youth, and sorrow over its fleeting nature. Indeed we all do that. But why do we not organise our society so that the joys of youth can be tasted to the full?

We should provide golden lads and golden girls with facilities for sexual fulfilment, just as we provide them with facilities for other forms of healthy exercise for body and mind. The use of these facilities must never be compulsory, for compulsion to undesired sexual activity is as bad as denial of desired sexual activity. Each youngster must be allowed to go at his or her own pace.

Under this wise regime ultimate pair-bonding will continue to be the likely experience, though now with much greater prospects of success. Marriage will continue to be the basic institution, but it will not be thought of as socially compulsory. That element will have gone. So too will the insistence that the bond should be life-long, and that those who feel conscientiously obliged to sever it have somehow failed in their journey along life's highway. Such divorces are likely to be few.

For teachers, budding sexuality is a nuisance. For parents it is more. Signs of sexual development are forerunners of a future maturity, when docile little darlings will complete the transition to ungrateful near-adults itching to fly the nest. The sexual growth of children is a reminder to parents that they are ageing. Their generation is passing. Sexual rivalries and tensions in the home are thus a disturbing factor. Where the attempt to wish away adolescent sexuality fails, its manifestations may be met with savage punishment.

The only way to cure this is by changing society's attitudes so that sexual fulfilment in adolescence is accepted; appropriate arrangements being made to accommodate it. This means recognising that the adolescent is a sexual target for other people. Most parents would say that if their teenage son or daughter has to be a sexual target, at least let the one who aims at the target be a person of the youngster's own age-group and of the opposite sex. For an older person to take aim at the teenager raises complex emotions in the parent, among which jealousy may predominate. For a same-sex lover to appear raises deep-rooted fears. For an older person of the same sex to enrol as the child's lover complicates and compounds parental hostility.

Though understandable, these feelings of antagonism cannot be regarded as acceptable from the point of view of the ordering of society. If we believe the adolescent should be sexually free, then he or she must be free to experiment, to make mistakes, to accumulate experience and learn from it – in the sexual field as in others. To argue otherwise is to display once again the all-pervading vice of sex-hate.

Of course the parent should stand ready to advise and warn – and to help pick up the pieces when things go wrong. The parent willingly does this in all other compartments of the son's or daughter's life; why not in this one?

Again, it must be clear that the genuine consent of the teenager is to be obtained before sexual activity takes place. With that consent, the teenager's sexual act with another person (of any age and either sex) should be treated as just as valid and acceptable as if the teenager were fully adult.

Child Abuse

This brings us to that most hated and pathetic figure, the pedophile or child-molester. Can he or she ever serve a socially useful function – for example when the child yearns to be, perhaps on one view needs to be, what the law calls assaulted and everyone else (except the pedophile) calls abused?

The fact that, as we have seen, sexuality is a human component from birth onwards creates moral difficulties that our culture prefers not to confront, or even acknowledge. It is easier and more comfortable to take the position that children are sexless. Then we can say with assurance that any act of a sexual nature committed by an adult with a child, however slight or remote the sexual component, constitutes child abuse and is to be condemned. This is not quite good enough, however.

Though it is a topic frequently discussed in the media, few pause to ask or discuss what child abuse consists of. This is assumed to be known, and to go without saying. To raise the issue at all risks an accusation that one is oneself an abuser, or would like to be. But, as we shall see, some definition is essential.

A treatise on sexual ethics, if it is to be comprehensive, needs to investigate this topic closely. We begin by looking once again at what is meant by the above statement that sexuality is a human component from birth. It can be expanded into five incontrovertible propositions.

1. Babies are born with a complete set of genitalia and other sex-related organs.

2. Children experience sexual sensations, and are capable of genital tumescence and orgasm, from the earliest age.

3. The curiosity of young children applies to the sexual side of life just as much as to other aspects, if not more.

4. The desire of infants to be cuddled and caressed is wholly sensuous, and when gratified may produce sexual sensations in the infant.

5. For its parent to deny or denigrate a child's sexuality by rejecting this aspect of its nature may inflict on the child grave emotional and/or psychological damage.

Since a child is then a sexual creature, what is one to say of the parents and others whose task is to rear it? They too are sexual creatures, and will often need to be in close contact with the child. Inevitably some degree of sexuality must enter into the interchanges.

So does the social concept of child abuse permit any margin for this natural expression of sexuality? Dr Robert Wilkins, a consultant in child and adolescent psychology, noted in a report in the *Independent* (23 May 1990) that for centuries in different cultures mothers have been known to soothe their baby sons by stroking and sucking their penises. Is this child abuse? In Arab cultures the young boy's genitals are a matter of interest, even admiration, on the part of nurses and others. They are displayed, caressed and pampered. Should that be condemned?

Michele Elliot, director of the charity Kidscape, has documented eighty cases involving so-called sexual abuse of children of both sexes by women, including at least one where the 'abuser' was the child's nanny. American studies suggest that the most common forms of abuse perpetrated by women are fondling of a child's genitals, oral sex, digital masturbation and vaginal intercourse. Francesca Corder, a child-care officer, says there is no particular type of woman who indulges in 'abuse'. Those she has known come from all backgrounds and a range of ages. They have 'abused' children of both sexes aged from infancy to fifteen. Some believe it is better for a child to be initiated into a sexual relationship within the family rather than in play with other children, or otherwise in the outside world. They argue that such experiences assist development.

It is a dangerous over-simplification to condemn any sexual activity involving a child on the ground that *ipso facto* it constitutes 'abuse'. Children have sexual needs of their own. A report in the *Independent* (13 October 1990) described a 'child abuse' ring in Australia involving 300 boys aged between seven and seventeen. The ring operated in a highly-organised way, and kept computer records of the boys. No doubt the operation was highly reprehensible, but one item in the report strikes a redeeming note. The computer records included *the sexual preferences of the boys*. A pederast interviewed for Dr Parker Rossman's book *Sexual Experience Between Men and Boys* said:

Kids love sex and become joyous when they are sexually happy. I'm not just rationalizing when I say that ninety per cent of the trouble we have with teenagers is the result of sexual frustrations. When I see a really happy well-adjusted boy I say to myself: 'He's getting some good sex somewhere.'

Rossman comments that 'a society which denies coitus with females to developing boys should not be surprised at their fantasies and substitute experiences'. His study leads one to conclude that many young boys become obsessed by sex simply because society has made it a problem for them. It should be no problem. Subject to the freedom of others, the boy should not merely be allowed but encouraged to act out what he thinks is right, expressing his sexual emotions in the way his heart and body tell him to do. As things are, however, he may well become society's victim, first as a pederast's boy and later as a pederast himself. 'I am sure', says one of Dr Rossman's subjects, 'I would not be a pederast today if society had permitted me to follow my natural inclinations when I was a young teenager.'

Granting the child freedom to develop its sexual capacity carries certain dangers, particularly in relation to adults who are themselves psychological victims of sex-negativism. Some of these find children sensually attractive, and are tempted to take advantage of sexual openness to exploit them as objects for their own gratification. Child sex abuse exists whether or not sex-negation flourishes, but anthropological comparisons suggest that adults who are themselves the victims of a sex-negative upbringing are the most likely to offend in this way.

In any case we need to be wary when using so catch-all a term as child abuse. Precision is required if any statement on this topic is to be meaningful. Ethical considerations vary according to the age of the child, whether the 'abuse' is committed on it by an adult or an older child, whether it takes place within or outside the family (incestuous or non-incestuous), whether it is heterosexual or homosexual, whether or not the child gives apparent consent to it, whether it is physical (e.g. rape or buggery) or psychical (e.g. the showing of pornographic pictures), and whether it is loving, cold or cruel.

The Wolfenden Committee referred, in the passage quoted above, to the 'special vulnerability' of youths between the ages of eighteen and twenty-one to sexual approaches from older men. The truth however is that all adolescents, of either sex, are vulnerable to sexual approaches from their elders, again of either sex. By means of such approaches, the young learn the practicalities of sexual functioning and those who are older can share the beauty and freshness of youth.

This vulnerability increases if there is a special position of dependence, in addition to that induced merely by the age difference. Parents and their children or step-children, teachers and their pupils, ministers of religion and members of their flock, armed forces officers and young recruits, all these and many others furnish examples.

This leads us to two important ethical principles. One is that approaches to the young by male or female homosexuals do not really call for any different treatment from society than is accorded to approaches to the young by male or female heterosexuals. The other is one we have already dealt with at some length, namely that the question of true consent is crucial in all sexual relations between adults and adolescents.

Rational sex morality is based on the consent principle, namely that in general no sexual act done to or with another person is ethically objectionable if done with the true consent of that other person. The reference to *true* consent excludes consent obtained by fraud, trickery or coercion. It also cuts out the case where the person apparently consenting did not understand the nature and quality of the act to which consent was given. This principle, though valid, may be difficult to apply in practice. Here is one more example drawn from life.

Peter is just thirteen. He is an only child, in the course of being well brought up by religious parents. Apart from infantile experiments with age-mates, he has never in his life engaged in sexual activity with another person. He has carried out the usual auto-erotic manipulation of his genitals but has not yet experienced an ejaculation. He is now on the verge of puberty, and his first emission of semen (whether by masturbation, a wet dream, or possibly some form of intercourse) cannot in the nature of things be much longer delayed. Peter has been competently instructed about these possibilities, but has no practical experience of them either in himself or in relation to other boys of his age.

Peter goes to stay with his Uncle Fred who, unknown to the family, is a pederast (a man sexually attracted by pubescent boys). Uncle Fred quickly wins the boy's confidence, being well versed in this art. One morning Uncle Fred enters Peter's bedroom while he is still in bed. He asks if the boy knows about masturbation. Peter hesitatingly says yes, but confides that he has not done it yet. Uncle Fred asks Peter if he would allow him to demonstrate how it is done. He adds that it is time Peter found out at first hand what masturbation is, and the most pleasurable way to do it. Peter is inclined to agree, and does not feel coerced. He gives his consent, and greatly enjoys the resulting first ejaculation of his young life.

This is a typical adolescent–adult sex incident. Family events of this kind, whether homosexual or heterosexual, and involving young people of either sex, occur with great frequency. The question for us is whether in such an incident the youngster's consent is 'true' or not.

Before it happened, Peter did not understand what male orgasm with ejaculation truly amounted to. Reading or being told about it could have communicated only a tiny fraction of the reality of this momentous experience. Does that mean the consent he gave Uncle Fred was unreal? Suppose this incident were repeated each morning for a fortnight, until the end of Peter's stay. By that time Peter would have more understanding of the nature of the act he was consenting to. Quite possibly he would be eagerly seeking its daily repetition. Is his consent by then more 'true'?

To answer these difficult questions we need to look again at that phrase *the nature and quality of the act* as applied to Uncle Fred's acts with Peter.

Each act could be described in one or more of the following ways.

1. It gave Peter a delightful physical sensation, coupled with a feeling of emotional release and fulfilment.

2. It taught Peter how to obtain similar welcome sensations and feelings for himself in the future.

3. It set up a special relation of intimacy between Peter and his uncle.

4. It exploited a child for the private gratification of a perverted adult.

5. It introduced Peter to a practice that is morally wrong and injurous to health.

6. It was a betrayal by Uncle Fred of the trust Peter's parents had placed in him.

7. It was a breach of the religous instruction Peter was receiving in his confirmation classes.

8. It was a serious criminal offence, punishable by imprisonment.

Additional formulations are possible, but these are enough to serve the purpose of the argument. We see that some of the above propositions (1, 2, 3, 7 and 8) are objectively true and incontrovertible, while the truth or falsity of the remainder depends on the moral stance of the observer. By the end of the fortnight, which of them could Peter have truly understood for himself?

We may surmise that he certainly understood 1, 2, and 3. He probably understood 6 and 7. He was possibly aware of 8, depending on what if anything he had been taught about the law. Deciding about 4 and 5 may well have been beyond him, but again this depends on teaching and indoctrination.

The law answers conundrums of this kind by taking the easy way out. Because Peter is under the relevant age of consent, namely twenty-one, his factual agreement to Uncle Fred's acts is deemed to be no agreement at all. In law the acts were indecent assaults, and punishable accordingly. That does not however answer the moral question, for the moralist cannot yield up his function to the legislator.

Provided the legislature fixes on a realistic age of consent, the moralist may be forced to admit it has taken the only practicable course. But we should realise that no one but a fully mature adult is capable of accurately assessing the moral nature and quality of a sexual act. People are ready for sexual acts some years before they reach this degree of maturity, if indeed they ever do reach it.

That time interval, which above we called the maturity gap, represents the nub of the problem. Sex-negaters would like to say that all sexual activity should be forbidden during the maturity gap. They cannot quite say this because our culture permits young people to marry during the whole, or at least the greater part, of this period. To do so is engrained in the institution of compulsory marriage, which thus allows the immature to engage in an important change of status the true nature and quality of which they are as yet unable to grasp.

We now see how illogical the sex-negating position is. It allows the immature to agree to engage in sexual activity within marriage, but forbids them to engage in the much less significant undertaking of sex *without* the responsibilities of marriage. It would make far better sense the other way round.

It is obvious that we have to revise our formulation of the consent principle in the case of youngsters who, being within the maturity gap, are not yet able to grasp the full nature and quality of sexual acts. We might do this by saying that for his or her consent to be morally valid the youngster must understand sufficient of the nature and quality of the act not to *regret* having consented to it when looking back at the incident once full maturity has been reached.

This exposes the nature of the problem, and the full operation of sex-negativism in our society. For the likelihood or otherwise of subsequent regret over an act *of that character*, as opposed to regret over an act of that character *with that person*, will almost entirely depend on how relations and friends, and society generally, view such acts.

Let us return to Peter and Uncle Fred. Suppose (it will be a considerable effort for most people) that these two were living in a society such as ancient Greece or modern Turkey or Holland where acts of that kind are fully accepted. Suppose it is regarded by society as a good thing for an uncle lovingly and considerately to induct his young nephew into the ways of sexual practice. Even suppose it is regarded as an uncle's moral duty to do this.

Immediately the position is transformed. In the light of that imaginary transformation, let us look again at the eight ways in which we found Uncle Fred's act could be described. We need not change the first two (relating to Peter's delightful sensations and feelings). The third (the special relation of intimacy) might remain as a verbal formulation, though it would have a different meaning. Because the act is now socially approved it would not involve the participants in the intimate conspiracy of guilt induced in our present society. The remaining five propositions would no longer apply.

The result is that in our hypothetical society there are no reasons why Peter should feel regret when at maturity he looks back on the acts with Uncle Fred that at the beginning of the maturity gap introduced him to delightful physical and emotional experiences. Under those conditions, Peter's consent to Uncle Fred's acts would have been a true consent.

In the conditions of our own society, however, the position is very different. Looking back on Uncle Fred's actions from say his mid-twenties, Peter will realise to the full the truth of many of our formulations, namely that the acts were indecent, exploitive, treacherous, morally wrong and illegal. He will know how gravely society would condemn them. He may feel that, since he gave at least apparent consent, he would share in that condemnation. Accordingly he would feel guilty, and regret having taken part. In those conditions, Peter's consent to Uncle Fred's acts would *not* have been a true consent.

The same analysis can be applied to any sexual act with an adult apparently agreed to by a youngster within the maturity gap. The reality of that agreement almost entirely depends on how society would view the act if made aware of it. This statement of the case supposes that society has a common opinion on such acts. If different sections of society have different opinions, then the position depends on which section the youngster belongs to.

This process of reasoning demonstrates the fluidity operating in the maturity gap. If we can rid ourselves of the irrational prohibitions induced by sex-negativism we are able to take a fresh look at that area lying between puberty and the end of adolescence. It becomes virgin territory, or perhaps more accurately cleared ground – cleared of cant and hypocrisy. We are then enabled to frame moral and legal rules related to the *true* welfare of youngsters at a critical stage of life's journey.

No time need be wasted in establishing that under present conditions the child abuser (or molester) is regarded by the unthinking, that is majority, sections of our populace with uncomplicated revulsion. Here the social standard is set by burglars, robbers and other sturdy prison inmates. These regard themselves as a distinct cut above child-abusers, and moreover authorised by some jungle law to administer corporal chastisement on them in addition to what the law supplies. As in other areas, many prison officers here abet their charges in malfeasance. The victims may be forced to take refuge in the notorious Rule 43.

The Home Office Rule 43 allows protected solitary confinement to any prisoner whose safety is threatened by fellow prisoners. It is useless for a newly-admitted child-abuser to pretend to a 'respectable' crime such as robbery with violence. The prison grapevine is merciless, and he is sure to be found out.

About two thousand English prisoners are under Rule 43 at any one time. Such a person is known in prison jargon as a 'nonce'. This is a term very near 'nance', an abbreviation for 'nancy boy' or homosexual. Yet nonces are usually pedophiles rather than homosexuals. They may also be victims from a different sphere, such as grasses (informers) or convicted police officers. Claiming the protection of Rule 43 is known as 'going on the rule'. It is fatal to the penitential reputation of the claimant, both among fellow prisoners and warders or 'screws'.

The theory is that prisoners on the rule are removed from all contact with fellow prisoners. The fact is that, often through the collaboration of prison officers, fellow prisoners continue to have their input. Prisoners on the rule are routinely assaulted, spat upon and otherwise insulted. Their food is contaminated by such matter as urine, faeces or squashed cockroaches. Their few possessions, such as family photographs, are mutilated or destroyed. One nonce, who asked the prison barber to make him look presentable before a court appearance, showed before the judge with bald patches on his scalp and a jagged fringe. When he complained he was told he should have bribed the barber with tobacco. The Chief Inspector of Prisons, Judge Stephen Tumim, is on record as saying that the prison service accepts this prejudicial treatment of the weak and inadequate.

Rule 43 is an illustration of how the rule of law breaks down in our society. For a child-molester there is not only the sentence of the court, but the additional sentence of the virtuous majority among the prison population. The first, at Parliament's behest, eschews corporal punishment; not so the second. Her Majesty's judges acquiesce in this state of affairs, and recognise it in their homilies addressed to the molesters they dutifully sentence.

Our task is to go into the matter a little further.

First, we define our terms. What is a 'child' when we are considering child abuse? This is very rarely stated. It would be sensible to take a 'child' in this connection as an infant who has not yet reached puberty, but this the law would not countenance. Nor would the law allow us to take it to be one who is below the sensible, as opposed to the legal, age of sexual consent, which is only the old, pre-1875, nubile year: fourteen for a boy and twelve for a girl. In this, as so often, the law is an ass – which only means those responsible for constantly adjusting it to current social conditions are asses. It needs to be changed.

The true child is one below puberty, whose body is unequipped as yet for sexual engagement. Older young ones whose bodies are so equipped must not complain (nor must their parents) if other people notice it, and act on the information this state of readiness transmits. Nor must more distant busybodies complain on their behalf. That is the natural law of propagation. The human law that governs fleshly congress must be always allied to nature's prime purpose. Sex, unless you are a voyeur, is for doing. We may adopt Peter Righton's statement that the stage of sexual maturation is a crucial emotional and physiological watershed, and thus limit the field of abuse to victims who have not yet reached that stage.

We are talking about the child-molester, so next we must ask: what is sexual molestation? What does it mean to abuse a child in this way?

In the true sense molestation is a breaking in on shrinking innocence. The perverted adult rudely thrusts aside the child's frail unknowing defences. Yet those very defences are set up to confront forces the child must in due time face. So is molestation but a calendar matter? Surely teaching cannot be molestation. Or can it? We are confused about this, yet the rule for youngsters is learning. Indeed that is the rule throughout life.

Two points arise. First, punishment should not be increased just because the convict's act was *sexual*. So to increase it smacks of sex-hate. The essence of a child-molester's offence is the commission of a physical act against the youngster's frail will and body by the thrust of a bigger and stronger force. In the most extreme example, the sex-murder, it is the killing which is important. If the child is raped, it is the frightening and painful violation of the infant body that counts. Sex must not overturn sense, when it comes to judgment and punishment.

The second point is that we must always remember the offender is also a victim. The more gross the offence, the more pathetic the offender-victim. To be a child-abuser is a pitiable thing. The archetypes are the Moors murderers Hindley and Brady. Who would not rather be one of their victims than one of them?

Sometimes an abuser obtains the child's apparent consent to what he or she does. This is the gentle molester, declining to use greater physical strength to obtain by force the warm fleeting intimacy desired. We have seen one example in Mr Whipp, who quietly asked a little girl by the river bank to touch his 'person'. Here is another.

Mr Speck (again a true name) was sitting reading when a girl of eight came up and put her hand on the part of his trousers that concealed the Speck penis. Its owner said nothing, and went on quietly reading. The girl's small hand remained where it was for five minutes. Beneath the serge, the manhood of Mr Speck gradually drew itself toward becoming erect. At last it achieved that condition, so far as the constrictions of the cloth permitted. From beginning to end of this episode, nothing else occurred. The appeal court held that Mr Speck had been properly found guilty of an act of gross indecency towards the little girl. His sentence of imprisonment was upheld.

Such is the operation of sex-denial in our society. Yet children ought not to be altogether separated from the force that brings them into being (as if that were possible anyway). By nature they are equipped with most sensitive antennae in this regard. They also have inbuilt means of protection. Despite the passionate response of his private possession, Mr Speck himself was not moved to take any liberties with the little girl. His control, matching his organ of generation towards the end of this little episode, was iron-hard.

The tale of Mr Speck is reminiscent of upright Eric. He, as we saw earlier in this chapter, believed it right to allow his small daughter to experience her progenitor in the nude, and was embarrassed when she innocently engaged in manual investigation of his interesting male appendage. Suppose that, like Eric, Mr Speck believed it might be harmful to discourage a child's natural curiosity. He may have heard the maxim of the Rene Guyon Society in America: avoid juvenile delinquency and divorce by allowing sex at a very early age. Was is fair to brand him for life with a criminal conviction as a child-molester?

That example shows the question we are engaged in discussing to be far from simple. Here is another.

Charlie is a pedophile. Now in his middle forties, Charlie is shy with women and afraid of men. His libido is fixated on little girls in the age-range five to seven. Only they can arouse in him any sexual feeling, but he is always gentle and loving with his 'victims'. He finds they usually respond warmly to his affectionate approaches. If they do not he at once desists, because he has a horror of forcing young children in the slightest way. We have seen that the concept of infants as sexless is false, and that indeed they have a real sexual need. This need is for play, for the satisfaction of curiosity, for experimentation, and for obtaining warm pleasurable sensations – precursors, one hopes, of adult sexual satisfactions to come.

Why, in a sanely adjusted society, cannot the supplier of these basic needs of infancy be an adult? Who else is so well qualified? As Lars Ullerstam says in a discussion of pedophilia: 'Children have a craving for physical contact, and if they do not get it at home they resort to outsiders.' Is the pedophile perhaps just one more type of social worker? Yet we recognise at once that ours is not a sanely adjusted society. It is a society run by sex-negaters.

We saw in the discussion of how to assess whether a child's consent is 'true' that the attitude of parents and others in authority profoundly affects the answer to this question. Charlie's little 'victims' are placed in an intolerable position. They sense from the sex-negating way in which they are being brought up that their artless frolics with Charlie must be kept a deadly secret. They are forced to go back to their doting parents with guilt in their childish hearts. This is far too heavy a burden to place on the very young, but who is truly responsible?

Parents too have a right to consideration. The burden of rearing the child is their's, and they are entitled to choose its playmates and decide on its activities. The fact that the parents would recoil in horror if made aware of Charlie's affectionate embrace strikes us as decisive. Sad though Charlie's fixation may be for him he is not, we may feel, entitled to a free supply of other people's children. Only a change in parental attitudes could ameliorate his plight.

So we conclude that our present society cannot be expected to allow Charlie the pedophile freely to indulge his propensity. How then should society treat him if he insists on doing so? Let us look at how society treats Charlie now. He is a pariah. If the court sends him to prison (as is most likely) then, no matter how hard Charlie tries to conceal from his fellow inmates the nature of his offence, they are sure to find out and add their own punishment to the state's.

What of the *official* treatment of the pedophile? Apart from, or in addition to, his prison sentence he may be required (or at least persuaded) to undergo medical treatment. The Home Office employ a medical team who experiment with sex-offenders. Sometimes the doctors seek to persuade them to accept treatment more barbarous than the offences for which they are imprisoned.

One of the modern treatments for child-molesters is by hormone drugs such as Androcur and Oestradiol. These reduce the sex-drive. The hormone implant operates by swamping the male hormone testosterone with the female hormone oestrogen. The offender's male sex-drive wilts, and often disappears, for as long as the treatment is continued. There are side-effects. The men find their breasts swelling. Not infrequently this becomes so embarrassing as to require surgical treatment. It is a straightforward operation: the offending breasts are cut off. One should not be too distressed about this however, since a clever technique enables the nipples to be reattached. After healing the scar tissue is not extensive.

Dr O. W. S. Fitzgerald, a psychiatrist at Dartmoor Prison who conducted many such operations, said on his retirement aged seventy:

I left Dartmoor with an easy conscience. I reckon that I have saved dozens of children from sexual assault: this treatment is the only possible answer we have to this social problem.

Another common treatment for sex-offenders against children is aversion therapy. An electric wire is wound round the man's penis so that his sexual response to stimuli can be exactly measured. If he is a pederast, and is shown photographs of naked teenage boys, his penis will enlarge and the faithful electric wire will accurately measure the rapidity and extent of his reaction by means of a pointer on a scale. There is a scientific name for this process. It is known as phallography, and the apparatus it employs is called a plethysmograph. Whenever the response goes beyond a certain figure on the scale an electric shock is administered through a band wrapped round the prisoner's wrist. Not surprisingly, this dampens his enthusiasm. The measurable penile response to naked boys grows less. In time, if enough electric shocks are administered, the prisoner's reaction may vanish. He is then pronounced cured.

In a television programme demonstrating methods of treating pedophiles, a number of prisoners were interviewed by a commentator who struggled to keep the disgust out of his voice. Their faces were kept in shadow throughout. Each freely admitted he had consented to undergo this aversion therapy. Asked why, each said, not unreasonably, that he wanted to stay out of prison and to lead a life as near normal as society would allow. This raises questions. The clever machine that measures penile volume enables it to be shown conclusively that the greatest sexual response manifested by certain adults is to children of a particular age and sex. This response is genuine. It is physiological. It is not something their wicked *minds* perversely lead these brutes to do. On the contrary it is a response which, however society might regret it, some of its citizens make as automatically as the beloved British dog wags its tail.

Society does not not like this response. It is totally unimpressed by the argument that the response is not sought, and is natural. Society imposes the severest punishment on those whose undoubted nature it is to behave in this way. In our present, more merciful, times society has come round to offering to moderate the punishment of its victims if they will agree to undergo such treatment as a course in Androcur (with a guarantee of free surgery if the breasts need removing) or electric shock aversion therapy.

There are other possible approaches. We might ask ourselves whether, if in a future, more enlightened, society some degree of sexual fulfilment were allowed to children (so that they came to expect it and it was openly accepted), the children would really be harmed by gentle pedophiles. It is possible the children might benefit. It might even be that adults who are drawn to children sexually have this attribute because children need such sympathetic attention from loving adults. After all, adults actively help children realise their potential in all other ways.

A further possibility is that adults brought up in such a sex-loving society would lack the pedophiliac impulse anyway. So in time it would die out. Would this also apply to pederasty? Let us go back once again to the Wolfenden Committee.

The retired judge Lord Devlin was invited to give evidence to this committee. He tells us in his book *The Enforcement of Morals* that this was because the Lord Chief Justice, Lord Goddard, considered it desirable that evidence should be given by one judge who thought the law should not be altered and by another who was in favour of reform. Surprisingly (in view of the opinions advanced by him in the book), Lord Devlin elected to testify as the judge in favour of reform. His reforming zeal, and the accuracy of his testimony, can be gauged from the following passage in his book.

I agree with everyone who has written or spoken on the subject that homosexuality is usually a miserable way of life and that it is the duty of society, if it can, to save any youth from being led into it. I think that that duty has to be discharged although it may mean much suffering by incurable perverts who seem unable to resist the corruption of boys.

Now the truth is that this talk of the corruption of boys is nonsense. It has been amply proved that seduction in youth does not cause homosexuality. The Wolfenden Report expressly accepts this. If hereditary and early environmental factors conduce to homosexuality the child will grow up to be a homosexual; otherwise not. No effective 'cure' is possible, and no act of seduction will make any difference. In the nature of things, for youngsters predisposed to homosexuality seduction of this kind is inevitable at some point in their lives. Like speaks to like. The duty of society is not to try to prevent it but to ensure that it is a happy experience.

This leads to two conclusions. One, the homosexual male adult will have had an adolescence during which he should have been entitled to exercise his right to sexual fulfilment in accordance with his true nature, that is with members of his own sex. Two, the heterosexual male adult will have reached that state regardless of the fact that (through the desire to experiment, or the absence of available females) he is likely to have had homosexual experiences in adolescence.

Both conclusions indicate that for males, as indeed for females, consenting homosexual experiences during the maturity gap are to be treated as allowable – even desirable. As we have argued, the legal age of consent should be the time-honoured one of fourteen for boys and twelve for girls, whether the sexual activity is heterosexual or homosexual.

Perhaps we should add a final word about that elegant reference of Lord Devlin's to 'incurable perverts who seem unable to resist the corruption of boys'. It has always been the case that for some men the pubescent youth is a creature apart – a third sex almost. Girls do not possess this distinct intermediate quality during adolescence, but pass direct from childhood to womanhood.

It is largely a visual effect. Visually, the youth proclaims that he is no longer a boy, nor yet a man. Now that we have ceased to crop our young males like convicts, we enable them to display a more girlish aspect if they wish. Often the youth has a tender look, as of one not yet hardened by life. Sometimes he may appear almost angelic; though the reality is likely to tend in the opposite direction. While still partaking of the feminine appeal a woman has for males, the youth already possesses something of the strength and vigour of his future manhood. For a few male beholders, the combination is irresistible.

Why this should be is not known. The most likely explanation is, once again, arrestment of the libido. The boy-lover is fixated at this very point in his own development (the ages from twelve to fifteen are crucial). Some event in his youth, such as a totally unexpected first ejaculation, or some continuing pattern of inadequacy within the stressful period of adolescence, supplies the fix. Thereafter, sex with a youth becomes, in a sense, sex with himself at that fraught age. For men so fixated, life is filled wherever they look with young mirror-images calling forth an urgent response.

As with all adults caught in a position where their most acute sexual feeling is aroused in unsatisfactory contexts, the pederast deserves sympathetic understanding. Not for him the sexual ideal, where passion is equally shared between two equally mature adults. Men with this nature are capable of giving tender love to boys not yet ready for sex with girls within their age-group. Indeed some boys who will end up heterosexuals have a temporary but pressing need for male intimacies of this kind. The pederastically inclined T.C. Worsley illustrated this in recounting an episode in his autobiography *Flannelled Fool*. He refrained from having sex with a thirteen-year-old boy when sharing a bed with the boy at the latter's instigation. Others, wrote Worsley, would have commended him for his moral firmness; his own considered view was that he was guilty rather of moral cowardice for failing to respond to the boy's openly expressed sexual need.

A boy may sense that he can find in this sort of way an outlet other than solitary masturbation. Provided he is not living in a censorious environment he can learn much about life from his older lover without being in any way 'corrupted', as the ancient Greeks and numerous other societies in the world's history have found. If, as in our present society, such actions do meet with opprobrium then benefit to the boy may be outweighed by guilt. Morris Fraser points out in *Perspectives on Paedophilia* that whatever we may think of it, children have to conform to society's major norms as they are – otherwise they will become ill, depressed or delinquent. However enlightened the society, a pederastic relationship must in any case be subject to moral norms, as Parker Rossman stressed in laying down no less than thirteen ethical principles for this purpose in his book *Sexual Experience between Men and Boys*.

It is immoral for a mature man to indulge himself at the expense of a puzzled adolescent who is not at all sure he likes what is going on. This is vividly shown in Mica Neva's essay 'Drawing the Line', published in 1984 in the collection entitled *Generation and Gender*. Phil, a heterosexual fourteen-year-old boy rejected by his parents, is befriended by his school teacher Mr Smith, aged forty-one. Mr Smith overbears the unhappy boy's resistance with alcohol and seduces him. The distraught Phil confides in Mary, a liberated woman of enlightened views. After much agonising, Mary decides she must lodge a complaint on Phil's behalf with his head teacher. Phil approves, but the results are unfortunate. Mary's well-meant action unleashes a bureaucratic nightmare which very nearly engulfs the boy.

On pederasty, as with all the other deviations that turn people into sex-aliens, the last word is this. In a society which had succeeded in eradicating sex-hate the deviation would almost certainly, in due time, vanish with it. Meanwhile we may take comfort from the fact that many boys sexually befriended by men rejoice in the memory even when they reach heterosexual adulthood. The Cornish painter Henry Tuke revelled in portraying naked boys, usually in marine settings. Patrick Leigh Fermor, one of this artist's youthful subjects, in later life addressed to an august male contemporary the following verse:

> You, my dear, are Prime Minister
> He, my dear, is a Duke
> But I in my day, I'm ecstatic to say
> Posed in Polperro for Tuke!

14

The Ethics of Homosexuality

Three Simple Precepts

To be a lifelong gay or lesbian is to be a person *all* of whose orgasms are doomed to take place at some distance removed from the fecund womb. Yet such dismissed persons exist. Irritatingly, they form a distinct segment of society – perhaps as large as one tenth of the whole. That does not save them. Where an individual's psychosexual makeup is such that desired activity can never, of its nature, result in procreation, then society's rejection is total.

Those who do not *feel* this perverse unfecund desire steadfastly decline to admit its validity. What I do not feel, I do not admit can be felt. Those whose dreams, however proper their lives, never feature a crucial act of same-sex love dismiss its possibility. What I do not dream, I do not admit can be dreamt.

Yet dreams are the true revelation of fact. What you dream is what you are.

Also to be considered are those whose homosexuality is partial or intermittent, usually called bisexuals. In her book *Bisexuality: A Study*, Charlotte Wolff maintained that 'bisexuality is the root of human sexuality, and the matrix of all bio-physical reactions, be they passive or active'. This is only to say that we are all sexual creatures before we are heterosexual creatures (if indeed we do end up that way). The wonder of sexuality imbues human creatures from birth. It is the wonder of human creation, and the question of who does what, and with which, and to whom is of lesser importance in the true scheme of things.

The ethics of homosexuality can be stated in three simple precepts.

It is not immoral to have sex with a person of the same gender.

It is immoral to discriminate against a person on the ground that he or she is a homosexual (whether practising or not).

It is not immoral to advance the view that homosexuality is a natural condition rather than a remediable disorder, that homosexuals are to be encouraged to enhance their life-style, or that a good family life is possible for homosexuals and others (including children) associated with them.

The rest of this chapter is devoted to showing how the truth of these precepts has emerged in the teeth of unrelenting opposition.

History of Homophobia

The universal detestation of homosexuals, nowadays known as *homophobia*, is fully documented. As a reminder for those who are familiar with this distressing story, and a glimpse of it for those who are not, let us look at some instances. They are chosen with the object of presenting as many facets as possible of this peculiar form of sex-negativism.

The origin of our society's taboo on homosexuality lies in the teaching of the Judaeo-Christian religion. This makes it strange that so many homosexuals are devoutly attracted to that form of spiritual consolation. They kneel and bow amidst clouds of incense, foolishly believing they are accepted. The Bible puts them right. It abounds with examples of the immemorial hatred of such pathetic sex-aliens. Here are two, drawn at random from each Testament.

If a man also lie with mankind, as he lieth with a woman, both of them have committed an abomination: they shall surely be put to death; their blood shall be upon them. [Leviticus 20:13]

and God gave them up unto vile affections: for even their women did change the natural use into that which is against nature; and likewise also the men, leaving the natural use of the woman, burned in their lust one toward another; men with men working that which is unseemly . . . [Romans 1:26–7]

Much that is good is unseemly. Despite the enlightenment we owe to Freud and other thinkers, such dismal tracts are trotted out still as gospel truth. Yet they are in reality the barbarous product of a distant, ignorant culture. Why do we put up with them? This is a very strange aspect of our educated society.

The Jews of the Old Testament interpreted that sudden destruction of the city of Sodom by an earthquake as God's just punishment for the wilful choice, by a minority of His creatures, of love between members of one sex. So the city's very name passed into the vocabulary of our criminal law. Another term in that vocabulary derives from an edict of the emperor Justinian promulgated in 544 AD. This refers to male homosexuality as abominable and impious conduct, deservedly hated by God. It describes the sexual love of male for male as a disease so base and criminal as not to be committed even by brute beasts. (An irreverent hearer might suppose this only showed such human love to be above and beyond the brute capacity of the said beasts.)

During the dark and medieval ages in Europe, the church punished homosexual acts by excommunication, torture, mutilation of the flesh and ecclesiastical murder. In the last case, death was usually by burning at the hand of the civil power. The church shrank from doing itself what it wanted done. Its comforting rites were withheld from the condemned. I decline to console you if you insist on disagreeing with me.

Burial of the sad corpse of an interrupted same-sex lover was required by ecclesiastical doctrine to be in unconsecrated ground, usually situated at a crossroads. The belief that a sacramental gesture might penetrate to every last worm-tunnelled inch of soil gladly admitted this exception. Consolations of holy penance were not opened to homosexuals. At the crossroads of life they had deliberately taken the wrong turning. There let them lie.

Many Christian kings of England have loved members of their own sex. Their rank has not saved them, and their punishment has invariably been severe. William II, son of the Conqueror, was a practising homosexual. 'Into the details of the private life of Rufus', wrote a Victorian professor of history in a happy phrase, 'it is well not to grope too narrowly.' Commenting on William's death in a supposed hunting accident suspected of being engineered by enemies of his way of erotic fulfilment, the professor observed that none wept for Rufus but the mercenaries who received his pay, and the baser partners of his foul vices. A contemporary monk, Ordericus, alleged that at William's court the effeminate predominated, and revelled without restraint. In this regal setting (the monk added) filthy catamites, fit only to perish in the flames, abandoned themselves to the foulest practices of Sodom. How different from the home life of our own dear Queen!

Another regal invert, Edward II, perished at Berkeley Castle in a horrible manner devised by his murderers as an entirely appropriate punishment for his life long vices. An iron bar was raised to white heat in a brazier and then thrust into the king's living rectum. His shrieks, we are told by a chronicler of the time, were heard throughout Berkeley Castle and beyond, forcing awestruck listeners to drop to their knees and pray to the God of mercy for the safe passage of his soul.

Edward's successors as practising homosexuals on the throne of England included James I and William III. Before leaving the topic of English kings we may mention a telling remark attributed to George V. On being told that one of his courtiers was homosexual, the king said: 'I thought men like that shot themselves.'

Naturally enough, the Christian kings and queens of England who chanced not to be homosexual made up in the virulence of their antagonism for the unfortunate minority who were. Parliamentarians followed suit. In 1631 the Earl of Castlehaven was tried by his parliamentary peers for homosexual offences. The report in the State Trials series shows no mercy being displayed by the House of Lords. The indictment tabled against the noble earl accused him of that detestable and abominable sodomitical sin *buggery* (not to be named among Christians). This the earl, it was alleged, devilishly, feloniously and contrary to nature did commit and perpetrate to the great displeasure of almighty God and disgrace of all mankind. (Such language was commonly used in criminal indictments up to the present century.) Their lordships had no hesitation in returning a verdict of guilty, spurred on by the Attorney General's warning not to give the least mitigation to so abominable a sin. It had, he pointed out, 'brought such plagues after it as we may see in Genesis xviii, Leviticus xviii, Judges xix, Romans i'. For his crimes against nature the Earl of Castlehaven was duly beheaded on Tower Hill.

Modern Examples of Homophobia

Today, though the methods have changed, ecclesiastical censure goes on unabated. Here are two recent examples.

Peter Elers, the kindly vicar of Thaxted in Essex, believed after prayer that if two Christian homosexuals earnestly wished to form a lasting union, and for that seek the Church's blessing, they should receive it. His superiors disagreed. One autumn day Elers performed in his ancient church a ceremony he called 'The Blessing of Lovers'. The subjects were two lesbian couples, each member wishing to commemorate by a religious symbol her desire for life-long linking. In a formal statement, this novel service was condemned by not one but two neighbouring ordinaries. The Lord Bishop of Chelmsford was the first to emit the ecclesiastical censure. His words were, with equal formality, echoed by the nearby Lord Bishop of Colchester. Both prelates earnestly explained that Elers's initiative fell foul of the beliefs and practices of the Church of England. They urged those unfortunates who found themselves to be of a homosexual inclination to understand and respect the sincerity and depth of conviction of that vast majority in holy Church who believe such acts to be sinful.

The second recent example of clerical censure comes from the preface to *Crockford*. This authoritative directory of the Church of England recounted the salutary experience of a Welsh Bishop. Having been caught in a regrettable posture with a consenting adult male, the bishop had meekly yielded up his crozier. Basing his text on this sad case, the anonymous preface-writer delivered a homily on how gay Christians should conduct themselves, and how society should treat them. Society, said he, should accept only those who are that way inclined by a deep-rooted and ineradicable nature, and then only if they are always discreet. It is unthinkable that people capable of true marriage should be turned away from its joys and social duties by corrupting influences. Christians should never be so charitable to deviants as to cease to oppose the flaunting of homosexual behaviour. For the clergy themselves, the only alternatives are faithful marriage or faithful chastity. This must mean that no priest with homosexual leanings should ever feel free to give any physical expression to those urges: the self-control must be iron. The word 'homosexual', continued the preface-writer, has many meanings. Most of them are still, to the general public, corrupt. Pastoral priests who do not obey the moral line liberate the power of evil. The writer concluded with a sage observation: the recent formation of a Gay Christian Movement 'seems to us worse than foolish'.

Foolish it may indeed be for homosexuals to cling to Christianity in the knowledge of the gross cruelties it has inflicted on their kind. As we have seen, even the highest have not been exempt.

Like their brethren in the Church, parliamentarians in both Houses have continued to the present day to show hostility to homosexuals. In the House of Lords in 1964 Earl Winterton said:

I am convinced that the majority of British people agree with me that few things lower the moral fibre and injure the physique of a nation more than tolerated and widespread homosexualism. I hope and believe that we have not reached that point and never shall. If we did – and here I think I should have the support of everyone in this House – we should lose our influence for good in the world, and we should go the way of other countries in the past, who were once great but became decadent through corrosive and corrupting immorality.

These remarks echo those uttered a few years before in the lower House by the then Home secretary, Maxwell Fyfe. This Scottish worthy had a sallow complexion and a slow, ponderous manner. A then-current rhyme ran:

> The nearest thing to death in life
> Is David Patrick Maxwell Fyfe.

Maxwell Fyfe, later ennobled as Viscount Kilmuir, described homosexuals as exhibitionists and proselytisers, and a danger to others – especially the young. He assured the House of Commons (the year was 1953) that so long as he held office he would do his best to prevent them being such a danger. Sir David would not have approved of the Act, passed shortly after his death, which in 1967 mitigated the penalties long inflicted by the criminal law on homosexuals.

The Labouchère Amendment

The 1967 Act undid some (but by no means all) the harm caused by the most devastating blow struck against male homosexuals in modern times. The perpetrator was Henry Labouchère MP, editor of the journal *Truth*. Instigated by W. T. Stead, wayward editor of the *Pall Mall Gazette*, Labouchère persuaded Parliament to insert in the Criminal Law Amendment Bill (later passed as the Act of 1885) the notorious section eleven, known thereafter as the Labouchère amendment. This rendered criminal a type of conduct which had never previously been punishable by the criminal law, namely what it called any act of *gross indecency between males*. The age of the participants was immaterial, and so was the place where the act was committed. This infamous measure brought police officers into the bedrooms even of the most respectable, discreet and faithful male lovers of males (lesbians were unaffected). What to such men was an expression and fulfilment of their mutual devotion became overnight, in the ugly phrase devised by Labouchère, an act of 'gross indecency'.

The Labouchère amendment was added to a government Bill concerned with other matters entirely. It was based on no enquiry or research, and was proffered without any proof that it was needed. All Labouchère said in moving it was that it was acceptable to the government and he therefore did not think it necessary to offer an explanation. The amendment was not debated in the House, though another MP proposed to double the proposed maximum penalty of twelve months' imprisonment. This improvement Mr Labouchère gratefully accepted. His clause (so amended) was added to the bill. During the ensuing eighty-two years, until it was repealed by the 1967 Act (though not completely), section eleven became known as the blackmailer's charter. It inflicted misery on thousands of men whose only offence was to act in accordance with the unwished nature of their sexuality.

In 1921 an attempt was made to introduce a clause extending section eleven to lesbians. In the debate on this clause, which was introduced by a backbench MP, there were many sex-negating speeches. In one of them, Sir Ernest Wild (an Old Baily judge) announced that he had the authority of a great nerve specialist for saying that no week passed but some unfortunate girl did not confess to the specialist that she owed the breakdown of her nerves to the fact that she had been tampered with by a member of her own sex. Sir Ernest added:

We do not want to pollute the House with details of these abominations. I have consulted many asylum doctors and they assure me that the asylums are largely peopled by nymphomaniacs and people who indulge in this vice.

In an unusual triumph of liberalism, the House of Lords had the sense to reject the clause. Lord Desart, a former Director of Public Prosecutions, rhetorically asked, anent lesbianism: 'How many people does one suppose really are so vile, so unbalanced, so neurotic, so decadent, as to do this?' The Lord Chancellor cautioned that if the clause were passed there would be a risk that innocent women, forced by the housing shortage to share a bedroom with one of their own sex, might be tainted by 'this noxious and horrible suspicion'.

A parliamentarian of the present time who should be mentioned in this context is the late Montgomery Hyde. Whether or not Hyde was homosexual himself one does not know. This sort of doubt is typical. Hyde clearly took great interest in the subject of male homosexuality. Equally clearly, he sympathised with those who are subject to this condition. Yet he felt obliged by the culture, perhaps coerced, to write as if he occupied the standpoint of the censorious majority. In his useful survey *The Other Love*, published in 1970, Hyde discussed a book by a Victorian homosexual, John Addington Symonds. Of Symonds's account of conditions prevailing at Harrow when he was a pupil there, Hyde said:

In Symonds's time the moral state of Harrow school indeed left much to be desired. Every boy of good looks had a female nickname, and a boy who yielded his person to an older lover was known as the elder lad's 'bitch'. According to Symonds, the talk in the dormitories and studies was of the grossest character, with repulsive scenes of onanism, mutual masturbation and obscene orgies of naked boys in bed together. There was no refinement, just animal lust, and it was little wonder that what he saw filled the young Symonds with disgust and loathing.

What a wealth of sex-hate lurks in that passage! If written by one with positive views of sexuality it would have been expressed quite differently. Setting the scene in its true context of Victorian prudery and hypocrisy, the writer would have remarked on the cruelty of that age in separating adolescent boys from their female contemporaries, on the heartlessness of leaving them in ignorance of what was happening to their bodies, on the wickedness of deceiving them grossly as to the consequences of masturbation. The positive writer would have sympathised with the boys' attempts to find sexual fulfilment in such unpromising conditions. Far from sneering at 'animal lust', he would have made allowances for the biological fact that in the youthful male the peak of sexual feeling comes earlier in time than the development of refinement and sensibility.

It can only have been because he was reared in a sex-negating society that the young Symonds found it necessary to say that he was filled with 'disgust and loathing' at the spectacles in question. It is unlikely that he truly was, if one may judge from his later writings.

The Judges' View

After kings and parliamentarians we pass, in this review of establishment haters of homosexuality, to the judges. These shape our laws, and bear a heavy responsibility for their oppressive nature. The choice is wide, and we must be brief. We pass over the innumerable judges who approvingly imposed sentence of death on homosexuals convicted before them until capital punishment for buggery was abolished in 1861. These judges could plead, after all, that they were enforcing the provisions of the law in accordance with the prejudices of the populace and their judicial oath. A random illustration of these prejudices is the treatment accorded to organisers of a homosexual club at the White Swan in Vere Street (off Oxford Street) in the early years of the nineteenth century. Sentenced to stand in the Haymarket pillory, the malefactors were conveyed from the Old Bailey in a cart. A contemporary account quoted in Montgomery Hyde's book *The Other Love* says:

it is impossible for language to convey an adequate idea of the universal expression of execration, which accompanied these monsters on their journey . . . Before the cart reached Temple Bar, the wretches were so thickly covered with mud that a vestige of the human figure was barely discernible. They were chained, and placed in such a manner that they could not lie down in the cart, and could only hide and shelter their heads from the storm by stooping. This, however, could afford but little protection. Some of them were cut in the head with brickbats and bled profusely. The streets, as they passed, resounded with the universal shouts and execrations of the populace.

The most notorious homosexual trials of the nineteenth century were those concerning Oscar Wilde, the first prominent victim of the Labouchère amendment. In one of these trials Mr Justice Wills began his summing up by telling the jury that the horrible nature of the charges ('gross indecency' with willing males above the age of consent, already experienced homosexuals) was such that 'I would rather try the most shocking murder case that it has ever fallen to my lot to try.'

Another trial concerning Oscar Wilde was that of Pemberton Billing for criminal libel in 1918. Billing was editor of a journal called *Vigilante*, the organ of an association dedicated to ensuring sexual purity in public life. He wrote an editorial revealing the existence of a 'black book' compiled by German agents and alleged to contain the names of 47,000 prominent Britons guilty of homosexual practices. The editorial said that the black book reproduced instructions 'regarding the propagation of evils which all decent men thought had perished in Sodom and Lesbos'. The *Vigilante* also published, under the heading *The Cult of the Clitoris*, an attack on the staging of Oscar Wilde's play *Salome* for members of a private club. Pemberton Billing alleged that most members of the club were included in the German 'black book', and insinuated that Maud Allan, who played the part of Salome, was herself a lesbian. Miss Allan brought proceedings for criminal libel against Pemberton Billing. The judge at the trial was Mr Justice Darling, whose biography by Sir Derek Walker-Smith makes it very clear that he disapproved strongly of Oscar Wilde and all his works. On *Salome* he told the jury that 'if it were a Lesbian play, it would be to the public advantage that it should be denounced'. Wilde he referred to as a 'great beast'. The jury found against Miss Allan and Pemberton Billing was acquitted, to the acclamation of a large crowd that had gathered outside the Old Bailey.

Recent examples of judicial prejudice include a case cited by Montgomery Hyde in which four teenage youths were convicted of 'gross indecency' with each other in private. The judge brushed aside the argument that in fixing twenty-one as the age of consent the 1967 Act had not intended to penalise youths below that age, but only older men who exploited them. While conceding that two of the youths had developed some strength of character and had prospects of establishing normal relationships with young women, the judge ordered the other two to be sent to Borstal. He felt they needed protection against the misery life would have in store for them if they failed to develop natural sexual impulses and desires. That misery is entirely inflicted by sex-negaters opposed to the widespread homosexual impulse. As Montgomery Hyde points out, it is difficult to see how the judge could have imagined that what he considered the necessary heterosexual desires would be fostered in the all-male environment of a Borstal.

The last English judge we will mention is Lord Devlin. In his 1965 book *The Enforcement of Morals* Devlin attempts to justify our society's adverse treatment of homosexuality. This rejection of a persistent human feeling is based, he argues, on deeply-rooted disgust. The presence of such disgust is, Devlin thinks, a good indication that the bounds of toleration are being reached. Not everything is to be tolerated. No society can do without intolerance, indignation and disgust. Moreover there can be no doubt that the total number of those who on balance disapprove of homosexuality is far greater than the number who view it with active disgust or indignation. Devlin goes on:

There is . . . a general abhorrence of homosexuality. We should ask ourselves in the first instance whether, looking at it calmly and dispassionately, we regard it as a vice so abominable that its mere presence is an offence. If that is the genuine feeling of the society in which we live, I do not see how society can be denied the right to eradicate it.

This is morality based on fallacy, namely that it is in the power of society to 'eradicate' homosexuality. The slightest knowledge of social history, in any country and at any period, reveals the core presence of a not insignificant proportion of homosexuals of both sexes. Devlin's respectable morality is the suspect morality, as indeed he confesses, of mass intolerance. It is the majority coercing the minority – always the sign of danger in a supposedly democratic human grouping.

What happens when the respectable majority successfully claim to feel painful, righteous disgust at the fulfilment by the despised minority of their innate, though unusual, sexuality? Simple. The majority can justly don the robe of morality as they set about their persecution. When judges prance in this dismal cloak they dismally betray their high office.

Things are no better among the United States judiciary. In his book *The Gay World* Dr Martin Hoffman shows that American judges are uneasy when called on to deal with cases involving 'abnormal' sexual behaviour. One judge, required to decide whether fellatio was, within the meaning of the Criminal Code, a crime against nature, lamented in his written judgment that his consideration of the point made it necessary 'to soil the pages of our reports with a subject so loathsome and disgusting'.

Judges in England are promoted from the ranks of senior barristers, and it is no surprise to find the Bar sharing to the full the judicial prejudice against gay love. Tony Palmer's book *The Trials of Oz* tells how in the notorious prosecution of the Australian magazine *Oz* for obscenity in 1971 the following interchange took place at the Old Bailey between Richard Neville, the editor of *Oz*, and Mr Leary, counsel for the prosecution, about a special homosexual number of the magazine:

Leary (reading from the magazine): 'Multiracial male kisses. Only 25 left of most controversial *Oz* ever. Selling in Earl's Court for £3 each. Save £2.5s. Rush your 15s now'. The suggestion there being that it was at a premium in the Earl's Court area. That's right, isn't it?
Neville: Yes, that is the suggestion.
Leary: The Earl's Court area being famous – or infamous, whichever way you like to put it – for male perverts.
Neville: It's famous for Australians.
Leary: Yes, but it wasn't the Australians that were rushing to buy the homosexual *Oz* because they were Australians, was it?
Neville: I always thought homosexuals were mainly centred around Piccadilly. But if you insist Earl's Court, then I'll settle for Earl's Court.
Leary: Isn't it Piccadilly for drugs, Earl's Court for queers?

Other Professions

Other professions adopt the same attitude as the law. Doctors, with notable exceptions, are in general no less sex-negating in this respect than in others. Montgomery Hyde cites one medical man who, discussing in a professional journal the Kinsey finding that more than a third of all males enjoy at least one homosexual experience to the point of orgasm after the onset of adolescence, remarked: 'It would be a cleaner world if Kinsey had stuck to his rats.' Dr Charlotte Wolff in *Love Between Women* gives the case history of a lesbian girl who decided to leave home to take up residence with her lover.

When I told my parents I was going, they made an appointment for me to see the doctor, so that he could give me a letter for a psychiatrist. He had been my doctor for about ten years, and I liked him. I thought I might be able to talk to him so that he could explain things to my parents, but when I went to see him he was horrible. He told me I was stupid and that the psychiatrist would soon 'knock all this nonsense' out of me.

Later in her account this girl relates poignantly that she feels wary and tense when in the company of heterosexuals. As she does not look obviously homosexual, sooner or later someone (not realising what she is) makes a sneering remark about 'pansies' or 'homos'. She thinks: 'That's me they're talking about – that's how they'd feel about me if they knew'.

This unthinking dismissal is one of the hardest crosses homosexuals of either sex have to bear. With race prejudice or sex discrimination the position is different. It is usually obvious that a person is black or female. A racist or sexist remark will not be made in their presence except with positive intent to wound. Most homosexuals are not obviously so, and the heterosexual majority blithely assume they are not present when bandying their prejudicial remarks.

We conclude this survey of establishment prejudice against homo-sexuals with a few samples from professions other than law and medicine. We have done no more than scratch the surface. As Bertie Wooster was wont to say, slice him where you will, a hell-hound is always a hell-hound. The remark aptly describes the total infection of society by the sentiment called homophobia.

The Victorian historican Lecky, writing of ancient Greece, felt it necessary to describe the accepted cult of boy love or pederasty. He confessed that he found the task an eminently unpleasant one, forcing him to explore what he called 'that lower abyss of unnatural love, which was the deepest and strongest taint of Greek civilisation'. Lecky conjectured that pederasty arose from the influence of public games. Accustoming men to the contemplation of absolutely nude male figures, these games, he said, awoke an unnatural passion, totally remote from all modern feelings.

Another Victorian, the poet Swinburne, was himself a sex-alien – but of a different kind. He was a masochist, spending a great deal of money on prostitutes who flogged him in the manner he fervently desired. In illustration of the fact that a sex-alien of a particular kind may be just as hard as a sex-citizen on a deviation he does not share, we have noted above Swinburne's elegant description of Greek boy love as 'besmeared by blood and dung by criminal lunacy'. How reminiscent that is of Samuel Butler's rebuke to the man who:

> Compounds for sins he is inclined to
> By damning those he has no mind to.

The last profession we look at in this discussion of the establishment dismissal of homosexuality is journalism. We have seen what the journalist Pemberton Billing thought about *Salome*. Here is James Douglas on Radclyffe Hall's lesbian classic *The Well of Loneliness*. This novel was written in a demure style, including no word or description that would have brought even a faint blush to the cheek of Douglas's maiden aunt. Yet the *Sunday Express* columnist of the time (true to the form of that newspaper since) described it as a seductive and insidious piece of special pleading, designed to display perverted decadence as a martyrdom inflicted upon those cast out by a cruel society. Douglas further attacked the book as flinging a veil of sentiment over the depravity of lesbians, and as suggesting that their 'self-made debasement' is unavoidable. With monstrous exaggeration, he ended by saying that rather than put the book in the hands of a healthy boy or girl he would sooner present them with a phial of prussic acid. More recent examples of journalistic prejudice are furnished by two contrasting yet essentially similar writers: Barbara Cartland and a staff member of *The Times*, Ronald Butt.

Mr Butt, before whose name one itches to write 'the egregious', is on record as saying that *any* sexual activity by young teenagers, even with one another, is 'beastliness'. Miss Cartland breezily dismisses homosexuality as a sin against God and mankind, adding:

The homosexual is an unhappy misfit in society and therefore extremely dangerous. He grudges the normality and happiness of those around him. His aim is to destroy everything that is decent and conventional.

In contrast to that, we may end with another columnist from *The Times*, Bernard Levin. He is writing about a scandalous incident concerning a Remembrance Day parade in 1978. The mayor of Wolverhampton had thought it right to accede to a request by the local branch of the Campaign for Homosexual Equality that they should be allowed to join the parade and lay a wreath in memory of homosexual service personnel of both sexes who died in the two world wars. The leader of their contingent was a regular army captain, a holder of the Military Cross. The homosexual captain had been three times mentioned in dispatches, and twice wounded. When the brave mayor's decision was made known all the other ex-service organisations in the town announced that they would boycott the parade in protest. They did so. A statement informed the world that they did not want to be associated with homosexuals in any way.

Bernard Levin devoted his column on 14 November 1978 to this incident. He asked why homosexuals who died in war should be commemorated *as homosexuals* at all. Answering his own question, he pointed out that homosexuals in our armed forces were often treated in a humiliating or cruel manner. Ironically, the Nazis against whom our service personnel fought were particularly vicious to German homosexuals, forcing them to wear a degrading badge equivalent to the yellow star imposed upon Jews and sending many to concentration camps for no other reason. It was appropriate therefore for English homosexuals to make a collective commemoration on our Remembrance Day. Continuing in his characteristic style, Levin said:

I presume that the town's heterosexual ex-servicemen did not, during the war, refuse to fight alongside homosexuals; I presume they would not claim that homosexuals fought less bravely; I take it they do not insist that heterosexuals who fell in battle should be segregated in death by being put in a different part of the cemeteries in which the war-dead lie. I presume, in short, that they would not say that homosexuals who died in the two world wars should not be remembered, and saluted, on Remembrance Day. Then why do they object to such commemoration being undertaken by the homosexuals of Wolverhampton?

In further answer, Levin said that the sad truth was that the boycott had nothing to do with the war-dead or their commemoration. It was based on an ancient and lamentable revulsion against homosexuals which was inexcusable *not* because no homosexual can help being a homosexual, though that, he said, is indeed true, but because 'there is nothing more "wrong" with being a homosexual than in being a Jew or for that matter being one-legged'.

Though the establishment, and society generally, is still riddled with sex-hate against homosexuals, there are many honourable exceptions. Bernard Levin is one of them. Others were those parliamentarians who in 1967 secured the passage of a reforming Act.

The Sexual Offences Act of 1967

The hatred for homosexuals is one of the most virulent and widespread forms of sex-negation. Although it has lessened slightly in recent years, this dire emotion is still widespread and intense. In the face of that it is perhaps surprising that any formal withdrawal of society's condemnation should have proved possible. Nevertheless in 1967, as a move in what are today widely condemned as 'the permissive sixties', Parliament was persuaded to go some way in this liberating direction. Based on the Wolfenden Report of ten years earlier, the Sexual Offences Act confines its relief to homosexuals who are (and whose sexual predilections therefore are) of more than twenty-one years' standing. In a previous chapter we considered the injustice of that age-limit. Now we look at other features that merit the comment that, despite its general relaxation of an oppressive law, the 1967 Act nevertheless reeks of homophobia.

First, the statutory relief does not apply if more than two persons are present. This is directed at 'orgies', and catches group sex not only where confined to males (or to females), but where both males and females are present. For example if two married couples share a bedroom and in the course of group sexual activity, even of a predominantly heterosexual kind, there is any contact between the two men the Act is infringed. This consequence was unintended. The true object was to deny homosexuals a freedom which the law has never withheld from heterosexuals.

Next, the statutory relief does not apply to a gay suffering from severe mental abnormality. A man disabled in this way can never fulfil his sexual impulses in the manner that is natural to him without being branded by the law as a criminal.

Thirdly, the Act extends to male *patients* the long-standing legal prohibition against the male *staff* of hospitals having sex with inmates. This prohibition does not apply the other way round. There is nothing in the criminal law preventing female staff having sex with male (or female) patients.

Fourthly, the relief conferred by the 1967 Act does not apply to members of the armed forces or merchant seamen. This exception is designed to safeguard service discipline, yet it is an obvious injustice not to treat sexual irregularities by service personnel in the same way whether they are heterosexual or homosexual in nature. This is particularly so where, as in modern units, the sexes are mixed.

Lastly, the 1967 Act increases the maximum penalty for sex by a man over twenty-one with a youth under that age from two years' imprisonment to five. Two years was the period fixed by the infamous Labouchère amendment for conduct which previously had not been a crime at all. For a 'relieving' modern Act to increase this penalty by 150 per cent is a staggering piece of oppression.

The 1967 Act contains other extensions of the criminal law in a way antagonistic to homosexuals, for example by applying anti-prostitution law to male brothels, and living on the earnings of male prostitutes. Furthermore the judges have gone out of their way to make it clear that the Act in no way renders homosexuality 'respectable'. In the eye of the judge-made common law of England any homosexual act remains, as it has always been, immoral, indecent and depraved.

Few passionate mortals are troubled, in the midst of their passion, by what the law proscribes. Social attitudes are more potent. For gays and lesbians both factors combine to rob their transports of the base of legitimacy that comes from general acceptance. Guilty excitement springing from consciousness of condemnation is a poor substitute. Sexual ethics is about acceptance, and a true ethical system must embrace all legitimate claims on it.

Clause 28

That homophobia is alive and well and living in Britain was confirmed by the enactment in 1988 of the notorious clause 28, which is in two parts.

(1) A local authority shall not intentionally promote homosexuality or publish material with the intention of promoting homosexuality.
(2) A local authority shall not promote the teaching in any maintained school of the acceptability of homosexuality as a pretended family relationship.

The first thing to be said about this is that it is illiterate. Homosexuality is defined by the *OED* as 'sexual propensity for one's own sex'. Sexual propensities are inherent, and cannot be promoted or otherwise by a statutory corporation such as a local authority. Nor can a propensity be a relationship (pretended or otherwise). The draftsman has fallen into illiteracy through the requirement of being mealy-mouthed. He was not allowed to say what he really meant.

Clause 28 was intended to rectify such supposed outrages as the 1983 publication by the Gay Men's Press of a child's picture-book, translated from the Danish of Susanne Bösche, entitled *Jenny lives with Eric and Martin* and its circulation among children by some local authorities. The furore to which this gave rise compelled the publishers to abbreviate their trade name for the future to the anonymous 'GMP'.

Jenny is five, and lives in a little house in Denmark with two young gay men Eric and Martin, the latter being her father. Her mother Karen lives nearby and 'often comes to visit'. The book, which is profusely illustrated by photographs and drawings, shows how the three spend a typical weekend at home. Nearly all the numerous illustrations depict the protagonists fully clothed, but there are five exceptional photographs which gave rise to heated objections. These show Jenny playing in the young men's bedroom early on the Saturday morning, just as any child of that age might play in its parents' bedroom. It is obvious the men are naked, though no genitals are shown. Jenny is fully dressed throughout. What caused scandal was the fact that little Jenny would have been able freely to see the men's genitals, since obviously no attempt was being made to hide them. One of these photographs even shows Jenny sitting with her back against her naked father's genital area while he lies on his side. In another, Eric lies with his arm round Martin.

The book shows typical family weekend situations. It is Eric's birthday, and Jenny helps decorate the cake. Karen comes with a present for Eric. The four hold a birthday tea in the back garden. Afterwards Jenny helps dig some potatoes for Karen to take home with her. Next day Jenny helps Eric mend a puncture in his bicycle tyre. Then she goes to her room and does a jigsaw puzzle. Later the two men bicker together, and make up with a kiss. It is all quiet and uneventful, which if anything increased the public sense of outrage. It suggests to the child reader that a little girl could lead her life in a gay household no differently, and no less happily, than in an ordinary heterosexual household. This accounted for that particularly vicious condemnation in clause 28 of a 'pretended family relationship'.

Jenny lives with Eric and Martin is undoubtedly gay propaganda. It asserts, both expressly and implicitly, the right of gays to be treated as ordinary people. At one point Eric draws for Jenny a story in chalk on the stone garden-path. In the first picture two men are shown, with speech balloons issuing from their mouths. One, who is clean shaven, says 'I love you Fred!', the other, who has a beard and is presumably older, says 'I love you too Bill!'. In the next picture Bill says 'Why don't we move in together?', to which Fred agrees. Under the heading 'Here comes grumpy Mrs Jones' the third picture shows a neighbour saying 'Oh no! What is this! Two men cannot live together! It is very wrong!' The two men reply that they really love each other, so why is it wrong? 'It just is!' ripostes grumpy Mrs Jones, adding that her husband would never kiss another man. However Mr Jones then comes along and says that is not correct, adding:

When I was young I was in love with a man and we lived together. But then I met you and it was you I loved most. And you loved me most. So we moved in together and got married.

Not unreasonably, Mrs Jones asks why her husband has not given her this piece of information before, adding 'I always thought it was wrong when two men love each other.' Mr Jones replies: 'There are so many things people think are wrong. It can never be wrong to live with someone you are fond of.' The scene ends with Fred and Bill going off hand in hand while Mrs Jones (no longer grumpy) waves an apology.

On the book's last page little Jenny asks Eric a question as she puts on her pyjamas.

'Can you and Dad have babies?'
'No, you silly. We can love each other in the same ways as anyone else, but we can't have babies. Only women and men can have babies together. You know that.'
'So it is lucky you have me.'

Now the harsh fact is that some marriages and other pair-bonds do break up, after children have been born, because one partner proves to be bisexual and goes off to live with someone of the same sex. This is regrettable, but it happens. The children need to be told that it has happened. Moreover they need to make a relationship with the homosexual couple, even if they do not actually live with them. Sometimes it may be necessary that they should live with them. These facts need to be taught to young children, not only when such a thing actually happens to them but generally. This is called education. The publishers of *Jenny lives with Eric and Martin* would have such things taught to children uncensoriously, even approvingly. The clause 28 establishment would have them taught censoriously, or better still not taught at all. That shows the enduring nature of the homophobic gulf.

It is a gulf that needs bridging.

15

The Ethics of Prostitution

Erotic Samaritans?

The harlot or whore has aroused scorn throughout the ages. The reasons are complex, but one of them clearly is that this useful creature takes money in exchange for the service rendered. It is held to be contemptible to trade one's body for hard cash, yet that is what everyone does in the labour market. All paid work, whether of hand or brain, is accomplished by the human body through one means or another. Why should commercial use of the sex anatomy be set apart as unforgivable?

This book rejects that lame-brained conclusion, and instead advances the following precepts.

It is not immoral to make or receive payment for a sexual service willingly rendered. The duty of sex-fulfilment may require a person to pay for what they need rather than go without.

The duty of sex-respect requires that prostitutes of both sexes should be well treated and never degraded. They serve a useful and valid social purpose.

To justify these precepts requires an examination of the reasons why sex for money is frowned on, and why we do not think of prostitutes rather as erotic Samaritans. This term, suggested by Lars Ullerstam, takes the parable of the Samaritan who did not pass by on the other side to its ultimate conclusion. Why should sexual need be regarded as unworthy to rank alongside other needs as calling for a charitable response? If we read the parable (Luke 10:25–37) we see that the point of the story is that the Samaritan looked at the man who had been mugged and *had compassion on him*. He paid the innkeeper to *take care of him*. For that he was praised as a good neighbour. The parable was said to have been used by Christ to illustrate the precept that we should love our neighbour as ourself. Sexuality is a ready means of indicating love, if only we could see it that way instead of constantly putting it down.

Hatred of Sex for Money

It was two o'clock in the morning at the Intercontinental Hotel in London's Park Lane. The soft door-chime woke Herbert from a sleep he needed. Throughout the next day he had both to chair a conference at the hotel and be the principal speaker. Herbert, a conscientious man, had made plans to stay overnight so as to be fresh and on the spot next morning.

If Joan had been attractive, Herbert might have reacted differently.

'Thought you might want a bit of company.' So Joan remarked when Herbert reluctantly opened his bedroom door. To her, Herbert looked almost as irritated as he felt.

'We could have a chat . . .'

Herbert shook his head, and shut the door. Later he lay in bed thinking of the rebuff he had administered, no doubt all in the day's (or night's) work to her. He felt ashamed.

Our society needs a radically different attitude to most aspects of sexuality, not least prostitution. The basic negativism that causes people to put down almost any manifestation of sexual desire runs riot over prostitutes. We start with language. They are harlots or whores, strumpets or tarts. Any new evasion is quickly besmirched. What do respectable people nowadays think of a 'call-girl' or 'model'?

The Oxford dictionary tells us that prostitution is 'the offering of the body to indiscriminate lewdness for hire, whoredom, harlotry, devotion to an unworthy use, degradation, debasement, corruption'. What drives men to prostitution is filthy lust, unbridled animal instinct. The English language is rich and varied. It has no shortage of abusive terms for what society hates and fears.

At bottom, what society hates and fears is sexuality itself. In this it changes little with the passing of time. As always, the origins are in the Bible. Chapter 23 of Deuteronomy says that there shall be no whore of the daughters of Israel, adding: 'thou shalt not bring the hire of a whore, or the price of a dog, into the House of the Lord'. Equating whores and dogs in this way was significant, for the Jews abominated dogs. Hunting in packs and covered in sores, these animals were regarded always with disgust and loathing.

A campaign was launched by the Moral Union in 1884 to combat the assumption that indulgence is a necessity of man and argue instead 'the better and true belief' that vice is capable of diminution. The Union opposed state regulation of prostitution because 'the path of evil is made more easy to our sons, and to the whole of the youth of England: in as much as a moral restraint is withdrawn the moment the State recognises, and provides convenience for the practice of, a vice which it thereby declares to be necessary and venial'.

This attitude is echoed in our own day by the Wolfenden Committee on Prostitution. Abraham Flexner's 1914 study *Prostitution in Europe* stated: 'A very large constituent in what has been called the irresistible demand of natural instinct is nothing but suggestion and stimulation associated with alcohol, late hours and sensuous amusement.' Citing this remark, the committee report that many men, especially younger ones, who now avail themselves of the services of prostitutes would be less inclined to do so if these services were less readily and obviously available. The fact that the youth of England (and their elders too) need and should reasonably expect adequate services for sexual fulfilment is ignored.

The Wolfenden Committee were realists, however, and did not seek to *ban* prostitution. It has never been a crime in England (unlike in the United States). Nevertheless they took a low view of current manifestations of sexuality.

At the present time, entertainments of a suggestive character, dubious advertisements, the sale of pornographic literature, contraceptives and 'aphrodisiac' drugs (sometimes all in one shop), and the sale of alcoholic liquor in premises frequented by prostitutes, all sustain the trade, and in turn themselves profit by it. With most of the evils the law attempts to deal so far as it can without unduly trespassing on the liberty of the individual; and, as in the case of prostitution itself, it is to educative measures rather than to amendment of the law that society must look for a remedy.

As if one can be 'educated' out of sexual desire!

In a recommendation followed by Parliament, the Wolfenden Committee argued that while prostitutes should be removed from the streets ('brushed under the carpet', sneered some moralists) their basic activity should not be made criminal, since 'criminal law is not concerned with private morals'. In *The Enforcement of Morals* Lord Devlin said: 'All sexual immorality involves the exploitation of human weaknesses.' He added that the prostitute exploits the lust of her customer, and the customer the moral weakness of the prostitute. We detect a rich seam of sex-negating words and attitudes there too.

With these attitudes around we cannot be surprised at the outcry that arose over Martin Cumella, the Birmingham social worker dismissed for placing a boy who was at the time in local authority care with a female prostitute over an Easter weekend. This woman was the only adult the boy had any kind of relationship with (and not a sexual relationship either). She was married and lived with her husband. But she was a working prostitute, and that was enough to condemn Mr Cumella for thinking his difficult charge might be happy living with her for a day or two.

In her 1975 study *The Prostitution Papers* Kate Millet presents a picture, based on taped interviews, what it is really like to be a prostitute. She gives a stark warning to those who write about this topic.

Everything I've read on prostitution, even the way it is discussed, pisses me off: the statistical approach of sociological texts, the cheerful rationalisations of popular accounts, the romanticised versions of literature. One is slowly forced to realise that for centuries a tremendous moral and sociological confusion has surrounded the entire issue, a phenomenon one can account for only by considering the monumental sexual repression within our culture, and its steady inability, after having created both the prostitute and her plight, to recognize her as human in any meaningful sense at all.

Kate Millet first approached the topic of prostitution as an ardent worker in the women's movement, wanting to liberate her enslaved sisters. They weren't having any. They liked the money and they were hooked on the life (some were hooked on hard drugs too). Kate Millett retired baffled. That is a measure of the difficulty society has got into over the question of sex for payment.

Any weapon will do to beat sex with, and the sex-negaters seize upon money. Pornography is bad because people make money out of it. Contraceptives are bad because businessmen trade in them. And prostitution is bad because the whore sells her body. Even the whores think this. Listen to one of Kate Millett's women:

But as soon as somebody paid me any money, that changed the women thing; made it the other thing. I see them as something else when they give me money. They might be the nicest people in the world, but it's something else, and you don't mix business with pleasure. I make a tremendous division between love and money. I don't get sexually turned on by somebody who gives me money . . . I would think it would be humiliating to buy a person, to *have* to offer somebody money. I felt the poor guy's gotta buy it; I felt sorry for him.

Now this thing about sex and money is illogical moonshine. As we saw in chapter 7, our society functions on the basis that people's demands will be met by commercial enterprise. Our food, our houses, our cars are provided in this way. Churches are put up by builders who make profit from it. Priests wear vestments on which some company is declaring a dividened. In a 1951 study of American sex offenders Albert Ellis pointed out that anyone who cooks, or makes shoes, or writes books, or does any kind of activity which he or she does not enjoy, but for which he or she receives socio-economic gains in return, is in no different position from the prostitute.

If sex itself is alleged to be the difference then, as Benjamin and Masters pointed out in their 1964 book *Prostitution and Morality*, one needs to remember that anyone who gives half-hearted sexual favours from a position of economic dependence can be equated to the prostitute:

It is scarcely practical . . . to label as a prostitute the wife who is not erotically responsive to her husband, but who copulates with him in order to safeguard her status and security, or even for outright payment. Neither are we always inclined to designate the mistress or kept-woman a prostitute; or the starlet climbing to name-in-lights fulfilment by way of the proverbial casting couch; or the waitress whose continued employment is contingent upon her 'being nice' to the boss. The motives of such women may be quite other than sexual, and even crassly commercial, but they are not customarily, especially not by the police, regarded as being prostitutes.

The anthropologist Desmond Morris puts it in a similar way in *The Human Zoo*:

Commercial sex of any kind also figures as an important function in many marriage situations, where a one-sided pair-bond exists: one partner simply provides a copulatory service for the other in exchange for money and shelter. The provider who has developed a true pair-bond has to accept a mock one in return. The woman (or man) who marries for money is, of course, functioning as a prostitute. The only difference is that whereas she, or he, receives indirect payment, the ordinary prostitute has to operate on a pay-as-you-lay basis. But whether the system is organised on long-term or short-term contracts, the function of the sexual behaviour involved is fundamentally the same.

A milder form of sex-for-material-gain is executed by stripteasers, dance hostesses, beauty queens, club girls, dancers, models and many actresses. For payment, they provide ritualised performances of the earlier stages of the sexual sequence, but (in their official capacities) stop short of copulation itself. Compensating for the incompleteness of their sexual patterns, they frequently exaggerate and elaborate the preliminaries that they offer. Their sexual postures and movements, their sexual personalities and anatomy, all tend to become magnified in an attempt to make up for the strict limitations of the sexual service they provide.

A final point on money is that, as Lars Ullerstam points out in *The Erotic Minorities*, some individuals find it absolutely necessary to have certain elements in the sexual prelude, for example that they are allowed to pay for intercourse!

Prostitution as a Social Service

Lars Ullerstam's customer is one type of person who definitely benefits from the service of prostitutes. Let's look at some others. John, a young businessman, went on a long business trip which took him to Bangkok, among other places in the Far East. He had never visited a prostitute before, but feeling rather jaded he decided to refresh himself at one of Bangkok's modern bath-houses. He was invited to look through a window and make his choice from among the kimono-clad girls, which he did. John's chosen girl smiled prettily and led him to a cubicle containing a massage table, a steam cabinet and a low sink. She gestured John to sit on the massage table, and then proceeded to undress him. She took off everything except his underpants and John got worried about his growing erection. (He was far from certain what to expect, and after all it might really be just a bath-house.) The girl did not pull John's pants down for him but delicately indicated, with a slim finger inside the elastic waistband, that he was to do this for himself. As he did so she turned and opened the door of the steam cabinet.

Twenty minutes steaming dampened John's ardour, and he emerged in a respectable state of detumescence. The next step was a hosing down in the low sink. The water was cold and John found it stimulating. As the girl dried him with a towel he decided to stop worrying about his erection. If she didn't like it she could turn him out. In fact she ignored it, dried him all over, and motioned him to lie on his back on the massage table. While she busied herself at a small shelf with her back to him John wondered what happened next. Would she take her clothes off? The massage table seemed too narrow for anything but massage. Should he initiate anything? He tried a smile as the girl returned, and she smiled coolly back. She began rubbing his leg with oil. He suddenly realised that above his head another girl, who had evidently just finished with her own client in the next cubicle, was looking over the partition and watching with interest. John, now rather enjoying the experience of being an exhibitionist indulging in indecent exposure, relaxed and encouraged his erection to let itself go. The feel of the girl's fingers sweeping up and down his leg assisted this.

John realised that very delicately the fingers were beginning to touch his genitals, always instantly retreating so that if he had wished to object the matter could have proceeded from there as an ordinary massage. He decided not to object, but to lie passive and see what would happen.

The touches grew more confident. When she found that definite strokes on his penis brought no resistance or objection from John the girl suddenly went back to the shelf and fetched a small towel, which she laid on his stomach. Then she got a bottle of different oil and skilfully and gently massaged the stiff penis, the scrotum and inner thighs. The girl above continued to watch absorbed. The orgasm when it came was full and satisfying, the body massage that followed utterly relaxing. As the slender girl completed the treatment in the tradiitonal Thai way by walking up and down along his back in her bare feet, expertly manipulating the vertebrae, John felt more completely rested and refreshed than he had done for a long time. What had happened was an act of filthy lewdness, in which the prostitute had exploited John's unbridled lust while in return he had exploited her economic need and, as Lord Devlin would have it, her moral weakness. Or is that really quite the right analysis?

Theodoor Van de Velde, in his pioneering book *Ideal Marriage*, wrote of 'too much joy untasted which could enhance life's worth'. Sexuality is a potent source of joy, but our official culture insists that sexual joy be restricted to what must necessarily be a limited portion of anyone's life and no portion at all of many lives: marriage. Even some more liberated people seek to confine sex to a loving, settled relationship. Well and good if you have one, but many do not and some cannot. The old, the ugly, the shy, the handicapped, have sexual needs just as urgent as their more fortunate fellows. What of those who are in the armed forces, or in longstay hospitals, prisons or other institutions? As we have seen, society is happy to deny them sexual outlets. Again, what of the young?

Adolescent boys have the strongest sexual urges of any, but are forbidden by moralists to give their urges any outlet. The film *Souffle à Coeur* shows with great sympathy a mother comforting her fourteen-year-old son. After beginning with trembling nervousness his first act of sexual intercourse, the boy was cruelly interrupted by older brothers bursting into the prostitute's bedroom and pulling him naked from the bed. Later, the mother takes him to her own bedroom and lovingly guides him to his first completed act – with her. She subdues her usual sound objection to incest out of overflowing maternal sympathy, thus (or so the film argues) preventing a life-long trauma.

R. E. L. Masters describes how as a fifteen-year-old attending a private school in the American middle west he went often to a local brothel with thirty or forty of his classmates. He became the 'pet' and confidant of the young madam, and learned much – as well as enjoying regular sexual intercourse with a variety of girls. In *Prostitution and Morality* Benjamin and Masters mention another brothel, this time in Missouri.

Marie's bawdy-house was somewhat unusual in that it did a thriving business among young students from a private school in the vicinity. These students for the most part ranged in ages from 15 to 17 years. She was especially interested in the youngest of her clients, many of whom were without any previous sexual experience when they first came to her establishment; and all of the girls who worked for her were given strict instructions not to patronize, ridicule, or in any way embarrass the youths. Sexual activity other than coitus was prohibited so far as these boys were concerned – although Marie herself occasionally violated the prohibition against oral intercourse with 'pupils' of long standing who initiated the activity. She, also, for the benefit of her few favourites (and of herself?), kept a basin of cold water beside the bed and would 'cool them off' when she sensed the ejaculation was near, in order to prolong the coition.

She impressed her girls with the necessity of making a boy's first sexual experiences good ones, and instructed them as to the damage that might be done if a youth were humiliated or disgusted by the intercourse. She had a good understanding of such matters, part of it intuitive and part of it based on her reading, and her instructions to her girls might have served as a model for any other establishment catering to a similarly youthful clientele.

That is sex education in its most enlightened form. It is also its most effective form: ordinary sex education is inevitably at second hand. Sex learning, like all practical learning, involves much trial and error. Advocates of compulsory marriage require this to be carried out entirely by two people after a legitimating ceremony. Yet, as Michael Schofield points out in his book *Promiscuity*, if a person has sex with different people he or she draws on all their experiences and passes on what has been learnt to the next partner. In this way sexual technique is developed, and one learns how to give pleasure to others (including the eventual spouse, if marriage does ensue). Schofield aptly calls seduction a private lesson in an advanced course of sex education. How much more effective the lesson can be when administered professionally by a trained erotic Samaritan!

Marie's lessons were far more than practical sex education. They gave happiness and fulfilment. That is what youth has a right to enjoy, but gratuitously and unnecessarily society forbids it. We buttress our prohibition with every weapon we can command: criminal law, family organisation, social attitudes, cruel words. Society is sex-hating, and we are society.

The position is not negative everywhere, even today. Enlightened countries such as Holland sometimes show they can handle sex for money as a respectable social service. In 1985 the American publisher Frank Torey interviewed a youth working in a 'boy bordello' in Amsterdam and found his life had its redeeming features, as the following extract shows.

I don't mind going to bed with older men, because I know when I get old I'll do the same thing, and there'll be a boy helping me – I hope! I don't care if they're young or old, so long as they're clean. And then if they're just gentle and don't treat you as if you're some kind of robot or something, that they see you as a human being. Because there are some people who say you have to do this and you have to do that because I'm paying you. We're not just sex machines.

What's nice is when someone's never had it before. This one man was leaving and he said, 'It was a feast, it was wonderful, I loved it, thank you so much.' And then I felt fine. I said to myself 'You've done a good job.' I like working with people. I worked in a clothes shop in Germany once. I like to help people, and see them looking good . . .'

Others who benefit from the service of prostitutes are sex-aliens who like their sex kinky, people so brilliantly portrayed in Genet's *The Balcony*. This is one more group savagely condemned by our social attitudes, often for fixations they have no power to do anything about. A compassionate society would understand that people with psychological problems have more need, not less, of adequate sexual outlets. Our society, with its stern motto *conform or abstain*, coldly turns its back on them.

So far we have been talking of joy untasted. There is in addition much positive *harm* caused by our sex-negating laws and attitudes over prostitution. They encourage profiteering, they encourage corruption, they encourage disease, they encourage intimidation, and they encourage blackmail. Worst of all, they damage the prostitute. Here are some examples of the application to prostitution of what in chapter 7 we dubbed the sleaze syndrome.

Profiteering. The Wolfenden Committee found the average rent of flats let to prostitutes was *fifteen times* the controlled rent. If the activities of prostitutes were regarded as normal they would pay normal rents.

Corruption. Kate Millett found that the Vice Squad in New York (known as the pussy brigade) function in the same manner as pimps, since their 'fat earnings' are acquired through methods of coercive protection. Benjamin and Masters report the American madam as generalising that all persons in authority are 'on the take'. They add:

That the policeman who arrests her, the attorney who prosecutes her, and the judge who sentences her, may have been customers or quite possibly 'freeloaders' at her establishment does not seem to her altogether compatible with her notion of justice.

Disease. Control of sexually transmitted disease depends on open reporting. If the circumstances in which disease is contracted are regarded as illicit, control becomes more difficult. Furthermore a regulated system of prostitution permits frequent medical inspection of prostitutes, thus saving their clients from infection.

Intimidation. The outlawing of prostitution leads to the pimp system by which men live off prostitutes and force them (very often by brutal violence) to hand over their earnings.

Blackmail. Those engaging in any illicit activity are inevitably exposed to blackmail, and this is a common hazard with the clients of prostitutes.

Damage to the prostitute. Regarded as outcasts, prostitutes are victims of pimps, madams, police and crooks. Their self-esteem is destroyed. Often they take to drugs. Kate Millett summed it up in writing of one of the women she interviewed, named 'J' in the book:

But I know what the years in sexual prostitution have cost J too, can see it in the damage in her eyes, at moments their blueness as dead as glass. It is no melodious or pietistic bullshit to see prostitution as a particular crime against her humanity. Her suffering comes back when I remember our long halting talks, both her admissions and her denials, the long pained hours, her sensitive face. How much it has all hurt her: the years of silence and repression, the secrecy so deep it forbade her even to remember for some years after. And at the time how deeply the pain required that she utterly anaesthetise herself, passive even to the point of numbness. Now too bitter to love anyone. That's a lot to pay even for $800 a week; it's a still more terrible sum for which to hold men liable.

Prostitution and the Future

So there are the problems. What are the solutions? We cannot change things overnight. For one thing we are all too deeply conditioned. We can't change ourselves, or not very much. That means we can't change society – yet. There is one helpful principle in such difficult situations. First work out exactly how things ought to be, how you want them to become. Only when you have done that can you see how to travel the difficult road that leads to your objective. So let's look into the future, when the inhabitants of this planet are not conditioned in the sex-negating way we are today. How would we like them to be?

First they should openly, honestly and fully accept that sexuality is a fundamental part of human nature. None of it is a matter for shame, only for sympathy and understanding. The future world will have full control over conception and venereal disease. Even the new scourge of Aids will be conquered in time. That's important. It means the twin obstacles to free sexuality are at last on the way to being removed. We are almost at that point now. Freed of bigotry and prejudice we could be there. Few would dispute the truth of that on conception. On sexually transmissible diseases we need only quote Dr Derek Llewellyn-Jones in his book *Sex and VD*.

Eight years ago, speaking in Denver, Colorado, one American authority, Dr Knox, said wryly that if as much money was put into venereal disease as went into research for poliomyelitis, which neither cripples nor kills as many people, a vaccine could be found in a few years. Nothing has been done yet. The public has a right to ask why.

Since that was written Aids has come along, and spending budgets have been transformed. Still not enough is done however.

Second, the future inhabitants of our planet will need to realise that sex is complex. It shakes our foundations, and it is not simple. It needs study and practice. It is both a science and an art. It has to be accepted as a life-long concomitant of our existence. There must be no nonsense about confining it to marriage. Here we come up against Christianity once more. There is a difference between Christ and Christianity. Christ was the one who said to those who jeered at the woman taken in adultery: 'Let him who is without sin cast the first stone.'

Third, our future inhabitants should organise life so that the fulfilment of sexual needs – at all ages and in all conditions – is openly recognised as a primary concern of society. Words like 'prostitute' will be forgotten, and the word 'lust' will be regarded as too obscene to be mentioned. Some people will feel a vocation to serve sexual needs just as people today feel a vocation to be lawyers or accountants or surveyors. The sex-servers will need to study both the theory and the practice of their chosen profession. Maybe they will pass out with diplomas from a professional body: perhaps the Royal Institution of Chartered Courtesans. Unlike today they will pay their taxes because they will be accepted, respected members of society.

That's all very well, you say, but what do we do right now? Fight to overcome your conditioning. Don't allow anyone to rob you of your right to sexual fulfilment (with due regard, it goes without saying, to the freedom of others). Fight to put sex in its proper place.

Think back to that night at the Intercontinental Hotel. Women should not need to stalk the corridors of West End hotels in the dead of night hoping for an economic reward. Guests in need of sleep should not be rudely awakened. This is how it might be in the distant future . . .

A Visit from an Erotic Samaritan

Peter arrived at the Central Hotel in the early afternoon, tired out. He slept, waking about five. He rang room service and ordered tea. While waiting he took a shower. Stepping out, he found himself with an enormous erection. He felt rested, refreshed – and randy. The buzzer sounded. Peter put on a bathrobe, then let in the waiter with the tea-ray. As the man put the tray down on a side table, Peter spoke.

'I feel like a little love-making. I take it that . . .'

'Oh yes, Sir. We have a number of qualified Sex Assistants on ready call. Just dial 69.'

'Thanks' said Peter. 'I can see the Central Hotel maintains its standards.'

'Would you be wanting a young lady Sir, or perhaps you would prefer to have . . .'

'A lady would be fine . . .'

'Then if I may, I would advise you to ask for Emily Foster. She only started work here last week, but we're getting very good reports of her.'

After dressing and finishing his tea Peter rang room service and asked for Emily Foster. She was free and came up straight away. At first Peter was disappointed at her appearance. She was not pretty, and her face had strong character. But clearly she was well trained. Like a hetera or Geisha girl, she knew how to charm a man without surrendering one iota of her own individuality. With the feeling of a pleasurable night to come, Peter set about making himself agreeable to Emily. He wanted her to like him. He was determined to make their brief intimate acquaintance satisfying for them both. It worried him not at all that her services would appear next morning as an item on his bill. She had to live, as he had to live. He knew that, and he accepted it.

Emily accepted it too. Her training had included instruction not only in the psychology of her future clients, but in her own. Unlike Kate Millett's subjects, she was not in a state of mental conflict. She did not feel guilty or degraded, because no one treated her occupation as materially different from that of any other career girl. She did not have a pimp, and lived in a flat for which she paid a normal rent. She belonged to a union, which protected her from exploitation. She had regular working hours.

Emily too set out to enjoy her evening with Peter. As with any other paid worker, job satisfaction was important to her.

16
The Ethics of Pornography

The word 'pornography' derives from the Greek *pornographos*, meaning writing which is about the sexual lives and ways of prostitutes or their clients. In this book it is given the wider and morally neutral meaning of *sexually explicit* material for reading, viewing or hearing. The complex questions surrounding the ethics of pornography concern not only the nature of the material but its creation, dissemination and reception. We look first at the categories into which it can be divided.

Categories of Pornography

By definition all pornographic material is *revealing*, in that it exposes to view or hearing, whether accurately or not, some aspect of human sexuality. Some such material, for example a medical textbook on genitourinary surgery, is good in itself (even though it may be used for an evil purpose such as the seduction of a child). Other such material, for example a 'snuff' movie which depicts the actual murder of a prostitute in obscene circumstances, is evil in itself (even though it may be used for a good purpose such as exhibition to a trial jury). A third kind of material, such as the straightforward sculpture of a nude human figure in full anatomical detail, is morally neutral (even though it might be used for either a bad or a good purpose). All this serves to remind us that given material may or may not be good in itself or evil in itself. Even if it is evil in itself, it may be put to good use on a particular occasion. When judging pornographic material we must always consider for whom it was intended and into whose hands it has fallen, or might fall.

In search of a reliable test of its morality we may divide pornographic material into five categories, as the following suggested precept indicates:

Pornographic, that is explicitly sexual, material can be divided into: (1) non-erotic material; (2) perverted or debased material, (3) stimulative or erotic material, (4) educational and artistic material, and (5) political or destabilising material. Given material may fall into more than one of these categories.

Though there is relatively little to be said about the first two categories, because there can scarcely be any disagreement as to the morally neutral nature of material in the first or the immoral nature of material in the second, the remaining three categories raise issues so complex that each needs a chapter to itself (see chapters 17 to 19). Before considering the five categories in detail we need to set the scene with an examination of the general nature of, and objections to, pornographic material. This comes next. Then there follow brief discussions of the first two categories. The chapter concludes with a reminder that *opposition* to pornography can in certain respects also be immoral.

The Nature of Pornographic Material

Material alleged to be pornographic may be written, visual or aural. It may be static (a book, statue or picture) or moving (a play, film or television production). It may be experienced in private (reading or watching a video at home) or in public (attending a cinema or theatre). It may or may not employ human models or actors. If it does, the representation may or may not be 'live'. The Defence of Literature and the Arts Society (DLAS) pointed out, in evidence to the 1979 Williams Committee on Obscenity and Film Censorship prepared by the present author, that there are differences in the essential nature of pornographic material. The DLAS subdivided it with the following headings and examples:

fact (e.g. a medical description of the human anatomy);

opinion (e.g. that sexual experience benefits young people);

factual scene (e.g. a photograph of a copulating couple);

imaginative realism (e.g. a novel not far removed from real life);

distorted fantasy (e.g. an extravagant essay which few could mistake for truth).

The DLAS suggested that it is much harder to justify censoring facts and factual scenes than wantonly cruel essays in fantasy, and that censorship of opinion raises different issues from censorship of fact. Their evidence pointed out that it is necessary to draw a distinction between the way pornographic material comes into existence and what is done with it. A particular item, however subjectively 'obscene', may in an objective sense be neutral. What matters from the viewpoint of social control is how it came into existence ('creation') and what is done with it ('dissemination'). Although dissemination may be harmless (if confined, say, to experienced adults), creation may be objectionable (for example where young children are used as models). In other cases the reverse may apply. If perverted material produced by using experienced models, who are thereby unaffected, is shown to unaware young people the latter may suffer.

Various recipients view pornographic material differently. Sex-aliens are turned on by whatever stimulus corresponds to their fixation, and may be repelled by stimuli which do not. It is a general finding that sexually explicit material of a type different to what one finds stimulating oneself arouses irrational feelings of antagonism, which may help to explain the feminist opposition to pornography articulated by writers such as Andrea Dworkin. Nudity and voyeurism seem to have little appeal for most women. In *Sex, Violence and the Media* (1978), the psychologists H. J. Eysenck and D. K. B. Nias report that males are far more permissive than females and less prudish. Again this may help to explain the views of feminists. Within either gender, personality differences affect the appeal of specific erotic matter. Eysenck and Nias group these differences under three headings: extroversion/introversion, neuroticism, and a degree of predisposition to psychosis (the 'P factor').

Again, there is likely to be a difference in the motivation of the creators of pornography (who may seek to serve a need, influence opinion or merely make money) and the receivers. A receiver's purpose may be to open the mind or please the senses: he or she may seek instruction or stimulation. Another possibility is that the receiver is undergoing medical treatment such as aversion therapy or the correction of a sexual dysfunction. The effect of pornography greatly depends on the previous experience of the receiver. The Weber-Fechner law shows the difficulty of attempts at moral judgement. It states that the perception of visual, tactile, auditory and other stimuli is a function of the amount of similar stimulation experienced on previous occasions. A single candle lit in a room where 100 candles burn will be unperceived; in a totally dark room it will transform the scene. However stringent the social controls imposed, we may be sure that no one will pass through life without some exposure to pornography. It is likely to begin in schooldays.

The Moral Framework

In 1971 a Roman Catholic hereditary peer, the Earl of Longford, set himself (in his own words) to improve the morals of the nation. Lord Longford was sure that sexually explicit material is harmful. He considered it a manifest evil, and therefore appointed his personal committee 'To see what means of tackling the problem of Pornography would command general support'. Longford persuaded fifty-two people, some well known, to sit on his committee. These included an archbishop, three bishops, seven other clergymen, a former chairman of the Trades Union Congress and a judge. Arts and the media were represented by Kingsley Amis, his then wife Elizabeth Jane Howard, Frank Gillard, Malcolm Muggeridge, Cliff Richard, Jimmy Savile and a sprinkling of journalists. Others included persons described as 'a housewife' and 'a student'. A former head of the Parliamentary Counsel Office in Whitehall, Sir Noël Hutton, volunteered to draft a Bill for the committee free of charge, and did so. No atheists or agnostics were included.

Before setting up his committee, Longford informed the House of Lords that 'pornography has increased, is increasing and ought to be diminished'. His committee found themselves in agreement with this. They proposed severe tightening up of the criminal law. The legal test of obscenity which then applied and still applies (requiring proof beyond reasonable doubt that the material tends to deprave and corrupt those likely to see it) should, they said, give way to the test of 'outrage to contemporary standards of decency or humanity accepted by the public at large'. The 'public good' defence, introduced by Parliament in 1959 to save works of genuine merit, should be abolished (this defence is discussed in chapter 18). Penalties on conviction should be severely increased. Kingsley Amis and his then wife propounded a further device. There should be an X-category of books and magazines for children under eighteen. A board of censors should decide which articles fell within this category and mark them with an X accordingly. It would be a criminal offence to contravene the censorship system thus imposed. Though tempted, the committee as a whole did not fall for that one.

For religious believers like Lord Longford, anything that contravenes the doctrines of their religion is necessarily 'immoral'. That pornography contravenes the doctrines of the Judaeo-Christian religion cannot be denied. The Longford Report contains a contribution from Malcolm Muggeridge (like St Augustine a late convert to the paths of sanctity). Mr Muggeridge cites St Paul's dictum that 'to be carnally minded is death, but to be spiritually minded is life and peace'. This, adds Mr Muggeridge, leaves no room for pornography 'in any form or guise'. Fine rhetoric, but carnal means 'of the flesh', and flesh is what we happen to be made of. All of us are carnally minded from the day we start breathing till the day we stop. That's because we are carnally made. Included among our carnal organs are those suited to sexual purposes.

Still, we sex-lovers must be careful. We mustn't fall into the error the sex-negaters make, of shouting abuse when they can think of no arguments. Like the Manchester theologian who in a letter to *The Times* talked of 'fatuous loss of judgement'. Or Dr Court from New Zealand, whose opponents are said by him to 'mouth' their arguments. Or Mr David Holbrook, who equates those who defend pornography with the Nazis who believed 'evil things may be done with a clear conscience'. Or Mrs Mary Whitehouse, who in her 1977 book *Whatever Happened to Sex?* accuses her opponents of 'blather', denies them any integrity or idealism, and dismisses them as cruel and predatory humbugs. On this passionate subject, dispassionate argument serves best.

If those who attack pornography need to be clear what they mean by it, they also need to declare their moral frame of reference. Here we come to another truth basic to any discussion of sex towards the end of the twentieth century. It is no use saying a thing is 'immoral' unless you make clear the moral code you are applying. No longer is there general agreement on what the moral code is. No longer is Christianity the groundwork for moral debate in the west – on sex least of all. For many now think the historic Christian doctrine of sex is positively *immoral* – indeed evil.

Today, whether we like it or not, we live in a plural society. Not only is it multiracial, but it is multireligious. It also embraces many who believe in no religion. Where agreement on moral systems is lacking there can be no agreement on whether any apect of sex is 'immoral'. How can a person who holds that sexual activity outside marriage is sinful agree on the morality of stimulative or erotic pornography with a person who holds that every human being has a right to sexual fulfilment throughout life? How can a supporter of the traditional family system agree on the morality of a piece of anti-family political pornography with a person who believes communes offer the best form of social grouping? The answer is they can't. Such people must be allowed to debate the issues in an atmosphere of tolerance, and if necessary agree to differ.

While it is possible to say that some acts, like murder, robbery or fraud, are 'immoral' without defining the moral frame of reference, it is not nowadays possible to say it truthfully about sexual practices freely entered into. Since there is no longer a common sexual morality, society should not behave as if there were. Its laws should only restrict and punish acts which contravene the generally accepted code, such as rape. To those who say 'no' to all forms of pornography because it is 'immoral', the response must be: check your frame of reference, check the clarity of your thinking and, if you still adhere to your opinion, respect the right of others to disagree. (Of course, some moral frames of reference leave no room for private judgment or the opinions of others: a Catholic cannot argue when a book appears on the *Index Librorum Prohibitorum*.)

We now examine one by one six objections frequently levelled against the creation, dissemination or reception of pornographic material. These are that it is harmful to those who experience it, that it enables people to make money out of sex, that it causes crime, that it wrongs models and actors, that it harms children, and that it undermines society.

'Pornography Harms People'

If, as current British law does, we define pornography as material likely to deprave and corrupt (that is, cause psychological damage) then the question of potential harm is answered by the definition itself. The only further inquiry needed is whether the material under examination falls within the terms of the definition. The fact that juries have convicted, and magistrates have made destruction orders, by applying the 'deprave and corrupt' definition does not establish that sexually explicit material really is capable of causing harm. Other explanations are possible. Juries and magistrates may have misunderstood the definition. Or (and this applies particularly to magistrates making destruction orders) they may have acted on their own feelings of outrage, without regard to the letter of the definition. To define pornography as material likely to cause psychological damage is elliptical. It omits any description of the factors alleged to produce the damaging changes. Nor does it describe the putative changes themselves.

The definition originated in the famous 1868 case of *The Queen v. Hicklin*, where Chief Justice Cockburn said: 'the test of obscenity is whether the tendency of the matter . . . is to deprave and corrupt those whose minds are open to such immoral influences and into whose hands a publication of this sort may fall'. This test was given statutory force in Rab Butler's 1959 Obscene Publications Act, and has thus applied for well over a century. In the 1968 appeal concerning the alleged obscenity of Hubert Selby Jr's book *Last Exit to Brooklyn*, Lord Justice Salmon said:

The depravity and corruption may . . . take various forms. It may be to induce erotic desires of a heterosexual kind or to promote homosexuality or other sexual perversions or drug-taking or brutal violence.

The notion that it is corrupting and depraving to induce ordinary heterosexual desire is absurd. On that basis even the respectable married woman who seeks to arouse a spark of ardour in her phlegmatic spouse is to be branded as a corrupting influence! Such rulings are made by elderly judges, and elderly people are prone to take a dramatic view of obscenity. In the same case the ageing Oxford bookseller Sir Basil Blackwell caused a sensation in court by testifying on oath that Selby's scabrous novel had depraved even him.

Legal practice follows the line indicated by Lord Justice Salmon. It equates a tendency to cause arousal with a tendency to deprave and corrupt. C. H. Rolph, in *Books in the Dock*, tells how he badgered a senior Treasury counsel at the Old Bailey to explain the way he decided whether a book should be prosecuted for obscenity. Counsel replied that the test was whether on reading the book he himself felt randy. An objective test was impossible, he added. 'When it comes to the crunch there's only me, and how I feel myself reacting.' Now whether it results in orgasm or is ended by turning attention to other things, mere sexual arousal is fleeting. It leaves no mental alteration. Afterwards the aroused person is pretty much what he or she was before. There is an addition to the memory store, and in rare cases this may be painful. Such pain is likely to be caused not by the nature of the arousing material, but by accompanying factors. There may be guilt at conflict with sex-negative conditioning. Or another person may discover what is going on and inflict punishment. Only one who regarded sexual arousal as bad in itself (that is, a sex-hater) could regard stimulative material as being corrupting.

Prompted by such sex-negativism, British law restricts obscenity in many ways. Acts of Parliament make it a criminal offence to bring 'indecent or obscene' objects into the country or send them through the post. Even today public displays of sexual material are caught by the Vagrancy Act of 1824 and the Town Police Clauses Act of 1847. As recently as 1961 the House of Lords, sitting as a law court (unelected by the people), invented the offence of conspiring to corrupt public morals in order to punish a man who circulated a directory of prostitutes. The backlash against 1960s 'permissiveness' has led to a series of represssive Acts of Parliament, in securing the passage of which Mrs Mary Whitehouse has been a prime mover. Nevertheless the 1959 Rab Butler Act, with its 'deprave and corrupt' test, remains the principal legal weapon against pornography.

In the 1970s juries increasingly refused to accept that to arouse someone sexually is to deprave them, and that degree of liberation has survived the swing against 'permissiveness'. Modern juries demand something more serious than arousal before they will convict of obscenity, as was shown by the 1977 trial at Leicester of Dr Arabella Melville and her boyfriend Colin Johnson for publishing the sex magazine *Libertine*, a case discussed in chapter 19.

The Longford Committee made strenuous efforts to find proof that pornography harms people, but failed. They were forced to fall back on what they described as 'the instinctive reaction of most people that what strikes them as revolting is likely to damage the individual'. Although they had mentioned earlier in their report that when Annie Besant was prosecuted for obscenity in 1887 even the *thought* of birth control struck people as revolting and that, when Radclyffe Hall was prosecuted for obscenity in 1927 even the *thought* of lesbianism struck people as revolting, the committee had forgotten these cautionary precedents by the time they drew up their conclusions. They relied on the similar thought processes underlying the rejection by the not-yet-disgraced President Nixon of the American Pornography Commission's finding that pornography is not harmful. After referring to the President's 'contemptuous and indignant' repudiation of that finding, the Longford Committee quote approvingly his exact words:

I have evaluated that Report, and categorically reject its morally bankrupt conclusions and majority recommendations. The Commission contends that the proliferation of filthy books and plays has no lasting harmful effect on a man's character. If that be true, it must also be true that great books, great paintings and great plays have no ennobling effect on a man's conduct. Centuries of civilisation and ten minutes of commonsense will tell us otherwise.

It might have been better if President Nixon's ten minutes of common-sense had been extended to a quarter of an hour, or even longer. The likelihood is that few people have gone out and done a noble thing after reading *Hamlet*, just as few have gone out and done an ignoble thing after reading an erotic novel. *Hamlet* is part of our lives. We are better for it, but scarcely 'ennobled'. Shakespeare has given us important tools to understand ourselves, our fellow men and women, and our place in the universe; but only a Nixon could think he has ennobled us. Some pornographic work might also have given us such tools, because from it we might have learned, as respects our sexual condition, a degree of insight. We might have learned truth about those who wrote or modelled the pornographic work, about those who felt they needed to buy it – and about ourselves.

Everything we experience affects us. There are some who think that everything we have ever experienced is stored away in our heads, and could be recalled if we had the means. Whether or not it can be recalled, it has had its influence in making us what we are. Sex-negaters, because they believe that sex is bad, think a child who picks up a pornographic picture will be scarred for life. In fact if such scarring occurs it will be because of the reaction of adults to their discovery that the child has had this experience. Left alone, the child would evaluate it according to the level of development he or she had reached. At one level it would mean nothing. At another it would stir interest. At another it might shock. In rare cases the shock could be severe, but only because of some lacuna in the child's past teaching or some false conditioning.

The Longford report can be dismissed as an amateurish hatchet-job perpetrated by people who had made up their minds before they started. Yet it is instructive. It shows how sex-negativism operates. It is full of confusions, but these are probably not deliberate. They usefully demonstrate that the first essential for any would-be reformer in the sex field is clear thinking.

The American Pornography Commission found that pornography was not harmful and recommended that all restrictions, except those protecting children, be lifted. This followed the fullest investigation ever carried out into the subject. It might therefore be accepted as conclusive by reasonable people.

Nevertheless, doubt remains. This mainly concerns the way the libido is 'fixated' by early sexual experience (possibly including exposure to pornography). Apart from this doubt (which we return to below), it is established that pornographic experience has no lasting effect. The finding is expressed by the American Commission as follows:

When people are exposed to erotic materials, some persons increase masturbatory or coital behaviour, a smaller proportion decrease it, but the majority of persons report no change in these behaviours. Increases in either of these behaviours are short-lived and generally disappear within 48 hours ... In general, established patterns of sexual behaviour were found to be very stable and not altered substantially by exposure to erotica. When sexual activity occurred following the viewing or reading of these materials, it constituted a temporary activation of individuals' pre-existing patterns of sexual behaviour.

This conforms to the psychological law expressed as $P = D \times H$, where P is performance (what is actually done), D is the strength of sexual drive or libido and H is the type of sexual activity habitually engaged in by the subject.

The doubt over fixation of the libido arises in this way. As we saw earlier, a single traumatic event in early life can 'fix' the libido in the direction of a particular deviation. If this traumatic event is exposure to a deviant form of pornography, the subject may become attached to that deviation. So runs the argument. It is presented by Eysenck and Nias in their book *Sex, Violence and the Media*, but merely as a hypothetical possibility. No findings confirming it are cited, and it appears that none exist. Moreover in other passages in the book the authors (without apparently realising it) contradict the theory. They say in one place: 'It is unlikely that exposure to pornography on its own is sufficient to lead to sexual deviations.' In another place they record the results of the only experimental field study they know of that investigates the effects of prolonged exposure to erotica. Twenty-three college students were the subjects. All but two moved towards a more permissive attitude to pornography. 'Another attitude change was the realisation that unconventional sex, specifically group sex and homosexuality, was not for them.'

Finally we may quote Dr Ivor Mills, Professor of Medicine in the University of Cambridge. In a letter to *The Times* answering the usual unproven assertions by the *soi-disant* Responsible Society, Dr Mills said: 'I know of no data supporting the view that erotic material is harmful to the young.' He urged that if the Responsible Society knew of such facts 'they should present them to us.' So far as we know, there was no response.

'Pornographers make Money out of Sex'

It is undeniably true that large profits are made by pornographers. David Waterfield, fined and imprisoned at the Old Bailey in 1976, was proved to have made more than £6,000 a week from showing pornographic films at two London clubs. At another Old Bailey trial in 1977 a senior police officer was proved to have received bribes totalling more than £50,000 out of profits made by pornographic bookshops in Soho. Police corruption is a grave matter. Large profits on pornography are objectionable if they escape taxation, but is there any other objection to them that does not equally apply to large profits on anything else? If so, what is it?

As is typical in this field, complainants regard the objection as self-evident. Why give yourself a headache trying to think it out? 'Pornography', say the Longford Committee, 'is business, and very big business . . . fortunes are being made out of pornography, of that there can be no doubt.' The truth of that is plain, but the social objection to it is not. Elsewhere the Longford Committee report a Bristol meeting of the Festival of Light, where a thousand people processed and signed a protest against 'the local exploitation of sex for commerical purposes'. Why? We are not told. Would the good people of Bristol have processed and signed a protest, aimed at Sainsbury's or Tesco, against 'the local exploitation of hunger for commercial purposes'? If not, why not?

If objectors to commerical pornography are short on reasons they are not short on rhetoric. The prophetic theologian from Manchester, referred to above, says that in our toleration of commercial pornography 'we will appear to posterity as sickeningly vulgar and tasteless, and as culpable, blind'. The noted private prosecutor Raymond Blackburn announces: 'There is no sacred right to the commercial exploitation of human weakness and vice.' The New Zealand expert Dr Court refers to the pornography industry as a 'multi-million dollar parasite'. A film censor says there is 'something frightening and distasteful' in the exploitation of sexual appetites by commercial interests. The Longford Committee go so far as to assert that where 'unscrupulous manipulation of sexual excitement' is employed for profit this *constitutes* pornography.

Other critics raise the bogey of capitalism. A correspondent in the fundamentalist journal *The Plain Truth* writes that it is no paradox that in Marxist regimes the display and sale of pornography is not permitted: 'Marxism teaches respect for and of the person, both one's self and others . . . we are living in a capitalist society, and capitalism can only exist by a cynical exploitation of people, by the use of people as "fodder".' This approach brings support from political pornographers such as Richard Neville of *Oz* fame, who considers the pornography trade 'an objection-able manifestation of capitalist greed'. Tony Smythe told the Longford Committee that the left-wing National Council for Civil Liberties was against the commercial exploitation of sex. So there are incongruous bedfellows (if that word is appropriate) in the opposition to commercial pornography: the publisher of the *Oz* School Kids issue and the instigator of the Longford Committee; the Festival of Light and the National Council for Civil Liberties. What chance then have the James Humphreys of this world? David Holbrook thinks the steam behind the movement for abolition of censorship is 'predominantly commercial'. James Humphreys, former pornography king of Soho, could not disagree more strongly. Conceivably he knows more about the subject than even Mr Holbrook, who has admittedly made a close study of it. James Humphreys told John Trevelyan, the chief film censor, that he was getting worried about Lord Longford's activities. When asked why he replied: 'I have an uneasy feeling that the end result will be to make all this stuff legal, and that wouldn't suit me at all.'

That remark gives the clue. It was under the Longford Committee's nose when they complained that 'magazines which can be bought over the counter in Denmark for 50 or 60p are sold in the British pornography shops for *ten times* that amount'. It derives from the ineluctable sleaze law mentioned in chapter 7: *Prohibition of a strongly demanded service merely ensures its provision at a debased level and high social cost.*

If pornography were legalised, so that excessive profits were not made and proper standards of quality prevailed, the only ground on which objection could stand would be the *marketing* of material designed to satisfy sexual impulses. As we have shown, there is nothing whatever in this objection. It is the product of unreasoning, confused emotion. What should concern us is not that commercial interests supply our pornography (as they supply our other wants) but that they are prevented by the criminal law from supplying it to an adequate standard, and at a proper price.

'Pornography Causes Crime'

Pornography certainly does cause crime; at least the fact that its distribution is forbidden does. This gives rise to protection rackets, blackmail, police corruption and other criminal offences. This is not what opponents of pornography mean, however, when they allege that it causes crime.

The only person President Nixon personally appointed to sit on the American Commission was a Mr Keating. One of the three who dissented from the sixteen-strong majority findings, Mr Keating did some research on his own account. He dug up the following cases to show that 'pornography causes crime':

Rape case. Seven Oklahoma teenage male youths gang attack 15-year-old female from Texas, raping her and forcing her to commit unnatural acts with them. Four of the youths, two the sons of attorneys, admit being incited to commit the act by reading obscene magazines and looking at lewd photographs. See Fellers case, Oklahoma City Feb 1, 1966.

Assault. Male youth, aged 13, admits attack on a young girl in a downtown office was stimulated by sexual arousal from a stag magazine he had previously read in a public drug-store, which showed naked women and an article on 'How to strip a Woman'. See affidavit of youth, dated June 30, 1965.

Attempted Rape. A 15-year-old boy grabbed a 9-year-old girl, dragged her into the brush and was ripping off her clothes. The girl screamed and the youth fled. The next day he was picked up by the police. He admitted that he had done the same thing in Houston, Galveston, and now in San Antonio. He said that his father kept pornographic pictures in top dresser drawer and each time he pored over them the urge would come over him. See report of Capt. G. E. Matheny, Juv. Off. San Antonio, Texas Police.

There are of course many such cases. What can never be proved is that *on balance* pornography causes more crimes than it prevents. The fact is that every healthy youth has a powerful sex-drive. If society offers him no adequate outlet for it, society will get what it deserves. Innocent victims will suffer. An individual case may appear to have been 'caused' by pornography. Perhaps none of the youths in the examples given above would have done those acts on that day if the arousing material had not come their way. But how many youths have been prevented from committing assaults by releasing their libido through masturbation aided by erotic material? How many non-sexual assaults have been committed by youths frustrated by the denial of any approved erotic outlet? We do not know, and we will never know, because the springs of human conduct are infinitely diverse. But we can guess.

There are further answers. Dr L. F. Lowenstein pointed out in 1977 that research shows alcohol to have far more effect than pornography in inciting to forcible rape. In 1975 Rada investigated seventy-seven convicted rapists and found no less than half of them had been drinking when the act was committed. Over a third were alcoholics. Yet alcohol, unlike pornography, is freely available. In 1973 M. Goldstein interviewed sexual offenders to assess the effect of their experience with pornographic material. He found that a control group of non-sexual offenders had significantly *greater* exposure during adolescence to erotic materials than did sexual offenders! Few of those investigated initiated sexual behaviour seen in the erotic material immediately or shortly after viewing it. Dr Lowenstein comments: 'That exposure to erotic materials during adolescence is associated with later sexual pathology has not been supported.' A number of other studies confirm that sex-offenders tend to have less rather than more exposure to pornography in their history than non-sex-offenders on non-criminal controls.

The clinching evidence on this point comes from Denmark. An official inquiry reported in 1966 that there was 'no evidence that exposure to or use of explicit sexual materials plays a significant role in the causation of social or individual harms such as crime, delinquency, sexual or nonsexual deviancy or severe emotional disturbances'. After this report, Danish law was altered in 1967 to repeal the ban on pornographic literature. By 1970 the restrictions on visual material (including films) had also been removed. Writing in 1978, Berl Kutchinsky reviewed the effect of these legal changes on sex crimes. Not only was there no increase in sexual offences to match the increased availability of pornography, but there was a very considerable *decrease*. This decrease applied to all offences except rape, for which the figures remained unchanged. More-over, adds Kutchinsky, the Danish experience has disproved the hypothesis that pornography is dangerous when consumed by 'pre-disposed' and abnormal individuals.

'Pornography wrongs Models and Actors'

Lindsay Kemp's production of Genet's *Flowers* opens with a row of nude men simulating masturbation. *Sebastiane*, a film of the life of St Sebastian, has a sustained sequence in which two Roman soldiers embrace naked on the shores of a lake; there is one brief glimpse of an erect penis. Rainer Wernher Fassbinder depicts a naked youth being strangled by a cannibalistic murderer in *Tenderness of the Wolves*. In *Heloise and Abelard* Diana Rigg appeared naked on the stage of Wyndham's Theatre. And so on. If you have nude sequences in films and plays you require nude actors and actresses.

Films and plays regarded as 'pornographic' usually have explicit sex all through. Take *Carte Blanche*, a successor to Tynan's *Oh! Calcutta*, which was staged at the Phoenix Theatre in 1977. In this revue every item was sexual. Here are descriptions of a few of them.

Afternoon contains simulated sexual intercourse. A handsome young couple, nude, make love in a variety of ways. Some of it occurs on stage, the rest in a colour film of the couple projected as background. This permits interior shots such as a bath sequence. The item is arousing, though there are distancing devices. The boy never gets an erection, on stage or in the film.

Earls Court Single. A flasher tells his tale. He is nude under a dirty mackintosh. At appropriate points he opens the mac and 'flashes' at the audience to emphasise a mock insult. He gets many laughs. The act, cleverly written, casts more light on what makes people sexual exhibitionists than many a work of scholarship. It shows the 'flasher' as a human being – even one capable of humour.

The Lady and the Gentleman. An upper-class youth entertains an upper-class lady to supper. He makes 'smart' conversation about how champagne should be served, the best place in London to go for pâté (Fortnum and Mason, inevitably). Suddenly the forced artificial conversation is switched off. The couple are on the floor making love and using the vocabulary, equally stilted, of the sex magazine. Love-making ended, they resume their supper. 'Slice of Camembert?' drawls the youth, instantly back in character. The five-minute sketch succeeds in both arousing laughter and sending up two sets of false attitudes.

Rochester's Revels. This masque written for Charles II by John Wilmot, second Earl of Rochester, is bawdy, earthy and real. The king, seated at the side of the stage, watches his courtiers perform sexual romps. The women avow their pleasure in sex, their concern at penile size. One girl initiates her fourteen-year-old cousin in vaginal intercourse (like all the males in this scene, he wears an artificial phallus). The court stud displays a sixteen-inch erection, and the ladies drool over it. Finally the king reveals his own weapon, even longer and tipped by a gold knob. The dialogue is light and witty. Its artificiality prevents any deep engagement of feeling.

Carte Blanche lets laughter into sex in a cathartic way, as well as providing arousal. The beauty of young bodies is displayed, but so are many truths. Pornography itself is often sent up. The writers are particularly severe on those who preach sexual gymnastics, multiple orgasms, orgies and other extremes. Truth in sex is well served.

Are actors and actresses harmed by participation in such plays and films? Certainly they have been found to need protection. The 'casting couch' is a notorious theatrical institution, by no means limited to shows involving nudity. Equity, the actors' union, has found it necessary to make rules restricting producers' demands for nudity at auditions. The theatrical profession is overcrowded, and the granting of sexual favours has long been a bargaining-counter for obtaining work. While the fact that a part is to be played in the nude may facilitate sexual advances by directors or producers, it is scarcely a decisive factor. If such advances are going to be made they will be made in any case.

No, the contention that actors are harmed arises in another way. It is expressed by David Holbrook in the Longford Report:

The 'stunning' nudity in *Oh! Calcutta*, by reducing individuals to the status of objects, has the effect of reducing human value, and, thus, human freedom – which depends upon our *counting* in the eyes of others. It is because they are affected by deep symbolic meanings of this kind, that actors and actresses become ill and impotent, by performing in stage 'sex' plays.

Now whether Mr Holbrook is correct in saying that actors and actresses become 'ill and impotent' through playing in live sex-shows one does not know. Certainly he gives no evidence for it. If it is correct then it answers the question, for *some* harm is caused to *some* participants. But without evidence we cannot be sure. All we can do is express surprise that a responsible body of people should make an important assertion without providing a shred of evidence to back it up.

Still, let us assume for the sake of argument that some actors and actresses do become 'ill and impotent' through participating in shows like *Oh! Calcutta* or *Carte Blanche*. It would be distressing if it were true, for such people perform a useful public service. But we need to ask *why* they suffer in that way, and Mr Holbrook himself provides the clue with his remark about 'objects'. The predominant feeling of many who go to see such shows is a deep sense of gratitude to the players. Never for a moment do they think of them as objects – quite the reverse. But others may go with a different attitude. So is that perhaps the reason why (if such be the case) some actors and actresses in sex-shows become 'ill and impotent' – because they sense from the auditorium the censorious eyes of the David Holbrooks of this world (what are they doing there anyway?) flashing the message 'you are an object'? If we think people are objects, and fix our gaze on them accordingly, they will respond. Like the rubber plant when someone at a party stubbed out a cigarette on one of its leaves, they will instantly wither and die – in spirit if not in fact. If the audience gaze on a nude actor thinking 'you should have kept your privates private', he or she will get the message. Just as he or she will if they are thinking 'thanks for letting us share in the beauty and reality of your youthful form'.

That's all right, but what of the real 'hard porn' show? During the Second World War, when stationed in Cairo or Alexandria, young servicemen heard tales of live sex-shows where girls were fucked by a donkey. Some plucked up the courage to go and watch them, being relieved to find that the donkey was at least fitted with a rubber washer to save the girl from being split open by the terrifying length and power of its penis. At the thought of something like that, most of us start to want to argue like a David Holbrook. But we must keep our heads and go on looking at the matter rationally. There are two alternative explanations for human sex with a donkey. One makes one angry and sick; the other makes one sympathetic and sad. Perhaps in the end they are the same explanation.

The first explanation is that donkey shows are the ultimate manifesta- tion of the titillating society we exposed in chapter 6. Robbed from the earliest days of natural sex, people have either no sex at all or unnatural sex. Thwarted in their yearning for simple happiness, some of them lose the natural touch. Out of anger at those who have denied them their birthright they attack the wrong target. They attack, not the sex-haters, but sex itself. They seek to put it down, and a donkey will do as well as any other means.

The other reason for sex with animals lies, as we also saw in chapter 6, in the area the law calls 'bestiality'. Many prosecutions for bestiality have concerned youthful farm-labourers who, denied legitimate sexual outlets, turned to the animals on the farm. One was even reported to have been desperate enough to experiment with a hen, which seems unlikely to have yielded him much satisfaction. Where animals are used because humans are not available one can only be sad – and sympathetic. Where their use has fixated the libido, so that sex with humans becomes second best, sympathy is redoubled. Pornography catering for such sex-aliens uses live models, including animals. In advanced countries the latter are protected by the legislation against cruelty to animals.

What of human models in hard porn productions? If they are degraded productions we can assume that all those taking part are degraded too. But their degradation comes not from what they do, but from how society regards it. In the Garden of Happy Emotions they would not need to do it, for there would be no demand. Even in our society, where there is a demand, we look on those who choose to help satisfy it with sympathy and understanding. Certainly we should never despise them, for they may well provide more true happiness than we shall ever do. They are erotic Samaritans in another guise.

Does the same apply when the actors and models are children? The very question calls forth howls of hysterical rage.

'Pornography Harms Children'

In the *Guardian* of 16 February 1977 a report by Jonathan Steele appeared under the heading 'Where to buy five pubescent girls for 75 cents'. The heading was grossly exaggerated; in fact it was a lie. The report began:

She thinks it must be close to the ultimate in pornography, if not the ultimate itself. Dr Judianne Densen-Gerber, a New York psychiatrist, went into an adult bookstore and peepshow near Times Square with her husband the other day. For 75 cents she was able to watch a nine-minute film featuring five girls not yet in their teens. The film was called First Communion and showed the girls receiving red wafers from a priest. Then there was a roar of engines and a motor cycle gang arrived. Five boys proceeded to tie the priest to a cross beside the altar and, in a closely filmed sequence, gang-raped the girls.

Last night on St Valentine's Day Dr Densen-Gerber was out picketing several book stores in New York which deal in what she and a growing number of Americans have suddenly realised has sprung up in their midst – a horrifying boom in child pornography. 'We have found children as young as three years old being posed in the nude', she told a press conference on Capitol Hill in Washington yesterday.

She displayed to reporters a cascade of glossy magazines with titles such as *Lollitots* and *Moppets*. Showing a picture of a three-year-old girl in a sexually suggestive position, Dr Densen-Gerber said she must have been used with the consent and participation of her parent or guardian. 'Parents provide their children and it may be for only 20 dollars a picture.'

The press conference was also treated to clips from two films. One starred a ten-year-old girl masturbating her eight-year-old brother and finally having intercourse. Another called *Ronnie, Bobby and Eddie* featured three boys aged about eleven to fourteen on a motel-room bed. The publicity literature for the film, entitled *Lollipops No. 9* and distributed by Kent Masters in New York, describes it as 'three preteens on a bed. A smooth three-way lollipop lick'.

At first sight this is sensational and wicked, but let us look more closely. The first case cited depicts a rape. No one denies that rape should be a criminal offence, whatever the age of the victim. If the filmed rape was genuine, a crime was committed even though no laws against pornography existed. The case resembles that of the 'snuff' film, where prostitutes ostensibly hired to act in a skinflick are murdered on camera for the greater titillation of high-paying viewers. As Professor Preston King has pointed out:

Here what is clearly offensive is the murder component. And laws against murder in every society are already on the books. It is questionable therefore as to whether one in any way needs censorship to place a check upon the production of films of this sort. A further point, of course, is that films of this kind are not, and in the nature of things will not, be publicly screened.

The second case in the *Guardian* report is a three-year-old girl in a 'sexually suggestive position'. What does this mean? The language reeks of sex-negativism. To 'suggest' sex is to hint at the existence of something there is a general conspiracy to pretend does not exist. Is that what worries Dr Densen-Gerber? Or is there something worse? We are not told. All we know is that three-year-olds will freely get themselves into 'sexually suggestive positions' if they are allowed to. That is because they are sexual creatures.

Then we have the ten-year-old girl having sex games with her eight-year-old brother. Not only harmless but right. If adults will pay to see a film of that going on it can only be because they were denied it in their own youth. The same goes for the last incident showing the three boys. So much for Dr Densen-Gerber.

But wait a minute. Isn't that a bit too quick? Aren't you saying that anything goes with kids? That can't be right. No, we are not saying that, not at all. If any photograph or film employs young children there must be strict regulation. Nothing should be done against the child's will, nothing to make him or her worried or unhappy. But let's be quite sure that what makes the child worried or unhappy is that pose it is asked to take up and not the reaction of parents and other adults. Children are sexual creatures, and if left to themselves they are happy in their sexuality and certainly not harmed by it.

Writing in 1978, Eysenck and Nias said that in the United States child pornography was one of the fastest-growing industries. They alleged that 300,000 children under sixteen were then involved in this industry. No evidence was cited for either proposition, which is remarkable for what purports to be a scientific work. Also remarkable is the fact that these two learned psychologists did not think it necessary to spend any time enquiring *why* there should be such an enormous demand by American adults for material of this kind. It surely says a great deal about the inadequate sexual upbringing of Americans that they should so avidly seek portrayals of childish sexual activity. What are the psychologists doing to ensure that the generation now growing up will not be similarly deprived?

Dr Densen-Gerber's campaign did not pass unnoticed in England. To Mrs Whitehouse it was (no doubt literally) a Godsend. Instantly that redoubtable lady sprang into action. In one of the most remarkable political campaigns in recent years she quickly mobilised opinion in both Houses of Parliament. The complete absence of evidence that this exploitation of child models existed to any significant extent in Britain was brushed aside. So too was the fact that the government-appointed Williams Committee was in the course of a general inquiry into what the law should do about pornography. Home Office advice that the existing law provided adequate protection was ignored. The result was the Protection of Children Act 1978. The Act makes it a crime to take an 'indecent' photograph or film of a child under sixteen, or to distribute or display such photographs or films. There is no limitation on the meaning of 'indecent' and the Act is not restricted to commercial activities. The proud father who takes the traditional family photograph of baby lying nude on the hearthrug thus falls within the ban. The maximum penalty for contravention is three years' imprisonment.

The only parliamentarian courageous enough to criticise this measure when it was being enacted was Lord Houghton (who first won fame as Douglas Houghton with his 'Can I help you?' radio broadcasts). He told their Lordships that pornography had corrupted far more policemen than it had children. He argued that the Bill was conceived in hysteria and was being passed because of political cowardice. The House ignored him.

Apart from their use as models or actors, does *exposure* to pornography harm children? We have reported the view of the Cambridge Professor of Medicine, who knows of no data supporting the view that it does. We have also reported the numerous findings that show sex-offenders to have had *less* adolescent experience with erotica than other adults. On the contrary side, Eysenck and Nias say that it seems likely that whatever effects pornography may have they will be strongest with children. Significantly, they add: 'but evidence for this belief is lacking'. In accordance with the argument of this book, we conclude by saying that if (which is not proved) any child suffers harm by exposure to pornography this is because of wrong attitudes by parents, teachers and others having a formative influence on the child's development.

The final objection to pornography is the vaguest of all.

'Pornography Undermines Society'

In the Longford Report Malcolm Muggeridge said that the increasing availability and tolerance of pornography in everyday life is one symptom of a sick society. The truth of this remark depends on what Muggeridge meant by 'pornography'. In her book *Coming of Age in Samoa*, Margaret Mead wrote that in Samoa familiarity with sex, and recognition of the need of a technique to deal with sex as an art, had produced a scheme of personal relations in which 'neurotic pictures' were unknown. The existence in our society of neurotic pornography, depicting such things as sadistic cruelty, human–animal sex, or activities involving excreta, is indeed disquieting. But it is a symptom, not a cause. The cause of the sickness, as we have seen, is sex-negation. The symptom is missing in Margaret Mead's Samoa because there the cause is missing too.

Stimulative pornography is said to threaten marriage. Husbands who turn to it compare their wives unfavourably with the attractive models depicted, or demand new varieties of sexual activity which wives are reluctant to engage in. Yet when in 1971 Byrne and Lambeth tested the effect of erotica on married couples they found the opposite result: sexual behaviour between the couples was little changed by the exposure to stimulative pornography. Such changes as did occur indicated 'increased love, increased willingness to experiment, and increased feelings of closeness'.

Political pornography, on the other hand, does aim to undermine society. Or rather it attacks the institutions favoured by the establishment. Great rage was caused in 1971 by the circulation among English children of a publication translated from the Danish of Hansen and Jensen called *The Little Red School Book*, which started off by saying, in a memorable phrase, that all adults are paper tigers. Its section on sex, couched in clear and vivid language, was ruled obscene on no other ground than that it could be understood by very young children. Other countries behave similarly. In Nicaragua for example the satirical journal *La Semana Comica* was banned by the Sandanista government three times in 1988 for pornography. One banning occurred over an attack on the official feminist organisation AMNLAE which consisted of a photograph of a naked woman shaving her vulva. The caption read 'One of the ladies of AMNLAE preparing herself for International Women's Day'. One recent English manifestation of political porn is *Blot*, a scurrilous magazine produced by the National Union of School Students. Teachers condemn it as subversive of school discipline, yet as with the School Kids issue of *Oz*, they could learn much from it about what troubles and concerns their pupils.

Political pornography runs counter to the indoctrination desired by parents, teachers, ministers of religion, or state agencies. It may make young people unsettled, confused or rebellious. But is that not part of healthy growing up? Does it justify the kind of censorship and suppression that may be, or develop into, nothing more or less than a resource of dictatorship? The questions surrounding political or destabilising pornography are investigated in chapter 19.

Non-erotic Pornography

Non-erotic pornography, namely sexually explicit material without erotic content, is morally neutral.

By non-erotic pornography is meant material which has no erotic content apart from being sexually explicit. A photograph of a nude male which shows his genitals is sexually explicit. If the genitals are not in a state of arousal, and the subject's pose has no other suggestion of sexual activity, the photograph may be called non-erotic. In a sensible world, where the duty of sex-acceptance was honoured, material of this kind would not be considered pornography at all. As things are, we have to include it in our discussion.

The reasons why non-erotic pornography should be treated as morally neutral are stated in the course of the discussion of sex-acceptance and nudity in chapter 4. That there is a long way to go before this sensible doctrine is generally accepted is shown by the fact that as recently as 1988 Parliament was induced to pass a provision, section 160 of the Criminal Justice Act, that makes it an offence merely to be in possession of an innocent photograph of a naked child under sixteen unless the defendant proves the existence of a 'legitimate reason' (undefined). As we have seen, an earlier Act passed in 1978, while the Williams Committee on Obscenity and Film Censorship was still sitting, had made it an offence to take such photographs or show them to anyone. In the sedate language one would expect, the committee criticised this hasty step:

The need for fresh legislation for this purpose was always in some doubt. Certainly no evidence was put to us that child pornography was a growing problem – indeed the Director of Public Prosecutions told us he had no evidence that there was any new problem, or one of any significance, and he considered the existing law was adequate to deal with it.

Perverted or Debased Pornography

Perverted or debased pornography is immoral because it contravenes the duty of sex-respect by denigrating human sexuality through associating it with violence, cruelty or bestiality, or otherwise depicting it in degraded form.

There can be no doubt that in so far as sexually explicit material is perverted or debased, it is to that extent immoral. This is because it infringes the duty of sex-respect discussed in chapter 6. Whether that means it should be censored is discussed in the next section of this chapter.

While the principle is easy to state, its application in practice may prove difficult. Opinions differ widely, and there is likely to be much dispute over whether particular material is truly 'perverted or debased'. Material that falls into this category may have its value in the study or treatment of disorders. It may be of high artistic merit, or for other reasons be justifiable as being for the public good. Nevertheless we should not shrink from recognising that there is much pornographic material in circulation that can only be condemned as filth. Its manufacture degrades the producer, its circulation degrades the distributor, and its consumption degrades the user. It is contrary to the public interest for many reasons, not least because it gives a spurious force to the arguments of those who are anxious to condemn all sexually explicit material.

Immorality of Some Opposition to Pornography

In the final section of this general chapter on the ethics of pornography we consider how in some respects the opposition to sexually explicit material can itself be immoral. We have seen one instance of this in the discussion above of non-erotic material. Since it infringes the duty of sex-acceptance, the general condemnation by society of such material is immoral.

Next we need to look at the morality of censorship. By condemning pornography as immoral, society calls for it to be censored. But when we try to smother what we do not like by censorship we run a risk. Someone else may try to smother what *we* believe to be right.

Feminists now seek to suppress pornography by censorship. A slight backing or filling in the political wind and people may try to suppress feminism by the same means. The apparatus of censorship, once set up, is there for the using. Arguments justifying it can easily be turned round. As David Ramsay Steele said (Libertarian Alliance, *Political Notes* No. 45):

It is dangerous that much of the argument about freedom for pornography is concerned with whether it be harmful. Libertarians say that pornography should be unrestricted by the state, no matter how harmful it may be. It is well-established that Roman Catholics are statistically more prone to crime than the average. Should Catholicism be denied the freedom to proselytize? Young blacks are more criminal, on average, than the population as a whole. Should young blacks be locked up? It is unjust to penalize everyone in a particular category because the category is statistically associated with something obnoxious. Therefore no 'research' into the 'effects' of pornography can ever justify its suppression, though it might help to justify an anti-pornographic moral code, voluntarily accepted and spread by peaceful persuasion. The case for freedom in any sphere does not rest upon a denial that harmful consequences may flow from some people's exercise of freedom. It rests on the view that *more* harmful consequences will flow from prohibition.

Free speech is recognised as a fundamental human right essential to any civilised society. It cannot be an unqualified right, but exceptions to it are to be kept to the minimum. The onus is on those who seek to justify an exception to prove the case for it. We are not surprised to find that the Longford Committee thought pornography should be one of the exceptions:

In defending free speech one has to defend a defensible line. And in most countries today it would be easier to defend freedom of speech if one did not have to include pornography. One can well imagine some cultural commissar making the point that freedom of speech is all very well, but as can be seen from the capitalist countries, it opens the way to a flood of pornography and the exploitation of the people by unscrupulous commercial interests. It is true that pornography, like blasphemy, expresses a point of view. But so does racialism and so do libels and slanders, all of which are placed outside the protection of free speech because they tend to bring particular people or groups of people into disrepute, hatred or contempt.

If pornography were censored out of existence what would we lose? If the present censorship were abolished and not replaced what would we gain? The different wording of these two questions reminds us of the sleaze law described in chapter 7. It is important enought to repeat. *Prohibition of a strongly demanded service merely ensures its provision at a debased level and high social cost.* In weighing the merits of pornography we should consider it not only in the debased form resulting from legal prohibition, but also in the form we might expect if no prohibition existed: not bootleg porn, but open-market porn.

The onus of justifying the exception of pornography from the principle of free speech has not been satisfied. That this supposed exception does not apply was argued by John Mortimer in his closing speech for the defendants at the *Oz* trial. The prosecutor, Mr Leary, had criticised John Peel, the disc jockey, for mentioning on the air that he had once had venereal disease. 'Are there not certain things better not spoken about?' Mr Leary demanded of Peel in cross-examination. John Mortimer referred to this incident, and continued:

Is that a view which you find sympathetic, ladies and gentlemen of the jury? Or do you not think that human dignity, and human responsibility to our fellow citizens, enjoins us to discuss everything as honestly and frankly as possible? It's very easy and simple to be tolerant and allow freedom of speech when what people are saying is that with which we agree. But if free speech and democracy mean anything at all, they imply tolerance and freedom for people with whom we disagree. And the odd thing is this: it is very rarely the people who are putting forward what Mr Leary would call 'the progressive point of view' who want to censor the opinions of others. Nobody, on behalf of the defence, is suggesting that the schoolmaster who says that people should not have sexual intercourse before they marry should be suppressed by law. The act of censorship is always one way. A great and wise Frenchman, who found himself in England, once said that he disagreed with every word his opponent said but would defend to the death his right to say it. And those words of Voltaire should be emblazoned in gold above the chair of every judge trying an obscenity case and should be emblazoned on the door of every jury room of every jury which has to consider matters of obscenity. Tolerance means protecting minority opinion, particularly the opinions of minorities with whom we disagree.

In line with this the Williams Committee on Obscenity and Film Censorship recommended that, although certain controls may be needed for pictorial material, the printed word should not be restricted since its nature makes it neither immediately offensive nor capable of causing lasting harm, and it is important in conveying ideas.

Should we admit an exception to free speech where material is to be seen by children? In putting to the Longford Committee their proposal for a children's censor, Kingsley Amis and his then wife attempted to formulate reasons. For this they deserve praise, since most people accept as beyond argument that sexual material should not be seen by children. Before we consider the Amis reasons here is a true story.

In the 1930s a boy of eleven named Alan found himself alone in the sitting-room of a family friend known as Auntie Florrie. She was a large, amiable woman to whom Alan was devoted. At that particular time the lad was obsessed with finding some picture of the nude female body, a thing he had never set eyes on either in the flesh or otherwise. There was a small glass-fronted cabinet of books in the room. On the top shelf Alan saw a volume entitled *Medical Cyclopedia*. Stealthily he opened the glass door and got out the book. Dropping to the carpet, he began to riffle through its pages. He did not hear Auntie Florrie come in. Kindly but firmly she took the *Medical Cyclopedia* from the boy's grasp. 'You mustn't look at that', she said, 'that's the ladies' book.' Alan received this information with baffled rage. Why, he asked himself, should ladies be so privileged?

Auntie Florrie, long gone from us, could not have explained. The Amis explanation is not very satisfactory either. They say with doubtful accuracy that a child's sexual nature is not fully formed and needs time to grow up. Then they make the mistake that is always made and assume that during this growing-up time the child should be sealed into an asexual vacuum. Why? Here is the Amis psychosexual theory, unsupported by evidence: 'By "uninhibiting" a child in certain sexual respects, one may suppress other good and natural instincts that he would certainly exercise if given the chance.' The Amis theory is that one of these suppressed instincts is *love*. If sex comes in by one door, love goes out by the other (a familiar sex-hater's theory). There is nothing else in the Amis argument but a tired military analogy.

A great many parents forbid their children to play with toy weapons or any warlike gear, on the grounds that to do so will corrupt children into accepting the violence, brutality and horror of something which, by the nature of their youth, they cannot understand. Surely younger children cannot be expected to read hard pornography in a strip cartoon or books without likewise being corrupted?

This gives away the level of argument. Because some parents think giving a small boy a toy weapon corrupts him into accepting militaristic violence, *therefore* giving children toy weapons does corrupt them into accepting such violence. Because some parents think giving a child hard pornography likewise corrupts it, *therefore* giving children hard pornography does likewise corrupt them.

As well as the right of free speech, another human right operates in favour of pornography. This is *the right to have one's needs satisfied*. Again, there must be exceptions. We have no right to have our needs satisfied at the cost of harm to others. But again, it is necessary to *prove* that this exception operates. The presumption is the other way. It is that if a person has a need they should be allowed to satisfy it. And they are to be the judge of whether they have a need or not. Other people may not agree that they have a need. They may be like the Bishop of Lincoln, who believes present-day pressures are driving many people to seek consolation in sex, unaware of being 'victims of a giant fraud'. If a man or a woman (or a child, if it comes to that) disagrees with the Bishop, and does not accept that sex is a giant fraud, then he or she has a right to seek consolation in that quarter. If, to do it, he or she feels a need for pornography then that establishes the need, whatever any bishop might say.

Widespread and serious consequences flow from our society's disregard of the sleaze law in the field of pornography. Any legitimate human demand should be met in the best practicable way. To know what that way is in the case of erotica we only need to look at how any comparable demand is met. Take the demand for adventure stories, or for history, or for scientific knowledge. Consider the quality of the books, plays, films and other materials produced in response to those demands. There is no inhibition on the production of such materials. The people involved risk no social disapproval. So what do we find? Not that all the materials are of a uniformly high standard, far from it. The quality varies according to the level of those producing any particular item and the level of those for whom it is intended. There are adventure comics and science fiction thrillers as crude in their way as anything in *Oz*. But there is another end of the scale. We have adventure stories like Scott's *Rob Roy*, histories like Macaulay's *History of England* (and, if it comes to that, we have Shakespeare's English kings); we have a huge collection of high-grade scientific works.

This is what is missing in the field of erotica. Either material of good quality is not produced at all or it is kept out of reach in locked-up museum collections or similar caches. The tawdry, the cheap (but not in price) and the vulgar are what are on offer. They are provided through a miasma of guilt and shame. The lifestyles of those involved are degraded. Behind it all loom the criminal courts and the prison cell.

The usual consequences of the criminalisation of an activity follow. Profits escape income tax. Quality controls do not apply. Social laws such as those governing conditions of employment are evaded. Criminals move in and operate protection rackets, blackmail and intimidation. Widespread police corruption follows.

Public opinion in Britain was horrified at the revelations in police pornography trials in 1976 and 1977. It was proved that for twenty years or more the Obscene Publications Squad at Scotland Yard operated a corrupt system of 'licensing' pornographic bookshops in return for huge bribes. 'Licensees' were tipped off about police raids. Material seized was sold back to them at half-price. The squad ran blue film-shows for police colleagues, using film confiscated in raids on 'unlicensed' premises.

After a six-week trial, five former police officers of high rank were given prison sentences ranging from four to ten years in December 1976, and that was but one of several cases. The matter only came to light when diaries kept by James Humphreys fell into the hands of *The Times*. Humphreys boasted that he had forty Scotland Yard men in his pocket. Ben Whitaker, former Labour MP and director of the Minority Rights Society, commented:

The experience common to all countries is that the bulk of police dishonesty occurs in connection with offences that are 'victimless' and which substantial parts of public and police opinion do not really regard as morally reprehensible, such as the sale of pornography, contraventions of the licensing laws, and (formerly in Britain) street-betting and prostitution: significantly areas where the police have wide discretion in deciding to prosecute.

If pornography is 'victimless' why is its propagation a crime? Certainly *criminalisation* makes many people victims, through deprivation or in other ways already discussed. Despite the current aura of disrepute, uses are being developed in the medical field which even its most determined opponents find hard to challenge. This, together with the 'public good' defence, calls in question the entire justification for criminalising pornography. Material that is 'good' for some purposes can scarcely be 'bad' for others. Judgements that it is 'bad' are very likely to be faulty, especially when based on nothing more than disgust.

Many people were disgusted by the unsparing descriptions of depravity in New York's East Side which were portrayed in Hubert Selby Jnr's novel *Last Exit to Brooklyn*. Readers who overcame their sense of disgust and allowed their minds to grasp the *reality* of what was described felt moved. Not only emotionally moved, but moved to action, to reform. A government committee might have inquired into the matter and produced a blue book. But no blue book could bring those terrible social conditions into people's minds with the immediacy and effect of literary art. A long-lived effect too. Few readers of that book will forget to enquire, when the question of social reform in New York comes up, 'Has anything been done yet about those *Last Exit* scandals?'

Again, many people were disgusted by *Oz* 28 (the issue prepared by schoolchildren). Let such people ponder the four following remarks taken from Tony Palmer's book on the trial:

By a medical witness:
These words are very commonly written on the walls of school lavatories. I think they are common currency among schoolchildren in secondary schools; there would thus be nothing surprising, or even out of place, in seeing those words.

By Caroline Coon:
The whole point about *Oz* is that it's young people talking to their peers. And you're not so likely to think it's just stuffy nonsense if it comes from your own contemporaries.

By George Melly:
I find it extremely useful in discussing things with my sixteen-year-old son because it is there; it's something concrete. One can read it and we discuss whether we agree or disagree about the contents. If I had to start a discussion on some broad moral front with him, I would find it much harder without *Oz* because *Oz* raises these questions in a way that is intelligible to both parent and child.

By Michael Duane:
An intelligent society would deal with this high-spirited prank in the way in which it deserves. But to blow it up into the form of a crime is, to me, one of the most destructive things that can be done to these young people. It was obscene that apparently mentally deranged people should bring the whole process of the law to bear on this schoolboy prank. If I found children in school who had scribbled sexual drawings on the walls of classrooms and lavatories, I would not immediately send for the police. I would be more likely to deal with those children myself and discuss with them what they were doing and why they had done it and explore with them the consequences of their actions. To send for the police would indicate that I was not fit to be a schoolmaster.

17

Stimulative Pornography

The Nature of Stimulative Pornography

If stimulative pornography does its job it induces sexual arousal. The need of an aroused person is for orgasm. Apart from triggering arousal, this kind of pornography serves to enhance the quality of the ensuing orgasm. Usually the orgasm in such cases is induced by solitary masturbation. Much of the antagonism customarily displayed towards erotic materials stems from that fact. Another ground of hostility is that they get in the way of romantic love (a concept discussed below).

But for sex-negative upbringing, people might not feel very much need for stimulative pornography. The philosopher Bertrand Russell said that nine-tenths of its appeal is due to the indecent feelings concerning sex that moralists inculcate in the young. (He referred to Christian, not secular, moralists.) Even would-be liberators of sexuality feel compelled to admit that this substitute is suspect and inadequate. For the real, it offers the unreal. For life, it parades fantasy. For the breathing lover we would ardently possess, it gives us coloured paper.

Once again, clear thought is necessary to arrive at the true analysis. Mrs Whitehouse is fond of quoting D. H. Lawrence's remark that pornography does dirt on sex. This is the Christian view (though Lawrence was far from being a Christian himself). Yet it is the pot calling the kettle black. Throughout history Christianity has itself done dirt on sex, placing it well below the cesspits and the sewers. Filthy lust is one of Christianity's kinder descriptions of our deep-planted instinct, ignoring the fact that the ready capacity for sexual desire is indeed a quality planted deep within every man and every woman, every girl and every boy – and every baby. It is powered by emotion, a warm, strong, elemental force. It is the one human characteristic spanning both the past and the future ages. Without it mankind would have no past, and could not hope to have a future. Lying within the core of everyone, sexuality announces that it is not to be ignored. If not fulfilled, it will reduce living to a pedestrian level or worse. The mark of its fulfilment is orgasm, but sexuality is no blind physical force. It reaches to the highest levels, and the orgasm it seeks connects with those levels too. The mystery of sexuality is that while a moment of physical release is indispensable, the force seeks to associate that with the highest elements of moral life. Sexuality feels it needs links with the noblest qualities: truth, beauty, eternity. Rooted in the flesh, it yearns for wide, universal spheres. Looking always outward, it reflects the aspirations of mankind. Wiser religions than Christianity perceived this and embraced sex as an element of holiness. What western archaeologists crassly describe as 'temple prostitutes' were one result.

Does not this exalted nature of sexuality mean that erotica necessarily degrades it? No. Erotic pornography is a mirror reflection of real life; an imitation for those unable to get nearer. Often the mirror is cracked and distorted. That should arouse our sympathy. Whether knowing it or not (and almost certainly not knowing it), every model in a crude pornographic film or photograph, every tawdry stripper in a clip joint, every backstreet whore in a sleazy cat-house, is an anointed celebrant of holy rites. It is as near as they can get, and it is not very near. But it is better than the turned back. Better than the pitiless Christian rejection of 'filthy lust'.

Nevertheless, uneasiness remains. Is not sexuality meant to enrich a full human relationship between two people? Is not any lesser use therefore degrading? If pornography aids auto-eroticism and facilitates solitary masturbation does it not encourage people to settle for second best? Does it not force them to become sex objects and lose their true human identity? Is not the real nature of sex (and of people) falsified, distorted and cheapened? So argue the critics. The answer is that there is no one for whom pornography is all of life. Flesh and blood people intervene to convince the lover of paper images of his or her mistake. Curiosity satisfied, the porno lover will often turn towards reality, as in John Quainton's poem *A Student of Pornography*:

> The trouble with real people is
> they interfere with my fantasies
> get in the way of images
> evoked by the magazines
>
> I like to stare at coloured girls
> coloured pink I mean, and honey
> with gold hair and smiles for me
> only me (they promise)
>
> Then a real dark woman comes
> askew across my fragile dreams
> with breasts that are not regular
> and breath that is not sweet
>
> She forces me to look at her
> in three dimensions, not just two
> reality, she says, is me
> don't live out of the real

> She shows me round her house of flesh
> in her crowded head we kiss
> I at last acknowledging
> the dark red cells in the skin.

Stimulative pornography is said by feminists and others to degrade humanity by treating women as sex objects. Let us test this against research findings. A number of experimental field studies were set up by the American Pornography Commission whose conclusions were so abruptly rejected by President Nixon. One of these reported psychological reactions to pornographic films. The subjects were college students. Included in the study was a test designed to find out whether exposure of males to the films increased their 'sex calloused' attitudes to women. Commenting on the results, Eysenck and Nias say:

It was thought that the erotic films would strengthen any such attitudes, but, contrary to prediction, 'sex calloused' attitudes were found to decrease. After viewing the erotica the male students were less inclined than before to approve the use of force or tactics, such as plying a girl with alcohol and falsely professing love, for the purposes of seduction. This is evidence contrary to the popular view that erotica tends to degrade or humiliate women.

This is one example of how popular beliefs turn out to be wrong when tested. It illustrates the folly (as well as the presumptuousness) of not letting people judge erotic material for themselves, and react to it as they will. We may put forward the following precept.

Stimulative pornography has the effect of initiating or enhancing sexual desire. The duties of sex-acceptance and sex-fulfilment, together with the principle of free speech, require such pornography to be treated as not immoral, provided the nature and provenance of the material does not infringe the duty of sex-respect or any other ethical principle, such as the duty of consideration for a spouse or the requirement of consent to participation by models. That this kind of pornography causes the commission of immoral acts such as rape is unproved generally. On balance more such acts might be committed if this material were not available for masturbatory use.

Written material designed to stimulate the erotic imagination is often condemned. So too are pictorial representations of sexual actuality, whether in the form of photographs, drawings, sculptures, or cinema and video films. Since, for many people, the emotional need is pressing, a market for the purchase of these despised materials always exists. Again, prices are exorbitant; the quality often abysmal; the guilt piled on. As purveyors risk imprisonment the sleaze law applies and the inevitable consequences of illicit supply arise: blackmail, intimidation, violence, police corruption. The life-style of all engaged in the pornographic trade is impaired. Creative imagination is stifled, though even so a remarkably high proportion of literary and artistic geniuses have managed to produce their hidden quotient of erotica. The upshot is that the public does not get the service it requires.

The Cult of Romantic Love

Sexuality is the victim of numerous cults. Many of these are religious, but not all. There is the cult of romantic love. This is a dominant cult of modern times, but has an ancient origin. It can be traced back at least to Plato, who in the *Symposium* produced the fable, not original even then, of the fractured being. A perfect, complete creature had at some remote time been broken into two halves. For ever after each half, in the guise of a man or a woman, sought the completing other half. Only one person in the world could be that other half. When found he or she had to be clasped for ever. The ring, once reunited, must not be broken again. What God has joined together let not man put asunder. Other cultures were more sensible. They believed in the arranged marriage, knowing that almost any young couple thought suitable by their respective parents are likely to prove as well matched as if they relied on their own immature, inexperienced judgment in choosing a mate.

The cult of romantic love has many pernicious, not to say dangerous, aspects. One delusion is that the happy couple, in the ethereal joy of their long-deferred reunion, will enjoy immediate sexual bliss instinctively. No instruction is necessary; and certainly no apparatus. Even the term 'sexual bliss' is crude, for this is a union mainly spiritual. Did Abelard procure for Heloise a clitoral orgasm, or was it vaginal? The question is offensive to the devotee of romantic love. As for the idea that either of them might, at any time in their lives, have indulged in 'self-abuse' – the mind boggles, and indignation mounts. Similarly with Christ. As we have seen, modern doctors regard masturbation as a harmless substitute. Boys are forced by their parents to rely on substitutes, and masturbate freely and frequently (if in secret). Jesus, the perfect man, must have been at one period the perfect boy. Did he masturbate like any other boy? If not, why not? Are we entitled even to ask such questions? The uproar over the public showing of the 1988 film *The Last Temptation of Christ* indicates that many people think not.

In attacking the cult of romantic love, one does not seek to deny lovers (whether married or not) the magic of true romance. This is a beautiful, enhancing quality. It is false romance we must deplore. Like anything else that is false, it can destroy a relationship. False romance despises masturbation. True romance welcomes it. Many ruined marriages might have been saved if wives temporarily incapacitated by menstruation or pregnancy had possessed the knowledge or native wit to love their husbands in this way. Such loving is as true and beautiful as vaginal intercourse.

Ideally, loving of this kind (or indeed full intercourse) does not need the accompaniment either of fantasy or of stimulative pornography. If love is perfect, the lovers and their present love-making fill each other's minds to the exclusion of all other images. Sexual love is perfect when each of the lovers *in present actuality* can fully arouse and satisfy the libido of the other. Often this is not possible, however, and substitute images are needed. These are provided either by fantasy or by stimulative pornography.

Substitutional Orgasm

As we have seen, the basic purpose of stimulative pornography is to improve the quality of orgasm. This applies whether the orgasm is solitary or accompanied. The pornography thus fulfils a similar function to fantasy. As explained in chapter 7, pornography and fantasy are the accompaniments of *orgasm on a basis of substitution*. They are alternatives: one cannot study a pornographic picture and fantasise at the same instant. Many people with strong imaginations consider fantasy superior to pornography as an accompaniment to orgasm, since it calls forth more mental participation and is their own product. Of course one may look at pornography and later fantasise about it, in the same way that one can fantasise about an actual past event. Study of *written* pornography involves contemporaneous mental activity akin to fantasising, as the imagination works on images induced by the author's text.

We perceive that the argument about stimulative pornography is part of the argument about substitutional orgasm. Those who condemn substitutional orgasm, and seek to confine orgasm to a basis of actuality with a partner who occupies the mind fully, will condemn stimulative pornography. (By the same token they ought also to condemn erotic fantasising.) The opposite view will be taken by sex-lovers who accept the need for substitutional orgasm. As we have seen, there is no valid objection to solitary masturbation; on the contrary it is to be approved of and encouraged. As regards orgasm with a partner, the principles applying to the use of pornography can scarcely be different.

Yet acceptance of orgasm on a basis of substitution cannot free the issue of stimulative pornography from moral questions entirely. These may arise for example on the use of models, on the exhibition of pornographic material in public, and on the suitability of certain types of material for certain readers (for example children). Furthermore the objections that use of the material may be *dehumanising* or may *degrade sex* can be regarded as raising moral questions. All these points are examined below. Subject to them, the production of stimulative pornography is socially valuable. Furthermore we can say that societal needs require it to be of the highest attainable standard. From this point of view, hard porn is better than soft porn.

Stimulative pornography is best understood as concretised fantasy. Probably all fantasy begins in the memory of an actual event. Very often this will be an event in early life, making its indelible imprint at the most impressionable age. Fantasy embroiders an erotic event, expanding it in directions actuality did not reach.

Guy de Maupassant wrote a short story about a youth who adored the wife of a friend. One Sunday the three young people picnic on the banks of the Seine. After lunch the husband goes to sleep in the sunshine, while the youth and girl stroll beside the river. There is a moment when the youth feels that his love is returned, that if he made a move the girl would be his. He does not make the move. Decorously the couple return to the sleeping husband. For the rest of his life the youth is haunted by this incident. He does not marry, and remains on terms of friendship with the couple. Indeed they inhabit opposite houses in a quiet street of a small provincial town. For forty years he nurses fantasies of what erotic delights might have been his if he had been bold (or unscrupulous) enough to act. One day he can stand it no longer. He walks across to his friend's house. He reminds the woman of that long-ago Sunday walk along the bank of the Seine. 'What would you have done', he demands, 'if I had put my arm around your waist and kissed you?' She smiles. 'Why,' she says gently, 'I would have yielded.' He leaves her, walks along the Seine to the identical spot, sits down on the river bank and weeps. Such is the power of fantasy over our lives.

A fantasy linked to an intense erotic experience of childhood or youth will have an intense erotic effect whenever called to mind. The same is true of pornography; just as it is of actuality. After a disastrous marriage a man or a woman will seek as a new partner exactly the same type of person as the former spouse: *On reviens toujours à son premier amour.* Unfortunates whose libido was fixated in attraction to, say, a young child will fantasise about a young child, or seek out pornography involving young children. They too indulge in actuality at times; and one more pedophile comes to court.

For each sexual category there is a corresponding category of pornography. The leather or rubber freak is most turned on by leather or rubber erotica, the boy-lover by pictures of nude boys. One can go further and say that each person has his or her distinctive response pattern, called by Sternback *individual response-stereotypy.* As we have seen, for males a method of calibrating response known as phallography has been devised, using measurement by a plethysmograph of penile volume changes in response to stimuli. Nevertheless intensity of emotional arousal does not necessarily relate closely to genital change. There are other physiological indications, such as increased pulse-rate, respiratory changes and sweating.

If stimulative pornography is equivalent to concretised fantasy it will be arousing to the same extent as the corresponding fantasy. Where this fantasy is socially undesirable so will the pornography be. For example a person who gains most erotic response from fantasies of spanking will seek out the pornographic literature of spanking. The less active his imagination (and therefore the more inadequate his fantasies) the more likely he is to want pornography. Here we come to a vitally important aspect of the fact that pornography is concretised fantasy. Just as fantasy often does not represent what the person would *actually* do, so the pornography relating to it is divorced from reality. A good example of this is given in the Longford Report. A middle-aged businessman felt sorry for himself because he was impotent.

However, one day he found himself very excited by reading letters about spanking in an American magazine and he could not now have sex relations unless he read stories about the spanking as a form of punishment; he abhorred cruelty and never practised the things about which he read. Indeed, he only liked spanking as long as it was not cruel. Seven years ago he had visited a psychiatrist who told him that he was not harming anyone by his dependence on spanking literature and that he had better learn to live with it.

It was said above that from the arousing point of view hard porn is better than soft porn. This does not mean that crude porn is better than subtle porn. (In fact most of what is usually described as hard or soft porn is crude, but this is because of the difficulties society places in the way of its production.) The best porn for any male is the porn which arouses him to the highest erotic intensity possible *for him*. If he is a crude individual, over-subtlety will be wasted. If he is of refined sensibilities he will gain from an approach commensurate with his own nature. The same applies to females. Technique and skill on the part of the producer have their effect here as in other fields. This brings us to a central feature of the argument: the allegation that stimulative pornography is dehumanising.

Here we must once again reflect on the simplistic nature of most attacks on pornography. They proceed as if all pornography were the same, whereas it is as varied as the thoughts and imaginings of men and women. They are worded as if the films, books and other material available today were the only possible types of pornography, overlooking the fact that the materials we have now are products of a sex-negating society. Current pornographic materials are what is offered in response to an irresistible demand, operating in a wholly repressive milieu. When, just after the First World War, the Americans were unwise enough to embark on Prohibition, there was no reduction in the *quantity* of alcohol consumed. The reduction was in its quality. Bootleg liquor was the impure and adulterated product of illicit stills and breweries. What the world gets today is bootleg pornography. Nothing else can be expected when society puts down those who act in sex-shows or films, pose for sex-pictures, write sex-books, manufacture sex-aids, edit sex-magazines, distribute pornography, or in any other way attempt to satisfy a genuine public need. Bootleg porn is of low standard, but nothing else can be expected until society amends both its attitudes and its laws.

With that point in mind, let us nevertheless face the actual state of the game. Take a typical hard porn magazine, which in Britain, unlike other countries, cannot lawfully be imported, sent through the post or sold. Nevertheless it circulates somehow. It has a vulgar title like *Cunt, Suck* or *Screw*. It consists almost entirely of colour photographs of explicit sex. The participants are not young: most are over thirty. The women, legs astride, display every feature of their vulva. They suck the erect penises of the men. Their faces get covered in semen. Through it all they smile glassily. Bodies tangle in unlikely and uncomfortable heaps. The furnishings, like the people, are tawdry. The overall effect is joyless and crude, but arousing. In pursuit of variety, every possible position and combination is tried, save one. Women are freely shown embracing each other, but no man embraces another man. This is a book for run-of-the-mill heterosexuals, and male homosexuality belongs to another and quite separate compartment.

Or consider a commercial porn film on show in, say, Paris. It may be straight porn or kinky porn. Either way, there are the following features:

1. Sexual action is explicit, constant and repetitive. It bears no relationship to character or situation, but is gratuitous. To enable the audience to see what it wants to see, every male orgasm takes place outside the body of the partner. The women's pubic areas are shaved (but not the men's).

2. The crudity of the presentation degrades the actors, who seem well aware of the fact.

3. The audience, consisting entirely of men, give no sign of enjoyment or humour, but share in the actors' sense of degradation. Some openly masturbate. A heavy sense of stirred emotion looms over the auditorium.

People who complain that pornography separates sex from love, or imputes qualities of sexual feeling that are untrue, or disregards the trust, commitment, affection and responsibility found in genuine human relationships can fairly point to publications and exhibitions of this type. Where the pornography is aimed at arousing people of a different sexual orientation from the critic his or her hostility is further increased. Where women are crudely featured in the material feminists condemn it as one more piece of exploitation. What is the answer?

The answer is to admit that, like anything else, stimulative pornography is capable of varying standards of quality, and that much that now circulates is of a very low standard indeed. We should bring to bear the techniques we use to improve standards in other fields, so long as these do not amount to imposing censorship. We should freely criticise (constructively where possible) the shortcomings of the erotica now produced. But we should not do so with the object of driving away stimulative pornography, but on the contrary of helping it to perform its true social purpose. In their book *Sex, Violence and the Media*, the psychologists Eysenck and Nias, despite their recommendation that there should be more censorship, nevertheless plead for greater permissiveness for what they call 'nice' pornography. They say:

Most viewers seem to like a pleasant story, told in sequence; pornographic films of the commercial kind seldom have much of a story, and what there is is often filmed in so hurried and perfunctory a fashion as to be meaningless. Whole chunks are left out, thus a couple is seen kissing, fully clothed, and naked in bed in the next shot. One consequence of greater permissiveness of 'nice' pornography might be an improvement in the standard of such films. *Film makers might with advantage seek psychological advice on what may 'turn on' their customers; they clearly only succeed at a very low level at the moment.* [Emphasis added.]

Elsewhere in their book, Eysenck and Nias point out that too explicit a presentation makes it difficult for the viewer to modify a scene in accordance with personal preferences. Direct attempts to make a film or book arousing are usually self-defeating. Something should be left to the imagination; and the producer needs to remember that anticipation is more stimulating than realisation. Whatever the quality of the pornography, it is important to realise that, being concretised fantasy, it will not necessarily reflect the way people actually are and behave. An ugly, ageing man may in fantasy win the love of a beautiful princess. Her hair may be more golden than any human tresses, her skin more fair than rose-petals. If his fantasies show him this vision why should not his books and pictures reflect it? He knows only too well where the truth lies. Perhaps it would indeed be wiser for him to destruct his fantasies and seek a real-life relationship with a female as ugly and ageing as himself. Maybe he has failed in the vital field of human relationships. Yet all people at some time in their lives, most people at many times, some people at all times, fail in their personal relationships. It is cruel to deny them consolation, and the best fulfilment they are capable of. It is simply untrue to say that such alternatives are 'dehumanizing'.

Another frequent complaint against stimulative pornography is rather like the complaint against cannabis: it leads to harder drugs. It is said that the law of diminishing returns applies. In the words of the Longford Committee, there is 'a progression from titillation to mild pornography, then to hard pornography, then to super-hard pornography and then there is always something beyond even that'. Admitting that it is true that there are persons who, because of their personal inadequacies, *want* pornography, the committee doubt whether they *need* it.

No doubt they get a certain passing satisfaction from it which – it is alleged – they can get in no other way; but are they really any better for it in the long run? Is it not much more likely to have the same sort of effect on them as a pathological addiction to smoking, alcohol or drugs – a desire for more and more indulgence, with a progressive intensification, rather than amelioration, of the malady from which they suffer?

The first thing to be said about this is that there is no evidence for it. The Longford Committee cite no research which has established, or even tended to show that people make this kind of progression. (So far as is known there has been no such research.) Second, it is a simple-minded error to equate the mental process involved in ingesting pornography with the physiological processes involved in ingesting alcohol or any other drug. It is an obvious confusion of psychology with pharmacology. The ill effects of prolonged intake of alcohol, according to Neil Kessel and Henry Walton's book *Alcoholism*, include: lack of appetite (anorexia), inflamed stomach (gastritis), diseased liver (cirrhosis), peripheral neuritis and acute tremulousness (on withdrawal). Severe cases may encounter *delirium tremens*, alcoholic epilepsy or alcoholic dementia. In another condition, Wernicke's encephalopathy, 'there is great difficulty in concentrating and slowness in answering questions'. No doubt those on a diet of pornography may suffer inflamed imagination, peripheral gratification or even tremulousness on withdrawal, but is there truly a parallel? It is the opponents, rather than the users, of pornography who seem likely to suffer from the equivalent of Wernicke's encephalopathy, judging by their confused reasoning and failure to respond to pointed questions.

A *Times* contributor, the theologian from Manchester University referred to above, really seems to think that in this field there is a law of diminishing returns (enacted by a Conservative government, no doubt).

It has already been pointed out by correspondents in *The Times* that pornography isolates sexual activity from personal relationships, concentrating upon the physical activity and excluding the fact that it is human persons who act. This is ultimately intensely boring, and the law of diminishing returns ensures that the physical activity must continually become more and more violent, more outré, more thrilling to counteract the boredom. Hence the appearance of bestiality in the programme. But it can also be destructive to the character and even demonic in its nature and effects. To regard the effects of pornography as harmless or even beneficial seems to me to represent the ultimate stage of a fatuous loss of judgment.

This is the level at which the debate is usually conducted by opponents of erotica. Unproved assertion, mythical 'laws', appeal to demons, and finally, when all else fails, straightforward abuse.

The truth is that sexual desire goes in cycles corresponding to orgasmic release. Does the theologian from Manchester believe that after each act of sexual intercourse an average husband and wife want something more highly flavoured next time round? Or does the cycle simply repeat itself? The answer is obvious, and it is the same with substitutional orgasm. The type of fantasy or pornography which conduces to the most intense orgasm usually corresponds to the fixation of libido occurring in early life. To repeat the orgasm the fantasy or pornography is repeated. Its exact form may be varied, but not its essential nature – otherwise it is ineffective.

Although its main purpose is to enhance the quality of orgasm in ordinary sexual activity, stimulative pornography also has other uses, which we now examine.

Other Uses of Stimulative Pornography

Sex training. Stimulative pornography has a part to play in sex-training. In a report published in 1975 the World Health Organisation state that the need for education and training in human sexuality has become 'increasingly obvious as a public demand for sexual health care'. As mentioned below, health workers need training themselves, and should be convinced that sexuality is useful and healthy.

Eysenck and Nias point out that in western society there is little in the way of direct training on how to make love. Erotic films, they say, fulfil an important role in depicting techniques of love-making which the viewer can later imitate. The need for this form of instruction is stressed by sex therapists. These frequently encounter patients who do not know the first thing about what they are meant to do in order to engage in sexual intercourse. One is reminded of the old Irish joke of the ignorant Kerryman about to set off on his honeymoon. His equally ignorant bride shyly asks him what he means to do when at last they are alone in the bedroom. The Kerryman scratches his head, then has an inspiration. 'First thing I'll do', he says, 'I'll feel ye're arse.'

Sex therapy. Prohibition of stimulative pornography, apart from diminishing the quality of some individuals' orgasm, interferes with sex therapy by clinical practitioners. As the World Health Organisation have pointed out, these need to use a variety of erotic materials as part of their treatment procedures. So do practitioners of aversion therapy, and other behavioural clinicians.

A result of sex-negative conditioning is that many people develop sex dysfunctions such as impotence or frigidity. The new approach to the treatment of these differs from other forms of therapy in two respects: first, its goals are limited to relief of the patient's *sexual* symptoms; second, it employs a combination of prescribed sexual experiences and psychotherapy. The crucial feature of this treatment is the carrying out by the patient of what are called therapeutic erotic tasks, either alone or with his or her sexual partner. Therapists, in the words of the World Health Organisation report, 'use a variety of erotic films and literature, masturbation, vibrators, and various techniques of erotic stimulation'.

257

The aim of these tasks is to dispel performance anxiety, fear of rejection by the partner, and feelings of guilt or shame. The report adds that these factors seem to be highly prevalent deterrents to sexual abandonment, 'which is a prerequisite of adequate sexual functioning'.

There is a large and growing literature on the techniques of using stimulative pornography in sex therapy. Much of it originates in the United States, but British practitioners are following suit. Results are promising, but the problem of obtaining suitable erotic material is acute. The ordinary kind of hard porn is both vulgar and illegal.

Treatment of deviations. Erotic pictures are used in aversion therapy for treatment of pedophiles and other sex-aliens. They can also be used as an assessment device. In a paper published in 1978, Patricia Gillan describes how female and male erotic sequences were used to study the responses of transsexual patients who had requested sex-change surgery. The patients tended to show larger galvanic skin (sweat test) responses to females, but greater penile volume responses to males! Gillan suggests the explanation that transsexuals have a greater overall interest in women, but a greater sexual interest in men. It is obviously important to carry out such tests before drastic and irreversible surgery is effected, but again obtaining suitable pornographic material presents a problem.

Training of medical students. Another 'respectable' use for erotica has been indicated by the World Health Organisation in a 1974 report describing the training of medical students. Having been conditioned by a sex-negating society, these young people need first to come to terms with their own sexuality in order to be able later, as general practitioners, to help their patients. One method, used in the United States, involves showing to medical students selected videos portraying explicit sexual behaviour. These display men and women engaged in such activities as masturbation, vaginal intercourse, homosexual fellatio and cunnilingus. The procedure is as follows. A number of videos are shown, one after the other, to a small class of students. Immediately afterwards the students take part, under a leader, in group discussion in which they share their emotional reactions to the video. There may be embarrassment, disgust or hostility. Talking over these reactions afterwards, the group becomes relaxed. The students find after a time that their apprehension and discomfort vanish. They are then given a second opportunity to see the sex videos, on which they usually discover that their anxiety levels have been lowered by the previous encounter. After a number of such experiences the students find themselves able to encounter sex in a way approaching that in which they are accustomed to view all other human experiences. They are able to be calm, and to get ready to receive their patients in a state of true professional objectivity so far as sex is concerned.

The 1974 report goes on to say that students in many parts of the world grow up in cultures that evade direct confrontation with sexuality; sex-acts are private and secret, and are referred to by indirect suggestion or by joking. The young people have no language which suits the subject and no practice in serious communication about it. The result is that they may come to fear the reality of sex because they feel shy and believe it will plunge them into a tumult of uncontrollable emotions. The report concludes that unless the doctor has overcome this anxiety, he or she will be ill at ease whenever a patient brings up the subject. This may lead the doctor into defensive attitudes, blaming the patient for inadequacies or over-emphasising organ dysfunction and avoiding any reference to feelings.

18

Educational and Artistic Pornography

Content of Educational and Artistic Pornography

The category of pornography considered in this chapter comprises sexually explicit material which on balance is regarded as morally good because it serves the interests either of education or of art, using those terms in the broadest sense. It will be seen that there are elements both of sex-negativism and hypocrisy in the concept. The unspoken thought is that while SEX IS BAD it may be redeemed by the presence of some worthwhile element. The idea that in conformity with morality sex may in its own right be interesting and valuable, even absorbing, is disdained.

We are cheated by this grudging concept, plausible though it may appear. This is because we are entitled openly to demand of *education* that it should teach all that is of importance to humanity. We are entitled openly to demand of *art* that through the exercise of skill and imagination it should enlighten us about everything that is human. The word 'educate' derives from the Latin *educere*, to draw out. True education draws out what is already within. Since sexuality is within every person, the educational system should draw out its significance for that person. The word 'art' derives from the Latin *ars*, made familiar to older cinema goers by the Metro-Goldwyn-Mayer Hollywood motto *ars gratia artis* (art for art's sake). We do not want art for art's sake. What we demand of artists is that they give us art for humanity's sake. That means a large slice of art should be devoted to depicting our sexual natures. And so it would be but for sex-negative conditioning, a force that coerces artists as it does everyone else.

Being grateful for the little we have, we need to consider what realistic meaning can attach to the concepts of educational and artistic pornography, regarding them in the light of what is actually available to us.

Educational pornography. This may be defined as sexually explicit material of which the predominant purpose is educational. Obviously the term covers material intended for use in sex education, but it goes much wider than that. Many branches of study find it necessary to include writings or other matter concerned with human sexuality. Examples are medicine, law, philosophy, history, sociology, literature and physical education.

In considering this category we need to distinguish fact and opinion. Each may be educational, but we should separate material which conveys facts about sex from material which advances a particular point of view about sex. It is an infringement of human rights to deny any person, of any age, the facts. To seek to do so is to confuse innocence with ignorance. That acquiring knowledge of a plain fact about the human make-up could cause psychological harm is inherently improbable. There is no proof of it, and it contravenes the ideal of self-knowledge. Furthermore we know from experience that it is the withholding, rather than the supplying, of facts that so often inflicts harm. Human beings are by nature inquisitive, especially when young. If a thing they need to know is not kept from them, they find it out at their own natural pace. Otherwise they can become obsessed by frustrated curiosity.

Admittedly the way a fact is learned may cause harm. The young girl whose first sight of an erect penis is when a large rough man is about to rape her will probably be harmed by the vision, even though rescue comes in time. That is not pornography, however, and if beforehand she had seen 'pornographic' pictures of penile erections the shock of attempted rape might be less. It is always immoral to deny people the facts. Even the immature are entitled to these. If we try to conceal them, mischief is likely to ensue. Truth will out. As another Latin tag has it, *magna est veritas et prevalebit* (great is the truth and it shall prevail). To hide truth from the young, with however splendid a motive, invites the reproach of deception. A third Latin tag tells us that *suppressio veri est suggestio falsi* (to suppress the truth is to suggest a falsehood).

Logic plays little part in this area, and it is not surprising to find that mere distance in time lends enchantment to the view taken by Establishment figures such as schoolmasters. Scabrous passages from Catullus or the Greek Anthology were cheerfully placed in the hands of public schoolboys at the height of Victorian prudery. That the nature of human sexuality remains unchanged through the ages was apparently unperceived by those pedagogues.

Artistic pornography. The notion underlying this category is the neat one that artistic merit redeems what otherwise would be a gross appeal to prurience. That pornographic material is bound to be more, rather than less, effective as such if written or depicted by an able artist is overlooked. For the purpose of this category the realm of artistry is taken to include not merely painting, drawing and sculpture but the literary arts, theatre, film and television; in fact everything that deserves or claims the name 'artistic'.

We need not spend time discussing the more obvious forms of artistic pornography. Even the prosecution counsel in the Bradlaugh and Besant case referred to in chapter 7, brought at the height of Victorian prudery, admitted that 'there are a great many publications of high repute in the literary productions of this country, the tendency of which is immodest, and, if you please, immoral ... there are in many standard and established works objectionable passages'. From Michelangelo to Beardsley, from Shakespeare through Fielding, Congreve, Wycherley and Smollett to Joyce, most creative artists have perceived their duty and produced their share of erotica; our misfortune is that so much of it has been destroyed or is kept locked away. Even fellow artists have joined in the destruction. A number of J. M. W. Turner's erotic drawings and paintings were at his death said to have been destroyed in disgust by his youthful friend and admirer John Ruskin, misguidedly acting on his own later teaching that art requires not only truth, nature and earnestness but *purity*. For many years the British Museum library (now the British Library) has kept what it demurely calls its 'Private Case' of obscene books deemed unfit for unrestricted reading, a matter we return to below.

The problem of judging the legality of alleged pornography usually arises with modern works which have not yet been granted the spurious sanctity of age. The acquittal of D. H. Lawerence's novel *Lady Chatterley's Lover* in 1961 opened some doors. More were opened when the *Last Exit to Brooklyn* conviction was quashed in 1968. As has been mentioned, this novel by Hubert Selby Jr presented a searing account of one of the poorest areas of New York. There were many descriptions of crude violence and sexual acts of the most horrifying kind. The literary style has been described as 'typewriter English', staccato and immediate. The distinguished novelist Anthony Burgess wrote in a foreword to the book:

The sad and ironic thing about the indictment of Selby's book as obscenity lies in the fact that true obscenity uses literary condiments to inflame the palate; Selby, committing himself from the very first page to an unedited recording, totally eschews the devices of titillation. Pornography is not made this way. The literary value of the book, on the evidence of the careful choice of verbal technique and the exactness of the notation (both of speech and act) cannot be gainsaid. It requires considerable artistic skill to induce in the reader attitudes of compassion and disquiet through the immediate presentation of speech, thought and action.

Views on this category of pornography were expressed by the artist Feliks Topolski at the *Oz* trial. 'Looking with your knowledge down the corridors of the history of art', John Mortimer asked him rather grandly, 'do you think that there is any human activity on which an artist has felt himself forbidden to comment?' Topolski made the obvious reply. 'No, definitely not. He wouldn't be worthy of the name of artist.'

The next chapter describes the film *Salo, or the 120 Days of Sodom*. For reasons given in that account, it may be regarded as a film that merits inclusion in the category of artistic pornography. So does another film the British public have not been allowed to see. *L'Empire des Sens*, written and directed by Nagisha Oshima, is based on an actual case which occurred in Japan in 1938. A geisha girl, named Sada, develops psychotic tendencies and strangles her lover San after he has permitted her to tie his hands together. She then cuts off his penis and stuffs the bleeding remnant into her vagina. Only in this way does she feel that she can effectively take him into herself. Earlier, the film shows Sada falling in love with San, who is already married. They make love very frequently, and Oshima patiently shows how their passion reaches overwhelming heights. It would be impossible to do this without frank erotic scenes, but there is a distinct difference from the commercial porn movie. The erotic element is given no greater prominence than it truly has in the theme of the film (and no less). Visually *L'Empire des Sens*, set in a geisha house, is beautiful. Almost every shot is precisely composed, the exotic costumes effectively contrasted with sombre interiors. The characters have depth, and are allowed to develop. Sexuality is never obsessional, though because of the theme it is seldom absent. What is absent is the inevitable commercial feature of *falsifying* sexual behaviour in order to let the audience see the action its sex-starved nature makes it want to see. Sex between Sada and San is presented as a real-life observer would see it, and the dialogue (judging from the French sub-titles to the Japanese) is truly directed to displaying Sada's deteriorating mental condition. The dreadful denouement, with a great deal of blood in evidence, is one from which many in the audience will avert their eyes. Some of the more disgusting episodes in commercial porn films cause averted eyes too, but with a different basic response. The end of *L'Empire des Sens* causes genuine horror, coupled with deeply-felt sympathy for the unfortunate lovers. The worst episodes of commerical porn films cause disgust at the actual people involved – the director, the actors, the audience. The one is art while the other is rubbish.

The Public Good Defence

The claim of educational and artistic pornography to moral acceptability is rather surprisingly recognised by current English law, though attempts are continually being made to overturn this. Section 4 of Rab Butler's Obscene Publications Act of 1959 introduced the 'public good' defence. Under this, the penalties of the Act do not apply to the publication of what it describes as an 'obscene article' if the defendant proves that the publication 'is justified as being for the public good on the ground that it is in the interests of science, literature, art or learning, or of other objects of general concern'. A similar defence for live productions was included in the Theatres Act of 1968, which abolished the ancient censorship powers of the Lord Chamberlain. Here the grounds specified are 'the interests of drama, opera, ballet or any other art, or of literature or learning'.

The wording of section 4 neatly highlights the confused thinking over the Act's 'deprave and corrupt' definition of obscenity, which was explained in chapter 16. If 'obscene' merely meant 'explicitly sexual' then section 4 would make sense. Explicitly sexual material can be justified if on balance its publication is for the public good, because for example it is embodied in a medical textbook or a work of art. If on the other hand, as now appears to be the case, the true meaning of the 'deprave and corrupt' definition is 'likely to cause psychological harm' then section 4 is inapt. Apart from the fact that it cannot be proved beyond reasonable doubt that *any* explicitly sexual material is likely to cause psychological harm, there is the incongruity of seeing public good in material which *ex hypothesi* may damage those who experience it.

Whatever its theoretical drawbacks, section 4 works in practice. It expressly allows the defence to call expert witnesses as to the merits of the impugned article. Despite restrictive rulings by the House of Lords, defence counsel usually manage to bring before the jury an array of impressively qualified experts to testify to the need of the public for the defendant's product. We shall see how this works in the next chapter, when considering the *Libertine* trial.

As one would expect, the Longford Committee recommended the repeal of section 4. While admitting that the public good defence had a respectable ancestry, they asserted that its moral and intellectual validity is open to the strongest doubt. Their report went on:

Its invocation does not arise save in relation to articles which are deemed to have that tendency to deprave and corrupt which is the essence of 'obscenity' within the meaning of the 1959 Act. So what, in effect, is asserted is that the literary or other merits of a work can nevertheless be such as actually to render it 'for the public good' that those who read it should run the risk of thereby becoming depraved and corrupted. Surely this is nonsense. Mr John Montgomerie, while advocating the repeal of all anti-obscenity legislation on the ground that there is no evidence that obscene works deprave or corrupt, has rightly said that, 'the balancing of depravity against literary merit is farcical. Presumably the better obscenity is written, the more it corrupts.'

We may put forward the following precept in relation to this category of pornography.

Educational and artistic pornography is morally good as being in the interests of science, literature, art (including drama, opera and ballet) or learning, or of other objects of general concern.

The Private Case

Certain difficulties may be encountered by libraries and other educational institutions which find themselves obliged, in order to fulfil their function, to keep pornographic materials. Readers are sometimes tempted to mutilate or deface these. Erotic plates may be abstracted from books. Magazines or prints may be stolen. Staff members or visiting workmen may spend time perusing titillating material when they should be working. If any material is considered depraving or corrupting, authorities may fear for the morals of students and others in their charge.

In the middle of the last century such considerations led the authorities of the British Museum library in London (now the British Library) to start locking up their obscene books and journals in what is still called the Private Case. Julian Roberts, who was formerly in charge of this and is now Deputy Librarian of the Bodleian Library, says the criterion used for determining which materials should be consigned to the Private Case is similar to that employed by English law, namely whether because of its sexually explicit nature the material is likely to deprave or corrupt persons encountering it.

Formerly such obscene works were excluded from the British Museum catalogue, so that no publicity was given to their existence and indeed that existence could if necessary be denied. In the 1960s however the practice was changed, and Private Case materials are now catalogued. This was in response to Peter Fryer's 1966 book objecting to the trustees' secretiveness entitled *Private Case – Public Scandal*.

Relatively few staff members have keys to the Private Case, and readers who require access to works in it are placed under surveillance. Except for special reasons, such as a particular reader's known propensity to deface or abstract material, access to books and journals kept in the Private Case is not prohibited to readers. A bibliography is given in Patrick J. Kearney's 1981 book, *The Private Case*.

At Oxford the Bodleian Library operates a similar system of control over its obscene books and journals. Except for materials dating from 1988 onwards, which are recorded on computer, these are catalogued in a small half-calf handwritten book known as the Phi Handlist. This is named after the Greek letter ϕ, possibly chosen because its sound echoes that old-fashioned term of rebuke *fie!* No published account yet exists of the Bodleian collection.

19
Political or Destabilising Pornography

For those who adhere strongly to the traditional Christian religion, advocacy of birth control or free love is corrupting because it attacks the faith, and therefore the psychological state, of believers. This is an important reason why the 'deprave and corrupt' test has survived so long. Really it is a criterion for bolstering the established order.

Sexually explicit material that advances a political point of view about sex, for example that religious restrictions should be disregarded or that the community should tolerate nudity, is an attempt to change society's attitudes. So too is material, such as the underground comics of the 1960s, which uses sex as a weapon to attack the Establishment or its values. Material of this kind may appropriately be called political or destabilising pornography. That label acknowledges its potential for creating social problems. It also reminds us that there are hard-won safeguards against its suppression.

Political or destabilising pornography uses explicitly sexual material to make political points, and may therefore be subversive. The duty of sex-acceptance and the principle of free speech require such pornography to be treated as not immoral.

Pasolini's Last Film

In January 1977 the Greater London Council refused a certificate to Pier Paolo Pasolini's last film, *Salo, or the 120 Days of Sodom*. It had already been turned down by the British Board of Film Censors, although freely available to the public in Paris and most other capitals. This film is a good basis for a general discussion of pornography, since it has many of the relevant ingredients. Some parts of it are sexually stimulative, while others may be found grossly offensive. The film is directed and photographed with artistry, and contains many shots of stunning beauty. Although centred on sadism, it displays most of the other extremes of sexual behaviour too. It has political points to make. The British public, unlike that of other countries, is not allowed to see it.

Four fascist aristocrats (the scene is Italy during the Second World War) find themselves in a position every sadist must dream of. From a collection of press-ganged youths and girls they pick twenty of the best-

266

looking. These are conveyed to an elegant palazzo, and in accordance with a set of 'rules' the four aristocrats have devised, and with every aid and accessory that the wildest imagination could invent, are subjected to a merciless regime of sadistic exploitation and sexual torture. They are kept in the nude, raped in every conceivable way, terrified by vivid threats of death and mutilation, served human excrement at a mock wedding banquet and forced to eat it, summarily executed if they pronounce the name of God. Survivors have their tongues cut out, or (like Gloucester in *King Lear*) their eyeballs pressed in. Their nipples are branded with white-hot irons. One girl has a hungry mouse sewn into her vagina. And so on.

It is dreadful stuff. Can its public showing be defended? The answer is yes. First, the film is brilliantly made. The sex is not gratuitous. Even the cruelty is not gratuitous, for this is a study in cruelty and no more of horror is displayed than is necessary to make the points. It is a film with points to make about human nature. Some of the victims are brave, some not. Some betray infractions by other victims of the infamous 'rules' in order to save their own skins. (In the end no skins are saved.) We learn much about the torturers themselves. Once embarked on evil in the company of others there is no turning back. One cannot disapprove or hold aloof from anything a confederate chooses to do, even though one might not choose to do it oneself.

In one incident the youthful victims, sunk in horrified gloom, are made to *laugh* by a determined and clever crosstalk act between two women. At the very end, after the climax of horrors has passed, we see two of the boyish soldiers who guard the palazzo. They are lolling about alone in one of the smaller rooms. A 1940s-style radio emits an anthem from a church service. One of the boys switches the programme over. Now a foxtrot is playing. He asks the other boy if he can dance. The other shakes his head. 'I'll show you, come on.' They dance woodenly. 'What's your girlfriend's name?', asks the first. 'Marguerita'. They dance on, the foxtrot continues, the film fades. The inevitable presence of normality even in the midst of extreme horror is re-established.

Today, torture is used politically by numerous regimes. Terrorists and sadistic criminals torture their victims. To fight torture we need to understand it. Documentary news treatment tells us something, but as with any other aspect of the human condition we also need the contribution of art. If art is not allowed to be specific, too much weight is thrown on powers of imagination. If we cannot see reality visually re-created, but have to rely on suggestion and implication, we may fail to grasp it. Furthermore, the presentation of the explicit image frees the imagination to work on other levels. The scenes in *Salo* of shit-eating and sexual arousal through having one's face pissed on are explicit. The imagination, not having to construct images from oblique hints, is free to roam in search of understanding. Is this a reversion to the infantile anal stage? Is it a revenge on parents who were too early and severe in toilet training? Is sadism itself a form of revenge on harsh parents or rejecting lovers? Certainly the devilish four in *Salo* could be seen as revenging themselves on the beautiful youths and maidens who in freedom would have mercilessly rejected their claims to be sexual partners.

By the cleverly pointed contrast between the sedate appearance and manners of the four and their fiendish acts a parable of family life is obliquely told. The four could be socially respected parents or uncles of the youths and girls they torture. Between acts of villainy they behave as such respectable relatives do. One is reminded of the smug Victorian paterfamilias who occasionally left his domestic fireside of an evening to patronise brothels filled with terrified children. Audiences of *Salo* leave the cinema feeling shattered. The reality of evil has been conclusively established, and they know more about it.

Although *Salo* has many facets, we mention it here for its political relevance. It throws a harsh light on dictatorship, terrorism and other political aspects of human living. Another medium through which this is done is the so-called alternative comic.

The Libertine Trial

A strip cartoon entitled *Home on Leave* particularly incensed the prosecution. The burly RSM, newly arrived from Northern Ireland, greets his decrepit, wizened mum. She offers him oyster pie, and crumpet for afters. 'Tell me son, how was it in Ulster?'

The bullock-stupid RSM replies: 'It was rough mum . . . there I was surrounded by them Micks, after my arse they was, so I cocks me automatic and POW! POW! POW! . . . he! he! . . . splattered her brains all over the place. That . . . he! he! . . . learned her!'

A crude, troops-out, political cartoon; but there is something more. Crumpet for afters means cunnilingus with wizened old mum. The drawing is competent, and first time round the psychic shock tells. 'Melvin just loves his mum's hot crumpet' croons the balloon issuing from mum's thin lips as she lies outstretched on the kitchen table.

An Old Bailey jury might just take that sort of thing, but weren't attitudes less permissive in the provinces? In quick time and unanimously the Leicester jury put paid to that idea. They acquitted *Libertine's* youthful editors and publishers, and the judge gave them their costs. They were free to go on running what one of them, Colin Johnson, was proved to have called 'an improper little cottage industry'.

Libertine started in 1974 as a journal of period erotica, mainly Victorian and Edwardian. Colin Johnson and Arabella Melville took it over after five issues as 'a labour of love and principle'. They kept the period erotica but added humour, current sex information, a reader's advice column and anything else their fertile imaginations could dream up. As Dr Bethlehem, one of their witnesses, put it, 'the magazine has a friendly air'.

It received an unfriendly response from the police when Colin and Bella cheekily opened a sex bookshop in Leicester's main thoroughfare, Granby Street. Within days, the shop was raided and 22 tons of magazines removed. Undeterred, the two went on producing and selling *Libertine*, helped by sympathetic printers and others willing to work for nothing in what they saw as an important cause. The entire printing of issue 10 was seized, so the young publishers reprinted most of it in issue 11. When the indictments were drawn up they were reproduced in facsimile on the back of the current number, reprinted with the slogan 'There are no obscene words . . . there is no such thing as pornography.' David Barker QC, prosecuting at the trial, disagreed rather strongly.

The old attitude to sex was fully displayed by Mr Barker, the judge nodding approval. *Libertine's* title-page described Arabella Melville (a Ph.D., B.Sc., of Birmingham University) as a consulting sexologist – 'whatever that means', said Mr Barker scornfully. Of the Ulster strip cartoon he asked: 'Would it be wrong to use the word vile?' *Eveline*, a Victorian tale of incest, cunnilingus, buggery and lesbianism, dealt with sexual matters in 'the coarsest and most explicit way'. Anything, said Mr Barker, seemed to go. At one point he caused surprise by saying that everyone in court accepted that sex is a joyful activity. The defence looked disbelieving. It ought to be, but is it in fact? Trying to make it so was *Libertine's raison d'être*.

The defence called expert witnesses in support of the new attitude to sex. Maurice Yaffé said *Libertine* was educational. Challenged over items on pedophilia, he told the court about *victimology*, a new subdiscipline of criminology which studies the contribution made by the victims of sex crimes to the events which happen to them. He thought it socially valuable to study sexual deviants, their fantasies and motivation. They were, after all, human beings. Mr Barker looked disbelieving. He showed the witness the cartoon of the RSM and his mum.

'Is that of educational value?'
'Yes, in the sense that it expresses taboo thoughts of incest.'
'Is that a desirable way of doing it?'
'Yes. It takes the heat out of the subject.'

The defence witnesses argued strongly that fantasy material for masturbation was of social value. The components of an individual's fantasies can be structured better with the help of items like *Eveline*. An adequate fantasy and masturbatory life will prevent the deviate going out and actually doing it. It's a safety-valve, a healthy release. The harder the porn the more valuable it is for this purpose. Humour is also valuable, for laughter helps to dispel anxiety. Anxious is what most of us are about sex.

Peter Webb, wearing more purple even than the judge, gave evidence as an art historian. His qualifications included authorship of a book on David Hockney. Mr Barker pounced, but Mr Webb parried. Hockney, he said firmly, is *not* an erotic artist. Many illustrations in *Libertine*, he insisted, were of artistic importance. Some originals are in the secret collection of the British Museum or the V & A. It is difficult to view them there. Until recently they could only be seen if the Archbishop of Canterbury was present too. Other originals are in the erotic collection of the kings and queens of England at Windsor Castle. 'Will they', asked John Mortimer QC for the defence, 'be opened to the public as part of the jubilee celebrations?' The witness doubted it.

Mortimer, who has led the defence in many post-war pornography trials, made it very clear to the jury what the 'deprave and corrupt' test meant. The prosecutor had insisted that *Libertine* was 'filth', and invited the jury to apply 'ordinary, decent and prevailing standards'. Mortimer retorted that if it was filth that had nothing whatever to do with the case. Nor had words like vile, disgusting or nasty. The only words that matter, he said, are *deprave* and *corrupt*. He pointed out that the lawyers in the court, including the judge, had read much pornography in the course of their legal careers. 'Do you see any sign that we are corrupted?' The jury had been required to read the magazines from cover to cover. 'Do you feel that you have been permanently depraved as a result?' Mortimer urged that to describe explicit sexual action in an erotic magazine is no more likely to make people rush out and commit rape than to describe murder in a detective story is likely to make them rush out and kill.

When we read we enter a world of fantasy. When we find from Conan Doyle that Sherlock Holmes sustained his nerves by taking cocaine, that does not turn us into cocaine-sniffers too. When we find from Ian Fleming that his hero 007 was 'licensed to kill', that does not turn us into assassins. So it is with descriptions of sex.

There was much more in this vein. Clearly the jury were impressed. Although the magazines complained of contained many items which would undoubtedly cause 'extreme offence to the great majority of people', as one much-promoted test for banning pornography puts it, the jury quickly and unanimously acquitted. Why? Surely because they accepted the argument that the 'deprave and corrupt' test as applied in a criminal trial requires proof beyond reasonable doubt that the material is likely to cause a permanent, or at least more than a fleeting, change in the psychological makeup of those encountering it. Such proof is virtually impossible to provide.

The Purpose of Political Pornography

To free the mind from its prison is an object of political pornography. Where the imprisonment involves suppression of sexuality, the use of sexual weapons is both apt and effective. This has been skilfully exploited by the underground magazines which in their modern form first appeared in the 1960s, headed by Jan Wenner's *Rolling Stone* in California and Richard Neville's *Oz* in Australia. By its concentration on sexual themes, *Oz* ran foul of the law first in Australia and later in Britain, whither it was transplanted by Neville in 1966. Convicted of obscenity by an Australian magistrate in 1964, Neville appealed. Surprisingly, the appeal court quashed the conviction on a plea that *Oz* was satirical and not pornographic in intent. A passage from Judge Levine's judgment indicates the approach taken by the court:

Satire is an important part of the literature of protest dating back to ancient Rome and Greece and before, and satirical magazines such as *Oz* have no doubt been published wherever protest was thought necessary. And whilst it may be a necessary part of the satire to be critical of human behaviour by using a wide variety of weapons, including shock, invective and even crudity, and techniques (such as) ridicule, lampooning and caricature, nevertheless, I cannot make it too clear that obscenity may not be used as a weapon. Indeed, the appellants do not contend otherwise than that the best piece of successful satire may at the same time be obscene. I am not unmindful that there can be a large element of cant and hypocrisy in attempts to justify an obscene publication on the basis of literary merit and social necessity. However, I am satisfied that the article is a successful satire, that it does not glorify or condone, but on the contrary would create in ordinary people feelings of revulsion, abhorrence and censure against such behaviour [as it depicts].

This judgment is a useful illustration of Establishment attitudes and confusion of thought in Britain as well as Australia. Discussing the weapons of satire, the judge without explanation rules out the use of obscenity. Then in the next breath, and almost with approval, he notes that 'the best piece of successful satire' may be obscene. He speaks of cant and hypocrisy in the justification of social necessity for satire while oblivious to the same elements in the justification advanced for suppressing obscenity. He notes a common feature of political pornography: its *aversive* effect. While using explicitly sexual material it often does so in a way which is the opposite of arousing.

Political pornography is used to attack certain institutions, attitudes or groups in society and promote rival institutions, attitudes or groups. Typically, the things attacked are established, conservative and elderly while the things promoted are underprivileged, radical and young. The have-nots assault the haves. The Establishment is attacked by attacking its cherished institutions: monarchy, business, law, religion, compulsory matrimony. Since suppression of sexuality forms a central feature of Establishment attitudes the sexual attack liberates explosive forces.

The Old Bailey trial of *Oz*, in the summer of 1971, was the longest obscenity trial in British history. Strictly it was not a trial of *Oz* itself but of three young men and a paper company who were its editors and publishers. The men, all in their twenties and wearing the newly fashionable shoulder-length hair were Richard Neville, Jim Anderson and Felix Dennis. The trial concerned *Oz* 28, the 'School Kids Issue' (as the front cover described it). The charges were conspiracy to corrupt public morals (the crime invented by the House of Lords ten years earlier), publishing an article tending to 'deprave and corrupt', sending indecent or obscene articles through the post and possessing such articles for publication or gain. The 'articles' in question were copies of *Oz* 28. The following account is taken mainly from Tony Palmer's book on the trial.

Oz 28 was remarkable for one thing if for nothing else. Its contents (except the advertisements) were almost entirely produced and edited by a group of children aged between fourteen and eighteen. They were from all over England, having responded to an invitation in an earlier issue of the magazine. Richard Neville, defending himself because he did not wish 'to hide behind the gowns and wigs of the legal profession', said this from the dock in explanation of his decision to produce a 'School Kids' issue:

During this case, we shall hear much more about the increasing agitation of children and the relevance and importance of their demands for all of us. If their demands strike you as impudence, remember that children do not even have the most basic freedoms. They do not have freedom of dress or appearance. They do not have freedom to participate significantly in deciding what they should learn. They do not have freedom of expression – this incident reported last week is typical: a schoolboy claimed in his school magazine that the meals were unhygienic. Instead of answering the allegations, the headmaster merely confiscated all the copies of the magazine and tore off the front page which contained the offending story. That example may seem rather trivial, but how would you like to be treated like that? What if you published a letter in your local paper attacking the council and the mayor came along and ripped the offending pages out of every copy? ... We felt it was of social value to find out what adolescents were complaining about, in the hope that when their complaints were published, someone might do something about them. Young people, as they go through the no-man's land between fifteen and eighteen, are socially impotent. Even if some of the criticisms expressed in *Oz* are crude and silly, we believe it was of sociological and educational value that they should have been openly expressed.

Oz 28 was mainly concerned, as one might expect from its authorship, with problems of school and family life, though rock music, sex, drugs and the alternative society featured also. Much of the material was shocking to established values, but what came through was its fierce honesty. To read it taught adults how kids felt, and that after all was its object. John Mortimer QC, for Anderson and Dennis, argued that the sexual shocks amounted to little more than adolescent cheekiness.

One of the contributors to *Oz* 28 was Vivian Berger, aged fourteen, whose mother was chairperson of the National Council for Civil Liberties. He caused a lot of trouble for the defendants with a strip cartoon about Rupert Bear. This was made as a collage by cutting out figures from the *Rupert Annual* and marrying them with cuttings from an American strip cartoon called Gipsy Granny. In the first picture, entitled 'Rupert finds Gipsy Granny', the bear stares up the skirt of the reclining old woman. The caption reads:

> It looks just like a ball to me
> Let us open it and see.

The second picture shows the beginning of Rupert's exploration, with the caption:

> Then Rupert starts to push and peep
> But finds the hole is much too deep.

Finally, Rupert, equipped with a drawn-on erect penis, charges the recumbent woman and achieves his fell purpose.

Middle-aged people remember Rupert Bear from their youth. His activities had a quality of timeless significance which belongs to the mysterious world of childhood. It is indescribable, but very real. Viv Berger's target was well chosen. As, by then aged sixteen, he said in the witness-box, replying to a question from John Mortimer: 'I subconsciously wanted to shock your generation: to portray us as a group of people who were different from you in moralistic attitudes.' He insisted that his Rupert cartoons were the sort of drawings that go around every classroom, every day, in every school.

Another drawing in *Oz* 28 shows a pipe-smoking schoolmaster masturbating himself while sticking his finger up the anus of a schoolboy, who is vomiting. The caption reads: 'Like – the ageing master who used to walk around the junior's showers "cleaning his glasses" as he looked at the kids' balls, saying sometimes "I don't think I've seen you before".' Can anyone doubt that that picture and comment by a schoolboy is based on actual observation and the drawing of irresistible inferences? Ought we not to be more affected by the reality behind it than the item itself, shocking though it be? And ought we not to be grateful for a glimpse of important truth, brought home to us in a powerful and effective way? Many schoolmasters *are* pederastic, and *do* feel sexual desire for their boys. That may well be the reason for their choice of a profession. Yet society prefers to pretend that no schoolmaster is a pederast, averting its gaze whenever scandal breaks the illusion. It would be uncomfortable and troublesome to deal with the actual truth. Certainly no schoolboy seeing this item would be tempted to try a homosexual experiment. As one of the expert witnesses testified, it is aversive.

The police officer in charge of the *Oz* case said in the witness-box that in his opinion the magazine attacked society. On reading it there was 'a general dirtying of the mind'. This takes us back to the SEX IS BAD syndrome discussed earlier. Establishment people such as police inspectors prefer to keep dirty things like sex out of their minds, except when it is time to swap dirty jokes at a stag party or similar gathering of 'the boys'. The concept of 'dirtying the mind' is a false one, for the human mind, whether we like it or not, consciously or unconsciously encompasses all aspects of the human condition. But what of the attack on society? Here the worthy inspector was nearer the mark.

The prosecution was a counter-attack. In his book *What the Censor Saw*, the late John Trevelyan spoke of the 'unrevealed purpose' of the *Oz* trial. The obscenity laws were used as an instrument to deter and restrain people who wanted a new kind of society, the sort of 'alternative society' encouraged by the underground press. Trevelyan added:

In a free society we must defend the freedom to express ideas, even if they are minority ideas, and we should therefore closely watch for any possibility of there being an 'unrevealed purpose' behind the use of the chaotic and confused obscenity laws.

Enid Wistrich, formerly in charge of film censorship for the Greater London Council, makes a similar point in her book *I Don't Mind the Sex It's the Violence*. Censorship, she says, is an authoritarian act of formal political repression. Art, entertainment and other cultural artefacts contain messages which either reinforce or disrupt the prevailing ethos. Interference with those messages therefore has a politcal aspect, even where this is not suspected by the censor.

It is perhaps more accurate, and certainly more charitable, to regard the kind of political pornography exemplified by *Oz* 28 as the putting forward of an alternative culture rather than as a negative attack on the culture that prevails. Caroline Coon, a defence witness, felt that what was on trial was young people's lifestyle. Dr Lionel Howard, Director of Psychological Services for West Sussex, another defence witness, testified that one of the problems of understanding youngsters today is that what is unacceptable to us may be perfectly acceptable to them. He added: 'For too long we have assumed that what offends us will necessarily offend or disturb them.' A third witness, Edward de Bono, considered that *Oz* served a useful purpose in the hippy subculture because it provided a window into the minds of a significant section of society. 'It's a window; and don't think windows create scenes. They are merely something you look through.'

The idea that *Oz* asserted in a positive way the idea of an alternative society was perhaps best expressed in a manifesto published during the trial by the Friends of *Oz*:

The pick-axing of this magazine is nothing less than political censorship. *Oz* has relentlessly promoted some elements of the new culture – dope, 'rock 'n' roll, and fucking in the streets; it is the only magazine in the country to consistently and constructively analyse the tension between the freak/drop-out community and the militant left, and to struggle to develop a theory from such antagonism. We see fun, flippancy, guiltless sex and the permanent strike of dropping out as part of an emerging new community, but painfully acknowledge the limitations of leeching on the present society and becoming stooges of its consumer junkyism. We appreciate that *Oz* antics are often adventuristic, escapist, dilettantish, narcissistic, and juvenile; but we are congenitally incapable of facing a solemn fun-free future, cutting cane beneath some spartan banner of liberation; we only want to play with our toys, not own them, and we are fumbling towards a solution of living and working collectively – not for profit – which there ain't – but because we love what we do and believe naïvely in a joyful tomorrow of spiritual, emotional and intellectual *coitus non interruptus*. Help whiplash the backlash. For while religiously executed, it is politically motivated.

The politically motivated *Oz* trial ended in predictable fashion. The defendents were convicted and sent to prison for terms varying from nine to fifteen months. As the verdicts were announced there was the sound of a boy sobbing at the back of the court. It was Viv Berger, the *Oz*-contributor turned prosecution witness. Even before sentence was passed the prison authorities had shorn the convicts' shoulder-length tresses. The prison rules required, after all, that hair should be cut 'as may be necessary for neatness.'

Oz has perished, just as *Ink, Frendz, IT* and other underground journals of the 1960s have perished. Thankfully for the health of society, others rise to take their place. One of these, now in its turn defunct, was Antonio Ghura's comic *Bogey*. This displayed some of the best features of the underground magazines; predominantly, honesty about what society is perennially dishonest about. In the *Oz* trial Mr McHale, defending the paper company, made a point in his closing speech which some members of the jury may have thought curious. He criticised the prosecuting counsel for putting to witness after witness the question 'Would you encourage this?' or 'Would you encourage that?' He went on:

Now, of course, there are all sorts of things that you don't encourage children to do; but these are not necessarily harmful. Picking your nose, for example. Do you encourage your children to pick their noses? The answer is presumably not. But does it do them any harm? Are they going to have their poor little psyches bruised forever because they see somebody picking their nose?

Mr McHale was unwise to say that. It didn't do his case any good at all. Juries at that time were of the Establishment, and the Establishment hates to be reminded of things we all do but spend our social lives pretending are not done. Especially things concerned with the bodily orifices. The Establishment would really prefer to have no orifices at all, because almost every one of them is embarrassing in one way of another.

Bogey took its name (and the cover of its first issue) from the controversial little habit Mr McHale courageously, though unwisely, drew to the jury's attention. The figure picking his nose on the front cover is of course Humphrey Bogart. The comic thus establishes its wit as well as its honesty. On the inside cover Bogart, in six drawings, continues the digital research into his left nostril. The final drawing shows the product he finally succeeds in extracting. It is a foot long, wriggles, and has eyes on stalks.

Wherever there is a conspiracy of secrecy about a personal habit, the political pornographer pounces. He or she considers such secrecy unhealthy, and so it is. Nothing natural is wrong, and nothing natural should be hidden or disguised. That way lies anguish and shame, made only more poignant by its pointlessness. Humour assists the cathartic process; as always an invaluable dispeller of embarrassment and anxiety. There are other targets too: snobbery, pretentiousness, the unspoken background to family life. So *Bogey* has a cartoon that punctures wedding-night myths. 'Don't switch on the light Mack, dawling!' drawls the new wife of a Prussian trooper, as the bedroom door opens (sex should be practised in the dark). Indecent balloons issue from the black background, using the hackneyed phrases of sexing. At the climax the doors opens again. Click! The light goes on to show the trooper in full uniform entering the room to witness his *horse* performing the office of a bridegroom.

A comic strip in *Bogey* echoes the Manchester theologian's disapproval of pornography in ambiguous terms also fitting the detested practice of masturbation.

Reading U/G comix weakens your eyeballs, and fucks your mind . . . after 6 months of constantly reading U/G comix . . . you might turn radical . . . or lose complete control – completely . . . and anyhow yer sister's on to you [here the youth is shown reading his comic seated on the loo] . . . besides everybody knows when you've just read a copy . . .

Further strips in *Bogey* hit at commercial exploiters who market sex-aids. (The porn-is-dehumanising brigade should welcome these cartoons.) The first strip begins by showing a seductive blonde lying nude on the bed, legs apart, while the boy removes his trousers. As he comes near and leers in her smiling face we notice, just below the generous breasts, the tell-tale nipple for inflation of the doll. The boy's body descends on her and his embrace tightens. BLAM! The couple hit the ceiling on their way to bursting through the window-pane and hurtling across the night sky. 'Help!' cries the by-now distant boy, silhouetted against the full moon . . .

A similar send-up of those who market devices for enlarging the penis follows. The Charles Atlas figure announces: 'I need 250 young gals a day!' He assures potential customers that they will have similar needs too

if you enter my 'tensile contraktion' course . . . only a few minutes a day for just 35 years. You will notice definite results in only 14 minutes! Thin, skinny and short pricks have gained 10–20 inches, even in a certain case 30 inches. So far I have tested 'tensile contraktion' on 200 or so high school students and about 500 sailors. The results have been little short of miraculous.

More serious social comment is made in the *Bogey* strip entitled 'Fatherly Love', which echoes the incest theme of *Libertine's* Ulster cartoon described earlier. Vanessa, a sixteen-year-old girl, comes home to the 'typical' family situation: coarse, brutish father reading the sports news in his vest; fat, blowsy mother in the kitchen.

'School shut TWO hours ago, where have you been?'
'I've been out with Mike Feldthem, he's a writer Dad!'
'WHAT! You hear that Mother, our own daughter a SLUT already!! Look here my girl, I don't want you mixin' with that NO-GOOD DOPE SMOKIN' FREAKO!'
'But Dad, I'm 16. I'm not a child anymore!'

This makes Dad pause. Stupid as he is, he had not caught on before to his daughter's growing nubility. The next frame distinguishes Dad's spoken words from his lustful thoughts.

'Er, . . . just keep away from that DEGENERATE, you hear?'
[It seems only yesterday she was a spotty little brat in pigtails.]
'Haw, but Dad . . .'
'SHUDD UP and get to your room!!'
[Look at her now, only 16 and she's a woman already. Fuck, she's really FILLED OUT, look at them TITS!]

'Fatherly Love' continues its predictable course. Mum goes out to the bingo. Lust all over his face, Dad climbs the stairs, and enters Vanessa's bedroom. We glean the rest of the incident from balloons issuing from the closed door. (It is one of the rules of underground comics that you do not show gratuitous sexual images: the sex is aversive, not stimulative.)

'You look STRANGE Dad . . . What's wrong?'
Why don't you SHOW Daddy how GROWN-UP you are?'
'WHAT are you doing Dad?! EEEEEK!'
'OH MY! You ARE a BIG girl aren't you? . . . He! . . . He! . . . Vanessa . . . Look at THIS!!'
'OH! . . . Daddy it's so HUGE!! NO! Daddy, you mustn't, NO! . . . NOOOAAH . . . AAAH.'
'Oh . . . Vanessa . . . OOH . . . OOOH . . . OOH . . .'
CREAK ! CREAK! CREAK!

Later drawings show Vanessa escaping to Mike's pad. That night Mike tries hard to please Vanessa – the best he knows how (PUFF, PANT, GASP). But when Mike's ardour is spent, Vanessa is left AWAKE and TENSE. She ends up back in bed with Dad, the only man who can satisfy her.

'Oh . . . DADDY! . . . DADDY! . . . I will never leave you . . . NEVER!!! OH! . . .
'OOOOH! . . . Come on Dad, SHOOT your LOAD . . .
'Mum'll be back from shopping soon! . . . OOOH!'

Of course this is crude, disgusting and shocking. But like Oz 28's drawing of the masturbating schoolmaster, it brings into the open things that are real, important and hidden. Incestuous wishes frequently arise in both daughters and fathers. Often they proceed to action. Sometimes they lead to court proceedings, with intense and prolonged distress for all concerned. Concretising incestuous fantasies in this aversive way has a number of valuable effects. It acknowledges the *existence* of a common situation, so that those who experience it do not feel they are unique, and uniquely guilty. It hits at some common stereotypes, provoking thought and discussion about them. It lets humour in, with its releasing effect. Finally, it tends to *discourage* the acting-out of incest fantasies.

The first issue of *Bogey's* major item is a twenty-page cartoon sending up the drug scene and the pigs/freaks conflict. At the height of the bust, when the youngsters are being questioned at the police station, doped buns are substituted for official ones on the refreshment trolley. This gives the chance to show authority figures releasing their 'true' thoughts and feelings in a full-page uninhibited drawing.

Finally the issue contains a strip headed: 'BOYS! Earn £5 to £30 a week by fellating in your spare time.' In the first three pictures a boy, Jimmy, and his father are shown having the following interchange:

'Dad, how can I make some extra money?'
'Why don't you do what I did as a boy – fellate! Lots of famous men fellated as boys – ball players, politicians, artists, writers, business men.'
'What's fellate Dad?'
'Fellatio, son, is one of Britain's favourite sexual pastimes. 70% of British people enjoy it every day, or night, as the case may be. It's easy to fellate! You make a clear profit on every fellation.'

The next picture shows Jimmy with semen dripping from his smiling lips and down his jersey. He is taking a £5 note from his 'client'. In the last scene Jimmy is shown clutching banknotes to his chest while father says: 'You get to meet influential people, you can advance your social position.' The final caption reads: '. . . so all you boys out there get fellating right now . . . what you need is a willingness to please perfect strangers, a tonsillitis-free throat, clean white teeth and an ability to gargle and swallow large amounts of dense liquid.' Horrifying? Of course. Repulsive and disgusting? Certainly. But *repulsive* is the key word. No boy reading this is going to be encouraged to emulate the victims of Roger Gleaves, soi-disant Bishop of Medway, whose evil practices were portrayed in the notorious 1975 television documentary *Johnny Go Home* and described by Michael Deakin and John Willis in their book of the same title. No boy is even told what fellatio is. All the strip does, in addition to its aversive function, is take the rise out of the capitalist ethic and also bring into the open a trade and a need that indubitably exist on a wide scale. Not a bad achievement for one little comic strip in a sleazy magazine that every right-minded citizen would demand should be prosecuted.

In the opinion of Mark James Estren, author of a study of American subversive publications in the 1960s and early 1970s entitled *A History of*

Underground Comics, this form of pornography is quite different from what he calls 'release pornography' (in the present book referred to as 'stimulative pornography'). In Estren's view the underground comics, far from providing an opportunity for sexual release in the reader and thus, as he puts it, 'helping society function more efficiently', use the sexual freedom they practise for the purpose of aiming overt, often vicious, attacks on conventional society. A well-known American example of this is Robert Crumb's large cartoon captioned 'The family that LAYs together STAYS together!' Estren says that this satirises the whole rosy concept of 'get together with your family and do things' that Middle America holds so dear. (The drawing shows a cosy living room in which family members of various age-groups, all fully dressed and with no genitals in view, are engaged in sexual intercourse with each other while doing humdrum things like watching television or taking a pie out of the oven. In one corner a little girl, who unperturbed goes on playing with her bricks on the hearthrug, is being sexually assaulted from the rear by the family dog.) Estren understates the import of Crumb's infamous cartoon. It was commonly suspected that, in the redneck community above all, incest was a way of life in Middle America. The dominant male in many a household was thought to be in the habit of taking his sex where it lay nearest, and that surely was Crumb's principal target.

It was this cartoon, published in a journal called *Zap Comix No. 4*, that in the early 1970s gave rise to perhaps the best-known underground comics prosecution in America, rivalling those of *Oz* in Australia and Britain. Crumb was one of the most popular and effective American underground cartoonists. The notorious *Fritz the Cat*, the first animated cartoon film to be given an 'X' certificate, was based on one of his creations.

Like *Oz*, *Zap Comix No. 4* was condemned by the court. Although under New York law the prosecution were required to discharge the difficult obligation of proving that the publication was 'utterly without redeeming social value' (a test reminiscent of the English 'public good' defence discussed in the previous chapter), it was held they had succeeded in doing this. Law courts represent and uphold the Establishment, and in the view of the Establishment attacks on it using sex as a vehicle are not to be permitted unless the sexual element is diffused and weak.

20
The Garden of Happy Emotions

We remember the Garden of Eden. That genetic place of happiness is barred to us now by various obstacles. Theologians may understand what these are, and why we are not able to surmount them. We do not.

The substitute peaceful garden which has been tentatively offered by this book may be called the Garden of Happy Emotions. It too is a difficult place to enter, for as has been said we do not have emotions: they have us. All we can seek to do is tame them, and conduce them into the service of our happiness. It is a worthwhile and possible enterprise.

What then is it like, this Garden of Happy Emotions – the new Eden resulting from sex-positivism? *Our* new Eden. We can see it is not a jungle, and not a wilderness. It has been carefully landscaped, ready for us to enjoy. It goes on being tended with care, for it is a continuing product of that human triumph known as civilisation. It results from knowledge rather than superstition, honesty rather than hypocrisy, courage rather than cowardice. Like everything civilised it has to be fought for over and over again, all the time, minute by minute. Its guardians never feel able to relax.

To construct the Garden of Happy Emotions a lot of earth-moving was needed . . .

Clearing the Site

The site of this beautiful garden was formerly a gloomy place. Prisons and houses of correction abounded. Lawns became swamps when you walked on them. The favoured vegetation was laurel and yew. Gates were padlocked. Enticing avenues bore NO ENTRY signs threatening penalties for disobedience. Therein many dark temples stood dedicated to the irascible gods who hate pleasure and love guilt. Though human sacrifices were constantly made to these gods, they were never propitiated. In the centre of the drab plain a huge monument of grey stone bore the legend OBEY.

But we should not delude ourselves by using the past tense, as if the site for the Garden of Happy Emotions had already been cleared. It hasn't. How then shall we go about it? The only way to clear this site is to cut

down the manifestations of sex-hate that infest it like brambles. This is
our huge task. Sex-hate, firmly entrenched, is bolstered by every device of
the Establishment, though no member of the Establishment would ever
feel confident enough to admit being a sex-hater. Most do not suspect that
is what they are. We need to be alert to spot sex-hate, for if we cannot
recognise it we certainly cannot clear it away.

We may blame the sex-hate in our society on the Judaeo-Christian
religion. Yet it has to be admitted that other belief systems are not
guiltless. Sexual fascists, as Dr Albert Ellis, author of *The American
Sexual Tragedy*, calls them, are found among atheists, humanists,
communists and agnostics almost as frequently as among the congrega-
tions of the religious. In the first days of the Russian revolution in 1917
repressive sex laws, including those against divorce, abortion and
homosexuality, were swept away. Within a few years they were back.
Sex-negative conditioning is strong.

In *Sex and Marriage in England Today* Geoffrey Gorer tells of his
research among young people about their attitudes to the contraceptive
pill. A seventeen-year-old market porter, who denied having any religion
and said that he had had intercourse twice in his life, considered the pill a
bad thing: 'It proves they only have intercourse because they like it.' In
Sex in the Adolescent Years, Dr Lester Kirkendall writes of people's
problems in overcoming many years of misteaching.

They have deep-seated feelings of fear and disgust, concerning sex. They regard it
simply as a physical, sensual experience which is always threatening to
overpower judgment and due regard for others. They judge morality in terms of
the presence or absence of sexual experience. For many adults the need is first to
unlearn, then to build a concept of sex on a new and broader foundation.

The medical profession has an important role to play in this process, as
Masters and Johnston point out. The physician, they say, should provide
reassurance that sexual activity, in all its varied forms, is proper and
good. They remind us that many women have been taught that only
certain specifics of sexual stimulation or certain coital positions are
acceptable. These women do not readily accept any deviation from what
they are conditioned to consider 'right and proper', regardless of the
interests of their sexual partners. Masters and Johnson added that
Victorianism, although vanishing from the American social scene, left a
residual influence that may well require attention for at least another fifty
years. What they call the Victorian influence manifests itself in unhealthy
mental states and improper restrictions (imposed by law, social attitudes
or religion) on the liberty of individuals. These include guilt, tension,
anxiety, shame, prudery (with its components voyeurism and exhibitionism), pretence, ignorance, suppressed curiosity, chronically unsatisfied sexual desire, and an urge for harmful forms of sexual release such as
sadism or rape. The restrictions on liberty affect the mind as well as the

body. They interfere with free speech and impose censorship. They inflict thought control. They overturn a fundamental sovereignty.

The Way Forward

The way forward may be to go back. Square one takes us to the animals. Lacking self-consciousness, they lack the ability to be other than natural. In an excellent contribution to the Longford Report, Dr Peter Scott of the Maudsley Hospital spoke of the help ethology can give to the solution of human sexual problems. Sex, because it requires interaction, is always a difficult exercise – perhaps the most difficult we will ever have to manage, says Dr Scott. We know we are dependent on learning in order to do well with it: 'Yet little appears to be taught'. For animals sex is a contained thing, by no means limited to reproduction. 'We mustn't fall into St Paul's mistake of supposing that sex is only to beget children. You may discuss whether this is morally desirable, but not whether it is biologically true, because it manifestly isn't.'

Next we can gain help from primitive peoples, sharing to some extent the unselfconsciousness of animals. Dr Eugene Scheimann expressed this well in *Sex Can Save Your Heart . . . and Life*:

How can we in our enlightened twentieth century account for the fact that the earliest peoples knew instinctively about the association between sexuality and health and protected themselves, while we don't? Thousands of years ago making love played an open and important part in community rituals. It was accepted naturally as a concomitant of ensuring health, vigor, fertility, and longevity. Unfortunately for us, centuries later, sex was redefined under a two-faced, double-standard morality as being sinful, self-indulgent, and dangerous. The positive association between sex and health decidedly has been too long under official suppression. This must end.

As many anthropologists from Malinowski onwards have demonstrated, primitive people, uncontaminated by incursive traders and missionaries, have an evolved sex-economy that even Wilhelm Reich would have found acceptable. They know that sexuality is a potent factor in human wellbeing. Where life is dangerous, uncertain and mysterious, warmth and pleasure are valued. Fertility rites develop not just to ensure the continuity of the tribe but to acknowledge what is truly powerful and important in human life. A deity is given sexual parts, in recognition of their overwhelming significance. The early Mesopotamians, according to the anthropologist John Allegro, believed that on the rare occasions when it rained 'somewhere above the sky a mighty penis reaches an orgasm that shakes the heavens'.

Our easiest access to primitive people is in the shape of small children. Edmund Burke said that the arrogance of age must submit to be taught by youth. The monumental certainty of the Victorian pedagogue has, thankfully, passed away. Today we realise how little that is certain there is in what we pass on to our children, how respectful and careful we must be before deciding that a child's natural, unprompted action is to be 'corrected' by our greater wisdom. So far as that 'wisdom' comes from inherited attitudes we need to question it rigorously. Sex-hate is a legacy, a *damnosa hereditas*. The law says that no one is obliged to accept an unwanted legacy. Here is one respect in which the law is not an ass, but wise and right.

The Positive Sex Culture

If by a strenuous effort of imagination we can conceive of the site cleared for the Garden of Happy Emotions, how shall we then proceed? By approaching sex positively instead of negatively.

The positive sex culture *reverses* our inherited morality, under which the presumption is that any particular form of sexual activity is wrong. Our inherited morality says 'condemn' – unless a justification is made out. Positive sex says 'approve' – unless an objection is made out. The Garden of Happy Emotions is not an amoral place, where anything goes. It is a moral place, where the morality is true. Not founded on superstition, but on reason. Not designed for a totally different society, but for our own society.

The sex-morality we have inherited derives from Israel in biblical times. In biblical times, as now, Israel was ruled by militarism. Slavery was then an accepted institution. Democracy was unheard of. Human rights had not been mentioned. Woman was an inferior creature, unfitted to enter the priesthood, unfitted to take any decision of consequence. Ignorance prevailed on many subjects we take for granted: biology, physiology, even anatomy. Knowledge of the world, of the stars, of human history was sketchy and often mistaken. Scientific and technological development lay in the future.

Yet this is the age and the place from which we take, unchanged, our official sexual morality. We are fools to do so.

To reverse the presumption imposed by inherited morality involves taking a fresh look at every aspect of sex. We need to realise its staggering variety, its complexity. Each sex-group and age-group has its distinctive needs. Often they differ; sometimes they conflict. They must be studied, learnt and understood. Sex can be crude, blind and brutal, particularly as manifested by the very young. On the other hand sex can be the ghostly essence that flows around, and binds, the highest form of human relationship. It can be anything in between. Sexuality has to be seen as a wide spectrum. At one end is the boy's crude hunger, demanding to be crudely satisfied. At the other is the high renouncing sexual passion of Abelard. Sexuality is large enough to accommodate them all, *for all are valid*. In the future, sexual expression will be seen as anything from a vital part of a vital relationship at one extreme to the mere satisfaction of a passing hunger at the other – just as eating can be anything from a mid-morning snack at the office to Holy Communion at the altar rail.

Displacing the Rule of the Old

Who can take this fresh look at sex? Certainly not the old, who usually dispose our affairs (often from beyond the grave).

Benjamin and Masters complain of the immemorial rule of the old when discussing the sexual deprivation of young men in the armed forces. The laws and regulations dealing with this, they point out, are always enacted without asking those most concerned a single question about what they would prefer and advise. Benjamin and Masters continue:

It is always the ageing and the old men and women who primarily decide how those who are sexually most active should behave. This is manifestly ridiculous and unfair. The old man too often has forgotten how youth feels and reacts and what the requirements are of a man with a male hormone production of an age level 20 to 30 as compared with that of 60 to 70. If the senescent legislator, moral reformer and even medical adviser were compelled to undergo some geronto-therapeutic measures with hormones, and perhaps vitamins – a treatment that modern medicine is well able to provide – it is possible that a more realistic and sober program for the solution of the sex problem could be found.

Old maids (both sexes) are hardly well-equipped to write a useful textbook on the 'sex life of men'. A color-blind judge of paintings would be a joke. A deaf or even partly deaf music critic would be a travesty. Men and women who sit in judgment as to proper sexual behaviour of young males in uniform may well ponder these analogies.

Yet the common law, which binds us all, continues to be made by old men (no old or other women have as yet been added to the Judicial Committee of the House of Lords). The judges who in 1961 invented the crime of conspiracy to corrupt public morals were all old men. Listen to their mode of reasoning in that crucial case:

Viscount Simonds (aged 70):

In the sphere of criminal law, I entertain no doubts that there remains in the courts of law a residual power to enforce the supreme and fundamental purpose of the law, to conserve not only the safety and order but also the moral welfare of the state, and that it is their duty to guard it against attacks which may be the more insidious because they are novel and unprepared for.

Lord Tucker (aged 73, and equipped with the ability to foresee the homosexual liberation Act passed six years later):

Suppose Parliament tomorrow enacts that homosexual practice between adult consenting males is no longer to be criminal, is it to be said that a conspiracy to further and encourage such practices among adult males could not be the subject of a criminal charge fit to be left to a jury?

Lord Morris of Borth-y-Gest (aged 65):

There are certain manifestations of conduct which are an affront to and an attack on recognised public standards of morals and decency, and which all well-disposed persons would stigmatise and condemn as deserving of punishment.

What infamous conduct was the subject of these old men's solemn strictures? Why, the publication of a modest handbook miscalled *The Ladies Directory*. This gave names, addresses and telephone numbers of women offering sexual services for payment, considerately explaining the particular skills supplied by each. Their aged Lordships concurred in the opinion that these persons were not entitled to the appellation *lady*, that their proffered services were immoral, and that any published directory of these services was criminal. They awarded the little handbook the awful dignity of being in law a conspiracy to corrupt public morals. Gleefully they upheld the prison sentence which had been passed on its publisher.

The Comfort of Sex

Freud said that in normal sex there is no neurosis; then demonstrated the wide diversity of the sexual impulse. Alvin Toffler, in his book *Future Shock*, warns that technological progress is proceeding at a pace too fast for human minds to absorb. One comfort available to us in facing future shock is true sexuality, which is, thankfully, independent of technology. All it asks is honesty to human nature. Men, women and children fortunate to dwell already in the Garden of Happy Emotions (and there are many of these) are not repressed or inhibited. They know they are free to avow at all times the way they are feeling, even if respect for the freedom of others restricts to some extent its physical expression. They know they are able to bring out and discuss with others that crucial emotion that obsesses us all, *the innermost desire*. This is the image, tinted always by sexuality, that haunts our dreams. It points our way to paradise, and if only we had it in possession paradise is where we would be. Or so we *feel*.

In our present world, if you make me angry I can say so – should say so. If I am jealous or envious, if I feel slighted or neglected, I can and should say so. And the 'you' in this context may be my closest companion or a stranger. So it should be with my sexual feelings. These are 'intimate' feelings. But they are not more 'intimate' than my feelings of rage or jealousy, and should be as freely revealed. But rage and jealousy are negative emotions, while sexual feelings are positive. We might plausibly be ashamed of rage, and seek to conceal it while we struggle for mastery. The same applies to that most futile emotion, jealousy. We cannot plausibly be ashamed of sexual desire, yet all our conditioning drives us to conceal it. That is reinforced by words we are early taught to despise: lust, concupiscence, lasciviousness and the rest.

In the Garden of Happy Emotions we speak often of our sexual desires because we experience them often. We innocently display our genitalia (whether tumescent or not) as freely as we display our noses. We describe to friends the orgasm we experienced last night as readily as we describe our pride at succeeding in some arduous task, or our exaltation on hearing a Beethoven sonata or observing the beauty of a sunset on the river. We ask after the sexual fulfilment of our dear friend as sympathetically and naturally as we ask after his or her bodily ailments or holiday excursions, and we get an easy reply. We give our sexual parts and natures their true value, neither exaggerating nor underplaying. We are able at last to stop pretending.

Why have humans not found this garden before? Perhaps they have, and we in the west of today do not know about it. But to us, situated as we are towards the end of the twentieth century, it seems that apart from the acceptance of sex-positivism as a leading ethic two other developments are also to be wished for. This is where our science, our technology, our medical advances come in. In addition to the predominating influence of sex-negativism, two other barriers have till now checked our entry into the Garden of Happy Emotions. One is uncontrolled fertility. The other is disease. Prime conditions for entry into the garden are the surmounting of these two barriers.

Fertility. In the Garden of Happy Emotions it is desirable that every adult should be in an infertile state unless he or she has deliberately chosen otherwise. Subject to control of disease, that would allow unfettered sexual fulfilment for all, at all times. Whether women are on the pill, or men or women are temporarily defertilised by some more sophisticated technique, is immaterial. The point is that everyone should at all times be freed to express themselves sexually, but always responsibly (that is conformably with sexual ethics). So they would have to do something deliberate and positive, such as taking a counter-pill, in order to render themselves fertile. Thus sexual intercourse will be enabled to take place without the slightest risk of unwanted conception. When on the other hand conception is wanted it can be deliberately sought – always with due regard to the necessary ingredient of sex-respect. Intercourse with the fervent desire to conceive, though necessarily rare, will always be on the highest level of joy. That arises from the very nature of sex, which must never be lost sight of.

Disease. In the Garden of Happy Emotions there is no such thing as sexually transmitted disease. Medical science has completely conquered it. You are no more likely to catch a disease from making love than you are from shaking hands.

Very soon, if we press hard enough and spend enough money, science will make it possible to comply with these two prime conditions. Already we are very near, despite the temporary setback of Aids. Already we should be preparing our attitudes. Especially we should be preparing to receive into the Garden of Happy Emotions those members of the human race who will be attaining maturity in the early years of the twenty-first century.

Free Sexuality

Sexuality is not free until these prime conditions prevail. Already it is possible, by suitable precautions and a wise choice of partner, to achieve a situation where we can be almost certain they do prevail. What then?

With the prime conditions, mankind enters the realm of free sexuality. The first of the prime conditions separates sexuality from procreation. Indeed, science already possesses the means of bringing men and women into the world without there having been, in their case, the slightest throb of sexual feeling. The Central London Hatchery described in Aldous Huxley's *Brave New World* could be erected tomorrow if we wished.

Mankind's progress on this globe has been marked by triumphant conquest of natural limitations and triumphant discovery of unsuspected forces. Mankind is continually evolving as our environment evolves under the pressure of the relentless human genius. Evolution is unpopular with popes, but the opinions of twentieth-century popes on sexuality are no more valid than the opinions of seventeenth-century popes were on the obvious fact that the earth is flat and the sun goes round it.

If the opinions of popes are valueless, whose opinions can we rely on? Psychologists, sociologists, anthropologists? Yes, to some extent. But really mankind is at large here. The future is wide open. It's real democracy: every man's opinion, and every woman's opinion, is of equal weight. You will have your own opinion; here is mine.

I think sexual emotion, and sexual expression, are deep and important. I hate to think of them being trivialised: and one of the most obvious indications of the fact that our society is hopelessly wrong about sexuality is the way it trivialises that potent force. In this book I have labelled that trivialisation *the titillating society*.

The guide I would follow, because it's the simplest and the most reliable, is *truth*. If a person makes you randy, tell him or her so. If you (a male) have an erection, let it show. If you want to touch someone, touch them. Of course you must not invade the privacy of others, and you must do nothing to them against their will. But in the Garden of Happy Emotions everyone understands these things. There are no hangups. Sex is trusted and liked. It is respected, as deep feeling. It is not trivialised. Nor, however manifested, is it a source of shame.

How can we landscape this wonderful garden, that each of us can glimpse? We must start with the children, that much is clear. We must begin with those who enter life *when* they enter life. Also we must begin with the human body as it really is. Not as fevered imaginations, starved of the truth, depict it. In *The Female Eunuch* Germaine Greer quotes a sentence from an 1809 book entitled *A Father's Legacy to his Daughter*: 'The finest bosom in nature is not so fine as what imagination forms.' Humans are entitled, from the earliest age, to the truth about their anatomy and that of their fellows. Forced poses and airbrush pictures rob them of this, yet it is the basis for a happy emotional life.

Next, we must accept the reality of sexual emotion even in the very young. We must say 'yes' to childhood sexuality. The children, as nascent adults, come first. Adults must stand back. Their role is to let the children blossom. This does not mean that sex education should not be undertaken. There is a pressing need for sex education at all ages from infancy onwards. Moreover it should extend to instruction in the various forms of sexual technique. It is essential however to let children develop naturally at their own pace, answering their questions honestly and factually as they are put.

Still in the region of the young, we come next to adolecent sexuality. Here is where the usurpation of the elderly assumes its most obscene form. The vulnerable young, powerful only in their sexual potency, confront the wily aged and lose. There must be a new deal for adolescents, and for the right of older people to accept any willingly offered share in their budding sexuality.

If it is agreed that the basic sexual need is for orgasm it is clear that the most common form of orgasm must be accepted. So we must say 'yes' to masturbation. Some will sneer at this as a 'wanker's charter', but that is only a manifestation of the old bad attitude to sex. The new morality rules out sexual sneers.

Mention of sex training brings us to sex-aids and variations. There is much in this field that could add to our joy if the culture would accept and encourage it. Similarly with pornography. As we have seen, there are different kinds of pornography. Stimulative pornography has an important role to play as concretised fantasy, enhancing the quality of orgasm. Quite different is political pornography, aversive in its effect. Censoring this raises important questions of democracy and freedom of speech.

Discussion of pornography naturally leads to the topic of prostitution. Both are widely condemned, not least because people make money out of them – a false objection, as we have seen. Sex for money has always been put down, but really it makes about as much sense to put down sex for money as it would do to put down poetry for money, or music for money, or art for money. So let us defend so-called prostitution, arguing that it should be accepted and developed as a much-needed sexual service.

We must ensure that we do all that can be done to make the Garden of Happy Emotions available to certain classes of people who in our culture are particularly deprived. Sex-hate operates fiercely against the old. They are not supposed to possess sexual feelings, let alone indulge them. This monstrous lie inflicts much unhappiness. In retaliation the old (who are often in positions of power) curtail the sexual rights of younger people. The truth is that the elderly have every bit as much right to be in the Garden of Happy Emotions as anyone else. So have people who are under mental or physical handicap. Here again sex-hate inflicts its withering blight. Thalidomide babies are now grown up. What sex-life do they enjoy, to help make up for the terrible damage society has inflicted on them? None at all, if most members of society get their way. Deprived of limbs, thalidomide children are to be deprived of sexuality as well. What arrangements do hospitals and other institutions make for the sexual fulfilment of their inmates? None. The same applies to prisons and young offenders' institutes.

Another deprived class are the sex-aliens: the homosexuals, trans-vestites, voyeurs, exhibitionists, sado-masochists and the rest. Society denies sex (or tries to) to the mental defective in an institution, but does not place a stigma (or tries not to) on his psychological condition. But until recently the male homosexual was imprisoned if he achieved sexual fulfilment *in accordance with his nature*. He is still imprisoned in many cases; and social condemnation of his sexual nature rages almost as strongly as it ever did. So we say 'yes' to sex-aliens. In doing this we do not argue that society should invariably tolerate what they want to do. We do argue that society should tolerate *them*.

We are privileged to live in the first enlightened age of mankind. Hitherto, the society of man has looked to physical strength, virility, fertility and conformism. Those who, for physiological, mental or emotional reasons, could not conform were rejected. Very often they had to be, in order to safeguard the society. Now things are different, and we should rejoice. The exceptional can be accommodated. The disabled are given proper care. Blacks are accepted in a white society. Homosexuals are no longer invariably penalised. Objectors, dissidents and non-conformists are not merely listened to; they are encouraged.

Finally, a Glimpse of the Future

We have outlined the new ethics. What then is sexual life like in this Garden of Happy Emotions, where the new ethics are universally observed? It is right, at the conclusion of so challenging a thesis, to attempt an answer spelling out the detail.

Some preliminary points must be made. In now demonstrating the new ethics in action we pick on no particular country, for the truths in this book are universal. We set the scene in no particular future period, for verities are timeless. One thing it is necessary to presuppose. This true system of human sexual ethics (or what we call the new ethics) has been complied with in our supposed sample society for many generations, and is by now generally accepted. The people of our imagined today have been born and bred in it. No one obeying its precepts is nowadays dismissed, like trusting flower-children of the 1960s, as aberrational. This is the life we all lead.

So let us follow from cradle to grave two particular future people living under the new ethics. Let them be identical twins named Hector and Hilary. They are progeny of a couple we might sensibly, though without any claim to originality, christen Adam and Eve. Adam and Eve are pledged to each other in marriage. These two accepted before any child of theirs was conceived that, whatever their past history, they should thenceforth be sexually faithful to one another. It was difficult, but they kept that pledge. Sexual fidelity, within its proper context, holds a prominent place in the new ethics.

Hector and Hilary experience a good babyhood. They are kept warm, and fed regularly. In the first months Eve breastfeeds them herself, as part of the process of making the new arrivals feel welcome and wanted. At this age feelings, Adam and Eve know, are everything. Eve enjoys with a good conscience the pleasurable relief breast-feeding affords her. Adam monitors this primeval process with approval. The babies imbibe milk from their mother with an inner certainty that they are on to a good thing. They have been lucky enough to start out on the right track. They are too young to realise that this elemental boon is owed not to luck but the new ethics. After each feed they sleep peacefully and dreamlessly.

When the babies begin to observe the outer world their parents strive to be good and accurate communicators in every respect. No first-hand experience is transmogrified. No perceived truth is distorted into falsehood or shamefacedly suppressed. If the growing child finds hand contact with items or products of his or her own body pleasurable, the parents accept that without express or implied reproof. Nevertheless they tactfully begin, as is their duty under the new ethics, that training process which shall ultimately render their young fit to become members of a civilised human society. Training, never to be confused with brain-washing, is a vital part of the new ethics.

Adam and Eve exhibit not the slightest embarrassment at any interest their offspring exhibit in the lineaments of their parents' bodies. Such interest is in any case slight, since the twins have been accustomed to seeing their parents nude from earliest days. A young child has a strong tactile sense, desiring above all contact with both its own and its parents' flesh. Adam and Eve have been instructed by the new ethics that this is to be not merely tolerated but encouraged. From it, they know, springs reassurance. Deprived of it, a child may spend the rest of life searching for what so early was missed.

So as the babies grow to be toddlers they smoothly undergo a learning process at the hands of their well-adjusted and skilful parents. The skills have been *taught*, for in a complex modern society parental instinct is insufficient for sound rearing. Within the sexual sphere, the toddlers learn the vital balance inherent in the new ethics. They are trained to take their place in society, but no part of their makeup is denigrated. Eliminatory incontinence must give way to control, but without any suggestion that these natural processes are 'dirty'. Interest in the genital organs is treated as obviously healthy, yet the child is gently taught that humdrum everyday life must go on without the intrusion of rampant sex. That is a part of civility. Sex, though a pressing urge, is special – and worthy at all times of respect. Reserving sex for meaningful, joyful interludes does not put it down. On the contrary, it elevates it.

Early in life, Hector and Hilary are encouraged to play and make friends with their age-mates outside the home. If, which is seldom, this play includes sexual experimentation, no parent is upset. On the contrary, parents expect and encourage sex-play. It happens rarely simply because there is no perceived inhibition on the sexual element of the children's lives. From the beginning, this has taken its proper place and therefore does not obtrude itself in infantile behaviour. At any age, only sex denied is troublesome.

When Hilary is seven an incident befalls the little girl. She is the subject of old-fashioned sexual abuse in the park by Arthur, an elderly man. Arthur persuades Hilary to take down her knickers, and lovingly fondles her genital region. He then takes out his ancient penis, which is tremblingly erect. He asks Hilary to stroke it, and she does so. No big deal, say the exponents of the new ethics. Afterwards, Hilary asks her mother about this experience which, like so much in her young life, is new to her. Eve takes the opportunity to explain that there are still a few people around, by now very old, who lived in the former era of universal sex-negation.

'They are very sad sex people, because they were taught wicked things about sex. We know better now, and we must help them as best we can.'
'Why did the old man want me to stroke his penis?'
'Because it made him happy, dear. I'm glad you did it. We should always try to make the old happy. The poor fellow must have suffered a lot of sexual misery in his day to get pleasure from the little you did, sweet though it was of you to do it.'

That is all that happens. There is no fuss. Hilary does not ask in an agonised way why Arthur's penis was erect because she understands about that. Her parents have already taught her the mechanics, and even something of the mental and emotional elements. Occasionally Hilary has glimpsed her father with an erect penis, and her brother too. That too was no big deal. It did not lead to intimacies such as Arthur requested since another thing Hilary has been taught is that, *except in certain contexts*, sex is something to be known about, sympathetically understood, but not actually practised. The concept of incest, as the protection of affectionate but not passionate family relationships, is understood by

Hilary even at so young an age. Well before the meaning of passion is known to her at first hand, Hilary has learnt its allotted place within a happy household.

The new ethics teaches that the highest possibilities of human happiness are reached within the bosom of a well-adjusted family. The quartet comprising Adam, Eve, Hilary and Hector are such a family. The family members have no sexual secrets from each other, but are nevertheless trained to observe proper reticence, sympathy, tact and self-denial. These are not stifling because the crucial element is freely accepted. *Each member of the family, at each age, has his or her sexual needs recognised and adequately provided for.*

For example, Eve often finds herself growing impatient with Adam. He lacks something as a lover, and is too inclined to go off drinking with his mates. As he nears puberty, Hector presents himself to Eve's imagination as an alternative lover. He adores his mother, and enjoys informing her of the fact. He is boisterous and playful. Often in their romps Eve feels the tug of an amorous connection with her young son, but desists. She remembers her training in the new ethics. For his own mother to become Hector's first lover would be a disaster for the familial relationship they both depend on for life-long happiness. Eve is well versed in the true sexual disciplines, so different from the old cramping confines of sex-negation.

Adam experiences similar emotions in relation to Hilary, and also resists the resultant temptations. The natural longing of a pubescent girl for emotional intimacy with her father must be translated into relationships with her male age-mates. That is what nature intended, and that is the true recipe for happiness. As instructed, Adam helps to further this.

Shrewdly, Eve and her husband thrust away foolish notions of forbidden passion with their offspring in favour of the mellow joys of long-standing matrimony and grandparenthood. Their devotion to each other has an integrity that overrides such temptations. The crucial factor is something different, however. *The two disclose their temptations to each other.* They do this in the same way that they disclose their mutual frustrations with each other. Both are well aware that a marriage, like any tender plant, needs to be nurtured continually. This does not require deception. In caring for each other, they care for their marriage. That is how it flourishes, despite all the contrary winds that strive to blow it away.

Sheltered by the new ethics, the two children arrive at puberty. They are well prepared for its physiological and emotional characteristics, and so for them there is nothing of the pubertal shock that so often afflicts children of our own day.

The new ethics recognises that where puberty is concerned, as in so many respects, girls and boys are different.

Hilary has been taught that a girl does not have to be dragged into the feverish sexual world many adolescent boys inhabit. She has learnt that she is blessed with command over her own body, so far as sexual practice is concerned. If desire has not yet stirred in her, she is warned in advance that she has the right to reject male attempts to arouse it. Possibly her destiny might lie in life-long unawakened sexuality. If so, she has a right to that destiny.

If her sexual destiny lies along more usual paths, Hilary has been made aware of her rights and duties. Her right is to fulfil her sexuality to the utmost. Her duty is to practise certain safeguards, mainly concerned with pregnancy and disease, and to observe moral principle. Hilary is competently instructed in the methods by which these aims can be secured.

What has the boy Hector been taught? First, to respect the sexual rights and duties of the females he encounters (including those of his sister Hilary). Second, to fulfil his own sexuality without needless guilt. In the Garden of Happy Emotions, it is important to grasp, no one finds sex intrinsically evil or guilt-arousing. The position is the reverse. From birth, everyone is taught that sex is a *positive* quality. There is to be no guilt about the possession of sexual desire, or the need for its release. On the contrary, people who seek to foment such guilt are to be condemned. There are persistent folk memories concerning the long years of suppression. In the Garden, sex-negation is a dirty word. There it is *expected* that an adult or adolescent will have sexual needs. They are catered for with complete understanding. If anyone seems to lack such needs, eyebrows are raised. Polite enquiries are made, rather as people of our own day uninhibitedly enquire about a friend's operation or job problems.

So the boy Hector has been faithfully prepared. He is aware, well in advance of puberty, that people will expect him from that point on to experience frequent and acute sexual urges. He knows that in the reproductive purpose nature has designed the adult male to void semen at frequent intervals, and, what is more, urgently to *desire* to do so. He has been taught that this desire, at least in its crude form, is never so powerful as in early adolescence. At the same time Hector has learnt that nature's sexual purpose commands utmost respect, and is never to be trivialised. Everyone around the pubescent Hector is aware of these things too. So he is sympathetically left to practise solitary masturbation, after being advised by Adam on the most effective techniques. It is recognised as suitable that on occasion one of his age-mates (of either sex) might add a comforting and assisting presence to these occasions of release.

Going beyond that, the new ethics welcomes the fact that adults may have an active part to play in the pubescent Hector's sexual per-formances. A tender woman outside the family may initiate Hector, even in his early teens, in the joys of intercourse. Recourse may be had to a female erotic Samaritan, whose fee is willingly paid by Adam. Even a man may have a legitimate part to play in Hector's adolescent development, along the well-tried lines of Greek love. What any such adult always keeps firmly in mind, as they have been taught to do by the new ethics, is respect for sex in general coupled with deepest respect for a child's burgeoning libido. (It goes without saying that they also respect the need to avoid unwanted pregnancy and disease.)

The result of all this is that so far as their sexuality is concerned both Hilary and Hector enjoy their childhood, their puberty and their adolescence. Growth does not, as with us, bring stress. On the contrary the youthful years are regarded by all who live under the new ethics as times of joy. In later life they wistfully apply to these years a phrase that merely arouses derision when used about them in the late twentieth century: the best years of your life.

It is likely that Hilary will stay in the world, and live a fully realised adult sex-life. For a while she will employ her sexuality, like her other attributes, in the course of a succession of close relationships with loved men. In time she is likely to decide to settle down with one man in some form of dedicated marriage or pair-bond. This is not compulsory marriage, the forced and sole opening for sexual fulfilment we have known in the past. Nevertheless it is a profound and serious relationship, which may well endure for the rest of life.

It is possible that Hector might decide to live out his life in what used to be regarded as an honourable condition: bachelordom. It is most likely, however, that, like his sister, Hector will pass through the stages by which balanced adults, under the new ethics, are taught to employ their sexuality to the optimum possible extent in the service of living.

What of sex-aliens in the Garden of Happy Emotions? The first thing we notice is that there are very few of them. The new ethics has drastically reduced their number. Sexual needs are openly and acceptably catered for to the full. Commercial provision of sex services is not merely tolerated but accepted, indeed demanded. Quality controls are imposed by law.

Are there then any sex-aliens in the Garden? Here the present author must confess his inadequacy as a prophet. If life in the Garden is what it is cracked up to be, some may ask, why should there be left any lesbians, gays, transvestites, sado-masochists, voyeurs, exhibitionists, pederasts, pedophiles, or others of that ilk? It is possible to take a different view, and say that some at least of these conditions have a validity that will ensure their continuance.

What we can be sure of is this. If any sexual condition is shown to have a validity transcending the sex-negativism, even sex-hate, of our own times then the new ethics, as time progresses, will accommodate, recognise and respect it.

The Sex Code

Summary

Note. Below is a collection of the sixty moral precepts which are set out in various places in the body of the book and constitute the Code. The number in square brackets after each precept is that of the page on which it appears.

Ethics and sex
1 The concept of secular morality.
2 Secular sexual morality.
3 The duty of ethical understanding.
4 The duty of ethical action.
5 The present Code.
6 Interpreting the Code.

Accepting our sexuality
7 The duty of sex-acceptance.
8 Sex-guilt.
9 Sex in the workplace.
10 Nudity and exhibitionism.
11 Toleration of harmless sexual disorders.

Respecting our sexuality
12 The duty of sex-respect.
13 The right to sexual privacy.
14 Sex with animals.

Fulfilling our sexual natures
15 The duty of sex-fulfilment.
16 Acquiring and improving sexual techniques.
17 Celibacy and chastity.
18 Sex for the disabled.
19 Sex for service personnel.
20 Sex for prisoners.

Sexual acts
21 Types of sexual act.
22 Consent to sexual acts.
23 Sexual harassment.
24 Solitary sex.
25 Troilism and orgies.
26 Sex between persons of different race.
27 Harmful sexual acts.

Pair-bonding and marriage
28 Pair-bonding.
29 The social institution of marriage.
30 Open sexual relationships.
31 Passing as single.
32 Adultery.
33 Sterilisation of a marriage-partner.
34 Incest.

Conception, pregnancy and lactation
35 The decision to propagate.
36 Every child a wanted child.
37 Propagation of mixed-race children.
38 Artificially induced pregnancy.
39 The defective foetus.

40 Adverse actions during
   pregnancy.
41 Breast-feeding in public.

Contraception
42 Morality of contraception.
43 Deceit as to possibility of
   conception.

Abortion
44 Abortion of non-viable foetus.
45 Abortion of viable foetus.
46 Anti-abortion campaigning.

The young
47 Parents' duty to rear their child.
48 Sex education.
49 Consent by young people to
   sexual acts.

Homosexuality
50 Same-gender sex acts.
51 Discrimination against
   homosexuals.
52 Promoting homosexuality.

Prostitution
53 Payment for sex.
54 Treatment of prostitutes.

Pornography
55 Categories of pornography.
56 Non-erotic pornography.
57 Perverted or debased
   pornography.
58 Stimulative pornography.
59 Educational and artistic
   pornography.
60 Political or destabilising
   pornography.

Ethics and Sex

The concept of secular morality

1. Though non-believers cannot accept religion, they acknowledge right and wrong. They wish to make the best of themselves, and out of common sympathy also wish the best for their fellow humans. Without any supposed divine command or revelation, they accept that human acts are moral, immoral or morally neutral. They perceive that this indicates the existence, in some sense that is real, of an objective standard of ethics (referred to in this book as 'the ethical code') whose sole base is in human reason and the human conscience. [4]

Secular sexual morality

2. In the sexual field we all have a duty to be good, that is to act morally. This is part of our general duty, laid down by the ethical code, to act morally in every area of our life. Because the ethical code requires us to strive at all times and in all ways to be virtuous, it follows that we should strive to be virtuous in our sexual life. Indeed, since sexual wickedness can cause untold harm and distress, the duty to be good is particularly strong in this area. [7]

The duty of ethical understanding

3. No one can be sure of acting morally in a given situation, or responding with moral correctness to the act of another, unless they know and understand what is called for by the ethical code. Therefore we should try to absorb its principles to the fullest extent of our capacity. This we may call the duty of ethical understanding. [7]

The duty of ethical action

4. We should comply with the ethical code not only directly but indirectly. It guides our own sexual acts and also our response to the sexual acts of others. What we must not do ourselves, we must not countenance others doing. What it is our duty to do, it is our duty to help others do also. All this may be called the duty of ethical action. [8]

The present Code

5. Because the ethical code cannot be known in precise detail its prescriptions may be unclear in particular cases, and cannot be free from dispute. The present text (referred to in this book as 'the Code') attempts to formulate the ethical code, so far as it relates specifically to human sexuality, in a form most likely to produce certainty and command agreement in the modern western secular culture. [9]

Interpreting the Code

6. It is important to bear in mind when reading the Code that its effect is intended to be cumulative. Each precept is subject to limitations stated elsewhere in the Code, and also by precepts of the ethical code not specific to sexual matters. The Code is concerned only with morality, and pays no regard to law or aesthetics. In the Code references to acts include omissions. [10]

Accepting our Sexuality

The duty of sex-acceptance

7. Since we are all sexual beings we should look upon our own or another's sexual organs, functions and desires positively, with welcoming acceptance that they exist and work (the duty of sex-acceptance). We should never look on them negatively, with dislike, regret or contempt. This does not mean that remediable sexual disorders ought to be accepted as they are, or that immoral sexual behaviour should be tolerated. [15]

Sex-guilt

8. Because of negative conditioning, guilt about the mere existence of sexuality (sex-guilt) is endemic in western culture. Yet the duty of sex-acceptance means we should eschew this guilt in ourselves. Moreover we are under a duty not to implant or nurture guilt in another person, particularly a child, because of their sexual organs, functions or desires, or because of their sexual acts where these are not immoral. When we encounter such guilt we should where possible help to alleviate it. [47]

Sex in the workplace

9. If we have a job to do we should not let sex interfere with its proper execution. While accepting our sexuality, we should not therefore allow a sexual relationship with a fellow worker to become so demanding or stressful as to obstruct the work. If things do reach this stage, it may be our duty to seek other employment. [50]

Nudity and exhibitionism

10. The duty of sex-acceptance requires us to tolerate the sight of the nude human body, even where because of the subject's advanced age or other factors it seems to us aesthetically unpleasing. We should refuse to countenance prudishness about the body or its functions, which can be harmful psychologically. On the other hand we need to recognise the effects of past negative conditioning, and not knowingly outrage another person by the sight or sound of any extreme sexual activity or display. [63]

Toleration of harmless sexual disorders

11. The duty of sex-acceptance requires us to tolerate the sexual disorders of others, except where they give rise to immoral acts. If however such a disorder is remediable we should where practicable assist in its cure. [74]

Respecting our Sexuality

The duty of sex-respect

12. Since sexuality is the source of all human life, and is of profound emotional concern to all human beings in the living of their lives, we should treat our own or another's sexual organs, functions and desires with respect, even reverence (the duty of sex-respect). We should therefore not commit any act that degrades or trivialises them. [75]

The right to sexual privacy

13. It is immoral, as contravening the right to privacy and the duty of sex-respect, for anyone, without the consent of the person in question, to gaze at or listen to the sexual activity of another person, whether directly or by means of a recording or listening device. [78]

Sex with animals

14. It is contrary to the duty of sex-respect for a human being to have sex with an animal. [86]

Fulfilling our Sexual Natures

The duty of sex-fulfilment

15. Because sexuality is an essential and vital part of the human constitution, we should develop and fulfil our sexual nature throughout life (the duty of sex-fulfilment). This does not mean that remediable sexual disorders ought to be accepted as they are, or that immoral sexual behaviour should be tolerated. However it does follow that we should help and encourage others, particularly the young, to achieve fulfilment in the sexual field as in any other area of life. Equally we should not deny old people sexual fulfilment or denigrate their pursuit of it. We should not condemn any sexual relationship on the ground of a disparity in the ages of the partners. [89]

Acquiring and improving sexual techniques

16. As with most things in human life, satisfaction in sexual intercourse depends on knowledge and improves with practice. It is our duty to our partner and ourself to learn and practise the techniques needed to make the best of our sexual natures. [103]

Celibacy and chastity

17. Because they contravene the duty of sex-fulfilment, enduring celibacy and chastity are undesirable in the way that any other failure to fulfil one's human potential is undesirable. This does not mean that young persons should be hurried into sexual experience before they are physically or emotionally ready. [104]

Sex for the disabled

18. (1) Apparent consent by a mentally incapacitated person to a sexual act cannot be taken as true consent where the incapacity is too great to permit the person to understand the full emotional and ethical significance of the act. Where however such a person would otherwise be condemned to involuntary celibacy or chasitity it is not immoral to afford them sexual fulfilment with no more than their apparent consent, since in such circumstances the usual requirement of true consent is prevented from applying. [122]

(2) The duty of sex-fulfilment indicates that it is immoral to deny people a full sex-life merely on the ground of their mental or physical incapacity. Those having charge of such people therefore have a duty to ensure so far as practicable that they are afforded suitable opportunities for such fulfilment, provided necessary contraceptive and other precautions are taken. [127]

Sex for service personnel

19. The duty of sex-fulfilment indicates that it is immoral to deny people a full sex-life merely on the ground of their service in the armed forces or other state services. Those having charge of such people therefore have a duty to ensure so far as practicable that they are afforded suitable opportunities for such fulfilment. [130]

Sex for prisoners

20. A sentence of imprisonment inevitably restricts the prisoner's freedom of activity; indeed that is its social purpose. However the duties of sex-fulfilment and sex-respect indicate that we ought not to deny people a full sex-life merely on the ground that they are state prisoners, just as we do not deny them food, drink and rest. Those having charge of such people therefore have a duty to ensure so far as practicable that they are afforded suitable opportunities for sexual fulfilment. [130]

Sexual Acts

Types of sexual act

21. Since the primary purpose of our sexual organs, functions and desires is reproduction of the species, contraceptive-free vaginal intercourse between a fertile male and female may be regarded as the primary sexual act. However healthy sexuality goes much wider than this, and no type of sexual act is to be condemned on the ground that it departs from the primary act. [131]

Consent to sexual acts

22. We ought not to touch another person sexually without their consent, whether explicit or reasonably inferred. Nor should we do any other act towards a person sexually (such as showing them a pornographic picture or exposing their nakedness) which is out of scale with any indication they have given regarding their willingness for this. Special considerations apply where the person is too young, or is otherwise unable, to give informed consent. [132]

Sexual harassment

23. We should not make sexual overtures to any person beyond a point where the recipient indicates refusal, disapproval or distress. If for any reason the other is or may feel coerced or otherwise subservient, we need to realise that the signs of rejection may be faint. That does not mean they are to be disregarded. [133]

Solitary sex

24. A sexual act (such as masturbation) is not immoral because done in solitude. Since young people are often ready for sex before they are mature enough to enter a sexual relationship with another person, solitary sex may for them be the most suitable form of early sexual activity and should not be condemned or discouraged by parents or others in authority. However, solitary sex may encourage narcissism, and lacks the richness that comes from a loving relationship with another. Where the subject is within a pair-bond, solitary sex may be immoral if it indicates a rejection of the partner. [136]

Troilism and orgies

25. The participation of more than two people does not render a sexual act immoral. [137]

Sex between persons of different race

26. It is morally neutral for a person of one race to have sex with a person of a different race, and it is therefore wrong to condemn persons of different races merely because they have sex together. [137]

Harmful sexual acts

27. (1) Where is it known or suspected by either party to a prospective sex-act that one or other is or may be infected with any sexually transmissible

disease it is their duty to ensure that adequate precautions are taken against infection. [137]

(2) If a person knows that an infected person is likely to contravene the previous rule (for example because they have themselves contracted disease from that person) is it their duty to help ensure that the infected person does not transmit the disease to others. [137]

(3) It is immoral for a person who knows or suspects that they are infected with any sexually transmissible disease to have sex with another person without first informing them of the fact. [138]

(4) It is immoral to have sex with another person by a method or technique that may cause either party physical or mental injury. [138]

Pair-bonding and Marriage

Pair-bonding

28. It is common for sexually mature humans, whether heterosexual or homosexual in orientation, to form themselves into pair-bonds, that is couples who choose to link exclusively by means of enduring emotional-erotic ties. This bonding originates with the need of the human young for settled parenting during their lengthy period of infancy, and now has a deep emotional significance for humans generally. Accordingly the parties should strive to make the relationship fulfilling and enduring, particularly where children are being nurtured within the bond. Except in the case of an open relationship, outsiders should respect a pair-bond and not intrude upon it with competing sexual demands. [139]

The social institution of marriage

29. The highest form of pair-bonding is secular marriage, whereby society formally recognises the tie and accords it special consideration in law and otherwise. Since married bonding is supported by social consensus and state institutions, since it increases the chances of happiness of any children of the union, and since it enhances the bond's prospects of permanence and success, it is morally preferable to unmarried bonding. The institution of marriage should not be withheld from homosexual couples or transsexuals. [142]

Open sexual relationships

30. An open marriage or other open sexual relationship is one in which the partners agree that the relationship shall not be exclusive, so that a partner is free to have sex with outside persons. Because it can lead to their unhappiness, children should not be propagated or reared within an open sexual relationship. [142]

Passing as single

31. It is immoral for a married person to enter into a sexual relationship without informing the other person that he or she is married. Similar considerations apply to an unmarried person within a pair-bond. [142]

Adultery

32. Unless a marriage or other pair-bond is an open relationship or has broken down, it is immoral for one of the partners to have sex with anyone except the other. [143]

Sterilisation of a marriage partner

33. One party to a marriage should not undergo sterilisation without the consent of the other, since this operation fundamentally alters the nature and significance of the relationship of marriage. [143]

Incest

34. Incest may be morally objectionable on one or more of three grounds. It may (1) risk producing genetically defective offspring, or (2) grievously disrupt relationships within a family unit, or (3) constitute immoral exploitation of a younger person by an older relative. Where none of these conditions exist, incest is morally neutral. [144]

Conception, Pregnancy and Lactation

The decision to propagate

35. One of the most important decisions a person can take is the decision to propagate, that is to bring a new life into the world. It is an awesome responsibility. Accordingly the decision should be taken with great care, having due regard to the likely quality of life of the child and the effect of its arrival on other members of the family. [145]

Every child a wanted child

36. It is wrong deliberately to propagate a child unless it is wanted and the parents are able and willing to rear it properly. A child needs both parents, and therefore needs both parents to want it. [145]

Propagation of mixed-race children

37. Before a person has sex with a person of different race in a way that could produce a child it is their moral duty carefully to consider whether, having regard to the social difficulties often experienced by children of mixed race, and the genetic factors involved, it is morally right to do this in their case. If their sincere answer is yes, their propagation of the child is morally neutral, but they have a duty to recognise the difficulties the child may experience and help it to overcome them. [147]

Artificially induced pregnancies

38. (1) If the natural parents, that is the man and woman from whose bodies the sperm and ovum respectively derive, are pair-bonded to each other, the fact that a pregnancy is caused by artificial insemination, or is otherwise artificially induced, is morally neutral. [147]

(2) Where parties to a pair-bond accept insemination or implantation

from a donor, this carries the same duties with respect to the resulting child as if both were its natural parents. [147]

(3) A woman who is within a pair-bond ought not to accept insemination from a donor without the consent of her partner, and a man who is within a pair-bond ought not to donate his sperm for another woman without the consent of his partner. [147]

(4) A man who donates his sperm, for example through a sperm bank, without knowing its destination, or a woman who similarly donates her ova, has no moral responsibility for the resulting child and is entitled to keep his or her identity secret from it. [148]

The defective foetus
39. A person ought not to take the decision to begin a pregnancy, or continue it while the foetus is still non-viable, when believing that the resulting child's quality of life is likely to be poor because of injury, disease or genetic defect. [149]

Adverse actions during pregnancy
40. Subject to the rules regarding abortion, during pregnancy the prospective mother ought not to take harmful drugs or other deleterious substances, or engage in any other activity that might endanger the wellbeing of the foetus. [150]

Breast-feeding in public
41. The duty of sex-respect forbids our objecting to breast-feeding in public. It is wrong to equate this, as some do, with the public performance of excretory functions. [150]

Contraception

Morality of contraception
42. It is not immoral to use any type of medically approved contraceptive method, whether natural or artificial. [151]

Deceit as to possibility of conception
43. It is immoral for a person to deceive their sexual partner by falsely saying or implying that they are sterile or have taken adequate contraceptive precautions. [151]

Abortion

Abortion of non-viable foetus
44. It is not immoral for a pregnant woman who does not want the child to abort her foetus before it has become viable, provided no pain is inflicted on the foetus and the woman has carefully considered, and rejected as too distressing, the alternative of bearing the child and then offering it for

adoption. Where the prospective mother and father are married to each other, or have a subsisting pair-bond together, the former should consult the latter before deciding on an abortion, and should carefully consider any arguments he may advance. [153]

Abortion of viable foetus

45. It is immoral for a pregnant woman to abort her foetus after it has become viable, except where this is necessary to preserve her life or health, because by that time (though not before) the foetus has developed into a person in its own right. [153]

Anti-abortion campaigning

46. It is immoral to distress a woman who is considering the abortion of her non-viable foetus by asserting that the abortion would be immoral, or by using dysphemisms such as 'baby' or 'child' for the foetus or 'murder' for the process of abortion. [153–4]

The Young

Parents' duty to rear their child

47. (1) The natural parents of a child should accept and discharge their responsibility to rear it unless circumstances render this impracticable.

(2) It is the duty of the persons rearing a child to give it a secure and loving upbringing till adulthood.

(3) If the child cannot be reared by its natural parents it is best that it be reared by a couple who are as near as possible in age and characteristics to the natural parents. To be reared by a lone parent, or by two persons of the same sex, may succeed. It is more likely however to be less than the best, since the child needs a close and extended view of rearers of both sexes in order to make sense of its world. [155]

Sex education

48. It is the duty of the persons rearing a child to ensure that it undergoes whatever sex education may be necessary to enable it progressively to learn the facts about human sexuality, and eventually to carry out its duties of ethical understanding and ethical action. Subject to this, a child-rearer who has not been proved to lack a genuine intention to promote the welfare of the child has the right to decide what it is to be taught about sex. [164]

Consent by young people to sexual acts

49. Apparent consent by a youngster to a sexual act with an older person is morally ineffective, and therefore counts as no consent, where the youngster is too immature to understand the nature and quality of the act, that is its physiological, emotional and ethical significance. Apparent consent by a youngster to a sexual act with an age-mate is however to be treated as morally effective. A test for whether a youngster who apparently consents to a sexual

act really understands its nature and quality is whether, when maturity is attained, he or she would be likely to regret having committed the act. [170]

Homosexuality

Same-gender sex acts
50. It is not immoral to have sex with a person of the same gender. [194]

Discrimination against homosexuals
51. It is immoral to discriminate against a person on the ground that he or she is a homosexual (whether practising or not). [194]

Promoting homosexuality
52. It is not immoral to advance the view that homosexuality is a natural condition rather than a remediable disorder, that homosexuals are to be encouraged to enhance their lifestyle, or that a good family life is possible for homosexuals and others (including children) associated with them. [194]

Prostitution

Payment for sex
53. It is not immoral to make or receive payment for a sexual service willingly rendered. The duty of sex-fulfilment may require a person to pay for what they need rather than go without. [210]

Treatment of prostitutes
54. The duty of sex-respect requires that prostitutes of both sexes should be well treated and never degraded. They serve a useful and valid social purpose. [210]

Pornography

Categories of pornography
55. Pornographic, that is explicitly sexual, material can be divided into: (1) non-erotic material; (2) perverted or debased material, (3) stimulative or erotic material, (4) educational and artistic material, and (5) political or destabilising material. Given material may fall into more than one of these categories. [221]

Non-erotic pornography
56. Non-erotic pornography, namely sexually explicit material without erotic content, is morally neutral. [239]

Perverted or debased pornography
57. Perverted or debased pornography is immoral because it contravenes the

duty of sex-respect by denigrating human sexuality through associating it with violence, cruelty or bestiality, or otherwise depicting it in degraded form. [240]

Stimulative pornography

58. Stimulative pornography has the effect of initiating or enhancing sexual desire. The duties of sex-acceptance and sex-fulfilment, together with the principle of free speech, require such pornography to be treated as not immoral, provided the nature and provenance of the material does not infringe the duty of sex-respect or any other ethical principle, such as the duty of consideration for a spouse or the requirement of consent to participation by models. That this kind of pornography causes the commission of immoral acts such as rape is unproved generally. On balance more such acts might be committed if this material were not available for masturbatory use. [249]

Educational and artistic pornography

59. Educational and artistic pornography is morally good as being in the interests of science, literature, art (including drama, opera and ballet) or learning, or of other objects of general concern. [264]

Political or destabilising pornography

60. Political or destabilising pornography uses explicitly sexual material to make political points, and may therefore be subversive. The duty of sex-acceptance and the principle of free speech require such pornography to be treated as not immoral. [266]

List of Sources

Note. In addition to the sources listed here a number of newspaper and journal reports were consulted, most of which are identified in the relevant place in the text. Matters for which no source reference is given are usually derived from the author's personal knowledge.

Ackerley, J. R. *My Father and Myself.* Harmondsworth: Penguin 1971.
Acton, W. *Prostitution considered in its Moral, Social, and Sanitary Aspects.* London: J. Churchill 1857.
Aristotle. *The Nicomachean Ethics* (translated by D. P. Chase; introduction by J. A. Smith). London: Dent 1911.
Arts Council. *The Obscenity Laws: A Report by the Working Party set up by a Conference convened by the Chairman of the Arts Council of Great Britain.* London: André Deutsch 1969.
Bailey, Paul. *An English Madam: The Life and Work of Cynthia Payne.* London: Jonathan Cape 1982.
Banks, J. A. and Olive. *Feminism and Family Planning in Victorian England.* Liverpool: Liverpool University Press 1964.
Bean, Orson. *Me and the Orgone.* Sydney: Angus and Robertson 1971.
Bébel, August. *Woman in the Past, Present and Future.* London: Zwan 1988.
Benjamin, Harry and Masters, R. E. L. *Prostitution and Morality.* London: Souvenir Press 1964.
Beiber, Irving *et al. Homosexuality.* New York: Random House 1962.
Blackwell, Elizabeth. *Counsel to Parents on the Moral Education of their Children in Relation to Sex.* London: Hatchards 1879 (8th edn. London: G. Bell 1913).
Bösche, Susanne. *Jenny lives with Eric and Martin* (translated by Louis Mackay). London: Gay Men's Press 1983.
Bradlaugh, Charles and Besant, Annie. *The Queen v. Charles Bradlaugh and Annie Besant.* London: Freethought Publishing Company 1877.
Brecher, Ruth and Edward (eds.). *An Analysis of Human Sexual Response.* London: Panther 1967.
British Medical Association. *Teenage Living and Loving* (booklet). 1976.
Brown, J. A. C. *The Social Psychology of Industry.* Harmondsworth: Penguin 1954.
—*Freud and the Post-Freudians.* Harmondsworth: Penguin 1961.
Calderone, Mary S. 'Sex Education for Young People – and for their Parents and Teachers' (included in Brecher, Ruth and Edward: *An Analysis of Human Sexual Response* – see above).

Cameron, Nigel de S. and Sims, Pamela F. *Abortion: The Crisis in Morals and Medicine*. Leicester: Inter-Varsity Press 1986.

Caprio, Frank S. *Variations in Sexual Behaviour*. London: John Calder 1957.

Chesser, Eustace. *Love Without Fear*. London: Rich & Cowan 1940.

—*Reich and Sexual Freedom*. London: Vision 1972.

Choisy, Maryse. *Psychoanalysis of the Prostitute*. London: Peter Owen 1962.

Cleland, John. *Memoirs of a Woman of Pleasure*. [The History of Fanny Hill, with introduction and notes by Peter Sabor.] Oxford: Oxford University Press (The World's Classics) 1986.

Connolly, Cyril ('Palinurus'). *The Unquiet Grave*. London: Horizon 1944.

Cousins, Jane. *Make It Happy*. London: Virago 1978.

Cousins-Mills, Jane. *Make It Happy, Make It Safe*. Harmondsworth: Penguin 1986.

Deakin, Michael and Willis, John. *Johnny Go Home*. London: Futura/Quartet 1976.

Devlin, Lord. *The Enforcement of Morals*. Oxford: Oxford University Press 1959.

Draper, Elizabeth. *Birth Control in the Modern World*. Harmondsworth: Penguin 1972.

Drysdale, George. *The Elements of Social Science*. London: E. Truelove 1886 (25th edn.)

Ellis, Albert. *The American Sexual Tragedy*. New York: 1954.

—'A Study of 300 Sex Offenders'. New York: International Journal of Sexology, August 1951.

Enby, Gunnel. *Let There Be Love* (translated by I. D. Morris). London: Elek/Pemberton 1975.

Epstein, Isidore. *Judaism*. Harmondsworth: Penguin 1959.

Estren, Mark James. *A History of Underground Comics*. Berkeley, California: Ronin Publishing Inc. 1987.

Eysenck, H. J. *Fact and Fiction in Psychology*. Harmondsworth: Penguin 1965.

Eysenck, H. J. and Nias, D. K. B. *Sex, Violence and the Media*. London: Maurice Temple Smith 1978.

Faulder, Carolyn. *Whose Body Is It?: The Troubling Issue of Informed Consent*. London: Virago 1985.

Finmore, Rhoda Lee. *Immoral Earnings* (The Messina Trial). London: M. H. Publications 1951.

Firth, Sir Raymond W. *We, the Tikopia*. London: Allen & Unwin 1964.

Flexner, Abraham. *Prostitution in Europe*. New York: Century 1914.

Ford, C. G. and Beach, F. A. *Patterns of Sexual Behaviour*. London: Greenwood Press 1980.

Forster, E. M. *Maurice*. London: Edward Arnold 1971.

Fortes, Meyer. *The Web of Kinship Among the Tallensi*. London: International African Institute 1949.

Fox, Robin. *The Red Lamp of Incest*. London: Hutchinson 1980.

Fraser, Morris (inter alia). *Perspectives on Paedophilia*. London: Batsford 1981.

Freedman, G. R. *Sexual Medicine*. London: Churchill Livingstone 1983.

Freud, Sigmund. *Interpretation of Dreams* (translated by A. Strachey). London: Allen & Unwin 1955.

—*The Psychopathology of Everyday Life* (translated by A. Tyson). London: Ernest Benn 1966.

Fromm, Erich. *The Art of Loving*. London: George Allen & Unwin 1957.

Fryer, Peter. *Mrs Grundy*. London: Corgi 1965.

—*Private Case – Public Scandal*. London: Secker & Warburg 1966.

Genet, Jean. *The Balcony*. London: Methuen 1982.

Goergen, Donald. *The Sexual Celibate*. London: SPCK 1974.

Goffman, Erving. *The Presentation of the Self in Everyday Life*. Edinburgh: Edinburgh University Press 1956.

Good News Bible. London: Collins 1987.

Gorer, Geoffrey. *Sex and Marriage in England Today*. St Albans: Panther 1973.

Greengross, Wendy. *Entitled to Love*. London: Malby Press 1976.

Greer, Germaine. *The Female Eunuch*. St Albans: Paladin 1971.

Guillaume, Alfred. *Islam*. Harmondsworth: Penguin 1954.

Hall, Radclyffe. *The Well of Loneliness*. London: Virago 1982.

Hansen, Soren and Jensen, Jesper. *The Little Red School Book* (translated by Berit Thornberry). London: Stage 1 1971.

Hastings, James. *Encyclopaedia of Religion and Ethics* (13 volumes). Edinburgh: T. & T. Clark 1908–1926.

Hegeler, Inge and Sten. *Living is Loving* (translated by David Hohnen). St Albans: Panther 1974.

Hernton, Calvin C. *Sex and Racism*. St Albans: Paladin 1970.

Hill, Maurice and Lloyd-Jones, Michael. *Sex Education: The Erroneous Zone*. London: National Secular Society 1970.

Hobbes, Thomas. *Leviathan*. London: Dent 1983.

Hoffman, Martin. *The Gay World*. New York: Bantam 1969.

Humphreys, Christmas. *Buddhism*. Harmondsworth: Penguin 1951.

Huxley, Aldous. *Brave New World*. London: Panther 1977.

Hyde, H. Montgomery. *The Other Love*. London: Mayflower 1972.

Isherwood, Christopher. *Christopher and his Kind*. London: Eyre Methuen 1977.

Kavanagh, K. H. *Sex Education: Its Uses and Abuses*. London: The Responsible Society *c.* 1972.

Kearney, P. J. *The Private Case*. London: Joy Landesman 1981.

Kelly, Audrey. *Life and Our Children*. London: Burns & Oates 1961.

Kessel, Neil and Walton, Henry. *Alcoholism*. Harmondsworth: Penguin 1965.

Kinsey, Alfred C. et al. *Sexual Behaviour in the Human Male*. Philadelphia: Kinsey Institute 1948.

—*Sexual Behaviour in the Human Female*. New York: Kinsey Institute 1953.

Kirkendall, Lester (co-ed.). *Sex in the Adolescent Years*. New York: Association Press 1968.

Knight, Margaret. *Morals Without Religion*. London: Dobson 1955.

Knowlton, Dr Charles. 'Fruits of Philosophy' (included in *Birth Control and Morality in Nineteenth Century America*; Salem, New Hampshire: Ayer 1972).

Laing, R. D. *The Divided Self*. Harmondsworth: Penguin 1965.

—*Self and Others*. Harmondsworth: Penguin 1971.

Lambert, Royston (ed.). *The Hothouse Society*. London: Weidenfeld & Nicolson 1968.

Lawrence, D. H. *Lady Chatterley's Lover*. London: Heinemann 1963.

Llewellyn-Jones, D. *Sex and VD*. London: Faber and Faber 1974.

Longford, Lord et al. *Pornography: The Longford Report*. London: Coronet 1972.

Mace, D. R., Bannerman, R. H. O. and Burton, J. *The Teaching of Human Sexuality in Schools for Health Professionals*. Geneva: World Health Organization (Public Health Papers No. 57) 1974.

MacIntyre, Alasdair. *Marcuse*. London: Fontana 1970.

Malinowski, Bronislaw. *Sexual Life of Savages in North Western Melanesia*. London: Routledge 1969.

Malthus, Thomas Robert. *Essay on the Principle of Population*. London: Dent 1982.

Marryat, Frederick. *Peter Simple*. London: Dent 1970.

Masters, William H. and Johnston, Virginia E. *Human Sexual Response*. Boston: Little, Brown 1966.

Mead, Margaret. *Coming of Age in Samoa*. Harmondsworth: Penguin 1943.

—*Sex and Temperament in Three Primitive Societies*. London: Routledge & Kegan Paul 1935.

Mill, John Stuart. *Utilitarianism* (selection edited by Mary Warnock). London: Fontana 1962.

Millet, Kate. *The Prostitution Papers*. St Albans: Paladin 1975.

Morris, Desmond. *The Human Zoo*. London: Corgi 1971.

—*Intimate Behaviour*. St Albans: Triad/Panther 1979.

Morton, R. S. *Sexual Freedom and Venereal Disease*. London: P. Owen 1972.

Neill, A. S. *The Problem Family*. London: Herbert Jenkins 1949.

—*Summerhill: A Radical Approach to Education*. London: Gollancz 1962.

Nichols, Beverley. *Father Figure*. London: Heinemann 1972.

—*The Unforgiving Minute*. London: W. H. Allen 1978.

Notcutt, Bernard. *The Psychology of Personality*. London: Methuen 1953.

Palmer, Tony. *The Trials of Oz*. London: Blond & Briggs 1971.

Parrinder, Edward Geoffrey. *Sex in the World's Religions*. London: Sheldon 1980.

Plummer, Ken (inter alia). *Perspectives on Paedophilia*. London: Batsford 1981.

Pomeroy, Wardell B. *Boys and Sex*. Harmondsworth: Penguin 1970.

Proops, Marjorie. *Dear Marje*. London: André Deutsch 1976.

Quentin-Burstein, Jules. *Conjugal Visits in Prison*. Lexington, Massachusetts: Lexington Books 1977.

Rae, Daphne. *A World Apart*. Guildford: Lutterworth Press 1983.

Reich, Wilhelm. *The Invasion of Compulsory Sex-Morality*. London: Souvenir Press 1972.

—*The Sexual Revolution*. London: Vision Press 1952.

Rolph, C. H. *Books in the Dock*. London: André Deutsch 1969.

—(ed.). *Does Pornography Matter?*. London: Routledge & Kegan Paul 1961.

Rossman, Parker. *Sexual Experience Between Men and Boys*. London: Maurice Temple Smith 1979.

Rubin, Isadore. 'Sex After Forty – And After Seventy' (article included in R. and E. Brecher's *An Analysis of Human Sexual Response* – see above).

Rubin, Isadore (co-ed.). *Sex in the Adolescent Years*. New York: Association Press 1968.

Schapera, Isaac. *Married Life in an African Tribe*. London: Pelican 1971.

Scheimann, Eugene. *Sex Can Save Your Heart . . . and Life*. New York: Bantam 1975.

Schofield, Michael. *Promiscuity*. London: Gollancz 1976.

Scruton, Roger. *Sexual Desire*. London: Weidenfeld & Nicolson 1986.

Selby, Hubert (Jnr). *Last Exit to Brooklyn*. London: Calder and Boyars 1966.

Singer, Peter and Kuhse, Helga. *Should the Baby Live?* Oxford: Oxford University Press 1985.

Slaughter, Frank. *Medicine for Moderns*. London: Jarrolds 1953.

Spock, Benjamin. *A Young Person's Guide to Life and Love*. St Albans: Mayflower 1973.

Steele, David Ramsay. Libertarian Alliance, Political Notes No 45.

Stekel, W. *Sexual Aberrations*. New York: Liveright 1971.

Sullivan, Harry Stack. *Clinical Studies in Psychiatry*. London: W. W. Norton 1980.

—*Fusion of Psychiatry and Social Science*. London: W. W. Norton 1980.

—*Interpersonal Theory of Psychiatry*. London: W. W. Norton 1980.

Thackeray, W. M. *The History of Pendennis*. London: Bradbury & Evans 1849.

Toffler, Alvin. *Future Shock*. London: The Bodley Head 1970.

Trevelyan, John. *What the Censor Saw*. London: Michael Joseph 1973.

Trobisch, Walter. *Love is a Feeling to be Learned*. London: Inter-Varsity Press 1971.

Ullerstam, Lars. *The Erotic Minorities* (translated by Anselm Hollo). London: Calder and Boyars 1967.

Van de Velde, T. *Ideal Marriage: Its Physiology and Technique*. London: Heinemann 1928.

Waugh, Evelyn. *Handful of Dust*. London: Eyre Methuen 1979.

Weeks, Jeffrey. *Sexuality and its Discontents* London: Routledge 1985.

Weiss, E. and English, O. P. *Psychosomatic Medicine*. Philadelphia: W. B. Saunders 1949.

White, Margaret (with Jennet Kidd). *Sound Sex Education*. London: Order of Christian Unity 1976.

Wildeblood, Peter. *Against the Law*. Harmondsworth: Penguin 1955.

Williams, Bernard et al. *Report of the Committee on Obscenity and Film Censorship (Cmnd. 7772)*. London: HMSO 1979.

Wilson, Robert Anton. *Sex and Drugs*. St Albans: Mayflower 1975.

Wistrich, Enid. *I Don't Mind the Sex It's the Violence*. London: Marion Boyars 1978.

Wolfenden, Sir John et al. *Report of the Committee on Homosexual Offences and Prostitution* (Cmnd. 247). London: HMSO 1957.

Wolfers, David and Helen. *Vasectomy and Vasectomania*. St Albans: Mayflower 1974.

Wolff, Charlotte. *Bisexuality: A Study*. London: Quartet, 1977.

—*Love Between Women*. London: Duckworth 1971.

World Health Organization. *Education and Treatment in Human Sexuality: the Training of Health Professionals*. Geneva: Technical Report Series No 572 1975.

Worsley, Francis. *Flannelled Fool*. London: Hogarth Press 1967.

Yaffé, Maurice and Nelson, Edward C. (eds.). *The Influence of Pornography on Behaviour*. London: Academic Press 1982.

Index